Faith, Rationality, and the Passions

Directions in Modern Theology Book Series

Born out of the journal *Modern Theology*, the Directions in Modern Theology book series provides issues focused on important theological topics and texts in current debate within that discipline, whilst looking at broader contemporary topics from a theological perspective. It analyses notions and thinkers, as well as examining a wide spectrum of "modern" theological eras: from late Medieval through to the Enlightenment and up until the present "post-modern" movements. Attracting distinguished theologians from a world-wide base, the book series develops what is a unique forum for international debate on theological concerns.

Titles in the series include:

Faith, Rationality, and the Passions
Edited by Sarah Coakley

Re-thinking Dionysius the Areopagite
Edited by Sarah Coakley and Charles M. Stang

The Promise of Scriptural Reasoning
Edited by David F. Ford and C. C. Pecknold

Aquinas in Dialogue: Thomas for the Twenty-First Century
Edited by Jim Fodor and Frederick Christian Bauerschmidt

Re-thinking Gregory of Nyssa
Edited by Sarah Coakley

Theology and Eschatology at the Turn of the Millennium
Edited by L. Gregory Jones and James Buckley

Catholicism and Catholicity: Eucharistic Communities in Historical and Contemporary Perspectives
Edited by Sarah Beckwith, L. Gregory Jones and James J. Buckley

Theology and Scriptural Imagination: Directions in Modern Theology
Edited by L. Gregory Jones and James Buckley

Spirituality and Social Embodiment
Edited by L. Gregory Jones and James Buckley

Faith, Rationality, and the Passions

Edited by
Sarah Coakley

WILEY-BLACKWELL

A John Wiley & Sons, Ltd., Publication

This edition first published 2012
Originally published as Volume 27, Issue 2 of *Modern Theology* (Blackwell Publishing Ltd) and
Volume 28, Issue 1 of *Faith and Philosophy* (reproduced with kind permission of The Society of
Christian Philosophers)
© 2012 Blackwell Publishing Ltd

Blackwell Publishing was acquired by John Wiley & Sons in February 2007. Blackwell's publishing program has been merged with Wiley's global Scientific, Technical, and Medical business
to form Wiley-Blackwell.

Registered Office
John Wiley & Sons Ltd, The Atrium, Southern Gate, Chichester, West Sussex, PO19 8SQ, United
Kingdom

Editorial Offices
350 Main Street, Malden, MA 02148-5020, USA
9600 Garsington Road, Oxford, OX4 2DQ, UK
The Atrium, Southern Gate, Chichester, West Sussex, PO19 8SQ, UK

For details of our global editorial offices, for customer services, and for information about how
to apply for permission to reuse the copyright material in this book please see our website at
www.wiley.com/wiley-blackwell.

The right of Sarah Coakley to be identified as the author of the editorial material in this work
has been asserted in accordance with the UK Copyright, Designs and Patents Act 1988.

Wiley also publishes its books in a variety of electronic formats. Some content that appears in
print may not be available in electronic books.

Designations used by companies to distinguish their products are often claimed as trademarks.
All brand names and product names used in this book are trade names, service marks, trademarks or registered trademarks of their respective owners. The publisher is not associated with
any product or vendor mentioned in this book. This publication is designed to provide accurate
and authoritative information in regard to the subject matter covered. It is sold on the understanding that the publisher is not engaged in rendering professional services. If professional
advice or other expert assistance is required, the services of a competent professional should
be sought.

Library of Congress Cataloging-in-Publication Data

Faith, rationality, and the passions / edited by Sarah Coakley.
    p. cm.
  Papers presented at conference held Jan. 11–13, 2010 at the University of Cambridge.
  Includes index.
  ISBN 978-1-4443-6193-3 (pbk.)
  1. Faith and reason–Congresses. 2. Emotions–Religious aspects–Congresses.
3. Religion–Philosophy–Congresses. I. Coakley, Sarah, 1951–
  BL51.F319 2013
  202′.2–dc23
                              2012022577

A catalogue record for this book is available from the British Library.

Cover design by Richard Boxall Design Associates.

Set in 10 on 12 pt Palatino by Toppan Best-set Premedia Limited

1   2012

CONTENTS

INTRODUCTION: FAITH, RATIONALITY, AND THE PASSIONS

SARAH COAKLEY

The question of the relation of passion to reason in the life of faith is a pressing one for contemporary theology and philosophy of religion, and that for a number of reasons. This volume is devoted to a selective exploration of that relation and those reasons—understood historically, systematically, and in interdisciplinary exchange with relevant recent scientific research. The chapters in this book were first presented as papers at the "Faith, Rationality and the Passions" conference, which I convened at the University of Cambridge, January 11–13, 2010.[1] The offerings were then judiciously divided between two relevant journals with rather different readerships, in order to maximize the immediate impact of the conference in the philosophy as well as the theology guild.[2] The result was a happy collaboration which enabled a remarkably quick and efficient publishing process. Such was the positive response to the two journal issues, however, that the decision was made that the papers should now be reunited here in book form, allowing for a more effective integration of their shared contribution to the topic.

In order to situate the chapters in a wider context of discussion, it is perhaps worth spelling out at the outset some of the reasons for the current intensified scholarly interest in the relation of faith, rationality and the affective realm. Let me highlight four "clusters" of such interest.

First, there are of course the jibes from exponents of the "new atheism," for whom religious commitment is precisely a manifestation of a *loss* of reason. To be reasonable would be to be "scientific," and to override misdirected affective nostalgia for an outmoded "God," as well as violent discharges of religiously motivated hatred. This atheistical charge requires an answer, both philosophical and theological, in terms of the very notion of scientific "rationality" at stake;[3] but it also requires a historical diagnosis

Faith, Rationality, and the Passions, First Edition. Edited by Sarah Coakley.
© 2012 Blackwell Publishing Ltd. Book compilation © 2012 Blackwell Publishing Ltd.

which can explain how and why "reason" and "religion" became rhetorically unhitched in the first place, and when this might have happened.[4] There is a seeming oddity about such a disjunction appearing so forcefully in the modern period. Admittedly the very term "religion" took on significant new meanings at this juncture, and "fanaticism" was a topic of serious concern in the light of what had earlier come to be dubbed religious "enthusiasm"; but this was just at the same juncture as some other leading Enlightenment philosophers were simultaneously doing their best to *defend* the notion of a reasonable "faith."[5] In other words, a genealogy that reaches back at least to the Enlightenment is required that will help explain why current hostilities about "religion," reason and emotion are taking the form that they now are.

Secondly, there are increasingly pressing new doubts today (amongst at least some in the guild of philosophical theologians) about the hostile reception of "Enlightenment" philosophy which has characterized recent post-foundationalist Anglophone theology. Not long ago it became fashionable for theology to blame the Enlightenment (or more generically, "modernity") for all manner of distorting philosophical moves which effectively "secular-ized" reason and so fatally side-lined the intellectual status of theology.[6] Whilst that large-scale story obviously still has some real historical point, it is beginning to be clear that the assessment of the Enlightenment heritage it promoted needs much more careful discernment, and perhaps especially in relation to its accounts of affectivity, will and feeling in the philosophers concerned.[7] A stereotype had here been created of "secular Enlightenment reason" which obscured the manifold differences and riches of thinking in a period in which "passions" and "affections" were still counted as signifi-cant and often positive forces with which reason had to do, and "emotions" were yet to be invented. Part of the move beyond a false scapegoating of "Enlightenment" or "modernity," then, is the recovery of a nuanced sense of how modern philosophers *differently* construed the affective realm, and also what happened when their notion of "passion" became replaced, con-siderably later, by the very different concept of "emotion." As Thomas Dixon spells out, it is surprising how *recent* is the evolution of a concept of "emotion" divorced from rational moorings.[8]

Thirdly, the feminist critique of "The Man of Reason" (which to some extent piggy-backed on the malestream scholarship which homogenized the "Enlightenment," and in other ways already corrected that homogenization) has drawn attention in recent decades to the place that feeling, passion, maternal nurture, and domestic pursuits play in the thought of the leading male philosophers of the modern period and their female interlocutors, and has sought to excavate the often-covert associations with stereotypical pic-tures of "femininity" thereby promoted.[9] This feminist discourse has not been taken up as much as it deserves into the fields of theology and philoso-phy of religion. On the other hand, as Western philosophy of religion in recent years has tended to withdraw from foundationalist and universalistic claims to rationality, and to embrace a stronger interest in religious affections and desires, one might argue that it has unwittingly "feminized" *itself* to some extent in terms of these inherited cultural stereotypes.[10] This leaves a paradoxical situation, and calls for deeper analysis of the relation of belief, rationality, affectivity and gender.[11]

Lastly, but by no means least in terms of intellectual significance, recent deliverances from the fields of neuroscience and experimental psychology have yielded remarkably interesting challenges to the idea that reason and emotion can be regarded as an oppositional binary in their disciplines. The old picture of the brain's clear division into more ancient, animal-based centers of primitive emotion, and more-recently evolved centers of rational decision-making, has been questioned or refined in various ways, not least by the discovery that the brain-processes involved in rational thought are inexorably interconnected with affective function, and indeed operate quite weirdly and dysfunctionally in terms of human behaviors if artificially cut off from them. Even to put the matter this way of course begs profound (and highly technical) questions in the philosophy of mind about the relation of brain and "mind" which theology also has to face; but the neuroscience debate about the relation of rational and affective function has, in principle, great intrinsic significance for theology in itself—for its own choices about how to expound the nature of the human person and her integrity before God, and for its potential response to the "scientific" scoffers about reasonable faith. If reasoning in its neurological manifestations is in some sense *essentially* also affective, in other words, it cannot be that belief in God is irrational simply because it too has affective dimensions. Of course, to draw that conclusion simultaneously requires some moves in the philosophy of mind which may prove contentious: a stark mind/body dualism would have to be ruled out to sustain it, and the intrinsic relevance to the "mind" of brain states and functions would also have to be defended, without any actual "eliminative" reduction.[12]

Such, then, are the clusters of thematic concern which intersect in this collection of revisionary essays on *Faith, Rationality, and the Passions*. As will be clear, the overall effect of this collaborative research has been to underscore the significance, however it be parsed, of the affective dimensions of religious rationality. It remains for me now briefly to sketch each chapter, and to indicate how the themes enunciated here fit into a rather more focused cumulative thesis. Since the latter dimension may not be so obvious at first blush, I shall allow more attention to it than simply giving a précis of the chapters themselves.

The chapters in the book unfold in the following way. First, Charles Taylor's broad-ranging introductory reflection on the very meaning of "rationality" presents a systematic assault on what he regards as the modern "myth" of "disengaged" scientific reason. He urges the reconsideration of affective "meaning-making" (including religious such meaning-making) as endemic to the pursuit of "rationality," *tout court*; and—*a fortiori*—he likewise trenchantly resists the idea that religious faith is necessarily set at odds with reason. These connected "illusions" (reason *vs.* commitment, reason *vs.* faith) are now in need of urgent countering, Taylor urges; and though he does not here attempt any sustained genealogy of the triumph of disengaged or instrumental reason in the late modern period, it is noteworthy that he (unlike Milbank, who later gives a positive rendition of Hume's reliance on "sentiment" to ground his ethics) reads Hume's disjunction of reason and sentiment as precisely "opening the door" to the false modern instrumental reason which has "held us captive."

William Cavanaugh's chapter, which follows, comes at some of the same issues as Taylor but with the focus now on what "religion" came to mean in the modern period, and why it progressively became associated with irrationality and violence. His first concern is the way that "religion" and "public reason" became progressively divorced in this period in various contexts; and there is a particularly American, and contemporary, message which Cavanaugh wishes to purvey: when "religion" becomes suspected of irrational affectivity and violence, this can ironically cloak and condone the continuing uses of violence in the name of secular rationalities and nation-states.[13] Cavanaugh draws attention to those voices in the modern period (particularly Locke and Voltaire) who, as he reads them, significantly contributed to a new notion of religious "fanaticism" averse to reason. Yet he acknowledges that other Enlightenment thinkers, especially Kant, trod a more complex path in carefully distinguishing negative from positive affectivity in the realm of religion, and sought above all to align reason and faith. The Enlightenment presents no unified voice on these issues, then; and whilst it may have spawned one sort of problematic divide between religious fanaticism and reasonable "religion," there was no one way in which it consistently drove a wedge between reason and affectivity *tout court*. There remains a more complicated story to be told on that front.

What then are the ultimate intellectual sources of these complex modern re-negotiations of faith, reason and the affections? One possible remote root is the Platonic one, which is excavated here by Catherine Pickstock in her "The Late Arrival of Language." In an ingenious new reading of the *Cratylus* she urges that Plato's theory of forms in no way denies an intrinsic connection between human cognition and (passion-filled) materiality. Rather, the account of language in this dialogue suggests a vital role for passion and embodiment, and it is the religious element in Plato, Pickstock argues, which sustains the right balance between materiality and reason. If this reading is correct, then Evagrius's later Christian monastic advice about reason and the passions (as analyzed by Columba Stewart, OSB, in the next chapter on this theme) departs rather less from its Platonic heritage than might be supposed. What Stewart demonstrates is the remarkably systematic account supplied by Evagrius of the confronting, naming and taming of negative passions and "thoughts" for the sake of the attainment of "pure prayer"—which is, according to Evagrius, the "proper activity of the mind." This is not however in any way a recourse to what, post-Freud, would now be called "repression"; rather it is an ascetical program of affective and noetic transformation which has to be arduously and repeatedly *practised*. Such an integration of rationality and bodily practice is precisely what modern and contemporary philosophical theories of "affectivity" for the most part seem to lack; and this makes the rediscovery of certain late antique theories of affective transformation especially suggestive for contemporary philosophical discussion.[14] To this point I shall return at the close of this "Introduction."

Stewart's compelling account of the contemporary relevance of Evagrius's approach to the passions is followed by a strikingly original set of readings of Western philosophical authors on the topic of reason and feeling, in which tradition Augustine naturally holds a formative position. Paul J. Griffiths's delicate chapter on tears in Augustine's *Confessions* shows how Augustine can venerate the act of weeping—when rightly understood—as a confessional acknowledgement of human vulnerability, and thus as a truly appropriate means of intimacy with God; in such cases weeping is not in any discord with the rationality that is also inherently drawn back to its divine source by grace. Rather, it is, as Griffiths puts it, "communicative" of the "world's transfiguration." In this way Augustine can be seen to have established a positive and graced account even of seemingly uncontrolled grief; he carefully distinguishes between the merely self-indulgent, and the authentically transformative, effects of powerful feelings.

Eleonore Stump's new reading of Aquinas on the passions strikes a somewhat similar note, deliberately challenging some currently regnant "Aristotelian" renditions of Aquinas's ethics in the process. If Stump is right, the presumption of some contemporary "virtue ethicists" that Thomas disjoins feeling and reason is further compounded by another, and distinctively late-modern, misreading: one that drives a wedge between "Humean" and "Kantian" assessments of feeling in the ethical realm, and thus assumes a similar disjunctive choice between the affective and the rational (an exegetical problem which is addressed by other contributors to this volume). Further, such readings also misleadingly bracket away the significance of the third part of the *Summa Theologiae*, Stump argues, and especially the treatment of pneumatology there, for Thomas's rich understanding of the virtuous life: "For Aquinas, there are passions, in an analogous or extended sense, which are infused by God into the intellective appetite or which are the fruits of the Holy Spirit. . . . These passions or analogues to the passions are foundational to all virtue and to the whole of the ethical life."

By now the reader may be wondering quite when it was that the reason/feeling disjunction *did* rear its ugly head. If it is not to be found in any of these classic philosophical forebears, and the "modern" period is seemingly so complex and diverse, could Descartes perhaps, with his formidable commitment to cerebral reflections on the foundations of knowledge, still be the one to be singled out for opprobrium? Yet once again, as John Cotting-ham's chapter demonstrates, we need to deconstruct the twentieth-century straw-man rendition of a complex and subtle thinker. Not only is it not the case, argues Cottingham, that Descartes was wholly preoccupied with skep-ticism in the project of his *Meditations*; he was also not denigrating of passion in his *Passions of the Soul*, but rather concerned to clarify the ways in which passions could, under the right conditions, be "valued auxiliaries of reason in the quest for goodness and truth." Descartes was, after all, an original pupil of scholasticism.

The exegetical issue about the reason/feeling division, then, and about whom to blame in relation to modernity, becomes yet more fraught and divided in the next two contributions to this volume. John Milbank, in char-acteristically gadfly mood (and wholly fulfilling Eleonore Stump's predic-tions on this score about the Hume/Kant division), lards *Kant* with blame, by playing off Hume's well-known prizing of the affective in the ethical realm against what he reads as "the contortions that Kant went through in relation to the role of feeling with respect to the ethical."[15] In a daring and undeniably contentious re-reading of the significance of Hume for the general fate of the affective in modern and contemporary philosophy, Milbank excavates Jacobi's original response to Hume in aid of his central thesis. He argues that feeling, conjoined with habit, are for Hume inextrica-bly and rightly connected to *faith*; whereas Kant in contrast (on Milbank's rendition) "ensured the corralling of nature and reason in the sterile hall of mirrors which is the epistemological universe of representation . . . precisely through the banishment of the mediating but ineffable third which is feeling."

Nothing could be further from John Hare's account of the same Kant. Painstakingly laying out the relations Kant sees between "feelings," "inclina-tions," "affects" and "passions" (all subtly different categories in Kant), he shows that there are at least two positive ways in which Kant thinks that "feelings" and "inclinations" enter into moral judgment, and two ways also in which they can go awry. "Passion" has, indeed, become for Kant a nega-tive word (in contrast to Descartes's account); but that is not to say that the affective realm in general is unimportant for Kant's ethical theory—far from it, on Hare's reading; indeed, it has a vital role to play in the moral life.

Whereas Kant has unjustly garnered the reputation for a lack of interest in the affective dimension of the human, de Maistre and Kierkegaard have, in their completely different ways, tended to be associated with the opposite tendency—whether of violent passion (de Maistre), or of faith-against-reason (Kierkegaard). Once again, then, our contributors present us with readings designed to correct standard or lazy assumptions. Douglas Hed-ley's account of de Maistre indicates how a lesser-known Catholic Enlighten-ment thinker has been wrongly pilloried as a defender of dark passions and violence, when his philosophical interests were, on the contrary, fuelled by neo-Platonic, and specifically Origenist, interests in a universalist theodicy. Rather differently, Merold Westphal's characteristically careful account of "Kierkegaard on Faith, Reason and Passion" shows that if we take attentive account of what Kierkegaard really means by "faith," "reason" and "passion," then we see that we are in no "position to say that faith is irrational [sc. for Kierkegaard] because it rests on feeling rather than knowledge."

Whichever of the readings of Hume and Kant we find more persuasive in this section of the book, what at least becomes clear through the various assaults on the modern history of "feeling" is that the consolidation of the concept of "emotion" as a *psychological* category (even though it was a word already occasionally already utilized by Hume with slightly different overtones) is, in contrast to the various vicissitudes of the terms "feeling" and "passion" in Enlightenment philosophies, a relatively late development. Thomas Dixon's chapter, "Revolting Passions," surveys the backcloth to this shift in nomenclature and association in the late nineteenth century, and demonstrates how, once launched as a secular psychological category, "emotion" swallowed up and encompassed all the earlier and subtler distinctions between passion, affect, feeling and sentiment which for the most part had originally had a religious locus. Dixon concludes, then, that the "main casualty" in this new semantic transformation to a "secular, scientific, and sterilized" idea of "emotion" was the older sense of the cognitive and moral *seriousness* of the affective life which had attended the traditional discussion of the "passions." Contemporary revisiting of that interest in integrative "seriousness" is in undeniable reaction to the sanitizing and scientizing developments of the nineteenth century. So we do well, too, as Dixon highlights, to remember just how *recent* is the phenomenon over against which there is such a notable contemporary reaction. It is not the "Enlightenment" which is the main problem *vis-à-vis* the denigration of feeling; it is its late nineteenth-century scientific outworkings which represent the problem.

Such a proposed re-integrative approach to feeling and reason as Dixon suggests, however, already finds an anticipatory, albeit only implicit, manifestation in the thought of Ludwig Wittgenstein on religion, as Stephen Mulhall demonstrates in his chapter on the topic. It is vital here to read Wittgenstein aright, Mulhall urges, and not as the sort of expressivist who is *merely* attending to "feelings, attitude and emotions" where religious belief is concerned. Such a rendition trivializes the important contribution Wittgenstein makes when he talks of the importance of "pictures" to religious believing. To require a "picture" to account for the subtle status of a religious belief is precisely, for Wittgenstein, to refuse the disjunction between intellectual inquiry on the one hand and feelings states on the other. Thus Wittgenstein's discussion of religious belief suggest a strongly affective dimension (the Kierkegaardian influence is writ large here), and a simultaneous resistance to any proselytizing in aridly intellectualist mode; yet it is also fully "reasoned" in its own proper sense, as Mulhall clarifies. Wittgenstein's capacity to combine the affective and the rational in his account of religious "forms of life" is well capable, when rightly understood, of escaping the false charge of "fideism." It also shows a retrospective awareness of what might have been lost, well after Kierkegaard, in the separation of "emotions" from rationality.

Followers of Wittgenstein (as we shall discuss in the "Postscript" to this volume, below) tend to be strongly resistant to the idea that messages from the brain sciences can contribute anything to the sort of philosophy of mind that Wittgenstein envisaged. Nonetheless our volume closes with two inputs from the realms of the natural and social sciences which address the central question: What do these disciplines currently have to say about the realm of "reason" and "passion" (or "emotion") and their relation? And what light— if any—might thereby be thrown on the philosophical and theological issues enshrined in these questions?

In fact a remarkable consensus emerges from these two disciplinary reports from a psychologist (Gerald Clore) and a neuroscientist (Michael Spezio). Both draw attention to the turn made in their disciplines in recent decades to seeking an integrated understanding of the relation of "thought" and "feeling." Clore, having stressed throughout his account of recent trends in psychological research that "reason" cannot properly be accounted for without its affective dimensions, avers that, "Rather than suppressing or controlling emotion, . . . the power of cognition in emotion lies in the fact that emotions *are* cognitively-shaped affective reactions" (my emphasis). Evoking once more a Platonic heritage for these ideas at the end of his chapter, Clore concludes that "rather than thinking of emotion and cognition as horses pulling in different directions, we should think of them as strands of a single rope, made strong by their being thoroughly intertwined."

The following contribution from Spezio has a not dissimilar message, but works from significant recent examples in neuroscientific research, many of them focusing on experiments with brain-impaired subjects. The field's current approach to the neuroscience of emotion is, as Spezio admits, torn between at least two different factions. "Dual process models" (which pre-suppose a strong distinction between neural functions involved in intellec-tual goal-directed activities, and neural functions that are virtually automatic) have been, on the one hand, staging something of a comeback in recent neuroscience research. On the other hand, Spezio points to important work also currently being done on the "integrative" function of emotion for rational decision-making and moral action. These studies by and large take their cue from analyses of people with brain damage whose affective responses are impaired in some way. It is not only the celebrated case of the brain-damaged railway worker Phineas Gage (memorably analyzed by Antonio Damasio[16]) which is relevant here, but a more recent plethora of studies on patients with brain lesions who show "real-life social deficits and moral insensitivity" given their failure to bring emotion into a "constitutive" relation to thinking and planning. Perfect utilitarian reasoning is a chilling capacity to observe in such patients, observes Spezio, and it is at the same time evidence of a clear "abnormality" in brain functioning. He concludes that, in the case of normally functioning human brains, there is "no clear evidence for dichotomous views of emotion and reasoning when investigating neural systems in detail." On the contrary, emotion seems to be in some sense intrinsic to effective rational functioning when examined at the level of neural circuitry.

Our collection ends with a reflection by the noted philosopher of emotion, Peter Goldie, which forms an apt recapitulatory "book-end" to the opening piece by Charles Taylor. Goldie supplies a survey of the field of recent secular philosophy of the emotions and concludes—almost against his own better judgment!—that theological ethics may have much to learn from it, despite its apparently reductive presumptions. Again, the task of an integrative approach to reason, feeling and faith opens up creatively to the future; since Goldie avers that, in the case of well-balanced religious belief, "we would find that having the appropriate religious virtues would involve having the appropriate emotional dispositions, so that one would not be able to think or act virtuously without having the right feelings, towards the right objects, at the right time . . . so emotional engagement wouldn't merely be an optional extra but a necessary part of what it is to lead a good religious life."

To conclude: I promised earlier in this "Introduction" to detail the cumulative force of the proposals which emerge in this volume on "Faith, Rationality, and the Passions." Perhaps the most important deliverances of the joint, interdisciplinary research to be found in this collection of studies may be expressed thus, albeit succinctly, in closing.

First, it is clear that important semantic distinctions in the affective realm ("feeling," "will," "passion," "emotion") carry very different freight in different historical and philosophical contexts, and that attention to those contexts is exegetically crucial in assessing whatever relation to "reason" and "faith" may be at stake. Secondly, the widespread assumption that it was the modern period that produced a new and stark disjunction between feeling and rationality is, as repeatedly shown, significantly flawed. It is much more truly the case that sophisticated thinking about "passion" and its implications (negative or otherwise) for reason was carried through from late scholasticism in one form or another into the modern period and continued to hold a position of some philosophical significance into the nineteenth century. The birth of "emotion," therefore, as a quite new and psychologized concept in the later nineteenth century, marks the point at which much stronger dualisms between reason and the affective realm start to become apparent in evolutionary, medical and philosophical thinking, and the earlier and sophisticated range of distinctions between *different* sorts of affect seemingly starts to atrophy. Thus the current reaction to this disjunctive emphasis in contemporary philosophy and science marks a new development of some interest to theology as well as philosophy, since, amongst other things, it may engender a reconsideration of the wisdom of *diachronic* and integrative theories of faith, rationality and the "passions," based in practices, which are to be found in pre-modern monastic texts such as Evagrius's. Finally, the potential significance of the disciplines of psychology and neuroscience for philosophical and theological reflection on reason and affect (whilst remaining a necessarily contentious matter methodologically in terms of philosophy of mind), does at least open alluring possibilities for further future interchange between the disciplines. That neuroscientists and psychologists are becoming increasingly aware of the *integral* significance of the affective dimension of everyday reasoning is at least food for philosophical and theological thought: if faith too is to be reasonable on this hypothesis, it must perforce also be affective. It is the delicate philosophical distinction between different *kinds* of rationality and of feeling which should thus exercise us, just as it did the ancients and the scholastics, and not the false presumption that "emotion" necessarily distorts and impedes a reasonable faith.

NOTES

1 I would like to record my particular gratitude to the John Templeton Foundation for generously funding the original symposium, and to Dr. Mary Ann Meyers of the Foundation for making all the practical arrangements for the conference with her customary grace.

2 *Modern Theology*, Vol. 27, no. 2 (April 2011), pp. 217–361, contained an earlier version of this "Introduction" and the contributions from Cavanaugh, Pickstock, Stewart, Milbank, Dixon, Mulhall, Clore and Spezio, followed by my "Postscript." *Faith and Philosophy*, Vol. 28, no. 1 (January 2011), pp. 3–101, contained another brief "Introduction: Faith, Rationality and the Passions" by me, and the contributions from Taylor, Griffiths, Stump, Cottingham, Hare, Hedley, Westphal and Goldie. I am indebted to the editors of both journals for permission to republish these articles together, and also to their peer review readers for making the original process of production both professional and smooth.

3 Charles Taylor makes a start at such a defense in his opening chapter, "Reason, Faith, and Meaning," arguing that rationality itself is intrinsically meaning-making and affective; it is thus an "illusion" to quest for a "disengaged reason" as an ideal of rationality, and a further illusion to define faith as "believing *without* good reason" (my emphasis).

4 An analysis of this development is importantly provided by William Cavanaugh in "The Invention of Fanaticism," and this provides the contextual backdrop for the closer studies of the divergent renditions of "passion," "feeling," "faith," and "reason" in Descartes, Hume and Kant in subsequent chapters.

5 On this point it is particularly instructive to compare William Cavanaugh's discussion of Locke and Voltaire with John Hare's close analysis of "passion" and "reason" in Kant in his "Kant, the Passions, and the Structure of Moral Motivation."

6 I am thinking here particularly in Britain of the late Colin Gunton's sustained attack on Cartesian individualism (as, in his view, intrinsically inimical to Christian "relational" theism) in his *Enlightenment and Alienation: An Essay Towards a Trinitarian Theology* (Basingstoke: Marshall Morgan and Scott, 1985); and then of course of John Milbank's celebrated assault on "secular reason" (especially as in Kant) in his *Theology and Social Theory: Beyond Secular Reason* (Oxford: Blackwell, 1997). But any number of other influential figures (most obviously Stanley Hauerwas in the United States) might be cited in evidence of this anti-Enlightenment revulsion in the theology of the 1980s and 1990s. While in this current volume Milbank now goes on to embrace a controversial, and highly positive, rendition of Humean affectivity over *against* Kant's "secular" rationality, John Hare in his "Kant, the Passions, and the Structure of Moral Motivations" argues in contrast for the

strongly theological dimensions of Kant's whole "Enlightenment" system, and for the overlooked significance therein of positive affectivity.

7 John Cottingham's "Sceptical Detachment or Loving Submission" presents a particularly powerful riposte to false readings of Descartes along these stereotypical lines. But what all the chapters on particular philosophers share is the commitment to *corrective* readings of figures long misunderstood: either because their views on "reason" have been read in abstraction from their accompanying profound interests in feeling or passion (Plato, Augustine, Aquinas, Descartes, Kant), or because their perceived tendency to "irrationality" has led to an obscuring of their true intent (de Maistre, Kierkegaard).

8 See, *intra*, in his "Revolting Passions," and, in more historical detail, idem, *From Passions to Emotions: The Creation of a Secular Psychological Category* (Cambridge: Cambridge University Press, 2003). Peter Goldie's "Intellectual Emotions and Religious Emotions" witnesses to the stretched (and largely secular) category of "emotion" which dominates discussion of the topic in contemporary analytic philosophy.

9 See, e.g., Genevieve Lloyd, *The Man of Reason: "Male" and "Female" in Western Philosophy* (Minneapolis, MN: University of Minnesota Press, 1984), and the survey of related literature in Sarah Coakley, *Powers and Submissions: Spirituality, Philosophy and Gender* (Oxford: Blackwell, 2002), chapter 5.

10 I have recently argued this point in Sarah Coakley, "Dark Contemplation and Epistemic Transformation: The Analytic Theologian Re-Meets Teresa of Ávila," in eds. Oliver D. Crisp and Michael C. Rae, *Analytic Theology: New Essays in the Philosophy of Theology* (Oxford: Oxford University Press, 2009), pp. 280–312.

11 This issue is regrettably only glancingly tackled in this present volume, and much work remains to be done. A revealing feminist-inflected account of the passions in the seventeenth century is provided in Susan James, *Passion and Action: The Emotions in Seventeenth-Century Philosophy* (Oxford: Clarendon Press, 1997).

12 I take a brief look at those issues in my "Postscript," below.

13 Cavanaugh spells out this contemporary thesis in much greater detail in his recent volume *The Myth of Religious Violence: Secular Ideology and the Roots of Modern Conflict* (New York: Oxford University Press, 2009).

14 Similar themes are however traced, for instance, in Martha C. Nussbaum, *The Therapy of Desire: Theory and Practice in Hellenistic Ethics* (Princeton, NJ: Princeton University Press, 1994), though without the attention to Christian contemplative practice and sustained monastic discipline which are the hallmarks of Evagrius's vision.

15 It should be noted again that Milbank's rendition of Kant on this theme departs radically from that proposed by John Hare in "Kant, the Passions, and the Structure of Moral Motivation."

16 See Antonio R. Damasio, *Descartes' Error: Emotion, Reason, and the Human Brain* (New York: Avon Books, 1994), esp. chapters 1–2 on the case of Phineas Gage, whose skull was pierced right through by a wooden railway stake and who subsequently underwent a profound character change.

1

REASON, FAITH, AND MEANING

CHARLES TAYLOR

1

There are two connected illusions, it seems to me, which have become very common today. The first consists in marking a very sharp distinction between reason and faith—even to the point of defining faith as believing without good reason! The second is to take as a model what I want to call "disengaged" reason. And these two are tightly linked.

To start with the first, since the Enlightenment, a notion has been developed of "reason alone" (I'm taking this from the title of Kant's book, *Religion within the Limits of Reason Alone*). By that was meant, reason no longer augmented (or disturbed) by revelation. It was in that way explicitly contrasted to reasoning which operates along with, or on the basis of, revelation.

Obviously, the proposal to dispense with revelation was something new, but there was still an important continuity with earlier understandings. For the scholastic tradition, reason was capable of establishing important truths on its own. It could demonstrate the rational nature of human beings, and the ethic which should follow from this. It could even establish the existence of a Creator. But it needed revelation to take us farther, for instance to bring us the insight that this Creator was the Triune God of the Bible.

What seems agreed between pre- and post-Enlightenment positions is that reason and revelation can be clearly distinguished as distinct sources of truth. Many post-Enlightenment thinkers took over this conception of the two sources, and simply discarded or denied one of them.

But I would like to argue that the vicissitudes of the appeal to "reason alone" force us to depart more radically from this tradition. For a whole host of important purposes, "reason" is not the name of a reliable source offering

Faith, Rationality, and the Passions, First Edition. Edited by Sarah Coakley.
© 2012 Blackwell Publishing Ltd. Book compilation © 2012 Blackwell Publishing Ltd.

univocal and reliable answers; and "revelation" itself is a category by which we try, rationally, to make sense of the truths we discern.

I have just said that "reason" doesn't offer univocal and reliable answers in a number of domains. But there are some in which it seems to come very close to this. Let's look at these, because they provide the basis on which the belief in "reason alone" has been grounded. (A) Reason gets pretty close to univocal validity when it comes to the kind of reasoning whose rules are codified in formal logic and mathematics. And we might see (B) the discovery of reliable truth in natural science as a fruit of reason. Being rational here involves applying a correct method; we painstakingly validate our observations; and then we infer from them to the best explanation.

But while the Vienna positivists in their heyday may have thought that this suffices to generate valid scientific theories, the reflections of philosophers of science like Canguilhem and Thomas Kuhn have shown us that we need more. Good explanation—and then the further rational discovery which this enables—depends on (C) an adequate conceptualization. Our explanations can improve radically with a shift in what Kuhn called our "paradigms." As well as painstaking observation (1), and explanatory inferences (2), we need the exercise of (3) the theoretical imagination which enables us to reframe our questions. Sometimes our grasp of some domain remains very incomplete, and full of unexplained anomalies, until we transform our understanding of the crucial questions through a paradigm shift.

One famous example can suffice to illustrate this. Post-Galilean mechanics arose through shifting the crucial question. According to the Aristotelian mechanics which had dominated for centuries, in order to explain the continued motion of a projectile after it has left the hand (or the cannon mouth), one had to find some agency which went on propelling it. All motion required a motor force contemporary with it. The crucial question was: what causes continuing movement? Various candidates were proposed which all proved unsatisfactory. Continued motion remained an anomaly. The adoption of the inertial perspective changed the question; now it was: what causes changes in velocity? At once it became possible to make sense of the whole domain of imparted motion. The anomalies were explained and thus overcome.

Reason in this domain of natural science must include this third dimension, a creative recasting of the problem, which can't be "delivered" through a reliable pre-existing method. It requires something in the nature of insight, which can be validated, but only afterwards, through the overcoming of anomalies. Now in the domain of natural science, this doesn't seem to exclude our arriving at solid and agreed conclusions. Because even if the new insights can't be generated at will, and we may labor a long time before someone hits on them, we can generally agree which paradigm shifts have been valid. These impose themselves because they resolve the anomalies which earlier theories generated, without creating equally difficult ones in their place. This kind of progress can thus be credited to "reason alone."

We should note, however, that this happy result is only possible through a stringent form of self-restriction; "scientific" language in the meaning of the act must be purged of all reference to its significance for us; it must be used to make "literal" claims, in a sense which excludes metaphor, except those which can be "cashed out" quite "literally." It is a special "insulated" form of expression.[1]

But when we come to those issues in which the explanation and evalua-tion of human life is at issue; when we come, for instance, to ethics, political theory, social science, history, literature, philosophy, aesthetics, and the like, we are in a very different predicament. "Insulated" language is no longer adequate. New creations of our theoretical imagination (we might call this our "moral-anthropological imagination") are not lacking. But we find it very difficult to arrive at the kind of universal consensus which we at least approach in natural science. On the contrary, people of different cul-tures, different ethical outlooks, different aesthetic and moral intuitions, adopt very different paradigms for their accounts of human action and the nature of our moral life; and they cannot easily convince each other, or converge on a favored view, except in certain milieux and often for a limited time.

Faced with this disagreement, some conclude to relativism, and claim that there is no fact of the matter. Human nature is shaped by the interpretations we offer of it, and there is no given basis on which we must eventually converge. I haven't got the space to argue this here, but this inference doesn't convince me. We don't need to assume that there is no fact of the matter. Continued disagreement springs rather from this profound connection between the explanatory paradigms we find convincing in explaining human life, on one hand, and our moral and aesthetic, or spiritual sensibility, on the other. It is very often extremely difficult even to understand each other when we are arguing over a significant gap in spiritual outlook, and actually changing someone's mind may involve a thoroughgoing reorientation of his/her spiritual life, and not simply a punctual shift in a particular opinion which leaves the rest of his/her being unchanged.

An example may help clarify this. Take a widespread paradigm (alas) in social science today, that is based on rational choice theory. The affinity with the ethical theory we call utilitarianism is fairly evident, and both share a faith in a kind of transparent rational grasp of our motivations and moral predicament, which others (myself included) believe is bought at the expense of a considerable distortion of human experience. The attraction of the explanatory account is obviously linked to the attraction of this construal of the human moral predicament, and both express the powerful draw of a certain notion of rationality. You need a big change in your stance towards the world to get out of this pervasive construal.[2]

So I would like to claim that there is a truth of the matter underlying this kind of dispute; I would like also to say that we can reason about it; for instance we can debate which view really makes sense of human action, and put rational choice theory under severe strain when it is confronted with certain human actions in history. We can also show a rational path from one to another moral construal, by demonstrating how the better account can free us to take account of important things which the inferior one was blocking out.[3]

But I can't argue this here.[4] I would like rather to say what this means for our understanding of reason. What this means is that our reasoning always involves a third dimension, beyond accurate observation and reliable inference, namely what I called "theoretical imagination" in connection with natural science, and what we could call the "moral-anthropological imagination" in relation to human affairs. Reason has, in other words, a creative component; it can and must generate new ways of conceiving the reality it is trying to understand. How do we generate these? There is no standard answer, no sure method, but in general we can say that we do so by articulating what start as barely definable hunches, or inchoate insights. These unformed insights draw us strongly; we are willing to engage our attention very deeply in them. We have an as yet unfounded and nonetheless powerful anticipatory confidence in them; we might even speak of this as a kind of faith.

Fides quaerens intellectum: it may seem shocking to invoke this formula in a discussion of scientific paradigms. But I believe that there is a distant but discernible analogy with the theological. There is, in other words, a similarity of structure which can be discerned in all uses of the imagination which leap ahead of and set the path for more certain knowledge. Of course, this structure is visible in an impoverished mode in the scientific "hunch." The impoverishment resides in the fact that the act of faith is not in the general case in God, in the love and fidelity of one (a Being? but God is not really a Being) who is capable of these. And correspondingly, our faith emerges from and is nourished by our whole sense of what is of ultimate importance in life, whereas the scientific hunch relates to a much more circumscribed area. Thus one can say that the faith in God which seeks intellectual expression defines a direction for the intellect only because and to the extent that this faith gives a direction to our whole being. But nevertheless a loose analogy holds. The dawning sense of a new paradigm leaps ahead of what we know, and defines the direction of further inquiry which aims to clarify what draws us to it.

This richer notion of reason has often been neglected or forgotten in recent centuries, but it returns us to Plato. His "logos," which we translate "reason," involves the articulation in words of insight, whose full nature can nevertheless not be fully communicated in words. Reason cannot be simply reduced to explicit reason*ing*, the methodical rational operations which we carry out on our already articulated insights.

It was Descartes among others who caused us to lose this broader understanding of reason. Descartes held that reasoning could be from start to finish guided tightly by a defined method. He had no place for the notion that reasoning relies on articulations, which then only justify themselves, if they ever do so, *post factum*, by the sense they manage to make of the reality under study. These articulations transform our understanding. So much so, that even the kind of sense we end up making may be undreamt of before the articulation is made.[5]

The path through reason to truth inevitably involves a phase of near-blind groping which only later may be ratified in the clarity of the sense-making that ensues. There are two facets to this ratification. The first comes from the clarity of the sense we make, which each one of us may experience for ourselves. The second comes from the general agreement of all those engaged in reasoning, that we have really made sense of things. Because reasoning is something we don't only do alone, but which also inescapably involves dialogical collaboration and exchange, these two facets can never be wholly separated from each other. Descartes not only neglected this interplay of groping and ratification, but he supposed the ratification as self-authenticating in the certainty of clarity and distinctness. The dialogical dimension dropped from sight altogether.

Of course, this two-step understanding of reason, moving from articulation to ratification, gives just the most general, abstract form of its progress. This notion has to be augmented and enriched as soon as we think of reasoning as situated in a tradition. I will return to this below.

But for the moment, we should ask: What does this understanding of reasoning do to the post-Enlightenment notion of "reason alone"? In fact, it makes it very problematic to say the least. If reason alone is defined in opposition to faith, then it threatens to collapse as a category when we see the role that faith in our inchoate insights must play. If it is opposed to revelation, then the problem is that "revelation" is a category which we come to articulate in order to make sense of our most fundamental insights. It is itself the fruit of reason-as-articulation.

Maybe we can salvage a category of reason alone as what is operative in certain everyday reasonings as well as in natural science (the categories that Vienna positivists were willing to declare as free from metaphysics). We can say that once the inchoate insight has been articulated in a new paradigm, and once this paradigm shift is ratified through the sense it enables us to make of things, the element of faith is transcended. But for this very reason, the category can't apply to that whole domain which I outlined above where the anthropological-moral imagination is ever-active. On the contrary, in this domain ratification is never clear without zones of puzzlement and obscurity, and in the dialogical dimension it never comes close to generalized assent.

2

So we begin to see how the too simple separation of reason and faith comes unstuck. It does, indeed, seem to hold in certain domains, for instance, in mathematics and natural science. But once we step beyond these, it breaks down.

Now this begins to make clear the connection of this first error with the second, the belief that reason must be disengaged. The domains in which reason can easily seem to dispense with faith are the privileged fields of disengaged reason. By that I mean a reasoning which in no way draws insight from the significances things have for us as embodied, social beings, who mark moral or aesthetic distinctions in things and actions. This pre-scinding from life meanings was the essential founding step of modern post-Galilean, post-Baconian natural science. This natural science can be convincing to everyone, regardless of culture, because its explanations recur to factors which are not defined by their meanings for us, but simply by their efficient-causal relations. Descartes for his part defines clear and distinct perception as a disembodied grasp of things, where our normal grasp of them as embodied beings counts as obscure and confused. Our seeing the color in the object, our sensing the pain in the tooth, these are obscure and confused; to objectify the process, and to see the pain as arising from some pathology in the tooth is to see things clearly.[6]

Now it is true that even in these domains, our hunches are often given force by their elegance and simplicity, and mathematicians' intuitions can be drawn to what they see as beautiful forms. But the objects studied in each case have to be defined without reference to these meanings.

When, however, we come to the domains I mentioned above, including ethics, history, social science, literature, this kind of disengagement is impos-sible. How do we come to understand the emotions and reactions, the sense of beauty and the good, whether of another person, or of a strange society, without drawing on our own reactions? This may sound strange, because precisely in the case of cultures very different from ours, the easiest and most damaging mistake will often be to see them as operating out of the same gamut of possible emotions and reactions as we do. This will often make them come out as espousing the worse rather than the better, as being rude rather than refined, as addicted to pleasure rather than disciplined, as pagans worshipping the devil rather than revering the true God, etc. And it is almost always the case that these too ethnocentric perceptions are mis-readings, and we have to come somehow to see these other cultures in their difference.

But precisely, this can't be done simply by setting aside our own reactions, and studying this alien group "dispassionately." We can't just neutralize our expectations, because that doesn't help us understand. To observe these people outside of any frame of human meaning is to see them as another animal species, opaque and enigmatic. True, our expectations make their behavior puzzling, and we have to get far enough to see that these expectations are wrong. But the only way beyond them is to go deeper into the puzzlement they awaken in us, to live in and analyze this until a liberating insight comes into where the differences lie. This kind of science can only be done while one "inhabits" the meanings things have for us, rather than by disengaging from them.

We come to a similar conclusion when we look at what it is to make headway in ethical or spiritual insight. We ask ourselves what is really important in human life, for instance. Or we ask ourselves whether our spiritual life shouldn't take a new direction. We can explore this kind of question only through our own sense of what is important, or where spiritual growth lies. Again, this sounds paradoxical, because we want precisely to *grow* when we ask these questions. So surely we need to set aside our present intuitions? And in one sense, this is true, but in another important sense, not.

We may indeed ask other people to guide us, or read books to get other points of view, but what we are trying to do here is to educate our sense of what is really important; we are not simply bracketing it and studying the question dispassionately. And indeed, what will help convince us that we are making headway is a changed insight into what is important, but this is also something that we feel. Such insights are not in the nature of things purely dispassionate. When we might want to use this term, it is because we sense that it is taking us beyond some passions, those for instance of narcissistic ego-satisfaction, not that we are coming to a pure, emotion-free perception of the meanings of things.

Such moments do exist—when we have a fleeting insight, for instance, that we are living on a much lower plane than we need to. But these are exceptional moments. Normally, our sense that X is important ethically is inseparable from our feeling its importance, from admiring those who follow it, for instance; or being inspired by it; or feeling relieved and grateful that this exists as a human possibility.

In other words, the perception of significance, of human meanings, can't be detached from the experiencing of these meanings, an experience which can only be rarely and fleetingly indifferent. We grasp these meanings through our partiality to them. To such a point that we can often say, with Plato, that one hasn't really understood the good unless one is drawn to it; unless one loves it—though one may be driven, and also drawn to incompatible ends.

This is what the disciples at Emmaus knew, when they said to themselves "did not our hearts burn within us?" (Luke 24:32). They meant: we ought to have known. Our hearts were recognizing the truth, even while we were resisting it.

But again, this sounds paradoxical. Does this mean that we ultimately judge by brute reaction? We feel this is good, so we judge it good? Does reason have no further role here? On the contrary. Just as in the case where we are trying to understand people very different from us, there can be reasons to mistrust our reactions. Maybe some of the things we are induced to do by our present ethical sense shock us or others in some way. Maybe we have reason to think that our reactions are coming out of something extraneous in us, that has no reason to be linked with a correct perception of *this* good. Thus my satisfaction with my reaction to some challenge may come not from a real perception of its rightness, but from a more narcissistic fulfillment: that I like the image of myself responding, giving the stinging rebuke to wrong-doing, for instance, or standing up with integrity. We can come to liberate ourselves from these irrelevant reactions, and the truer perception of what's important that thereby emerges is all the more convincing, because it comes out of such an error-reducing move.[7]

In other words, just having the feeling that X is important doesn't resolve the issue. Questions, puzzlement may remain; and they may be raised by others. This hunch can't be fully ratified as long as these questions remain, and others disagree. The process of reasoning goes on. And this process involves the two phases of reasoning we identified above. Partly, it involves a re-articulation of our original insight: for instance, to distinguish what in it is really valid from what comes from narcissistic satisfaction. And articulation of inchoate insights is the first phase of reason. And we re-articulate in order to resolve anomalies and contradictions, which is the second phase: the good insight seems to have bad fruits, or our feelings of self-satisfaction are uncomfortably strong.

But without a perception which proceeds through a *feeling* of importance, there is no insight at all; neither the first off one which must face objections, nor an eventually more satisfactory one which has answered these. The whole process cannot go forward in disengaged mode.

The process of rational critique that I have just been describing is central to moral development. Moral growth involves, among other things, a change in our emotional reactions to people, acts, predicaments, making these reactions more accurate and insightful. But this doesn't mean that the standards which we aim at in this process are—or even could be—set by an utterly disengaged form of rationality, such as might suffice to calculate utility consequences, or to check if a maxim could be coherently applied universally. The temptation to resort to such abstracted forms arises from the mistaken belief that our sentiments are brute, non-cognitive, uninformed by insight, whether accurate or not. I will take up this error in the next section.

Needless to say, the process of surmounting anomalies is never finished. I remember going to see the film *Cabaret*, made on the basis of Christopher Isherwood's novel of late-Weimar Berlin. At one moment, a young man in uniform stands in the street and sings a song, "Tomorrow belongs to me." To my horror, I felt my feelings being recruited, by the music, the singer's youth, his wonderful confidence. Am I becoming a Nazi? Well, no, but it was an uncomfortable reminder: of lots of things, including how easily we respond to certain appeals towards a beautiful future. And I also reflect: I will not be a Nazi, because I have 20/20 hindsight where that leads. But what if I had been a young German in Berlin in 1932?

All of the above shows the crucial link of reason with the "passions": let this term stand here for our perception of life meanings through feeling— through the way that these meanings *move* us. Not seeing this is a fruit of making the disengaged uses of reason the only ones that deserve the name. So our two errors connect: the separation of reason and faith, and the separation of reason from the passions which are inseparable from the perceptions of certain meanings. There are certain domains where both separations (more or less) work; and others where they are both crippling. And we can see what distinguishes the two kinds.

3

Ideally, I would like to trace the origins of these connected errors: that of "reason alone," and that of a necessarily "dispassionate" reason. But unfortunately, there isn't space for this massive task here. I will just be able to take up the latter here, and relatively briefly, because the error is (perhaps) easier to see through.

A widespread mistake in modern philosophy is to lose sight of the distinction between an emotion and what might be called a sensation or a "raw feel." An emotion, like fear or despondency, joy or hopefulness, involves a perception. The emotion is a response to its "intentional object," and as such essentially involves a "take" on this object. I fear some impending disaster, or I am despondent at some disappointing outcome which has already befallen. The emotion is an apprehension of the object, threatening or actually present, but in the register of feeling.

This contrasts with what I'm calling a sensation, like pain, or a tingling in my foot, or the pleasurable feeling of entering a warm bath after trekking through deep snow. Of course, you also perceive the bath, and perhaps the cut which causes the pain, but these two are distinct. The sensation can be exactly this feeling, an acute pain in my hand, for instance, even if one has no idea what causes it. One rushes to a doctor to find out.

One of the distortions introduced by the modern objectified philosophical anthropology was to split emotion from its constituent perception, and thus assimilate it to sensation. On this view, the fact that a given emotion attends a certain kind of event—despondency in face of a disaster, for instance—can be judged neither appropriate or inappropriate; it is just a brute fact about us, like that fact that pain attends some kinds of changes in our bodies, and not others, or that some substances cause nausea and not others. The relation between event and affect is purely causal, and as such contingent.

Thus Hume will argue, in one of the most fatefully influential passages of his philosophy, that our moral sentiments are not ultimately grounded in reason. It is just a brute fact about us that we respond with approbation to what conduces to utility, ours or that of others. He is making a clear rupture with the ethical tradition of the ancients, which saw the good as an object of rational perception, an object which cannot be rightly perceived without being loved.

On this view, the rational perception of reality is by its very nature independent of our emotional reaction. It can proceed quite dispassionately. Passion can disturb us, if it is too strong, or too subtly seductive of our reasoning powers, but it cannot help.

But surely this mistrust of passion is not itself a modern error. Does it not go back to the ancients, who in general did understand our emotions correctly as perceptions in the register of feeling? Yes, but the mistrust of passion didn't involve a declaration of independence from all emotion. Take the Stoics, for instance. They did declare all passions as illusions. But they saw that these passions claimed the status of perceptions, that is, that they involved "opinions" (*doxai*) about their objects. To fear something was to see it as noxious. But the opinions intrinsic to the passions were all false. We had to liberate ourselves from these erroneous views, and hence of the passions which they animated.

But this didn't mean that our perception of the true order of things was utterly without affect. On the contrary, the correct grasp of things was accompanied by joy (*chara*). In a similar way, the correct grasp of the Good for Plato must move us to love it.

So the venerable doctrine that true rational understanding was "dispassionate" didn't amount to the modern view that it was affect-free. This is not to say that we will necessarily agree with the different traditional ways in which "passion" has been defined and distinguished from the affect inherent in the perception of truth. We couldn't, of course, agree with *all* of them, but we might well disagree with them all, and still not fall into the crucial error of the moderns, which is to fail to see the intrinsic epistemic content of emotion.

I invoked Hume above as the originator of the view that our moral opinions are grounded ultimately in brute reactions. Now there are many readings of Hume, and in this volume John Milbank proposes another. The one I am espousing here is the one which has made Hume a founding thinker of modern naturalism. I'd like to spell out a bit more what this reading involves.

The dominant tradition from the ancients sees ethical meanings as discernible by reason. Some modes of action, together with the motives inherent in them, are objectively higher; they are the object of a strong evaluation. Examples are: Aristotle's *theôria*, or else the citizen life, where you exercise and perfect your *phronésis*. You are actuated by love of truth, desire to know (*theôria*), or you seek honor, but also the common good. But another example is the Christian vision of a life actuated by *agape*. Or think of modern notions of career: aspiring to be a composer, writer, artist. These higher modes of being can also be described in terms of virtues. To have virtue is to be spontaneously disposed to act in the highest way from the highest motives.

On this model, reason can discern the order of higher and lower activities. This is quite understandable with Aristotle and Plato, where reason is precisely the faculty which can discern orders in things.

It follows that there is such a thing as getting it wrong. You fail to see what is higher in the citizen life. Or you misidentify what makes the citizen life *kalos* (noble-beautiful). You think it's just getting power, or fulfilling desires, or enjoying prestige.

There is a clear contrast with the reaction-triggering properties of things: e.g., shit is nauseating. There is no such thing as rightly/wrongly identifying this property. You can be unusual in not finding excrement disturbing, and/or in having nausea triggered by other things; but you can't be wrong. What nauseates is just a brute fact about you and other agents.

Now Hume denies this model. In the *Enquiry*, he poses the question about the foundations of morals, "whether they be derived from Reason, or from Sentiment."[8] His first answer is that both seem to have a case. We do *argue* about moral issues, about right and wrong. But on the other hand, it seems that

the final sentence, it is probable, which pronounces characters and actions amiable or odious, praise-worthy or blameable; that which stamps on them the mark of honour or infamy, approbation or censure; that which renders morality an active principle and constitutes virtue our happiness and vice our misery: it is probable, I say, that this final sentence depends on some internal sense or feeling, which nature has made universal in the whole species.[9]

This sentiment, then, is the ultimate basis of morality. This is a brute fact about us, not the deliverance of reason that we approve virtue and abhor vice. But this sentiment is quite different from our reaction of nausea, because it is directed towards certain human qualities, and we sometimes need to reason in order to determine whether these hold or not in given cases. The contrast case, for which I have chosen nausea as an example, is represented for Hume by "some species of beauty, especially the natural kinds, [which] on their first appearance, command our affection and approbation; and where they fail of this effect, it is impossible for any reasoning to redress their influence, or adapt them better to our taste or sentiment."[10]

But "in order to pave the way for [the moral] sentiment, and give a proper discernment of its object, it is often necessary, we find, that much reasoning should precede, and nice distinctions be made, just conclusions drawn, distant comparisons formed, complicated relations examined, and general facts fixed and ascertained."[11]

We thus have something here which is intermediary between, on one hand, the Platonic-Aristotelian rational perception of a higher way of being, and, on the other, mere brute reactions. What, then, do we, as a matter of brute fact, approve? Hume turns to examine this question, taking the example of the "benevolent or softer affections . . . [which] wherever they appear, engage the approbation and good will of mankind."[12] "No qualities are more entitled to the general good-will and approbation of mankind than beneficence and humanity, friendship and gratitude, natural affection and public spirit, or whatever proceeds from a tender sympathy with others, and a generous concern for our kind and species."[13]

Here he speaks of qualities "entitled to" our approbation, but this is to speak with the vulgar, to offer an expression of our common sentiment rather than an ultimate justification. For Hume this sentiment can be explained as a joint creation of two other motives which we universally share: we value "utility," that is, whatever conduces to life, health and the fulfillment of (non-harmful) desire; and we experience sympathy for other human beings. Utility alone makes us like beneficent acts of which we are the object and dislike the disutilities imposed on us by others. But utility in the context of sympathy induces us to respond positively to beneficence, and negatively to malefaction, whoever the recipients are or may be. Here Hume is following Hutcheson and the Scottish tradition of moral sense. Approbation and blame are *distinct sentiments*, immediately recognizable as such, and different from liking and disliking. It is these sentiments which can be explained (but not shown to be higher) by the joint operation of utility and sympathy.

But just because it is the real occurrence and not just the semblance of beneficence which gains our approbation, there is always room for argument, for probing, to establish that this object really exists in a particular case. Perhaps the supposed philanthropist is actually weaving some careful scheme to bring the apparent beneficiary under his control. Perhaps what we take as a case of one man inflicting terrible pain on another turns out really to be a surgeon removing a potentially fatal tumor. Our first off reactions can be revised. This revisability explains certain historical changes in Hume's view. The ancients disapproved of "luxury, or a refinement on the pleasures and conveniences of life," because they thought it to be "the source of every corruption in government, and the immediate cause of faction, sedition, civil wars, and the total loss of liberty." We moderns who now attempt to prove "that such refinements rather tend to the increase of industry, civility, and arts regulate anew our *moral* as well as *political* sentiments, and represent, as laudable or innocent, what had formerly been regarded as pernicious and blameable."[14]

That humans value utility goes without saying, but moral sentiments show that our concern goes wider.

> If usefulness, therefore, be a source of moral sentiment, and if this usefulness be not always considered with a reference to self; it follows, that everything, which contributes to the happiness of society, recommends itself directly to our approbation and good-will. Here is a principle, which accounts, in great part, for the origin of morality: And what need we seek for abstruse and remote systems, when there occurs one so obvious and natural?[15]

A footnote to this passage adds: "It is needless to push our researches so far as to ask, why we have humanity or a fellow-feeling with others. It is sufficient, that this is experienced to be a principle in human nature. We must stop somewhere in our examination of causes; and there are, in every science, some general principles, beyond which we cannot hope to find any principle more general."[16]

In other words, the positive evaluation of utility needs no explanation, and sympathy is a brute fact about our nature. What need have we to look further, for some supposedly rational insight which shows the love of the general good to be "higher"? We can see right away that the conception of reason has changed. The reason Hume invokes is not the discernment of an order of higher and lower; it is reasoning about consequences. That some character trait in fact conduces to the general utility, if this is sufficiently evident, is enough to explain why it is valued as a virtue. We see this with the case of justice (Section III). With some virtues, we might judge people by their intentions, rather than the actual results of their actions. This would be the case with benevolence, for instance. But then the issue is what good results they were striving to encompass.

The reason involved here is instrumental reason, what causes what? In particular, what brings about utility for human beings in general, severally and individually? Its relevance to our motivation is no longer the same as with Plato and Aristotle. For them, the reason discerning order was thought to motivate us to live up to this order. Indeed, we can't really be said to grasp the order if we are not appropriately moved by it. But with Hume, we now have a perception of causal relations which by itself would be motivationally inert. What it lacks as a motivating force is precisely a desire to encompass certain ends, which would set us about producing the means. That is the ultimate principle which Hume invokes. Reason establishes "factual" connections. These are motivationally inert. So what can move us, if not "some internal sense or feeling, which nature has made universal in the whole species. For what else can have an influence of this nature?"[17] This is the ultimate clincher. Or as Hume put it in the *Treatise of Human Nature* (2.3.3.4): "Reason is, and ought only to be the slave of the passions."

So Hume (a) eliminates reason as a perception of higher/lower, and (b) refocuses reason as the inquiry into what makes for utility. One can see how this outlook by a slight shift could mutate into Benthamite utilitarianism. And indeed, Bentham credits Hume as his major inspiration in the introduction to his *Principles of Morals and Legislation*. We simply start from the obvious importance of utility, and the fact of sympathy, and then we can ask: what else might justify any act as the right one, other than its having the greatest utility consequences? For any rival criterion has been displaced from the scene, and especially the outmoded ancient theories of virtue.

4

So a concatenation of errors has contributed to a Wittgensteinian picture which has "held us captive."[18] The powerful model of natural science has convinced many that true knowledge of the world has to be in "neutral" terms, that is, in terms which are purged of human meanings. Theoretical reason must operate in such a purified mode. But this means that practical reason cannot find the grounds for action in a world of "facts" alone. "Neutral" facts, by definition, can't tell us what we should do. They can only guide us once we have espoused certain goals, in the light of which these facts can become relevant to action. But since theoretical reason cannot establish these goals, they must come from ourselves, from our de facto inclinations. A neutral world is given practical shape by the "values" that human agents project onto it. Our values may arise from "faith," and they will almost certainly engage us emotionally, except in the most trivial contexts. But both faith and feeling can't arise in reason. They can only guide practical, that is, instrumental reason as ungrounded premises. The very possibility of a close relation between reason, faith and feeling becomes invisible. And so it remains for great numbers among our contemporaries.

NOTES

1   See Nicholas Lash, *Theology for Pilgrims* (South Bend, IN: University of Notre Dame Press, 2008), pp. 30–33.
2   This wide gap in the understanding of what is at stake can be seen in the public arguments which have been sparked by Angry Atheists. The God denounced by Dawkins, Hitchens, etc. doesn't seem to bear a close relation to the God of Abraham that Christians, Jews, etc. worship.
3   I have argued this point at greater length in "Explanation and Practical Reason," in *Philosophical Arguments* (Cambridge, MA: Harvard University Press, 1995).
4   In fact one recurring theme of the "adventures" of reason since the Enlightenment has been the flip-over whereby the exaggerated hopes for certain knowledge reposed in one or another method generate a far-reaching skepticism or relativism once it becomes clear that they cannot be met. This theme deserves much fuller treatment than I can give it here.

5 The importance of such articulations is central to Gadamer's critique of the omnicompetence of "method." Hans-Georg Gadamer, *Truth and Method*, second edition, translation revised by Joel Weinsheimer and Donald G. Marshall (New York: Continuum, 1993).

6 See *Meditations* III, in *Oeuvres de Descartes*, eds. Charles Adam and Paul Tannery (13 vols; Paris: J. Vrin, 1964–76), Vol. IX-1, p. 34; and also *Principles* I.68 in IX-2, p. 56.

7 I have talked about this kind of reasoning through transitions in "Explanation and Practical Reason"; see note 3.

8 134 (170). See Hume's "Enquiry Concerning the Principles of Morality" in David Hume, *Enquiries Concerning the Human Understanding and Concerning the Principles of Morals*, ed. L.A. Selby-Bigge, second edition (Oxford: Clarendon Press, 1902 [reprinted 1970]). Numbers out of brackets refer to the sections in the text, those in parentheses to the page number in this edition.

9 137 (pp. 172–173).

10 (p. 173).

11 (p. 173).

12 139 (p. 176).

13 340 (p. 178).

14 143 (p. 181).

15 178 (p. 219).

16 (pp. 219–220).

17 137 (p. 173).

18 "Ein Bild hielt uns gefangen," L. Wittgenstein, *Philosophical Investigations*, Section I, paragraph 115.

2

THE INVENTION OF FANATICISM

WILLIAM T. CAVANAUGH

It is common these days to say that the "secularization thesis" has been challenged by a global "resurgence" of religion. While not everyone accepts that the secularization thesis has been decisively refuted, the resurgence of religion seems to be a fact, one that can either be lamented or celebrated. Those who lament it often invoke the specter of religious violence: religion has a dangerous tendency to provoke and exacerbate violence wherever it is not domesticated and removed from public power by the secular state. According to this line of thought, religion has this lamentable tendency because it is an essentially non-rational impulse, a passion that frequently eludes or exceeds the attempts of reason to tame it. The frightful specter of religious fanaticism in the modern world is offered as evidence of the dangerous extremes to which untamed religious passion can tend if not brought to heel by a secular social order.

In my recent book *The Myth of Religious Violence*, I argue at length that the opposition of religion and reason was not diagnosed but invented by the modern West. The religious/secular distinction is a modern invention that directly parallels the invention of the modern state. Religion is not in fact a transhistorical, transcultural, and essentially non-rational feature of human life. As religion was invented in the early modern struggle between ecclesiastical and civil powers in Europe, it was envisioned as occupying an essentially non-rational and non-public sphere to which the concerns of the church should be confined. As the liberal state developed, "religion" became a category into which to dump ideologies and practices that are judged antithetical to the liberal state's goal of excluding substantive ends from the public sphere. As William Arnal writes, "This very definition of the modern democratic state in fact creates religion as its alter-ego: religion, as such, is the space in which and by which any substantive collective goals (salvation, righteous-

Faith, Rationality, and the Passions, First Edition. Edited by Sarah Coakley.
© 2012 Blackwell Publishing Ltd. Book compilation © 2012 Blackwell Publishing Ltd.

ness, etc.) are individualized and made into a question of personal commitment or morality."[1] Religion is a special *political* category that marginalizes and domesticates whatever forms of collective social action that happen to retain a positive or utopian orientation.[2]

Religion as passionate and non-rational is not a fact but a construction of the modern West. In this chapter I will examine this construction by first summarizing, in drastically brief form, the history of the category "religion" and the creation of the myth of religious violence. I will then examine the construction of one of the stock characters of modernity, the religious fanatic. I will close by showing how the construction of "religious fanaticism" can promote secularist rationales for violence.

Religion and Violence

The myth of religious violence is the idea that religion is a transhistorical, transcultural, and non-rational impulse that is inherently more prone to violence than so-called secular phenomena. The violence of religion is tamed by secular social orders that remove religion from public, which is the sphere of reason.

If we examine the concept of religion, however, we find that it is not a transhistorical and transcultural dimension of human life, but a category with a history tied up with the rise of the modern state in the West. Wilfred Cantwell Smith's landmark study *The Meaning and End of Religion* demonstrated that in the premodern West and in non-Western cultures previous to contact with the West, there was nothing equivalent to what we think of as religion, as a discrete human activity separable from culture, politics, and other areas of life.[3] The ancient Greeks, Egyptians, Aztecs, Indians, Chinese, and Japanese all lacked an equivalent term for religion, because it was not something separable from other areas of life.[4] It would be nonsense, for example, to ask whether the Aztecs' bloody human sacrifices were "religious" or "political"; there simply was no such distinction. The ancient Romans employed the term *religio*, but it covered all kinds of civic duties and relations of respect that we would consider "secular." As Augustine says in *The City of God*, "Religion (*religio*) is something which is displayed in human relationships, in the family (in the narrower and the wider sense) and between friends; and so the use of the word does not avoid ambiguity when the worship of God is in question. We have no right to affirm with confidence that religion (*religio*) is confined to the worship of God, since it seems that this word has been detached from its normal meaning, in which it refers to an attitude of respect in relations between a man and his neighbor."[5]

In the medieval era, the religious/secular distinction was primarily used to differentiate clergy who were members of orders from diocesan clergy. The ancient meaning of *religio* to which Augustine refers is rare in the medieval period. As John Bossy says, "With very few exceptions, the word was only used to describe different sorts of monastic or similar rule, and the way of life pursued under them."[6] In 1400, the "religions" of England were the various orders—Benedictines, Franciscans, Dominicans, etc.[7] In Christendom there was no separation of religion from a secular realm of politics, economics, and so on. Secondarily, *religio* named a virtue inculcated by disciplined practices within the Christian social order. For Thomas Aquinas, *religio* is one of the nine virtues annexed to the principal virtue of justice. The object of *religio* is the rites and practices, both individual and communal, that offer worship to God. *Religio* was not a purely interior disposition, not a set of beliefs, and not a universal genus of which Christianity was a species.[8] With the dawn of modernity, however, a new concept with a much wider and different significance came to operate under the term "religion." Religion in modernity indicates a universal genus of which the various "religions" are species; each religion comes to be demarcated by a system of propositions; religion is identified with an essentially interior, private, impulse; and religion comes to be seen as essentially distinct from "secular" pursuits such as politics, economics, and the like.

Why was "religion" invented? Within the West, religion was invented as part of the ideological apparatus necessary for the reduction of ecclesiastical power in the modern state. Church authority was gradually delimited to pastoral supervision of a non-rational impulse embedded in the human heart, essentially distinct from "secular" pursuits, the public business of government and economic life. The religious/secular divide thus facilitated the transfer in the modern era of the public loyalty of the citizen from Christendom to the emergent nation-state, the "migration of the holy" from church to state, to use Bossy's phrase.[9] The myth of religious violence helped and continues to help facilitate this process by making the secular nation-state appear as necessary to tame the inherently volatile effects of religion in public life.

Outside the West, religion is an even more recent creation. There is, as Wilfred Cantwell Smith has shown, no "closely equivalent concept in any culture that has not been influenced by the modern West."[10] Russell McCutcheon, Timothy Fitzgerald, Derek Peterson, and a host of other scholars have demonstrated how European colonial bureaucrats imported the concept of religion in the course of categorizing non-Western colonized cultures as subrational and submodern.[11] The creation of religion and its secular twin accompanied the attempts of colonial powers and indigenous modernizing elites to marginalize certain aspects of non-Western cultures and create public space for the smooth functioning of state and market interests. Hinduism, for example, was classified as a mystical and non-rational religion. As Ronald Inden writes, "Implicit in this notion of Hinduism as exemplifying a mind that is imaginative and passionate rather than rational and willful was, of course, the idea that the Indian mind requires an externally imported world-ordering rationality. This was important for the imperial project of the

British as it appeared, piecemeal, in the course of the nineteenth century."[12] What came to be called "Hinduism" was the entire Indian way of life, including what we would separate into religion, economics, politics, and culture. When British colonists classified Hinduism as a religion, it meant that to be Indian was to be private, while to be British was to be public.

The idea that religion has a peculiar tendency to promote violence is a variation on this idea that religion is an essentially private and non-rational human impulse, not amenable to conflict-solving through public reason. In the contemporary context, the idea that there is something called "religion" with a tendency to promote violence continues to marginalize certain kinds of discourses and practices while authorizing others. Specifically, the idea that public religion causes violence authorizes the marginalization of those things called "religion" from having a divisive influence in public life, and thereby authorizes the state's monopoly on violence and on public allegiance.

Religion, then, emerges as the Other against which the secular nation-state is defined, and against which a secular social order appears as necessary. The secular is established as the sphere of rationality. The secular nation-state also appears as natural and inevitable, the answer to a universal and perennial truth about the inherent danger of non-rational religion.

The Invention of Fanaticism

Accompanying the rise of religion was the rise of the religious fanatic, one of the stock characters of modernity. Although the term, derived from the Latin *fanum* or temple, is used by Cicero, fanaticism only becomes an important term in the sixteenth and seventeenth centuries, where, as Dominique Colas has demonstrated, it is often opposed to the term "civil society," which is here synonymous with, not opposed to, the "state." Colas traces the modern concept to Martin Luther's use of the term *Schwärmer* to describe Thomas Müntzer and the peasants whom he led in violent revolt in 1524–5.[13] As Luther and his followers used it, the term was more than a mere insult, and it described more than a peculiar *intensity* of violent passion. Writing in Latin, Luther's friend Philip Melanchthon used the term *fanaticus homo* to describe his Anabaptist opponents, who, as pacifists, were not engaged in any such violent action. What the leaders of the Peasants' Revolt and the Anabaptists had in common was a desire to eliminate any interval between the city of God and the terrestrial city. Melanchthon was the first figure to oppose the terms *fanaticus homo* and *societas civilis*, or "civil society," in a commentary on Aristotle's *Politics*. In using Aristotle against the Anabaptists, Melanchthon insisted on the theological legitimacy of political authority and decried the Anabaptists' confusion of church authority with political authority. What fanaticism meant precisely was the attempt to eliminate the mediating role of civil society or civil rulers, and to put the coming of the Kingdom of God on earth directly into the hands of the church. The novelty of the Lutheran Two

Kingdoms approach to the question of the relationship between civil and ecclesiastical authorities required coining a new term to name the peculiar heresy of trying to establish the Kingdom of God unmediated by the state.

We must be clear, however, that opposition to fanaticism in the sixteenth century did not mean the removal of Christianity from coercive power. The state that emerges in the Reformation period is not yet the liberal state, with its marginalization of "religion" from public life. There is as yet no separation of church and state, but rather the increasing absorption of the church into the state. The building of confessional identities was part of the state-building project, as Heinz Schilling and a host of other historians exploring early modern confessionalization have attested. As Luther Peterson writes,

> The confessionalization thesis is a fruitful instrument in explaining the transformation of medieval feudal monarchies into modern states, in particular how the new states changed their inhabitants into disciplined, obedient and united subjects. According to the thesis, a key factor in that change is the establishment of religious uniformity in the state: the populace was taught a religious identity—Catholic, Lutheran, or Calvinist—through doctrinal statements (confessions and catechisms) and liturgical practices. This distinguished "us" as a religious and political community from "other," often neighboring, religious-political societies. The ruler was sacralized as the defender and—in Protestant lands—leader of the church, rightfully overseeing the church of his land. These state-led churches also aided state development by imposing moral discipline on the communities.[14]

Fanaticism was in its origins a challenge to the power of the civil authorities to mediate Christian identities to the Christian masses.

Although it originally indicated a kind of theological heresy, from its earliest uses in the sixteenth century "fanaticism" also connoted a kind of pathology, associated with passions like "rage" and "fury." Because it was often spelled with a "ph-," the term was mistakenly thought to be of Greek origin, and the spelling *phanatique* in French linked the word with *phantasme*, *phantôme*, and *phantaisie*. In English "phanatik" was linked with "phantasm" and "phantom," with their connotations of hallucination.[15] The fanatic was one under the influence of a false light or hallucinogenic vision. Melanchthon, for example, attributed the "fanatic ravings" and "rabid reveries" of the Anabaptists to the fact that they "imagine it necessary to wait for new revelations and illuminations from God."[16] A century later, Bossuet would describe the English Society of Friends, derogatorily known as "Quakers," as "fanatical people who believe that all their reveries are inspired in them."[17] It is important to note, however, that for churchmen such as Melanchthon and Bossuet, fanaticism was not so much opposed to reason as it was opposed to the truth. Fanaticism was not thought to typify prophecy *tout court*, but only false prophecy. Fanaticism was not yet a transgression of the proper limits of reason, nor yet was a rejection of fanaticism an argument for the limitation of theological reasoning as such to an interior or private sphere.

As we move toward the creation of a liberal social order, however, two movements in the meaning of fanaticism can be detected. First, fanaticism came to be used to denote not heresy but rather intolerance of doctrinal difference. As it was used to denounce rival Christian sects, fanatics were false prophets, indicating a belief in true prophets. With the advent of liberal thought, however, "fanatic" came to indicate one who refused to remove such judgments from the public sphere.[18] John Locke was an important figure in the opposition of toleration and fanaticism. Locke was instrumental in the establishment of a strict separation between true religion, which belonged to the private conscience of individuals, and the coercive power of the magistrate that pertained to the possession of outward goods. Corresponding to the private/public distinction was the distinction of opinion and reason; tolerance was based precisely on the limits of human understanding in matters of religion. The magistrate had no business interfering in the manner of worship of God, provided it had no effect on my relationship to the prince or to my neighbor. The magistrate did have the right to interfere with the expression of religious opinion if it threatened public order; the magistrate could react with force when "men heard them selves into companys with distinctions from the publique," especially in matters of religion, because "the ties of religion are stronger, & the pretences of conscience fairer, & apter to draw partisans, & therefor the more to be suspected & the more heedfully to be watchd."[19] Though uncivil passions may be met with force, Locke advocates toleration for "Fanatiques," in which he includes Protestant sects dissenting from the Church of England, despite their wish to realize their vision of the Kingdom of God on earth, because they are easily divided and conquered by the state. "For the Fanatiques taken all togeather being numerous, & possibly more then the hearty friends of the state religion, are yet crumbled into different partys amongst them selves . . . People therefor that are soe shatterd into different factions are best securd by toleration," for persecution will be apt to unite them.[20] "Papists," on the other hand, were not to be tolerated, for they owed allegiance to a "foraigne & enemy Prince."[21]

The second shift in the meaning of fanaticism as we enter the Enlightenment was the opposition of fanaticism as a passion to the operation of reason. For Immanuel Kant, for example, fanaticism was involved (as it was for Locke) in transgressing the proper bounds of reason; as Kant writes in his *Critique of Practical Reason*, "fanaticism in its most general sense is a deliberate overstepping of the limits of human reason."[22] As in its earlier theological use, fanaticism is linked to vision and hallucination. In his *Critique of Judgment*, Kant defined fanaticism as "the *delusion of wanting to* SEE *something beyond all bounds of sensibility*, i.e., of dreaming according to principles (raving with reason)."[23] For Kant—unlike for Melanchthon, for example—all prophecy that had not been brought within the bounds of reason alone was suspect.

Establishing those precise bounds was, of course, not simply a philosophical project but a political project. The identification of fanaticism as an anti-rational pathology was accompanied by a vision of a political order against which the fanatic served as threat and alter ego. For Kant, political community could not be based on a kind of vision that was not communicable to others by the standards of public reason. The attempt to bring religion within the bounds of reason alone was accompanied by Kant's insistence that an idea, to be thought, must be thought in common with others. Fanaticism in thinking beyond the bounds of reason could only bring with it a kind of lawlessness. As Alberto Toscano comments, "In Kant, the defence of authority that we encountered in Luther reemerges: denial of any right of rebellion and the requirement in politics for a respect of authority, laws, and representative institutions. This is explained not only by Kant's cautious disposition, but by one of his possible definitions of fanaticism, as the confusion of a regulatory idea (the republic, for example) with a constituent plan that may be affirmed materially and subjectively."[24] In the wake of the French Revolution, Kant carefully distinguished between enthusiasm and fanaticism. Kant embraced the enthusiasm unleashed by the French Revolution, understood as a passion for a universalizing regulatory ideal. Enthusiasm for Kant is not an intensity of passion or emotion, but an aesthetically-appreciated affect for the sublime in history. The enthusiasm of the French Revolution indicated that humanity was being drawn toward its self-improvement in the establishment of a republican ideal. Enthusiasm was a movement of aesthetic judgment in the *observer* of the Revolution, but Kant distinguished enthusiasm from the fanaticism of the *sans-culotte*, who mistakenly attempted to achieve the ideal immediately in the here and now.[25]

As the example of the French Revolution makes plain, for Kant fanaticism is not necessarily religious, though it often is. Kant distinguishes religious fanaticism from a more general moral fanaticism, which is the tendency to exhort moral action on the basis of the supposed purity of the will, not on the basis of duty alone. Moral fanaticism transgresses pure practical reason, which forbids placing the subjective ground of duty in anything but the law.[26] Among Enlightenment figures, it is in Voltaire that the careers of the terms "fanaticism" and "religion" most closely coincide, and thus most closely anticipate contemporary uses of the charge of religious fanaticism.

Voltaire's entry on "Fanaticism" in his *Philosophical Dictionary* begins, "Fanaticism is to superstition what delirium is to fever and rage to anger."[27] Superstition, in turn, is defined in exclusively religious terms. "Almost everything that goes beyond the worship of a supreme Being, and the submission of one's heart to his eternal commands, is superstition."[28] Superstition is said to be endemic to paganism, Judaism, and Christianity, but the various sects cannot agree on what superstition is. "It is therefore plain that what is fundamental to one sect's religion passes for superstition with another sect."[29] The "mental disease" of superstition is least in the sect with the fewest religious rites. And "the fewer superstitions, the less fanaticism; and the less fanaticism, the fewer calamities."[30]

Voltaire describes fanaticism as an impassioned state of madness that inures one to reason. Reason is indeed the only hope for a cure; by contrast, "religion, far from being healthy food for infected brains, turns to poison in them."[31] Like Kant, Voltaire distinguishes between enthusiasm and fanaticism, but Voltaire draws the link closer. Enthusiasm is a condition of being "passionately moved,"[32] which he likens to a disease and to drunkenness. "Enthusiasm is exactly like wine; it can excite so much tumult in the blood vessels, and violent vibrations in the nerves, that reason is completely overthrown by it."[33] It can also, nevertheless, be tamed by reason, as it is among poets. Religious enthusiasm, on the other hand, is often incurable, and leads to fanaticism.[34] All fanaticism adds to enthusiasm is violent action: "The man visited by ecstasies and visions, who takes dreams for realities and his fancies for prophecies, is an enthusiast; the man who supports his madness with murder is a fanatic."[35]

It is obvious that Voltaire opposes fanaticism not to true prophecy but to tolerance of all opinions, even false ones. The "men whom centuries of fanaticism have made powerful" all "detest toleration" and hire fanatics to oppose it.[36] Toleration, however, is the only remedy to the constant dissent and strife produced by religion. In fact, as much religious diversity as possible should be encouraged by the state: "if there are two religions in your country, they will cut one another's throats; if there are thirty of them, they will live in peace. Look at the Grand Turk: he governs Ghebers, Banians, and Greek, Nestorian, Roman Christians. The first man who stirs up a tumult is impaled, and all is peaceful."[37]

As the last sentence makes clear, Voltaire's opposition to religious fanaticism is accompanied by an exalted idea of the efficacy of state coercion. Although Voltaire's target is often religion, he carefully distinguishes between "state religion" and "theological religion." The former he defines as an official class of ministers of religion—under the watchful eye of the ministers of state—that maintains a regular public cult established by law and teaches good morals to the people. "A state religion can never cause any turmoil. This is not true of theological religion; it is the source of all the follies and turmoils imaginable; it is the mother of fanaticism and civil discord; it is the enemy of mankind."[38] Though Voltaire does not directly define a "theological religion," it is presumably one that attempts to "inundate the world with blood for the sake of unintelligible sophisms."[39] Violence is produced by wrangling over abstruse doctrinal distinctions whose definitive solution lies beyond reason's grasp. State religion may not necessarily be truer than theological religion, in Voltaire's way of thinking, but it does a better job of preserving order by emphasizing decorous public ritual and morals over doctrinal hairsplitting. For Voltaire, the solution to religious violence was the subjection of the church to the oversight of the state and to the service of civic order. According to Voltaire, the absolutist monarchy of Louis XIV brought an end to the wars of religion and ushered in the Enlightenment.[40]

Voltaire's most extensive treatment of fanaticism was his play entitled *Fanaticism, or Mahomet the Prophet*, which depicts Mohammed as a "gross, uncouth camel driver"[41] who declares "I will have nothing to do with men who are bold enough to think for themselves or to look with their own eyes!"[42] Zopir, the ruler of Mecca, thus accuses Mohammed, "By means of bloodshed and terror you intend to order mankind to think as you do!" and Mohammed does not deny it. He recruits Seid to kill Zopir, telling him it is God's will. Seid hesitates, confessing himself "prey to this storm of passions" and declaring "How terrible and powerful is religion!"[43] In the end, however, he is swayed by Mohammed and plunges a knife into Zopir, only to discover too late that Zopir was his own father, a fact that Mohammed knew all along.

In the play, Mohammed is not so much a fanatic as a cynic; fanaticism seems to be for the credulous mob, who need to obey. As Mohammed says of them, "They need deceit. My cult, be it true or false, is needed by them . . . My faith creates heroes."[44] Ironically, Mohammed's cynicism is not far from Voltaire's own. Voltaire was willing to tolerate and even encourage organized religion provided it maintained order among the masses. As Voltaire wrote to Frederick the Great, "Your majesty will do the human race an eternal service in extirpating this infamous superstition [Christianity]. I do not say among the rabble, who are not worthy of being enlightened and who are apt for every yoke; I say among the well-bred, among those who wish to think."[45] Voltaire's condemnation of fanaticism is inseparable from his promotion of state religion to maintain civil order.

We have seen how, from its origins in the sixteenth century, the concept of fanaticism migrated from an accusation against heretics to an accusation against intolerance, and from an indictment of false prophecy and belief to an indictment of an irrational and violent passion. In the course of these migrations, "fanaticism" became closely associated with "religion," such that, as it is today, adding the qualifier "religious" to "fanaticism" became almost unnecessary. What does not change in the course of these migrations is the fact that the discourse of fanaticism is used consistently in the service of justifying the power of civil authority. This is crucial. The invention of religion and religious fanaticism is not simply a philosophical or theological project but a political project. The creation of the modern state and the policing of a realm of public reason seem to require the creation of their irrational alter egos.

Fanaticism in the Twenty-First Century

It is sometimes said that the real target of Voltaire's play was not Islam but the church, but it is not a mere coincidence that the enlightened Western world has continued to define itself over against the Muslim world. The myth of religious violence has continued to reinforce a dichotomy between, in Samuel Huntington's phrase, "the West and the rest."[46] As John Esposito has pointed out, the very use of the Western term "religion" to describe Islam immediately marks Islam as an abnormal religion because it does not conform to the Western notion of religion as a matter of private belief, inherently distinct from politics.[47] The Western notion of religion is, from a secular point of view, simply part of the way things are. Muslim societies are supposed to be peculiarly prone to fanaticism and violence because they have not yet learned to separate religion, which is inherently volatile, from politics. The myth of religious violence is a type of Orientalism that opposes Western reason against the irrational, benighted, non-Western world. The opposition of religion to public reason implies the inherent superiority of our political system over theirs.

The chief danger in this opposition is that it is used to justify violence against such irrational Others. Religious violence is fanatical and irrational; secular violence is rational and peace-loving. At times we must regrettably bomb them into the higher rationality, as we are currently doing in Iraq and Afghanistan. The logic of this position is spelled out with bracing clarity by new atheist Sam Harris, a rationalist with a special disdain for Islam: "There are other ideologies with which to expunge the last vapors of reasonableness from a society's discourse, but Islam is undoubtedly one of the best we've got."[48] According to Harris, there is no use trying to reason with such people. They must be dealt with by force.

> Some propositions are so dangerous that it may even be ethical to kill people for believing them . . . Certain beliefs place their adherents beyond the reach of every peaceful means of persuasion, while inspiring them to commit acts of extraordinary violence against others. There is, in fact, no talking to some people. If they cannot be captured, and they often cannot, otherwise tolerant people may be justified in killing them in self-defense. This is what the United States attempted in Afghanistan, and it is what we and other Western powers are bound to attempt, at an even greater cost to ourselves and innocents abroad, elsewhere in the Muslim world. We will continue to spill blood in what is, at bottom, a war of ideas.[49]

Harris is especially blunt, but his is not a marginal voice. His book has been enthusiastically endorsed by academic superstars Alan Dershowitz, Richard Dawkins, and Peter Singer. If we don't want this blood spilling to continue, however, we would do well to see that Harris and others like him, despite their claims, are not the true voice of reason, but the voice of a peculiarly virulent Western chauvinism. Western images of religious fanatics are, in Roxanne Euben's phrase, the "enemy in the mirror," constructions that can tell us much about our own fears and unreasoning fanaticisms.[50] We need to see that the opposition of religion and public reason is not simply the way things are, but a contingent modern Western construction that authorizes and excuses certain kinds of Western pathologies. We will then perhaps be able to see that there is no *essential* difference between violence on behalf of a god and violence on behalf of a secular nation-state, even though we tend to condemn the former as "fanaticism" and the honor the latter as "patriotism."

NOTES

1   William E. Arnal, "Definition," in *Guide to the Study of Religion*, eds. Willi Braun and Russell T. McCutcheon, (London and New York: Cassell, 2000), p. 32.
2   William Arnal, "The Segregation of Social Desire: 'Religion' and Disney World," *Journal of the American Academy of Religion*, Vol. 69, no. 1 (2001), p. 5.
3   Wilfred Cantwell Smith, *The Meaning and End of Religion* (New York: Macmillan, 1962), pp. 18–19.
4   Ibid., pp. 54–55.
5   Augustine, *City of God*, trans. Henry Bettenson (Harmondsworth: Penguin Books, 1972), X.1 [p. 373].
6   John Bossy, "Some Elementary Forms of Durkheim," *Past and Present*, Vol. 95 (May 1982), p. 4.
7   "Religion," *Oxford English Dictionary*, second edition (Oxford: Clarendon Press, 1989); see also Smith, *Meaning and End*, p. 31.
8   See Thomas Aquinas's treatment of *religio* in the *Summa Theologiae*, II-II, q. 81. See also Smith, *Meaning and End*, pp. 15–32, and Talal Asad, *Genealogies of Religion: Discipline and Reasons of Power in Christianity and Islam* (Baltimore, MD: The Johns Hopkins University Press, 1993), pp. 1–54.
9   John Bossy, *Christianity in the West 1400–1700* (Oxford: Oxford University Press, 1985), pp. 153–171.
10 Smith, *Meaning and End*, pp. 18–19. Smith goes on to say that the case of Islam might be a partial exception to his "no," but only because of a link with Judeo-Christian developments in the origin of Islam.
11 See, for example, Russell McCutcheon, *Manufacturing Religion: The Discourse on Sui Generis Religion and the Politics of Nostalgia* (New York: Oxford University Press, 1997); Richard King, *Orientalism and Religion: Postcolonial Theory, India, and "The Mystic East"* (London: Routledge, 1999); Derek Peterson and Darren Walhof, eds., *The Invention of Religion: Rethinking Belief in Politics and History* (Piscataway, NJ: Rutgers University Press, 2003).
12 Ronald Inden, *Imagining India* (Oxford: Blackwell, 1990), p. 128.
13 Dominique Colas, *Civil Society and Fanaticism: Conjoined Histories*, trans. Amy Jacobs (Stanford, CA: Stanford University Press, 1997), pp. 1–5. Colas's book, while exploring the term "fanaticism" in helpful detail, is framed by a political argument in favor of liberal society. For Colas, fanaticism is "the threat that the sky will crush the earth, but also the imagined possibility of a human community not regulated by the sum of individual selfishness, where the distribution of power would cease to be radically unequal"; ibid., p. 6.
14 Luther D. Peterson, "Johann Pfeffinger's Treatises of 1550 in Defense of Adiaphora: 'High Church' Lutheranism and Confessionalization in Albertine Saxony," in *Confessionalization in Europe, 1555–1700: Essays in Honor of Bodo Nischan*, eds. John M. Headley, Hans J. Hillerbrand, and Anthony J. Papalas (Aldershot: Ashgate, 2004), pp. 104–105.
15 Ibid., pp. 12–13.
16 Philip Melanchthon, "On the Number of the Sacraments," quoted in ibid., pp. 12 and 373n8.
17 Jacques Bénigne Bossuet, *Oraisons funèbres*, quoted in Colas, *Civil Society and Fanaticism*, p. 14.
18 Colas, *Civil Society and Fanaticism*, pp. 8–20.
19 John Locke, *Essay Concerning Toleration and Other Writings on Law and Politics, 1667–1683*, J. R. Milton and Philip Milton, eds. (Oxford: Oxford University Press, 2006), p. 285.
20 Ibid., p. 298.
21 Ibid., p. 292.

22 Immanuel Kant, *Critique of Practical Reason*, trans. Lewis White Beck (New York: Macmillan, 1956), p. 88.

23 Immanuel Kant, *Critique of Judgment*, trans. Werner S. Pluhar (Indianapolis, IN: Hackett, 1987), p. 135.

24 Alberto Toscano, "Fanaticism: A Brief History of the Concept," *Reset*, Vol. 97 (2006), trans. Anna Wolf, found at http://www.eurozine.com/articles/2006-12-07-toscano-en.html.

25 Ibid. Also Colas, *Civil Society and Fanaticism*, pp. 264–266.

26 Kant, *Critique of Practical Reason*, pp. 87–88. Kant calls such incentives "pathological" because they are located in sympathy or self-love, not in the law.

27 Voltaire, *Philosophical Dictionary*, trans. Peter Gay (New York: Harcourt, Brace, & World, 1962), p. 267.

28 Ibid., p. 473.

29 Ibid., p. 476. Voltaire says that "There is only one religion in the world that has never been sullied by fanaticism, that of the Chinese men of letters"; ibid., p. 269.

30 Ibid., p. 478.

31 Ibid., p. 268.

32 Ibid., p. 251.

33 Ibid., p. 252.

34 Ibid.

35 Ibid., p. 267.

36 Ibid., p. 487.

37 Ibid., p. 485.

38 Ibid., p. 448. The example of "theological religion" he gives to contrast with the sobriety of state religion is a fanciful account of two parties who come to the Dalai Lama asking him to settle a dispute about the divinity of Fo (the Buddha). The Dalai Lama gives each of them some of his own feces, which the two parties revere, but when the Lama decides in favor of one of the parties, they proceed to "assassinating and exterminating and poisoning each other." The Dalai Lama laughs and continues to hand out the contents of his stool to his grateful adherents; ibid.

39 Ibid., p. 445.

40 Voltaire, *The Age of Louis XIV*, trans. Martyn P. Pollack (London: J. M. Dent, 1961), pp. 394–415; see also pp. 1–19.

41 Voltaire, *Mahomet the Prophet, or Fanaticism*, trans. Robert L. Myers (New York: Frederick Ungar Publishing, 1964), p. 11.

42 Ibid., p. 35.

43 Ibid., p. 46.

44 Ibid., p. 23.

45 Voltaire, quoted in S. J. Barnett, *The Enlightenment and Religion: The Myths of Modernity* (Manchester: Manchester University Press, 2003), p. 40. As S. J. Barnett points out, in the Enlightenment "almost all those radical in religion or politics also recognized the vital role of the Church in preserving the status quo. Thus Voltaire, famed as a deist, could crusade against all organized religion, yet he also argued that religious observance was to be tolerated and even supported amongst the masses. It was to be tolerated, however, not because of its value as legitimate divine worship, but as an aid in the maintenance of social stability, including the maintenance of the social and economic status of the philosophes themselves, who, for the most part, were drawn from the moneyed classes"; ibid., p. 17.

46 Samuel Huntington, "If Not Civilizations, What?" *Foreign Affairs*, Vol. 72 (November/December 1993), p. 192.

47 John L. Esposito, *The Islamic Threat: Myth or Reality?*, third edition (New York: Oxford University Press, 1999), p. 258.

48 Ibid., p. 136. Harris regards Muslims as essentially backwards people, clinging to a bygone era: "Any systematic approach to ethics, or to understanding the necessary underpinnings of a civil society, will find many Muslims standing eye deep in the red barbarity of the fourteenth century"; ibid., p. 145.

49 Sam Harris, *The End of Faith: Religion, Terror, and the Future of Reason* (New York: W. W. Norton & Company, 2004), pp. 52–53.

50 Roxanne Euben, *Enemy in the Mirror: Islamic Fundamentalism and the Limits of Modern Rationalism* (Princeton, NJ: Princeton University Press, 1999).

3

THE LATE ARRIVAL OF LANGUAGE: WORD, NATURE, AND THE DIVINE IN PLATO'S *CRATYLUS*

CATHERINE PICKSTOCK

In his dialogues *Symposium* and *Phaedrus*, Plato makes a subjective emotional dimension for cognition a crucial aspect of his argument for the possibility of objective knowledge. That might seem paradoxical, but for Plato, if stable truths can only exist beyond the vicissitudes of time and space, our only access to them is via desire. Even by desiring such truths, we attain a dim intimation of their reality. This is one of the considerations that give rise to his doctrine of the recollection of the forms. Desire mediates the cognitive tension between the unknown, which one seeks to know, and fully realised understanding.*

It is in relation to this issue that I here present a version of what Robert Harrison has called the "other Plato," at odds with the "terminal" Plato of Vernant, Detienne, Derrida and Lacoue-Labarthe, on the one hand, and the "epistemological" Plato of Anglo-Saxon analytic philosophy, on the other. For both these schools, despite their differences, Plato sets running an unbroken lineage of rationalist metaphysics which eschewed bodily and emotional mediations, culminating in the enthronement of an indifferent supra-linguistic λόγος by Cartesian metaphysics.[1] Robert Harrison suggests that a critical and literary attention to the primary sources can yield a rather different approximation of Platonic metaphysics. From this perspective one finds not a neutral philosophical gaze, but a presentation of philosophy as a kind of terrible and physical anguish which yearns to see again and again intimations of the highest reality within material and beloved reality. In the *Phaedrus*, for example, recollection triggered by material encounters in time induces physical pain as Socrates describes the sprouting of the feathers of

Faith, Rationality, and the Passions, First Edition. Edited by Sarah Coakley.
© 2012 Blackwell Publishing Ltd. Book compilation © 2012 Blackwell Publishing Ltd.

the soul's wings,[2] and far from philosophical speculation enthroning a detached model of knowledge as vision, ἔρως is described as a liquid pouring into the eyes and overflowing into others.[3]

One might mention here the apparent significance in the *Phaedo* of Socrates's bodily disposition, the exact orientation of feet and hands and his bodily composure in the face of death, as informed by philosophy as a particular way of life.[4] If knowledge implies a pre-understanding through desiring-to-know, then, inversely, desire itself may be regarded as an obscure mode of comprehension. Far from adulating merely abstract truths (and perhaps he regarded even mathematical entities as ethereal concretions),[5] Plato, by appealing to the forms, invokes a primarily unknown, hidden, eternal concreteness of cognitive being. The mediative detours via the beloved individual and beautiful material particulars which we take in the course of seeking to recollect the forms do not stand in a hostile relation to the reality of those forms in which they participate. For it is ἔρως which conjoins our affinity with limited particulars with our affinity with the specificity of the forms themselves. One might suggest that our distance from, and motion towards, material particulars is correlated with our distance from the transcendent Forms. For if the forms are the "true realities" of material things, and yet the latter are not pure illusions, then a knowledge of the forms does not simply lead us away from the realities which participate in those forms. Rather, it gives us these realities, since they are, in themselves and without remainder, participations. Moreover, since our souls cannot fully divest themselves of embodiment for Plato, it is only a loving, attentive concern for particulars—whether beautiful material particulars or persons, or the specificity of dialectical conversation—which opens our souls to recollection. So a mutually confirming circle pertains, for all the admitted priority of the intellectual realm.

"The other Plato" involves an interlinked attention to three things; first, to the literary idioms of the dialogues: the dialogue form, the patterns of imagery and metaphor, and the deployment of myth and reference to ritual; second, to the religious background that is constantly invoked, as well as to the revisions of religious practice that are recommended. In general, the irreducibility of the literary dimension signals the equal irreducibility of the religious dimension. Because this involves concrete images and bodily ritual practices, it turns out—perhaps counter-intuitively—that insistence on the religious dimension in Plato encourages, third, a more positive view of his understanding of the material realm than is often ascribed to him. This is because it is material pictures and practices that are seen to play a vital mediating role in terms of ascent to the forms. At the same time, the latter tend to be construed in more apophatically transcendent terms: since we perforce have recourse to mediation while in the body, the forms are seen to exceed our mental capacities as currently constituted and also to contain in an eminent fashion all of what we find in material things but to a partly unknown and excessive degree. Together, these two emphases place *methexis* or participation more firmly centre-stage than some accounts allow. We have to pass through participatory means as triggers of recollection; but what is recollected is but dimly apprehended. Thus the merely intellectual is out-flanked for the "other Plato" both from the material and from the spiritual side.

This model stands in opposition to three inherited readings. First, the neo-Kantian reading which tends to reduce the forms to *a priori* structures of understanding which are seen as both immanent to our minds and as fully comprehensible; second, the analytic reading, according to which Plato is seen as posing genuine problems of epistemology but as proposing implausible solutions in terms of the doctrine of the forms. There is some continuity with the neo-Kantian reading here insofar as *Phaedo* and *Meno* tend to be read as trying to explain innate knowledge, rather than as concerned with how we can have the impulse to search for that which we do not yet know. What is taken to be innate knowledge is seen as explained excessively in terms of transcendence where either Humean naturalist immanence or Kantian transcendentalism would suffice. But if, on the contrary, the problem is not one of innate knowledge but of an obscure pre-understanding of the unknown, then one obtains to a philosophically irreducible ἀπορία which can only be religiously resolved in terms of the myths of pre-existence of the soul and recollection of this estate. The third way of reading Plato is the post-modern way of regarding him as "terminal" in the sense of offering a closed account of a replete presence accessible to intellectual sight. This way makes the mistake of projecting back Cartesian and Kantian attitudes of certainty and of eliding the religious dimension. The association of intellectual sight with domineering grasp overlooks both spiritual mystery and the need for material mediation in order to approach it.

By contrast, knowledge of the forms linked with an obscure and aporetic knowing in advance which is a *desire* to know them, is for Plato a knowledge respectful of the nature of material things, but also one which stays in motion from thing to thing, as passing from imperfect example to imperfect example, because it understands their true nature as only to be glimpsed in the realm of forms. Knowledge as erotic is both specific and dynamic. Interestingly, at *Cratylus* 420d–e, Socrates suggests that a willing ἔρως and the process of naming are stronger than fate (ἀνάγκη) which dominated even the gods for Homer. To desire is to "progress through a ravine" and to overcome "the necessary and resistant" which, since they are contrary to our desire (understood as true desire), "imply error and ignorance."[6] Socrates identifies this piercing ἔρως with the "force" or "power" of λόγος as dialectic, because after invoking the passage through the ravine, he says "while my strength lasts let us persevere and I hope that you will persevere with your questions."[7] We can understand by this that the λόγος of understanding is also the proceeding and persisting λόγος of language: material words indicating material things in time and place are forever in the motion of discourse. In the *Cratylus*, therefore, Plato shows that his concept of knowledge as linked to desire and motion is also a concept of knowledge as linguistic. Language in fact turns out to be a certain threshold between understanding and sensation and ultimately between the forms and the particulars which share in their nature.

The foregoing discussion of different interpretative schools of Plato's thought—one kind of Plato, and an "other" Plato—leads me to offer a word about the particular hermeneutic circumstances which surround the reading of Plato's dialogues. These works are characterised by a primary idiom of demur and indirectness. The dialogic genre itself is one which draws attention to, and problematises, claims to interpretative certainty. And if one attends to Socrates's own presentation of philosophy within the dialogues, one finds neither statement of doctrine nor dogmatic assertion, but rather a series of often unanswered and sometimes unanswerable questions. Socrates invokes peculiar and unplaceable sources of authority, from untraceable myths, nymphs and strange gods, likenesses and unlikenesses, strange analogies and images; he attends to the mysterious prompting *daimon* who whispers hesitations into his ear and holds him back from certainty; he admires the wisdom of the people at Dodona who were prepared to take heed of the prophetic promptings of oak trees and rocks.[8] (One might mention here the way in which Timaeus holds back from speaking directly of the Form of the Good at *Timaeus* 48a).[9] If one is to negotiate texts so inflected by demur, and attempt to avoid crunching anachronisms, then one might usefully follow the advice of Jacob Klein in attending to every word, every myth, every textual resonance that one can find, and try to piece together a pattern or a shape as best one can from one's crude and hopeless retrospective vantage point.[10] The dialogues often open in the middle of a discussion, on the way to somewhere, and are many-layered and digressive: these features of the dialogues make us silent participants, and draw attention to the proneness of the text, its lack of completeness, even if there is a risk that our interpretative contribution of reading might be too heavy-footed an intervention, and close the hermeneutic circle. There is even a risk that attending to demur itself has its own anachronistic crunch, and yet perforce less extreme than an approach which does not do so? A common criticism is that those who attend to the literary form, theological character, and mythological elements of the dialogues are readings into, or beyond Plato himself. Whilst it could be said that those interpretative strategies which do otherwise must surely do the same in their arguably unwarranted hermeneutic simplicity and certainty, one might consider whether the reading of any text at all, quite apart from the self-problematising genre of the Platonic dialogue, is always a reading-into, or a reading-beyond, the text. Could it be otherwise? But Plato's dialogues are self-consciously incomplete or enigmatic. What he has written down invites interpretation, seems intended to demand it. This does not necessarily presume interpretative audacity, but is perhaps in accord with the

Socratic method: something must come from the reader if we are not to be debased, passive recipients of an impersonal, written record, our souls divided and unawakened, our pockets full of *obols*,[11] and our cloaks bulging with the dubious stockpile of others' written traces.[12] Perhaps it is as the Delphic Oracle advised, that in order to receive its enigmatic utterances, one must know oneself.

In what follows, I seek to examine the discussion of language in the *Cratylus* as a way of illustrating an approach to "the other Plato." For as we shall see, language brings together the three essential dimensions of the alternative reading: the literary, the religious and the material. Words are somewhat material, they compose the literary, and, on Plato's view, they are inherently incantatory. Determining language's connection to the phenomenal world is crucial to the question of the accuracy of our knowledge of the world, and so it should not surprise us that this enterprise summons not only questions concerning the origin of names, but also the forms and our ability to gain knowledge of the form of the Good.

The *Cratylus* later gave rise in Western tradition to the term "Cratylist," meaning the view that linguistic signs are naturally appropriate to what they signify and are not merely conventional.[13] It is a view whose rejection is one of the foundation stones of modern linguistics, since Saussure, although there may be reasons to question it: it is notable that highly archaic languages such as Basque and Gaelic seem to be more onomatopoeic in character.[14] The traditional ascription, however, can be regarded as partially ironic, since Cratylus, a late entrant to his own dialogue,[15] is not straightforwardly represented as a "Cratylist." His extreme claim that a name which does not conform to the rules of natural correctness is not really a name at all,[16] is deconstructed by Socrates who shows, in effect, that such extreme naturalism forces the name to be so identical with the thing named that it disallows any gap at all to pertain between word and thing. The word here becomes onomatopoeically transparent to such an extent that it is effectively subsumed within the thing named.[17] If the name fails, then the thing named fails also, since it depends upon the name to be shown to us. This does not allow language to be language, and leads to the denial of the possibility of falsehood, as Cratylus explicitly indicates, declaring that no name can be better than any other, since they are all equally part of the law. For Cratylus, both names and laws are identical with the things and imperatives that they represent because in both cases what is given is so manifestly obvious that it cannot be mistaken.[18] Cratylus' position is seemingly opposite from that of Socrates's earlier interlocutor, Hermogenes, who regards language as separate from reality. This means that for Hermogenes, names are imposed in an entirely arbitrary fashion: they are just "a piece of [a person's] voice applied to a thing."[19] But his extreme relativism can also be taken as not allowing language to be language because it does not allow language to offer a disclosive λόγος.[20] Although, unlike Cratylus, he admits of a gap between sign and thing, he makes the gap so ultimate that this engenders a dialectically identical occlusion of verbal reality.

Neither Cratylus nor Hermogenes offers a "Cratylist" sense of a mimetic similarity between things, on the one hand, and words separate from things, on the other. The "Cratylism" of the dialogue, and so Plato, is also uncertain. For the dialogue ends in ἀπορία as to its central question which suggests that one must be wary of attributing either conventionalism or naturalism to Plato. However, tradition has often deemed him to be sympathetic with a form of linguistic naturalism, while in modern times that view has been questioned.[21] In this chapter, I nonetheless argue that the tradition had it essentially right, with certain qualifications.

The most important qualification to the usual readings is that Plato was not able to affirm the natural signification of language as a matter of reason alone.[22] Rather he did so in an explicitly inspired fashion that involved the supplementary mediations of ἔρως, inspiration from without and religious invocation. The "cratylist" view of language involves something like the view that language itself is coterminous with religion, if we take this term to imply belief in gods and the importance of myth, ritual and divine oracular disclosure. Language in this dialogue seems to be regarded as being a naming of the gods whose possibility is granted by the gods themselves.[23]

If, for Plato, language mediates between reason and the senses, it also links reason to passion. Moreover, it is in terms of this link that, in the *Cratylus*, the invocation of the transcendent forms becomes necessary. Access to the forms, I shall argue, does not take us outside language: rather, the forms can be deemed "superlinguistic" in the sense that they are in one aspect ontologised names, just as, for Plato, mathematical entities are ontologised symbols or diagrams. For while Plato appears to speak of a pre-linguistic knowledge of things,[24] he also indicates that the truest names participate to some degree in the stasis of the forms.[25] Since knowing things in themselves must mean by dint of their participation in the forms, this does not involve a knowing without speaking. Language is involved in the process of the recollection of the forms which is the means by which their existence may be intimated. Nothing is known, beneath the realm of the forms, save through copies. Material things are copies of the forms, and they themselves are only known through the copying of copies which is human art, and especially the eminent art of λόγος.[26] Accordingly, it can be seen that the doctrine of the forms upholds, even at a transcendent level, a Platonic link between reason, emotion, language and the divine.

The crux of the debate concerning the "Cratylism" or otherwise of the *Cratylus* is the following: at the outset of the dialogue, Plato establishes a correlation between an arbitrary theory of signification and sophistic Protagoreanism for which there is no intrinsic truth and no possibility of human concepts approximating to the essences of reality.[27] Socrates appears to suggest that the defence of such a possibility means that one must uphold the natural appropriateness of words to things.[28] This amounts to a mimetic or onomatopoeic theory of language: in some sense, words correctly imitate the things they betoken. From this perspective, a "Cratylist" account of language is seen as a necessary aspect of philosophical realism.

This might seem like a strange claim. But Plato could make this claim because he already ascribed to what one might call "a linguistic turn." For him, and for ancient Greek thought generally,[29] the word λόγος means both reason and speech; he upholds a mythical-magical mode of thought which binds the two together in such a way as to regard a thought as a word, and a word as a kind of effect-inducing or presence-invoking spell. It is true that Plato distinguishes "the form" from "the matter" of language and allows that the form of a word can stay the same even though the matter, which is to say the physical syllables used, may alter.[30] It is tempting to suppose that by "form" here Plato means what we would mean by the word "meaning," or perhaps what we would mean by the word "signified." However, it is clear that he does not entirely exclude the material signifier itself from the domain of form, because his examples of the mutation or variation of the signifier do not extend to total alteration: he is referring rather to etymological development or variation of cognitive-linguistic perception, in such a way that at least some phonetic aspect of the original word is sustained. Thus Socrates declares that "so long as this intrinsic quality is present, even though the name have not all the proper letters, the thing will still be named; well, when it has all the proper letters; badly, when it has only a few of them."[31] We can infer that in the case of Plato's example of the second of the two names for Hector's son—Astyanax—it is important that the letter "tau" remain in common.[32] (In addition, this name is well-chosen because it conveys the appropriate quality or state of its bearer as "lord of the city").[33]

In this way Plato appears to sustain a mimetic or onomatopoeic theory of linguistic equivalence. Of course, any such theory has to admit of the existence of cultural variation of different words for the same things—as for the two names for Hector's son—and to accommodate this fact.[34] Plato does so through a comparison of language to the use of material by a blacksmith: the smith can make the same tools out of different metals.[35] Letters and syllables are the equivalent here of the metals, but, if form is the equivalent of the tool, then it has a physical shape which is not simply invisible, like meaning, or abstractly positional, like a signified. It has to remain recognisably the same, despite etymological shifts.[36] He also compares language to a drug at 394b: the knower of names is not confounded by a variety and a varying of names, just as a good physician is not confounded by small changes in drugs. Here one sees that Plato indicates a continuity in material genealogy and not just arbitrarily different nomenclatures.[37]

Again, for us today to suppose that the "linguistic turn"—which is a modern semi-materialist insistence that all thought requires language—requires "Cratylism" seems absurd. Are they not quite distinct theses? If one says that we only think in speech, then that surely does not require that speech have a mimetic relationship to reality. The modern linguistic turn is not supposed in any way to invoke a "magical" dimension. Indeed, it is usually seen to be quite compatible with a "sophistic" arbitrariness of usage. What is more, there are two reasons that could be urged for the incompatibility of the two theses.

The first is a point made by Hans-Georg Gadamer with respect to this dialogue. If we can only think of things within language, then we are never in a position to compare, shall we say, the word "breath" with breath in actuality, because we do not have extra-linguistic access to the reality of breath. Hence there would be no way of verifying the "Cratylist" theory of onomatopoeic signification. It should however be said that Gadamer concludes that there would be no way of falsifying it either, and suggests that Plato implicitly sees this. Faced with this insight, on Gadamer's account, the dialogue *Cratylus* is striving towards an account of signification that transcends the contrast between onomatopoeic and conventional signification.[38] With some qualification, this is the reading of the dialogue which I will uphold. For if we cannot think things without the words which we fabricate, then neither do we have access to those "given" or donated things before the advent of language: we cannot "disprove" our sense that the Germanic-derived work "dark," for example, is like the actual darkness and yet that the Latin-derived "obscure" is also like this darkness, capturing it under a different aspect. In consequence, we cannot confirm the mere arbitrariness of language, to the exact measure that we cannot prove its appropriateness to things by a process of comparison. And since it is made up or contrived words which "give" us things, and since also every human being enters into language as something "pre-fabricated," it becomes spontaneously natural to view language also as a "given," in the sense of a gift which discloses the reality of things to us. For this reason, perhaps, we discover a religious understanding of the nature of language in many cultures (in Hinduism, for example, this idea is developed with great philosophical sophistication by the "Hindu grammarians") and its fabricated character is not so much ideologically disguised as rather interpreted as being the work of divine inspiration. This seems to be the perspective of Plato in this dialogue: one could say that for him speaking is fundamentally "in the middle voice"; it is willed and active, volunteered and intended, and yet also passively received. The sense of divine descent into our fabrications that is summoned here was later understood by the neoplatonists Iamblichus, Proclus and Damascius as the "theurgic" dimension that exceeds philosophy at its very heart. The linguistic turn cannot confirm Cratylism, but it cannot disprove it either.

The second objection is that Cratylism assumes a noun-based representative theory of language, involving a one-to-one equivalence of word to given thing—the kind of account which was criticised by Wittgenstein.[39] However, when Socrates imagines a dumb-show mimetic language, this does not consist in pointing to things and attaching classificatory labels to them, but rather in raising and dropping the hands in active imitation of the motions of rising and falling.[40] He associates the activity of naming, which he uses as a synonym for speaking, with the *motion* of the soul itself towards the beautiful, excellent and good, a motion which is shared by the soul of the world. He says that the word for excellence or virtue, ἀρετῇ, means "a good flow of the soul."[41] The act of speaking, for Plato, is not so much a matter of mirroring as of συμφέρον: of going with and furthering the teleological movement of reality.[42] Furthermore, he sees thinking-naming as a species of *action* which he variously compares with a craft,[43] with teaching and with political legislation; words have "force" and are a "mighty tribe."[44] He also compares it with biological generation and teasingly invokes the question of whether it is right or not to name a child after its parents: this will turn out fine if the child takes after his parents, but otherwise will seem literally anomalous.[45] The implication here is that the name is itself in the position of the child; it has to be derived genealogically, yet as a non-identical repetition of its source, or of that to which it refers, it can be faithful to it or it can "betray" it. Yet the risk of the action of generation is unavoidable and involves a certain "judgement" of appropriateness of name to thing named. It is never a matter of mere representational copying or of theoretical labelling or classifying—which Socrates associates with the sophists.[46] Plato makes more explicit the association of child and name when he elaborates the idea that the onto-genesis of the gods is shadowed by an onoma-genesis of their names as willed by the gods themselves.[47] In the course of this double generation, we eventually come to the figure named "Hermes" who is at once a messenger, and so an interpreter, and a thief and so a liar or distorter of meaning. His son is named "Pan" and inherits his father's ambiguity, being half sublime and half brutal or "goatish." As such he is not only "all things," but by virtue of his name, "speech [that] signifies all things" which is "always turning them round and round."[48] This speech like the god has two forms, "true" and "false." Hence language, like reality, is a matter of generation and non-identical repetition and this process is not necessarily coterminous with debasement, as on both conventional and post-modern readings of Plato. Not necessarily, because a hermeneutic work of non-identical repetition is essential to the way in which speech develops, is generated as speech from being and meaningfully conveys to us that being.[49] Betrayal is merely an unavoidable risk, and that it is not an impersonal and inevitable fate is conveyed by the personification of the ambiguity of transmission.[50]

Plato's deployment of etymologies can be cited as an indication of his seeking to trace the origins of words to fixed sources of meaning, and so seems to suggest an alignment between his position and that of Cratylus. However, as Gérard Genette has argued, whereas etymology traces words back to historical origins according to the accountable laws of filiation,[51] in the *Cratylus*, Socrates traces eponymic lineages which allow for imaginative licence. Socrates's eponymies try to show how a given designation is well chosen or in alignment with its signification.[52] He analyzes words by supplementing, removing, exchanging or bending letters or syllables according to sometimes whimsical rules of phonetic resonance and crude punning. Rather than excavating a fixed origin, the eponymic runnels seem potentially endless and in no way find a foothold in certain knowledge of the world. If anything, the eponymies might appear to underline the impossibility of such a foothold.[53] And yet the words summon a web of associations which do not exactly lie, and which the eponymist seems genuinely caught up in. But the further he strays into its web, the further he seems from the ideal of perfect truth. Some scholars have seen this distancing from truth as part of Plato's critique of the contemporary over-valuing of words,[54] and as consonant with an "essentialist" view of truth.[55] But one could see the tradition in terms of a more allegorical epistemology: instead of failing because the eponyms do not succeed in denoting one concept or object, or sometimes deliver unanchored or ironic chains of resemblance, a name can give allegorical access to a plethora of meanings none of which entirely exhausts the truth, but none of which betrays it either. Who is to know whether meanings of words arise at different stages of their history because they are at the centre of a web of allegorical echoes and these resemblances reach back to earlier meanings and forward to future ones?[56] The chain between words and things has already been broken, or rather, one could say, things were always words and words were always things. The eponymic exercises open up a continuity or chain, like the magnetic connections of inspiration in Plato's *Ion*, semantically across space, from word to word, and genealogically across time, tracing the earlier meanings and forms and associations of a word. For example, Socrates sets up a chain between the words for body, sign, tomb and safe: the body can be understood as the outer sign of the inner soul, and can be said to be the tomb of the soul, as well as its safeguard. The series of sound symbolisms appears to confirm that the elements of the chain are essentially connected and that words can give substantive indication of this relation.[57] Later in this article it will be suggested that the chain between words and things in the world does not entail a leap from one order of reality to another, but forms a continuum on a single but variously-articulated plane, since all the components of the phenomenal world are themselves signs of the higher realities in which they participate; the sensible realm is made up of signs or words in its entirety, with no substantive sublunary end-point for words to reach the consummation of their semantic or genealogical chain. Socrates's comparison of words with craft and characterisation as action have already underlined for us that words are part of the reality which they signify.[58]

Such an analysis is somewhat confirmed by Proclus's assessment of Socrates's "etymegories," as he calls them, which he says are issued with an eye on the form (*eidos*) of life, rather than on its material signifier.[59] So whilst Plato's eponymic allegorising might not be rooted in a scientistic excavation of original fact or essence, neither is it rooted in mere rhetoric or random wordplay: a name is an allegory of its meaning. It cannot point unequivocally to one correct sense but it does not mislead us entirely either.[60]

Having questioned the arguments that would render the linguistic turn incompatible with Cratylism, one can try, against modern fashion, to see merit in Plato's case that, on the contrary, the linguistic turn requires Cratylism. If the signifier is arbitrary, then the stable element of language is excarnated and language is reduced to thought after all, because its essence consists in a series of abstract relations, combined according to a set of rules. Physical words become in consequence no more than instrumental conveniences without any lure of particularity. Meanings and signifiers still require physical codes because we are embodied creatures, but only in a sense which reduces the bodily factor to something mnemonically and calculatively useful, like the matrices of a computer. If the essence of language exists apart from its sounds and the images which sounds conjure up, can one really say that thought is linguistic? In principle, it could dispense with language, for any view that makes language essential for thought would seem to require that the expressing, uttering aspect of thought is indispensable to thought as such. Thought without language might go unexpressed outside the thinker. But thought that has to be in language is always expressed in a public fashion outside the thinker's own domain. A reserved, private thought is only, on this view, a secondary and temporary act of enclosure of what was originally common terrain. Perhaps Wittgenstein was right: the linguistic turn implies that there can be no private language. However, the non-Cratylist view of the sign as arbitrary imposition would seem to reinstate the latter position.

So it is possible that there could be a case for saying that a real linguistic turn would require an onomatopoeic theory of signification. But, all the same, does such a theory not seem absurd and lacking in scholarly warrant? Plato himself never argues that it can be proven.[61] Indeed, he avers to its seeming absurdity.[62] He presents Socrates in this dialogue as "inspired" by the absent Euthyphro, in the manner of an initiate of a mystery religion and links the half-admitted apparent absurdity of an onomatopoeic theory of language to the mystery of religion.[63] Because of this apparent absurdity, which seems nonetheless demanded in order to uphold cognitive realism (as we have seen), Socrates, like the tragic poets, requires divine help.[64] And insofar as he sees λόγος or thought-language as corresponding to things, this is a matter of corresponding through desire to the disclosed excellence of things in the light of the form of the Good.[65] Λόγος as thought-language is a performance before it is a theory, because it is a giving birth to the concept-word under the prompting of desire.[66] We are told that the very name for "name," ὄνομα, means "being for which there is a search,"[67] and that the first men, who were semi-daemonic in their giant-power to name and legislate, were named "heroes" after the mediating god Ἔρως.[68]

As driven by desire, the process of thinking-naming seeks to express the good of that which it understands. The mimetic continuity of thing with word is therefore grasped more by feeling than by comparative knowing. When discussing etymologies, Plato confirms that we can, to a degree, know, for example, the phenomenon of breath in a bodily and sensory way and so compare it with the word "breath" and thereby test the suitability of this word. Yet the sensory experience is never entirely apart from its verbal expression.[69]

This can be tentatively inferred, because Plato links language with synaes-thesia.[70] It is easy to see the other arts and crafts as mimetic because they involve or invoke one sense alone: painting imitates the visible, music the auditory, and so forth. But the combination of sensory information in that "common sensing" which engenders thought is a more mysterious represen-tation of the entirety of a natural thing which is its "essence," invisible to us outside this synaesthesic access.[71] It is for this reason that naming is for Plato the work of the "super-artist" who is the legislator of the city. He crafts not any specific thing, but rather the instrument that discloses to us the inner actuality of all things.[72] The latter is inseparable from language, because it is realised through words which, though they are in sound, have the unique power to invoke visible images and other "imagined" sensations as conveyed by the other senses. Our experience of breath as a phenomenon is synaes-thesic, and inseparable from the articulation of the word "breath." Words somehow bind the different senses together.

The question is: what would justify a sense of felt *mimesis* as between word and thing? Whatever the answer here, this justification is crucial for Plato's mode of philosophical realism, because truth to the thing has to be truth to its goodness, and this has to be expressed by a conceptual act that perpetuates such excellence. But a conceptual act is always for Plato an act of naming: the thinker is always the teacher and the teacher is the one who names.[73]

In consequence, all language is for him a kind of poetry, divinely inspired, which discloses being because it belongs to being's "dynamic" impetus towards self-disclosure.[74] It begins with the partially revealed names of the gods,[75] and continues to trace an onoma-genesis which keeps pace with onto-genesis by proceeding to name daemons and then heroes of the golden age and men of the bronze age with all their parts of soul and body.[76] Finally, it inscribes a circle by naming "name" itself—ὄνομα—as the supreme instru-ment of human thought.[77] This instrument is created by one man, the legis-lator who founds the city,[78] but it is then used by dialecticians and secondarily by teachers in the way that a musician plays a lyre created by a lyre-maker.[79] It is the user who must guide the maker, if the instrument is to have the right shape and other qualities. Therefore it is the philosopher who must guide the legislator who is also, it would seem, the first poet and musician, the first shaper of meaningful sounds, like Orpheus.[80]

The philosopher guides the making of the instrument of naming in terms of the guidance of the realm of forms and especially the form of the good.[81] This demands that names be true to realities if they are to be in keeping with their excellence.[82] And being true to reality means above all being true to reality as a process of moving generation,[83] in such a way that a parallel is hinted at between a word as the child of the mind, and things as the offspring of other things.[84] All things should be named in terms of their origins: the first god *Uranus* from his looking up to the forms; his children and grandchildren after him; daemons from the gods; the heroes from the daemons and bronze age men after the heroes.[85] Such appropriate naming follows, first, the conventional names given to fathers. But, secondly, those names themselves are eventually named according to nature. As we have seen, this means in terms of a certain constancy of verbal form that endures, despite variations.[86] And it is clear that what secures this constancy is the flow of true desire, because the first heroic men acted as "guardians," partaking of the erotic power of the daemonic realm. This, says Plato, is why they were named "heroes," after ἔρως.[87] The true judging legislation of names (and so of social reality) is a work of love.

Yet this cannot mean, for Plato's realism, that isolated letters and syllables are by themselves merely conventional. He speculates that lying beneath the genealogical grounding of language, elemental building blocks form the basis for primary human language through basic onomatopoeic sound-elements:[88] "Rho" betokens physical motion as in the words for flow (ῥεῖν), current (ῥοή), rend, (ερείκειν), crush (θρπύτειν); "phi," "psi," "sigma" and "zeta" make use of an expenditure of breath in imitating shivering (ψυχρόν), seething (ζεον), shake (σείεσθαι) and shock (σεωμός);[89] by contrast, a binding or hindering of motion can be imitated by compression and pressure of the tongue by pronouncing "delta" or "tau,"[90] a gliding motion of the tongue in pronouncing "lambda," as in glide (ὀλισθάνειν) and sleek (λιπαρόν); but when a "gamma" is added to a "lambda," the gliding motion is curtailed or detained, as in gluey (γλοιῶδες) and glutinous (γλωχρόν);[91] a "nu," as an internal sound, can indicate interiority as in inside (ἔνδον).[92]

This is the heart of Plato's case for the mimeticism or sound-symbolism of language. And again, as with Socrates's eponymic lineages which unsettle one's confidence as to the presence of any anterior truth underlying the analysis of words in contemporary usage, so in Socrates's attempt to show that the basic sounds of language imitate reality at a fundamental level, one hesitates in answering the question, is he serious or is it all a joke? Or perhaps it is both: Socrates's exploration of the sound-elements and their significance suggests that everything has meaning or is motivated, not necessarily directly or with semelfactive reference to things, but more indirectly by a layering or digressive relay between letters and sounds belonging to still other words. Whilst one could see this as an humiliation of meaning and a confirmation of the essential arbitrariness of signs, one could equally see it as an indication of

the meaningfulness and interconnectedness of the web of reality as significant in its entirety.[93] And besides this uncertainty as between arbitrariness
and interconnectedness, the theory faces further problems.[94]

The first problem relates to the gradual historical obscuring which
such mimophony charts.[95] For Plato this problem is twofold. First, there is
a genuine decline, because human beings become forgetful of the true, the
good and the beautiful. But, secondly, he emphasises that, were a copy a
perfect copy, it would no longer be a copy, since it would be identical with the
original.[96] Plato is conventionally read as saying that all mimetic copying is
degeneration.[97] Yet for him the copying of material things is the space of truth
itself. Were he, to use modern jargon, to "disquote" this space by saying that
perfect truth would be identical with being, then he would have lost the idea
of truth as the space of beautiful manifestation.[98] Yet for Plato this space is
fundamental and irreducible. The copying of material things has a positive
valency. And this means that for him imitation has to be non-identical in
character.[99] It follows that the conventional element in naming can paradoxically belong to onomatopoeia itself. In the same way that motion, falling
motion and lapse in time can be positive, so conventionality can be seen as
positive with respect to the natural naming of essences. If the non-identical
character of a copy makes it a better copy, as inexact, then the conventionally
imposed character of a sound can form part of an onomatopoeic economy. It
is as if the gap between an essence and its inexact copy is occupied by all our
human striving: both our physical motions forwards, backwards, upwards,
but also the psychological motion of ἔρως. Such a gap might be seen to open
up a chasm which renders all our images and copies and strivings hollowed-
out or doomed from the outset. And yet the gap is the place where meaning
occurs: wisdom is the "touching of motion."[100] The continued desire to know
a thing surplus to its image corresponds with the fact that one can only fully
know the thing in the light of the forms which can never be encompassed
in this life. Our feeling ἔρως can recognise an intrinsic bond, affinity or
bringing-forth[101] between, as has already been discussed, the word "dark"
and the phenomenon of darkness or equally between the Latin-derived word
"obscure" and the same darkness. It is as if we see the one through the other,
the thing through the word, and vice-versa, in an inextricable fashion. In
consequence not every distancing from original linguistic mimesis involves a
loss of onomatopoeia.

The second problem with Plato's case for the mimeticism of language is the
inconsistency of the linguistic report. The most ancient elements of language
seem to hesitate as to whether a Parmenidean stasis is more fundamental, like
the sound-element "delta" or "tau,"[102] or a Heraclitean flux, like the sound-
element "rho."[103] Do we live on the earth as ἐσσία or the earth as ὠσία?[104]
If language is divinely revealed, how is it that the gods have originally spoken
with a divided voice which hesitates between movement and stasis, stop and
go?[105]

Leaving in suspense Plato's solution to this problem, let us mention the third problem. If we only think within language, how did human beings think language and so invent it in the first place?[106]

Plato presents the same solution for both the second and the third problem. It is the doctrine of the forms. In the case of the tension between stop and go, Plato sees language as like a loom which blends or interweaves rest and motion, same and different, in beautiful patterns.[107] Likewise, it blends rising and falling in order to reflect our ascent to the divine and the divine declension towards us. Plato's attention to language brings out clearly the fact that ascent to the forms involves a positive movement through their various particular imitations which clarifies the nature of these particulars by not tarrying too long with them. For just as the movement to the forms does not obliterate particulars, so also the same movement does not tend to dissipate time because recognition of the ephemeral nature of things requires that we embrace time as flux and welcome the arrival of the future. It is only in this way that, as the *Timaeus* puts it, we can grasp time as "the moving image of eternity."[108] Moreover, it would seem that this is the only image of eternity that we can have.

It is the element of divine descent and donation which paradoxically saves both time and particularity by rendering them significant as participatory. If language were merely our fabrication, it would have to build an artificial spatial fortress against time and the chance of the singular that would have to be made as immune and secure as possible, though it could never be made secure enough.

Language is always, for Plato, corrupted by the lure of a false *stasis* which offers the illusion of a pure artifice, entirely under our control. This *stasis* disconnects meaning from desire, and divides the soul. The sophists are presented as guilty of this separation, since they attach arbitrary labels to things merely represented.[109] It is the sophists, and not Plato, who seem to refuse change, and who disallow a dialectical admixture of truth and falsehood in language.[110] While Heraclitus observed the ontological river, Plato actively follows that river to its source. But language is also corrupted by an avoidance of pauses, or a conversion of stoppages into false flux, in the same way that it is corrupted by a languishing counter-divine fall on the part of human beings. The most constant factor of true naming, it seems, must be lateral and upward motion of varying speeds, co-ordinated with well-timed intervals.[111]

But a correct judgement of the bringing-together of stop and go, up and down, to and fro, is only possible if one attends to the forms.[112] This attention explains the human ability to invent language, which Plato appears to ascribe to the work of legislating individuals rather than to incrementally accrued folk wisdom.[113] So at the end of the *Cratylus*, he seems to forego language in favour of the pre- or supra-linguistic.[114] But one could argue that this is a misreading. The attention to nature which he advocates focuses upon the way in which one thing within nature "signifies" another—even unlike—thing. The signification of unlike things perforce involves a detour for us through human articulation. And the slavery to language that is refused at the end of the dialogue is that of the sophists who are trapped within language because they are trapped within wilful arbitrariness, whether of rule-following fixity or unhinged randomness.[115] Instead, Plato's thinking here is of a piece with his thinking about the access to the forms themselves. This requires the mediation of true desire and occasions of recollection. Words can function as such occasions. As to the question of the birth of words in the first place, it should not be supposed that the form is simply a kind of more primal "thing." The fact that the truth of material things lies in their forms as exemplars is the reason why one has to hold open for the sake of truth the distance between the name of a finite thing and that thing itself. Such distance allows for the recursiveness of our approximations, and allows these to be disclosive and resonant. Not only does the "distance" of the particulars from the forms, and of time from eternity, disclose the eternal forms; one can also say that for Plato this distance has an ultimately positive and not merely privative relationship to transcendence, because outside transcendence, only distance, and the motion which traverses distance, can give access to transcendence.[116] And since "for itself" transcendence is not such, but simply "is," one can also say that there would be no transcendence (which is always transcendence "for us") without distance and motion.[117] The temptation when reading Plato is to imagine that the "next best thing" to the forms would be the quasi-forms of stasis, perhaps on the model of Plato's own mathematical entities. Yet while these indeed for Plato supply a vital and necessary image of the forms themselves, they are not the sole or even the main means of access to them. Rather, one must be reconciled to the seemingly paradoxical yet necessary detour via time, recursiveness, embodiment and particularity. We can only be shaped by or guided towards the forms if we stay within our finite perspective. Yet to be reconciled to a finite perspective does not mean throwing ourselves headlong into the welter of Hermogenes's voluntaristic relativism, nor the infinite regress of Protagorean perspectivalism. The way to offset the instability of the transmission of truth via names, or via other means, is to receive it through motion, both prospective and retrospective: Socrates warns us to heed Homer in looking both forwards and backwards at the same time.[118] M. M. Mackenzie warns that this citation of Homer should be read as an hermeneutic instruction, recommending that we attend to the dialogue as a whole, both retrospectively and prospectively; and yet, at the same time, she notes that the instruction, and the dialogue as a whole, are so riddled with Euthydeman ἀπορίαι that the theory of forms is effectively refuted.[119] One might argue, however, that rather than indicating a refutation of the forms, as Mackenzie concludes, this instruction and the aporetic quality of the dialogue as a whole, are not Euthydeman at all, but are "resolved" (without resolution) by appeal to the forms whose transcendence is beyond the dichotomy of forwards and backwards, and beyond perspective altogether, but is reached through recollection whose dynamic is both retrospective and prospective at once, since the forms, as transcendent, do not reside semelfactively in the past, and since the act of recollection is itself embedded in the prospective movement of time.[120] Socrates's own repeated "turning back," his rehearsal of his former arguments and his retrospective appeal to earlier authors at *Cratylus* 428d, in order to have better hope of moving forward in their discussion of the correctness of names, itself bids the reader to look both backwards and forwards, not as an invitation to abase ourselves before the ἀπορίαι, but rather in an appeal beyond the dichotomy of both extremes. Such retrospection and prospection, in close succession, might be seen as a kind of repetition, or as a dialectical means in time to rise above the limits of successiveness.

One could further submit that the references to motion in this dialogue are suggestive of a redeemed perspectivalism. In contrast to Socrates's critique of perspectivalism in the *Theaetetus*, where appeal to an immanent stability of substance without invocation of the forms concludes in ἀπορία, one could argue that the *Cratylus* makes resolution seem closer to hand. Perspectivalism need not be obliterated in favour of stable substance if it is articulated by the forms. Indeed, the reality of the forms means that the alternative of finite perspectival regress, on the one hand, or seized or contrived immanent stability, on the other, is overcome.[121] In time, our finite perspective must be guided by the elective affinities of ἔρως which mediate between movement and stasis, between our prone angledness and the perspectiveless transcendence of the forms.

A recurrent structure can be seen in the way in which words are willed and yet not arbitrary, motion decides where to go, and yet is led; ἔρως is intended and yet arrives, as it were, from without.

This is not merely the time of human invention, because, according to the third ἀπορία, while language is a rational human work, it is impossible for human beings to work rationally without language. The answer to this dilemma is that just as participation in the forms enables a balance between stop and go, so also language is both active and passive, and the very fabrication of language is something oracularly revealed. The existence of language must "originally" have been the divine gift of the capacity to speak, the capacity to make up words.[122] This accounts both for the "impossible" existence of language and for our "impossible" power to judge language, which is the organ of judgement itself—to judge when to stop and when to go. Without this judgement, language could not really be improved upon, nor could there be any counter to the inherent tendency to degeneration, already mentioned. In proposing a reform of the over-Heraclitean (or "going") character of inherited language, Socrates implicitly appeals to the recollection of forms as the possibility of judging the very organ of judgement itself. Yet this recollection and reform can only occur through the deployment of existing human language, since the power of naming and reflecting on names has already been identified with the operation within us of the λόγος as such.

If our reason is also language, one could go so far as to say that the forms as embodying the real λόγοι of things are hyper-words, not reasons without words. The form as embodying the λόγος of the thing is at once "the real thing" *and* "the real name of the thing." It follows that appeal to the forms as the origin of language is not, for Plato, an appeal to the pre-linguistic. It is rather an appeal to what one might call the "superlinguistic."[123]

One can lend some credibility to Plato's view that language is more akin to a wise work of art than a collective, spontaneous and gradual folk production, even if it was collectively engendered. Wittgenstein was perhaps wrong to see language as innocent of metaphysics. One might alternatively aver here to Wilfred Sellars's as-it-were Platonic legislator "Jones" whom he imagined as inventing a language that included all our current notions of mind, willing and intentionality.[124] In effect, one could suggest, Plato is offering a Platonic theory of language that is also the theory that all human language is inchoate Platonic philosophy, since it recognises a spiritual mind guided by the extra-natural realities of truth, goodness and beauty and it is this guidance that generates language.[125]

Given these considerations, both *Cratylus* and "Cratylism" remain relevant for philosophy today. Plato postulated, in accordance with implicit traditional assumptions, a radical "linguistic turn" that includes the mimeticism of language, because he saw reason as linked with a desire for the good through the beautiful.[126] It is for this reason that for him the word "supplements" thought, just as, in the dialogue of *Euthyphro* (the presiding genius of the *Cratylus* due to turn up on the following day, which never arrives), the will of the gods "supplements" the good by which they are nonetheless guided.[127] This supplementing can invite betrayal, as for Socrates's main interlocutor Hermogenes, supposed son of Hermes, who is a thief as well as a mediator.[128] But not necessarily so, *pace* Derrida. As we have seen, the necessary erotic interval of supplementary copying can be benign, insofar as it witnesses to the gap between material thing and form which allows the thing to participate in the form's truth, its λόγος.

For Plato, it is the role of ἔρως which requires us to see λόγος as language, as well as reason. But this means that it is real, material language which links thought to feeling. Language is the constant work of synthesis between reasoning and emotion: in this way it both "pauses for thought,"[129] and desiringly moves forward to new conceptual discoveries and better articulations, as well as constantly re-addressing earlier moments,[130] like the light about the moon which shines as both old and new.[131] This retrospective and prospective motion, like the loom's shuttle,[132] forms part of a complex interwoven web of references: later names show us the nature of things by means of earlier ones,[133] every name appeals beyond itself to what it imitates,[134] and beyond that to the highest realities themselves. Every glance is shown to be always already a layer, a thread leading one elsewhere, a motion.

In making this synthesis between reasoning and emotion, neither empirical evidence nor *a priori* categories offers any guidance. Rather, judgement, truth and right desiring are only possible by virtue of the lure of the forms. And these also speak, or seem to be given personal voice by virtue of supplementation which is the will of the gods, according to the dialogue *Euthyphro*, with which the *Cratylus* is eponymously linked. The resolution of the "Euthyphro dilemma" in the former dialogue would seem to be that although the gods love the holy because it is holy, rather than the holy being holy because it is willed by the gods, all the same the gods love the holy because it pleases them. Likewise, in the *Cratylus*, it is said that the divine essence is named from the words for "moving and running," suggesting erotic motion, despite the stability of the divine.[135] It seems that ἔρως operates as a medium and as an element in intellectual recognition. In effect one can say that even though the holy (the good, the true, the beautiful) is not merely something fabricated by the gods, it is still "uttered" by them even as it compels them. A certain proto-personalism in Plato's theology, an unwillingness merely to ditch the gods in favour of the Good, seems to go hand in hand with the idea that all thought is language. For the *Euthyphro*, the good and the true precede desire and yet they *are* not, without desire. The question of feeling and the question of religion are for Plato inseparable. And there is for him no λόγος without either phenomenon.

I began this chapter by suggesting that the linguistic character of reason as λόγος is linked to Plato's theory that ἔρως dynamically mediates between knowledge of the particular and knowledge of the forms. Now it seems possible that attention to language in Plato further secures the connection between reason and feeling in terms of the religiously revelatory power of language. It is the true work of human beings insofar as it is also the work of the divine.

At the end of the dialogue we are presented with a negative circumstance and a positive assertion. The negative circumstance is that Euthyphro has not yet arrived and is only expected on the following day. The positive assertion is Socrates's claim that if there is only change there will be no knowledge, because while transition occurs, one cannot know its upshot and therefore if it perpetually occurs there will be nothing to be known and also no one to know it, as there will be no stable subjects of understanding.[136] How might these two things be linked?

The whereabouts of Euthyphro are only one example in the dialogue of metaphors of arrival and belatedness. First, Cratylus withholds his voice from the dialogue, suggesting perhaps that his refusal to permit a gap between the name and the thing named ends up causing him to lag behind in the truth, or miss the moment, since the subsuming of the name in the thing occludes the thing as much as its name.[137] By speaking late, it is as if he has missed the essential supplementarity of words, or overshot them, as represented by the words of the written dialogue itself. Second, Hermogenes appears to withdraw from dialogic exchange before the discussion is finished, with Cratylus taking his place as interlocutor, and his earlier words are recalled seemingly by secondary report (even though he apparently remains present).[138] He falls silent too soon to be part of the discussion concerning the essential link between convention and nature. Because Cratylus and Hermogenes are both half right, and the truth stands between them, the fact that they do not speak together, save in the briefest exchange,[139] could be taken as a metaphor for the truth that the synthesis between their positions lies in the transcendent realm, and that we must look to a dynamic temporal reflection of this realm in which the truth cannot appear all at once; our approximations to the truth must be made by means of successive variation of emphasis,[140] and by looking both forwards and backwards.[141]

Third, Euthyphro, who never arrives at all, stands in a "middle-voiced" way, both for the priority of eternal stable truth *and* for the non-eliminability of language. We can infer, *after* Socrates's final philosophical word about stability, that he is yet to turn up on the following day when we can assume that his words will be confirmatory of Socrates's verdict and yet not superfluous. We are told at 433a–b that the person who fails to admit, against the sophists, a realism of naming which includes an onomatopoeic dimension is in danger of being "punished like travellers in Aegina who wander about the street late at night after the curfew." The danger is that such a person will be "told by truth herself that we have arrived too late."[142] What can this *topos* import? Surely that if, according to the final positive affirmation, there is only change and journeying, we will always be "too late" for truth, for something will have shifted by the time we get there. On the other hand, the *topos* is not supposed to negate journeying, because the deluded traveller denies not only stable essence but also the necessary "supplement" of onomatopoeic correspondence. The curfew is of course for Plato not called down within time, nor in any earthly place. In time there is only perpetual travel and no abiding place.[143] The "evening" is eternal and through participation admits of a certain twilight and spatial enclosure in the realm of shadows. Here there can be calendars and cities. Yet because the enclosure is only relative and therefore a continued journeying through linguistic signs is required, Cratylus may not have added his voice too late after all: it is up to him to make a belated recognition of the truth; and Hermogenes's premature silence may not mean that all is lost. Likewise, Euthyphro is not too late, even though he has missed the curfew. Arrival on the following day always remains possible: the day, when truth in time will rise again with the dawn and shine both forwards and backwards.[144] The sun is said to collect men when he rises.[145]

NOTES

*   Sections of this chapter were delivered as part of the Stapledon Lecture Series, Department of Philosophy, University of Liverpool, April 2010. I am grateful to members of these audiences, and especially Professor Stephen Clark, Professor Charles Taylor and Professor John Cottingham, for their helpful comments and discussion. Profound thanks are owed to Professor David Sedley for his detailed critique of my interpretation of the *Cratylus*. His criticisms are insufficiently met.

1   Robert Pogue Harrison, "The Ambiguities of Philology," *Diacritics*, Vol. 16, no. 2 (Summer, 1986), pp. 14–20, 18.

2   *Phaedrus* 251b–e.

3   *Phaedrus* 255c–d, *Crat* 420a–b (ἔρως is not inherent, but introduced through the eyes).

4   *Phaedo* 59d–60c, 115b.

5   *Crat* 432a–b.

6   *Crat* 420d–e (The translation given here and elsewhere is that of H. N. Fowler, Harvard University Press, 1926, 1992).

7   *Crat* 420e. See also 405e.

8   *Phaedrus* 257b–c.

9   See also *Apology* 31d, 40a. The epistemological background to this pervasive "demur" has been much discussed. Hans-Georg Gadamer indicates that the Platonic dialogues are to be seen not as an example of philosophy itself, since contemporary culture is not morally equipped for its truths, but as representing a therapeutic stage on the way to philosophy (*Dialogue and Dialectic: Eight Hermeneutical Studies on Plato*, P. Christopher Smith (trans.) (New Haven, CT: Yale University Press, 1980)). It is because of these polemical circumstances that Gadamer puts the case for an "hermeneutical" reading of the dialogues; see *The Idea of the Good in Platonic-Aristotelian Philosophy*, P. Christopher Smith (trans.) (New Haven, CT: Yale University Press, 1986), Chapter 1. One might see further reasons for the Platonic-Socratic "demur" in Socrates's problematisation of writing, and his favouring of perpetually self-revising and self-supplementing (*pace* Derrida) orality (*Phaedrus* 278c ff), which is a staging-post to the higher "writing on the soul" which is open-ended yet continues forever (*Phaedrus* 277a).

10   Jacob Klein, *Plato's Trilogy: Theaetetus, Sophist and Statesman* (Chicago, IL: University of Chicago Press, 1977), pp. 1 ff: the texts are more akin to *mimes* than to treatises or lectures.

11   On the association of the written word and sophistry with money, see, for example, *Euthyphro* 3d; *Apology* 19e, 26d–e, 30b, 31b, 33b, 36c, and elsewhere in the dialogues.

12   *Phaedrus* 228d–e; see also 257d–258c.

13   *Crat* 383a, 384d, 391b.

14   Even Ferdinand de Saussure, founder of structural linguistics, who introduced the notion of the "arbitrariness" of the sign, was intrigued by what he called anagrams and paragrams, and wrote dense eponymic analyses of Vedic and Homeric verses and inscriptions, discovering the names of gods and heroes mysteriously concealed in letters and sounds. See Jean Starobinski, *Words upon Words: The Anagrams of Ferdinand de Saussure*, Olivia Emmet (trans.) (New Haven, CT: Yale University Press, 1979), p. 16–17. One might wish to argue that Saussure was a "secondary mimologist," as Gérard Genette dubs Socrates, for his hovering between conventionalism and naturalism. See *Mimologiques: Voyage en Cratylie* (Paris: Éditions du Seuil, 1976), Chapter 1.

15   Cratylus appears to be present throughout the dialogue (see *Crat* 383a), but is only a participant in the discussion during the second half (427e).

16   *Crat* 429b ff. On Cratylus as a sophist, see *Crat* 428b; also Timothy M. Baxter, *The Cratylus: Plato's Critique of Naming* (Leiden: E. J. Brill, 1992), pp. 25 ff.

17   *Crat* 424e.

18   *Crat* 429b–c.

19   *Crat* 383a; see also *Crat* 384d ff.

20   *Crat* 435a.

21   See, for example, M. M. Mackenzie, "Putting the *Cratylus* in its place," *The Classical Quarterly* (New Series), Vol. 36, no. 1 (1986), pp. 124–150; Imogen Smith, "False Names, Demonstratives and the Refutation of Linguistic Naturalism in Plato's *Cratylus*

427d1–431c3," *Phronesis*, Vol. 53, no. 2 (2008), pp. 125–151; Rachel Barney, "Plato on Conventionalism," *Phronesis*, Vol. 42, no. 2 (1997), pp. 143–162.

22 See Sean D. Kirkland, "Logos as Message from the Gods: On the Etymology of 'Hermes' in Plato's Cratylus," *Bochumer Philosophisches Jahrbuch für Antike und Mittelalter*, Vol. 12, no. 1 (2007), pp. 1–14.

23 *Crat* 391d, 396a ff, 400e, 438c; see also 383b–d.

24 *Crat* 438c.

25 *Crat* 440c–d; see also 389d–e, 397b. That the theory of forms is present, latent or anticipated in *Cratylus* is disputed. It is supported by R. H. Weingartner, *The Unity of the Platonic Dialogue: the* Cratylus, *the* Protagoras, *the* Parmenides" (Indianapolis, IN: Bobbs-Merrill, 1973), pp. 15–43; C. H. Kahn, "Language and ontology in the *Cratylus*," *Exegesis and Argument; Studies in Greek Philosophy Presented to Gregory Vlastos*, E. N. Lee, A. P. D. Mourelatos, R. M. Rorty (eds.) (Assen: Van Gorcum, 1973), pp. 152–176; and J. V. Luce, "The Theory of Ideas in the *Cratylus*," *Phronesis*, Vol. 10, no. 1 (1965), pp. 21–36. But see Gilbert Ryle, *Plato's Progress* (Cambridge: Cambridge University Press, 1966), p. 2. Mackenzie contends that the theory of forms is undermined in the *Cratylus* by the insuperable ἀπορίαι; see "Putting the *Cratylus*."

26 *Crat* 432a–e.

27 *Crat* 384d–e; 386a; 386c–391c.

28 *Crat* 386d–e; 434b.

29 I am grateful to an anonymous reader for this observation.

30 *Crat* 432e–433b; "Hector" and "Astyanax" are the same in "power" (δύναμις): 394b–c; see also 393a–394c; see 438d–e on the variability and unreliability of the "matter" of names for learning.

31 *Crat* 433a.

32 *Crat* 394b. It seems that alteration of the form of words through time is compatible with the integrity and continuity of meaning, and that the man who knows about names is not confused by variety or variation: "[. . .] if a letter is added or subtracted, that does not matter [. . .] so long as the essence of the thing named remains in force and is made plain in the name," *Crat* 393d; "the variety in the syllables is admissible, so that names which are the same appear different to the uninitiated [. . .] the man who knows about names considers their value and is not confused if some letter is added, transposed, or subtracted, or even if the force (δύναμις) of the name is expressed in entirely different letters," *Crat* 394a–b; see *Crat* 432e–433b on the historical mutation of the "matter" of words, and *Crat* 414c on primordial languages as more intensely mimetic.

33 *Crat* 392 ff.

34 *Crat* 393a–394c. For references to cultural and geographical variations of words, and to the foreign origin of certain words, see *Crat* 385d–e, 390a, 400e–401a, 401c–e, 410a, 412b, 416d, 419c–d, 434c. See Thomas Harrison, "Herodotus' Conception of Foreign Languages," *Histos* Vol. 2 (March 1998) (http://www.dur.ac.uk/Classics/histos/1998/harrison.html#n*); and R. H. Weingartner, "Making Sense of the *Cratylus*," *Phronesis*, Vol. 15, no. 1 (1970), pp. 5–25, 23 ff.

35 *Crat* 388b–c, 389e. See Aristotle, *De int.* 4.17a 1–2.

36 *Crat* 390a, 393d–e. See B. Williams, "Cratylus' Theory of Names and its Refutation," in S. Everson (ed.), *Companions to Ancient Thought 3: Language* (Cambridge: Cambridge University Press), pp. 28–36, 32–33.

37 *Crat* 390a.

38 *Crat* 435a–d. Hans-Georg Gadamer, *Truth and Method*, Joel Weinsheimer and Donald G. Marshall (trans.) (London and New York: Continuum, 2004), pp. 357–370, 410.

39 Ludwig Wittgenstein, *Philosophical Investigations*, G. E. M. Anscombe (trans.) (New York: Macmillan, 1958), on Augustine's *Confessions* I.8: 2e–3e, 1; see also 4e, 6; 5e, 7; 15e, 26.

40 *Crat* 423a.

41 *Crat* 415c–416b.

42 *Crat* 417a.

43 *Crat* 387d, 388c, 389d–e.

44 On thinking-naming as teaching: *Crat* 388c, 428e, 435d; as political legislating: 388c, 390c; naming as a species of action: 387a, 408b–c, 391c; on names as having "force": 405e.

45 *Crat* 393c.

46 *Crat* 440c; 432b.
47 *Crat* 401b–d. For further discussion of the link between naming and genesis, see Baxter, *The* Cratylus, pp. 136 ff.
48 *Crat* 408c–d.
49 *Crat* 428e.
50 *Crat* 428d, 430c–d, 431a–d. It seems that the only way to offset the instability of the transmission of truth via names, or via other means, is to receive it through motion, both prospective and retrospective, upward and downward. See, for example, *Crat* 428d–e where Socrates cites *Iliad* I.343, III.109. See also *Crat* 394b.
51 Gérard Genette, *Mimologics* (Lincoln, NB: University of Nebraska Press, 1995), p. xxiv.
52 Genette, *Mimologics*, p. 17; Davide Del Bello, *Forgotten Paths: Etymology and the Allegorical Mindset* (Washington, DC: The Catholic University of America Press, 2007), p. 55.
53 Baxter, *The* Cratylus, pp. 45, 119.
54 Franco Cavazza, *Studio su Verrone etimologo e grammatico* (Florence: La Nuovo Italia, 1981), p. 6; see also Baxter, *The* Cratylus, p. 92.
55 Cavazza, *Studio*, pp. 24–25; Baxter, *The* Cratylus, p. 6.
56 See Jean Lallot's concept of "pluralistic truth" in "L'étymologie en Grèce ancienne d'Homère aux grammairiens alexandrins" in Jean-Pierre Chambon and Georges Lüdi, *Discours étymologiques* (Freiburg: Max Niemeyer, 1991), pp. 135–148, 138. I am grateful to Thomas Harrison for pointing out that Plato's use of etymology (or allegorical eponymy) was not a peculiarity but formed part of an ancient Greek cultural tradition which hoped for words to be meaningful and sought to discover meaningful associations and first origins of word-chains. Harrison cites many parallels in Herodotus's *Histories* (e.g. 4.45.2–5, 1.139) and elsewhere. See Harrison, "Herodotus' Conception of Foreign Languages."
57 See Thaïs E. Morgan, "Invitation to a voyage in Cratylusland," in Genette, *Mimologics*, pp. xv–lxvi, xxxiii.
58 See above in main text and n. 44.
59 Proclus, *Lezioni sul "Cratilo" di Platone*, Francesco Romano (trans.) (Catania: Università di Catania, 1989), p. 89.
60 Plato frequently admits more than one etymological explanation for each given name. See, for example, *Crat* 400 c–d.
61 *Crat* 384c, 407b–c, 409d, 413a–c, 425c, 421c–d.
62 *Crat* 425d, 426b. See also 414c, 415d–e and 418a on the non-dogmatism of Socrates's position. As already indicated, the absurdity of the etymologies need not preclude the possibility of their seriousness. See Weingartner, "Making Sense of the *Cratylus*," p. 24, and Simon Keller, "An Interpretation of Plato's *Cratylus*," *Phronesis*, Vol. 45, no. 4 (2000), pp. 284–305. But above all, see David Sedley's argument that the etymologies are "exegetically correct" in "The Etymologies in Plato's *Cratylus*," *Journal of Hellenic Studies*, Vol. 118 (1998), pp. 140–154.
63 *Crat* 428c.
64 *Crat* 396d–e; 400e; 425d–e.
65 *Crat* 386b–389d–e; 397b.
66 On generation, names and words and offspring, see *Crat* 393d and 397b.
67 *Crat* 421b–c.
68 *Crat* 397e–398a–d.
69 *Crat* 426c–427d.
70 See the frequent comparisons of elements of words with pigments, as well as with music, rhythm and shape: *Crat* 423d–e, 424c, 425a, 430b, 430e, 432b, 434b.
71 *Crat* 423d–424a.
72 *Crat* 388c–e.
73 *Crat* 388c–e.
74 *Crat* 396d–e, 413a. See T. E. Jones, "Plato's *Cratylus*, Dionysius of Halicarnasus, and the Correctness of Names in Pope's Homer," *The Review of English Studies*, New Series, Vol. 53, no. 212 (2002), pp. 484–499. One might note Roman Jakobson's observation that "parallelism" or systematic similarities on phonetic, morphological, grammatical and semantic levels are characteristic of the "poetic function" of language, and that this poetic

function may become dominant in everyday language. See Roman Jakobson, "Linguistics and Poetics," in *Style in Language*, Thomas A. Sebeok (trans.) (Cambridge, MA: MIT Press, 1960), p. 357.

75   *Crat* 391d, 396a ff, 400e.
76   *Crat* 397e–398d, 399a, 400c.
77   *Crat* 421a–c.
78   *Crat* 429a.
79   *Crat* 388c, 388e–390c.
80   *Crat* 388e.
81   *Crat* 389c.
82   *Crat* 422c–d.
83   *Crat* 436e.
84   *Crat* 393d.
85   *Crat* 396b–d; see also 410e, 397b, 426a.
86   *Crat* 432e–433b.
87   *Crat* 397e–398a–d.
88   *Crat* 424b–425b, 434b.
89   *Crat* 427a.
90   *Crat* 427b.
91   *Crat* 427b–d.
92   See also *Crat* 434c ff.
93   Jacques Derrida observes that it is no accident that the consonantal cluster *gl-* should appear in the original sound symbolism in the *Cratylus*. *Gl-* stands for things which are "sticky" and "gummy," and he claims it imitates its own articulation as a speech sound. Built upon "association, [eponymy] is a sort of gluing [which] not only takes hold in the signifying paste," or the physical qualities of words, but "also sticks . . . to the sense" to such an extent that sound and meaning seem to cohere in every case. See Jacques Derrida *Glas*, John R. Leavey and Richard Rand (trans.) (Lincoln, NB: University of Nebraska Press, 1986), pp. 37, 142, 149.
94   As already mentioned, Socrates acknowledges its seeming absurdity at *Crat* 425d, 426b.
95   *Crat* 431a, 432e–433b, 439c.
96   *Crat* 430a–b, 431e–432d.
97   "An imitation of an imitation, in the third rank," Gadamer, *Truth and Method*, p. 115 (re. *Rep* X).
98   *Phaedrus* 250d–e.
99   *Crat* 432d: if imitation were exact in every way, it would be misleading. For discussions of non-identical repetition, see Catherine Pickstock, *After Writing* (Oxford: Blackwell, 1998), pp. 18, 25, 35, 109, 160.
100   *Crat* 412b–c.
101   Gadamer, *Truth and Method*, pp. 112–115.
102   *Crat* 437a–d.
103   *Crat* 438c, 426c–427c.
104   *Crat* 401b–d.
105   *Crat* 438c.
106   *Crat* 438a–b.
107   *Crat* 440c.
108   *Timaeus* 37d.
109   *Crat* 431e–432d, 440c.
110   *Crat* 423a. On the positions of Cratylus and Hermogenes as excluding the possibility of expressing falsehood in language, see Baxter, *The* Cratylus, p. 18.
111   The references to motion of these various sorts are too numerous to list here, but some examples include: *Crat* 396bc, 399c, 409a, 409c, 410b, 414a, 423a, 417a, 419a, 439c, 418e, 437a–d, 440b, 440c. True wisdom is described as the "touching of motion" (412b–c; see also 404d).
112   *Crat* 423a.
113   *Crat* 429a.
114   *Crat* 438e. See Keller, "An Interpretation of Plato's *Cratylus*."
115   *Crat* 431e–432d.

116 There is a suggestion at *Phaedrus* 250d that this distance saves us, for if true wisdom were to come to us directly, in unmediated form, it would arouse "terrible love" (δεινοὺς [. . .] ἔρωτας).
117 See *Crat* 401a for the human perspective of the discussion.
118 *Crat* 428d, citing Homer, *Iliad* i. 343 and iii. 109.
119 Mackenzie, "Putting the *Cratylus*," p. 128.
120 For a suggestion that recollection combines retrospection and prospective movement, see *Phaedrus* 249c–250d, 251a–252b. J.-L. Chrétien argues that, in contrast to the Kantian or neo-Kantian *a priori* which resides as a given truth in the mind, for Plato, recollection is not simply a matter of introspection. Rather, it is preceded by forgetting, and is triggered by the physical reality of loving something in the world. Insofar as for Plato recollection does not entail knowing identically an anterior moment, as it entails a memory of the pre-existent estate of the soul, but non-identically, through inspiration via ἔρως, one can infer a partial dynamic of prospectivity. See J.-L. Chrétien, *L'inoubliable et L'inespéré* (Paris: Desclée de Brouwer, 1991), pp. 9–56, 22. At the opening of her article, "Putting the *Cratylus*," M. M. Mackenzie describes those who interpret the arguments of the *Cratylus* as consistent with a theory of forms as downplaying the ἀπορίαι of the dialogue as "mere camouflage for the hidden dogma," the latter all too often being the theory of the transcendent forms (p. 124). One could argue, however, that the theory of the forms enables one to overcome dogma; in this case, that of relativism, on the one hand, and unreflective realism, on the other.
121 *Crat* 394b.
122 See *Crat* 438a–c.
123 See *Crat* 389b, 389d–e, 397b; on the gods as giving naturally correct names, see 391e, 392a–b, 397bc.
124 Wilfred Sellars, *Empiricism and the Philosophy of Mind*, Herbert Feigl and Michael Scriven (eds.) (Minneapolis, MN: University of Minnesota Press, 1956), Volume I, sections 48–63.
125 See Sedley, "The Etymologies," pp. 149–150, for a discussion of the way in which the seemingly haphazard structure of the etymologies apparently dictated by the vicissitudes of Hermogenes's and Socrates's discussion (390e–421c) in fact follows a calibrated philosophical scheme, from cosmology or physics, through ethics and logic, anticipating the Indo-European tripartition of philosophy into logic, physics and ethics, and echoing the bipartition in the *Timaeus* of λόγος into δόξα and ἐπιστήμη (29b–c).
126 Gadamer, "Plato and the Poets," *Dialogue and Dialectic*, pp. 39–72; Gadamer, *Truth and Method*, p. 115.
127 *Euthyphro* 11a, 14e.
128 *Crat* 384a, 407e–408a, 391c.
129 *Crat* 439e–440a–b; see also 412b–c.
130 *Crat* 428d.
131 *Crat* 409b.
132 *Crat* 390c–d.
133 *Crat* 422e; see also 387d, 408c and 432d.
134 *Crat* 423c.
135 *Crat* 397d; see also 419c–d, 420a, 421b–c, 436e.
136 *Crat* 440b–c.
137 *Crat* 427e.
138 *Crat* 433a, 434c, 435c. Hermogenes's physical presence is alluded to in Socrates's closing words at 440e.
139 *Crat* 428a.
140 The things of the earth are variegated. See *Crat* 409a.
141 *Crat* 428d–e.
142 *Crat* 433a–b.
143 *Crat* 411c, 415cd, 417ab.
144 *Crat* 428d–e; see 409c on the light of the moon as "a new and old gleam."
145 *Crat* 409a.

4

EVAGRIUS PONTICUS AND THE EASTERN MONASTIC TRADITION ON THE INTELLECT AND THE PASSIONS

COLUMBA STEWART, O.S.B.

This chapter is devoted to the contribution of Christian monastic writers of the fourth and fifth centuries to the study of faith, rationality, and the passions. Their names will be less familiar to most readers than those of other great philosophers and theologians who have studied the passions and emotions, though to an Eastern Christian audience they would be far better known than Augustine, Aquinas, Descartes, or Kierkegaard. I suggest that the philosophical and theological sources used by these monastic thinkers position them solidly in the great tradition of reflection on "Faith, Rationality and the Passions," and, furthermore, that even in the West their influence has been greater than one might realize. They played a key role in the further development of the strong ascetic dimension of Christian thought and practice, providing the conceptual basis for the monastic form of asceticism that would reshape the Christian Church in profound ways in the coming centuries. They also show us a particular Christian version of the general Late Antique concern with emotions and their management, placed within an explicitly theological and social framework.

The central figure I will consider is Evagrius Ponticus (ca. 345–399). Though not as famous as Antony the Great, celebrated hermit of the Egyptian desert, Evagrius was a prolific and systematic writer whose influence was to prove immense but tangled. I will also refer to Antony's contribution to the Egyptian monastic culture that shaped Evagrius during the fourteen years he spent in Egypt at the renowned monastic settlement of Kellia, the "Cells."

Faith, Rationality, and the Passions, First Edition. Edited by Sarah Coakley.
© 2012 Blackwell Publishing Ltd. Book compilation © 2012 Blackwell Publishing Ltd.

Evagrius's achievement was to join Hellenistic philosophical understandings of the passions to the acute diagnostic techniques he learned from masterful practitioners in the Egyptian monastic movement. The result was a systematic and pedagogically-oriented model of the spiritual life, in which sustained attention to the passions was the necessary precondition for loving relations with other people and for the fullest experience of prayer.

Introducing Evagrius

Evagrius brought to his task a formidable background in philosophy and theology, having been a pupil of two of the most gifted Christian theologians of the fourth century, Basil the Great and Gregory Nazianzen.[1] Born in Pontus, a region of northern Asia Minor, Evagrius moved to Constantinople when Gregory Nazianzen became bishop in 379, was ordained a deacon, and stayed on after Gregory's dramatic resignation two years later. With Gregory, he was part of an international intellectual community joined by their interest in the writings of the third-century Alexandrian theologian Origen (ca. 185–254). This community, united by frequent exchange of letters and texts, included the brilliant and philanthropic Roman widow, Melania (known later as "Melania the Elder," alleged to have memorized 3,000,000 lines of Origen's writings and 2,500,000 of works by other theologians),[2] and Rufinus of Aquileia, translator of Origen and monastic writings, and legendary friend and foe of Jerome. Their interest in Origen was based on a solid philosophical education and expressed a degree of comfort with Hellenistic thought not always shared—or admitted—by their contemporaries and successors.

Evagrius's great ambition, his outstanding intellect, and his personal charisma brought him to a crisis. Having fallen in love with a married woman of high social standing, he had a dream in which he was commanded to leave Constantinople. He then spent time in Jerusalem with Melania and Rufinus at the monastery they had founded on the Mount of Olives, though without revealing the reason for his departure from the capital. According to the biographical sources, Evagrius soon began to have troubles in Jerusalem as well, taking special care of his dress and spending much of his time sauntering through the streets of the cosmopolitan Holy City. Falling mortally ill with a fever, he confessed his struggles to Melania, who was evidently wise as well as intelligent. After Evagrius's unexpected recovery, she told him that he must adopt the monastic life, and in its strict Egyptian semi-eremiticial form. She then packed him off to the desert, there to be sorted out by monks who knew how to deal with particularly difficult cases like his.

Evagrius went to the monastic settlement of Nitria in Lower Egypt, which in his day was accessible by boat via the canal system connecting Alexandria to the Nile. He soon moved more deeply into the desert, to the remote hermit colony of Kellia ("the Cells"), where he spent the last fifteen years of his life. He apprenticed with the notable teachers of his day. The hermits of Kellia lived singly or in small groups; the day was ideally spent in prayer and manual labor (Evagrius worked as a scribe, copying texts for hire). These were surprisingly sociable anchorites, who sought wisdom from famous masters and travelled great distances to consult those who were especially renowned. Evagrius once travelled hundreds of miles to ask John of Lycopolis about the extraordinary light he sometimes experienced in prayer. Very quickly Evagrius himself became a sought-after discerner of thoughts and teacher. His substantial corpus of writings included works carefully designed for monastic instruction at various levels of emotional and spiritual development, as well as copious biblical commentaries. These are among the earliest surviving monastic texts in the Christian tradition. Evagrius's writings also preserve the earliest examples of monastic *apophthegmata*, the pithy aphorisms that have become popular spiritual reading in recent decades.[3]

The Egyptian Monastic Background to Evagrius's Work

When Evagrius arrived in Egypt around the year 384, Antony the Great had been dead almost thirty years.[4] Antony's biographer, Bishop Athanasius of Alexandria, had published his *Life of Antony* in 357, the year after the monk's death at the age of 105.[5] Athanasius's vividly written story was indescribably successful. It was immediately translated into Latin in two different versions, and eventually into Syriac, Coptic, Armenian, Arabic, and Ethiopic as well. One of the Latin versions played a key role in the conversion of the troubled African rhetorician Augustine, who learned about Antony from a friend who had become a monk after reading the *Life*. The story of Antony, able to storm the gates of heaven despite his lack of intellectual and social graces, precipitated Augustine's final crisis, famously resolved by the child's *Tolle, lege* (*Confessions* 8.6–12). Evagrius arrived in Egypt in about 385; Augustine was baptized in Milan on Easter 387. Despite the great difference in their subsequent careers, both lives were changed by what was happening in the Egyptian desert.

It is now widely acknowledged that the *Life of Antony* showcases Athanasius's own theological and monastic agenda, and deliberately distorts the facts of Antony's life by portraying him as an unlettered peasant.[6] Nonetheless, the central section of the work (chapters 16–43), a discourse delivered by Antony, contains teaching on discernment and "demons" that echoes other texts that come from within the monastic movement. In the *Life*, Antony explains how to unmask the wiles of the demons with various analytic and ascetic strategies. The demonology echoes that of early Christian writings, which had themselves developed themes found in Deuterocanonical, Inter-testamental, and Jewish sectarian texts grappling with the perennial questions of theodicy, viz., the origin and enduring presence of evil in a world created by a beneficent God.[7]

In the *Life of Antony*, as in other monastic literature, demons are hard at work trying to foil the monks' efforts to practice the "discipline" (*askēsis*) believed to restore the original human condition intended by God.[8] Demons in these stories play both a theological and a psychological role. Theologically, they represent forces of evil that linger even after the Incarnation and the Resurrection, now robbed of real power but highly skilled at deception and able to play on the weakness and fears of vulnerable human beings.[9] Psychologically, demons represent the mix of memories and passions that subvert a monk's spiritual intentions by suggesting alternatives to the harsh disciplines of monastic life. By externalizing and objectifying these powerful counter-forces as "demons," one can fight them more successfully.[10] Antony himself wrote several letters imbued with the struggle against the demons, which, though not as widely diffused as Athanasius's *Life*, complement its teaching with a more explicitly Origenist theological outlook.[11]

The *Life of Antony* and other Egyptian monastic texts also describe these temptations and powers as "thoughts" (*logismoi*). These thoughts, which may be prompted by demons, lodge within the psyche and become one's own. As we will see, Evagrius prefers "thought" to "demon" but uses both concepts. The diagnostic and therapeutic techniques that Antony proposes owe something to both Hellenistic philosophy and Christian ritual practice. The *diagnostic* techniques include vigilant self-awareness, interrogation and dissection of demonically-inspired thoughts, narrating one's struggles to a wise elder, and writing down particularly irksome temptations. These would have been familiar to any reader of Epictetus or Pythagorean literature.[12] The classic stance was to challenge the demon directly: "Who are you?" "Where have you come from?," thereby piercing the illusions and fear which alone give the demons their power.[13]

The techniques for *resistance* lie more, though not necessarily exclusively, in the realm of religious practice. They include the invocation of the name of Christ, making the sign of the Cross, and chanting biblical texts to block out and also to neutralize spiritually the unwholesome suggestions of the demons.[14] Underlying all of these practices, of course, was a preliminary realization that something was wrong with the way humans navigate their daily lives. The successful deployment of these techniques, in turn, depended on gaining a reflective distance from the immediate experience of temptation; they also helped secure and extend such distance once it had been gained.

Evagrius learned to employ what had become these standard monastic diagnostic and therapeutic techniques while he was at Kellia, where his principal teacher was Macarius the Great, who had been a disciple of Antony, and lived at the similar monastic colony of Scetis some 25 miles away. He placed them within a model of the Christian life that offered a theological trajectory of personal development that moved from a starting-point of fear and anxiety about one's own salvation, to a goal of love and knowledge directed outwards toward God and the whole of Creation. This saga of personal development was in turn placed within an elaborate cosmic story patterned on Origen's speculations in *On First Principles*. Both the personal and the cosmic frameworks that Evagrius devised would prove controversial, though his development of sharper analytical tools for monastic asceticism would prove both helpful and influential.

Evagrius's Development of the Egyptian Monastic Tradition

Evagrius wrote for both newcomers and advanced monks. He helped the former to acquire the detachment and perspective that would permit them to make their way through the progressive phases of the monastic life. For the more experienced, he provided a roadmap to chart their development and deeply challenging nuggets for extensive meditation. He wrote in several literary genres, including biblical commentary, manuals of ascetic practice, advanced treatises, speculative theology, and letters. Many of his writings employed a distinctive format, that of the *kephalaion*, or brief chapter, and the closely allied *scholion*, or brief commentary on an authoritative text. Familiar from works such as Epictetus's *Manual* and from commentaries on classic philosophical texts, *kephalaia* and *scholia* served Evagrius's pedagogical purposes well.[15] Many of them closely resembled the biblical proverbs typically memorized by ancient monks.[16]

Evagrius keyed most of his work to a model of the monastic life consisting of three stages: asceticism (*praktikē*), contemplation of creation (*theōria physikē*), and theology (*theologia*). Sometimes he used a simpler distinction between the "practical life" (*praktikos bios*) and the "contemplative life" (*theōrētikos bios*). Such a division of human activity has a venerable ancestry in Greek philosophy, where Platonic and Aristotelian distinctions between the active life and the contemplative life, or Stoic models of ethical, natural, and logical/rational aspects of life, were commonplace.[17] Origen had adopted it as a scheme for biblical interpretation, suggesting both different *kinds* of meaning and different *levels* of spiritual insight. He famously correlated these to the biblical books of Proverbs, Ecclesiastes, and the Song of Songs.[18] Evagrius applied the model to interpretation of biblical texts and used it as a way to conceive of the monastic life as a whole. A particular biblical text could be read in multiple ways, each keyed to a particular stage of monastic experience (an exercise he illustrates in his surviving *scholia* on Psalms, Proverbs, Ecclesiastes, and Job). His most fundamental work is a trilogy containing collections of *kephalaia* intended for reflection by monks in each of the three stages of monastic life.[19] In Evagrius's understanding, these stages were progressive and developmental, in the sense that they described advancement from beginning steps in the life to monastic perfection. They were not, however, strictly chronological or necessarily successive: even beginners could have experiences of a more advanced kind, and mature monks never abandoned ascetic practices or contemplation of God's creation.

Our concern here is primarily with the "practical life" of ascetic discipline, the focus of Evagrius's extremely influential and widely copied *Praktikos*, the first volume in his fundamental trilogy.[20] He develops the psychodynamic elements further in the more advanced treatise *On the Thoughts*.[21] The *praktikē* fundamentally consisted of sustained attention to the "thoughts" (*logismoi*), especially those that were "impassioned," i.e., preoccupying or linked to problematic behaviors.[22] Although Evagrius often used the demonological idiom favored in the *Life of Antony* and other monastic texts, he generally referred to these provocations as "thoughts." By using both "demon" and "thought," however, he was able to keep in play both an external (i.e., non-human) origination of disturbing suggestions and an internal (i.e., human and personal) responsibility for harboring them. Such ambiguity allowed him to address theodicy at the micro-level of human psychodynamics.

As Evagrius explored that micro-level, he employed two further tools. First, and most fundamental, was Platonic tripartite anthropology. Evagrius adapted a Late Antique version with wide circulation in manuals designed for teaching and self-help.[23] Following this tradition, Evagrius divided the soul into two irrational parts, desire (*epithumia*) and repulsion/resistance (*thumos*), and a rational part (*logistikon meros*), also termed the intellect or mind (*nous*). All three were essential and original to human nature as created by God, and each had a necessary use. The *nous* was meant to guide the effective operation of the whole self (Plato's charioteer stands in the distant background here); *epithumia* was to fuel love for God and neighbor; *thumos* was the capacity to resist evil and injustice. Each could also be misused. The irrational parts were the realm of the "passions," a term Evagrius uses to describe desire and repulsion when they are engaged destructively, and also employs as a synonym for *logismoi* when a thought has become engaged with desire or repulsion. These irrational energies required particular care in their management. Easily aroused, enmeshed in bodily activities in complicated ways, they readily seized control from the intellect. Evagrius describes it most simply when he notes that the intellect is meant to be dominant in all rational creatures, but only angels get it right. Humans are typically controlled by *epithumia*, and demons are completely mastered by *thumos*.[24] In fact, however, the human situation is unstable, with dominance cycling among *nous, epithumia*, and *thumos* as moments of clear insight yield to grasping or resentful obsessions.

Evagrius's second tool was a system of "eight generic thoughts" (*genikōtatoi logismoi*), comprising gluttony, lust, avarice, sadness, anger, accidie (*akēdia*, a bored restlessness), vainglory and pride.[25] Though not as ubiquitous in his works as the tripartite anthropology, the system of eight *logismoi* would prove to be more significant for the later tradition. The first three *logismoi* can be mapped to the desiring part of the soul, the next three to the repelling part of the soul, and the final two to the rational or intellectual part. Their sequence is based on observed interconnections between specific thoughts: overindulgence in food and drink excites lustful thoughts; failing to get desired money or material goods leads to anger or sadness, etc.[26]

The system of eight generic thoughts was largely Evagrius's own creation, though he relied heavily on the pioneering work of Origen. Origen was arguably the first Christian thinker to situate a sophisticated understanding of human psychodynamics within a theological (and more specifically, biblical) frame of reference.[27] Evagrius's list of eight generic thoughts owes much to Origen's biblical homilies and commentaries, in which he retold the story of Israel's ups and downs as allegories of the human journey from spiritual exile and alienation to a reunion with the Creator. Thus, for example, in his *Homilies on Joshua*, Origen interprets the account of the conquest of the Promised Land in a spiritual (i.e., non-historical and personal) manner as a description of every Christian's effort to re-conquer the terrain of the heart from the hostile demonic forces that had taken it captive. Origen characterizes these forces with various names and qualities, which in turn suggested most of Evagrius's eight generic thoughts and much of their sequencing as well.[28] Evagrius's innovation was the introduction of accidie, the "Noonday demon," which hardly figures in Origen's writings but was evidently a major problem among the anchorites.[29] Often alone, reliant on their own discipline to provide structure and momentum to the day, they were susceptible to boredom and depression, especially as the day grew hot and their hunger more urgent before the mid-afternoon meal. Evagrius's descriptions of accidie are among his most vivid literary creations.[30]

Beyond the Passions

As we have seen, Evagrius followed the traditional Christian understanding, prevalent in the *Life of Antony*, that malevolent forces outside the self, personified as demons, generated many of the thoughts that distract and tempt us. He also believed that the monastic techniques mentioned above, such as interrogation of the thought or demon, sharing thoughts with a spiritual guide, and using biblical phrases for "talking back" (*antirrhēsis*), combined with traditional ascetic disciplines such as fasting, keeping vigil, singing psalms, patience and generosity toward other people, and of course avoiding particular objects of either desire or aversion, could liberate one from domination or confusion by the passions, and restore the proper balance among the various parts of the soul. Evagrius called this healthy psychic condition *apatheia*, "freedom from passion," a repurposed Stoic term.[31]

With Evagrius's *apatheia*, we face an acute problem of terminology in the many ways in which ancient writers used the term passion (*pathē, passio*) and modern ones use "emotion." As a Late Antique Christian author, Evagrius's understanding and descriptions of human psychology were a mix of various strands of Greek philosophical thought and Christian anthropology. This is evident, for example, in the key chapter of the *Praktikos*, which describes the parts of the soul with their virtues and passions. Seemingly cribbed from a first-century Peripatetic treatise, it is a typical mishmash of terminology from different schools, with Christian adaptations by Evagrius.[32] Despite Evagrius's careful explanations, his use of *apatheia* proved to be confusing and also vulnerable to willful distortion by his critics. Evagrius did not in fact suggest that problematic thoughts or demonic suggestions could be entirely eliminated.[33] Temptation and susceptibility to sinful engagement with thoughts remained part of the human condition even for skilled monks. Nor did Evagrius imagine that *thumos* and *epithumia* would be shut down entirely. Far from it: they would now be able to fulfill their natural functions, under the restored authority of the *nous*.

The fundamental issue for Evagrius was clear thinking, which meant, with his Platonic epistemology, clear *seeing*. Thus, free from the distorting effects of unmanaged passions, a monk would begin to see more clearly the revelation of God's purpose as found in Scripture and in creation, both the visible creation of the material world and the invisible one of demons and angels (Evagrius's *theōria physikē*). Such *logoi* of God's self-expression brought the monk closer to knowledge of God as God truly is, as Trinity. By "knowledge" Evagrius did not mean the mere acquisition of information, but the Platonic sense of knowledge as participation in spiritual realities, a contemplative union between the human person and God the Trinity.[34] Such a person could relate to other people on the basis of love rather than fear, and become a help to others struggling with their thoughts.

Following Origen, Evagrius placed a special emphasis on the link between spiritual development and more insightful biblical interpretation. For them, the Bible is God's principal form of self-revelation, and the contemplation of nature in *theōria physikē* normally proceeds from the biblical text. As one advances from being a *praktikos* monk to being a "Knower" (*gnōstikos*) and teacher of others, the primary medium of instruction is biblical interpretation suited to the pupil's particular stage of development.[35] Evagrius added to this emphasis on deeper insight into scripture a groundbreaking exploration of the theology and practice of "pure" prayer, understood to be standing in the presence of God without the intrusion of thoughts or images of any kind, including—and especially—mental depictions or representations (*noēmata*) of God.[36] Evagrius's treatise *On Prayer* has arguably been as influential as his teaching on the eight thoughts and *apatheia*.[37] Pure prayer was the pinnacle of spiritual experience: first came discernment of *logismoi*, then their management, and finally the transcendence or "laying aside" of *logismoi* and *noēmata* in an unmediated encounter with God. Evagrius compares such (admittedly rare) episodes to Moses's experiences of theophany on Mount Sinai. He includes intriguing descriptions of the "light of the mind" or the "sapphire blue heavenly light" experienced in prayer. Such light-mysticism was characteristic of the neo-Platonic intellectual culture in which Evagrius and so many other early Christian theologians were formed, and anticipates the references in later Byzantine mystical literature to seeing the "uncreated light of Tabor" during prayer (Tabor being the mountain where Christ's chosen disciples saw him brilliantly transfigured before them).[38]

Because Evagrius set his teaching about passions and thoughts in an explicitly Christian theological framework, the freedom of *apatheia* was not selfish. It meant the opening of the self to others and to God, the unclenching of the hand grasping what it desires or fending off those who are a threat. Evagrius's *Antirrhētikos*, a compendium of hundreds of scenarios arranged according to the eight thoughts, with biblical texts to be employed in each instance, draws us into some of the daily challenges of life in his monastic environment. It becomes clear that even as they strove for perfection, monks fought over possessions, slandered one another, and generally acted much like other human beings.[39] Love, Evagrius reminds us, is not easy anywhere.

The Legacy of Evagrius's Teaching on the Passions

Evagrius's legacy is tangled. Like his theological mentor, Origen, Evagrius elaborated an esoteric cosmology (or more precisely a protology and eschatology) that was viewed suspiciously in the climate of increasing theological precision and controversy from the late fourth through sixth centuries.[40] The formal condemnation at the Fifth Ecumenical Council in Constantinople in 553 of propositions alleged to be Origen's views also caught Evagrius in its net.[41] Even earlier there were signs of trouble, with criticism—more accurately, willful distortion—of his teaching on *apatheia* by Jerome in the early fifth century.[42]

For both Origen and Evagrius, the consequence was the loss of much of their work in its original Greek. Even so, both of them had a tremendous impact on later theologians and writers. In the Greek-language monastic movements of the Mediterranean region, Evagrius's writings on the *logismoi* and on prayer proved to have enduring value. These foundational works, containing little of his esoteric speculations, were copied frequently and survive in many manuscripts of the tenth and later centuries from Mount Athos and other monastic centers, though the cloud over Evagrius's orthodoxy meant that sometimes his writings were attributed to other monks (most often Nilus of Sinai).[43] His exegetical *scholia* were incorporated into anthologies, sometimes with correct attribution, sometimes not (those on the Psalms were typically attributed to Origen). Such camouflage obscured his significance until the twentieth century, when scholars began to discern the true proportions and influence of the Evagrian ascetic corpus.[44] In the Latin world, Evagrius's friend Rufinus is known to have translated several of the works into Latin in the early fifth century, and others were translated decades later by Gennadius of Marseilles. Although these were the very first translations of Evagrius's works, they have been entirely lost;

only later Latin versions of two collections of proverbs (the *Sentences for Monks* and *Sentences for a Virgin*) and the treatise *On the Eight Thoughts* survive. The *Sentences* were popular in Benedictine circles, ironically often attributed to "Evagrius the bishop." The latter text was always attributed to Nilus.

Only in the Syriac monastic communities of the late fifth and sixth centuries, farther from the controversies of Egypt and Palestine, did Evagrius's work, under his own name, find a warm and lasting reception. Thanks to industrious efforts of translation, the works now lost in Greek have survived in Syriac, sometimes even in more than one version. The Armenian tradition is also rich, usually translated from the Syriac. Some of the Syriac manuscripts date back to the sixth century, antedating by centuries the surviving Greek copies.[45]

Direct transmission of texts is not the only, or necessarily the most significant, means of influence, and this is especially the case with Evagrius. Within the Greek literature of Byzantine monasticism, Evagrius's presence is obvious in both the content and the format of works by Diadochus of Photike (fl. ca. 450), Maximus the Confessor (d. 662), John of Damascus (d. 749), Symeon the New Theologian (d. 1022), and Gregory Palamas (d. 1359). The fullest flowering of Evagrius's influence in the Syriac world was in the spiritual writings of Isaac of Nineveh (d. ca. 700), arguably the most profound mystical author of the first millennium, who relies heavily on Evagrius's teaching on both the passions and prayer. The Latin world benefitted from the extensive syntheses of Evagrius's most faithful disciple, John Cassian, who carefully preserved and propagated the basic elements of his teaching on the stages of the monastic life, tripartite anthropology, and the eight thoughts. Cassian had the wisdom to rebrand *apatheia* as "purity of heart," and brought his own spiritual experience to bear on the elucidation of a "prayer of fire" complementing the Evagrian teaching on pure prayer.[46] From Cassian it passed to Pope Gregory the Great (d. 604), and the Evagrian schema of eight generic thoughts afflicting the monks of Egypt was transformed into a list now famous as the Seven Deadly Sins.[47] But even by the time of Cassian's writing (ca. 415), Evagrius's reputation was tainted. Cassian never mentions him by name, a remarkable and poignant silence in an otherwise prolix author.

The twentieth-century rediscovery of Evagrius by textual scholars occurred as researchers in other scientific disciplines were exploring anew the workings of emotion in human existence, and the relationship between conscious, reasoning faculties, and the more elusive aspects of personality. The investigations of modern psychology remarkably parallel Evagrius's efforts 1600 years earlier. His effort to craft a comprehensive view of the human person using the intellectual tools available to him, and to do so in a manner deeply imbued with Christian ethics and theology, makes him worthy of our attention. Perhaps he will inspire us to do the same.

NOTES

1 On Evagrius's life, see Antoine Guillaumont, *Un philosophe au désert. Évagre le Pontique*, Textes et traditions, Vol. 8 (Paris: J. Vrin, 2004), pp. 13–75; Columba Stewart, "Evagrius Ponticus on Monastic Pedagogy," in John Behr et al. (eds.), *Abba: The Tradition of Orthodoxy in the West. Festschrift for Bishop Kallistos Ware* (Crestwood, NY: St. Vladimir's Seminary Press, 2003), pp. 242–253; Julia Konstantinovsky, *Evagrius Ponticus: The Making of a Gnostic* (Farnham: Ashgate, 2009), pp. 11–19.

2 According to Palladius, *Lausiac History* 55.3, ed. Cuthbert Butler, Texts and Studies 6.1–2 (Cambridge: Cambridge University Press, 1898 and 1904), Vol. 2, p. 149, ll. 13–15. English translation in Robert T. Meyer, *The Lausiac History*, Ancient Christian Writers; the works of the Fathers in translation, Vol. 34 (Westminster, MD: Newman Press, 1965), pp. 134–135.

3 These conclude his two manuals, *Praktikos* and *Gnōstikos*; these will be described in more detail below.

4 See Columba Stewart, "Anthony of Egypt," in Philip Esler (ed.), *The Early Christian World* (London/New York: Routledge, 2000), Vol. 2, pp. 1088–1101.

5 The critical edition (with French trans.) is by G. J. M. Bartelink, *Athanase d'Alexandrie. Vie d'Antoine*, SC 400 (Paris: Cerf, 1994); English translation by Robert C. Gregg, *Athanasius: The Life of Antony and the Letter to Marcellinus*, Classics of Western Spirituality (Mahwah, NJ: Paulist Press, 1980).

6 See David Brakke, *Athanasius and the Politics of Asceticism* (Oxford: Oxford University Press, 1995), pp. 201–265. Antony's letters, seemingly authentic and preserved in various translations, show more than a passing acquaintance with philosophy and Christian writers such as Origen.

7 See Columba Stewart, "Evagrius Ponticus and the 'Eight Generic *Logismoi*'," in Richard Newhauser (ed.), *In the Garden of Evil: The Vices and Culture in the Middle Ages* (Toronto: Pontifical Institute of Medieval Studies, 2005), pp. 5–16.

8 See David Brakke, *Demons and the Making of the Monk: Spiritual Combat in Early Christianity* (Cambridge, MA: Harvard University Press, 2008).

9 *Life of Antony*, Chapters 13.1–2, 22–23, 30, 41 (Bartelink, pp. 168–170, 194–200, 218–220, 246–248; Gregg, pp. 41, 47–49, 54, 62).

10 See the insightful analysis by Kevin Corrigan, *Evagrius and Gregory: Mind, Soul and Body in the 4ᵗʰ Century* (Farnham: Ashgate, 2009), pp. 92–96.

11 See Samuel Rubenson, *The Letters of St. Antony: Monasticism and the Making of a Saint*, Studies in Antiquity and Christianity (Minneapolis, MN: Fortress Press, 1995), and David Brakke, "The Making of Monastic Demonology: Three Ascetic Teachers on Withdrawal and Resistance," *Church History*, Vol. 70 (2001), pp. 19–22 and 46–48.

12 As classically outlined in Pierre Hadot's "Exercices spirituels" and "Exercices spirituels et 'philosophie chrétienne'," English translation of both by Michael Chase in Arnold I. Davidson (ed.), *Philosophy as a Way of Life: Spiritual Exercises from Socrates to Foucault* (Oxford/Cambridge, MA: Blackwell, 1995), pp. 81–125 and 126–144.

13 *Life of Antony*, 43.1 (Bartelink, p. 252; Gregg, p. 64).

14 See Stewart, "Evagrius Ponticus and the 'Eight Generic *Logismoi*'," p. 15.

15 See Stewart, "Evagrius Ponticus on Monastic Pedagogy," pp. 258–268.

16 Especially true of the "sentences" he wrote for monks and nuns. On these, see Jeremy Driscoll's *The "Ad monachos" of Evagrius Ponticus: its Structure and a Select Commentary*, Studia Anselmiana, Vol. 104 (Rome: Abbazia S. Paolo, 1991) and his translation of the *Sentences for Monks*, Ancient Christian Writers series, Vol. 59 (New York: Newman Press, 2003). On the *Sentences for a Virgin*, see particularly Susanna Elm, "Evagrius Ponticus' *Sententiae ad virginem*," *Dumbarton Oaks Papers*, Vol. 45 (1991), pp. 97–120. These are translated by Robert Sinkewicz in *Evagrius of Pontus: The Greek Ascetic Corpus* (Oxford: Oxford University Press, 2003), pp. 131–135; he also translates those for monks on pp. 122–131.

17 See Pierre Hadot, "Les divisions des parties de la philosophie dans l'Antiquité," *Museum Helveticum*, Vol. 36 (1979), pp. 201–223, and Columba Stewart, *Cassian the Monk* (New York: Oxford University Press, 1998), pp. 49–55 and 92–99.

18 See the prologue to Origen's *Commentary on the Song of Songs*, in W. A. Baehrens (ed.), *Origenes Werke*, Vol. 8, GCS (Leipzig: Hinrichs, 1925), p. 75; English translation by R. P.

Lawson, *The Song of Songs: Commentary and Homilies*, Ancient Christian Writers series, Vol. 26 (New York: Newman Press, 1956), pp. 39–42.

19   These are the *Praktikos*, *Gnōstikos*, and *Kephalaia Gnōstika*. Only the first survives complete in the original Greek; the others have been recovered largely through the Syriac and Armenian versions, with some Greek fragments. See the discussion of them, with references to the editions, in Antoine Guillaumont, *Un philosophe au désert*, pp. 99–105.

20   The complete Greek text with a French translation and commentary can be found in Antoine and Claire Guillaumont (eds. and trans.), *Évagre le Pontique. Traité pratique ou Le moine*, Sources chrétiennes 170–71 (Paris: Cerf, 1971); a complete English translation (along with many other of Evagrius's works which survive in Greek) is in Sinkewicz, *Evagrius*, pp. 95–114.

21   Text, translation, and commentary by Paul Géhin, Claire and Antoine Guillaumont, *Évagre le Pontique: Sur les pensées*, Sources chrétiennes 438 (Paris: Cerf, 1998); English translation in Sinkewicz, *Evagrius*, pp. 153–182.

22   See the extensive discussion in Guillaumont, *Un philosophe au désert*, pp. 205–265; cf. Richard Sorabji, *Emotion and Peace of Mind: from Stoic Agitation to Christian Temptation* (Oxford: Oxford University Press, 2000), pp. 357–371.

23   As outlined in *Praktikos* 89 (Guillaumont, pp. 680–689; Sinkewicz, pp. 111–112). See also Stewart, "Evagrius Ponticus and the 'Eight Generic *Logismoi*'," pp. 17–26. This was one of his major departures from Origen, who preferred a more biblically-based model of the human person.

24   *Kephalaia Gnōstika* 1.68; Syriac text and French translation in Antoine Guillaumont (ed. and trans.), *Les Six centuries des "Kephalaia Gnostica" d'Évagre le Pontique*, PO Vol. 28 (Turnhout: Brepols, 1958), p. 49.

25   The classic descriptions are in *Praktikos* 6–14 (Guillaumont, pp. 506–535; Sinkewicz, pp. 97–103). See Guillaumont, *Un philosophe au désert*, pp. 213–220; Stewart, "Evagrius Ponticus and the 'Eight Generic *Logismoi*'," pp. 26–34; Corrigan, *Evagrius and Gregory*, pp. 73–101.

26   He has two versions of the sequence: in most of his works, including the *Praktikos*, sadness follows avarice and precedes anger, while in his treatise *On the Eight Thoughts*, a collection of maxims about each of the *logismoi*, anger and sadness are reversed. The latter order will be used by Cassian.

27   See especially *On First Principles*, 3.2, as in Henri Crouzel and Mario Simonetti, *Traité des principes*, Vol. 3, SC 268 (Paris: Cerf, 1980), pp. 152–183; English translation by G. W. Butterworth, *Origen on First Principles* (London: SPCK, 1936), pp. 211–222. On Origen's views and influence, see Sorabji, *Emotion and Peace of Mind*, pp. 343–356.

28   For Origen's contribution see Stewart, "Evagrius Ponticus and the 'Eight Generic *Logismoi*'," pp. 27–29.

29   See now Andrew Crislip, "The sin of sloth or the illness of the demons? The demon of acedia in early Christian monasticism," *Harvard Theological Review*, Vol. 98 (2005), pp. 143–169.

30   See, e.g., *Praktikos* 12 (Guillaumont, pp. 520–527; Sinkewicz, p. 99); *On the Eight Thoughts* 14 (*PG* 79:1160; Sinkewicz, p. 84).

31   See the characterizations of *apatheia* in *Praktikos* 63–70 (Guillaumont, pp. 646–657; Sinkewicz, p. 109). On the Stoic use of the term, see Martha Nussbaum, "Extirpation of the Passions," in *The Therapy of Desire: Theory and Practice in Hellenistic Ethics* (Princeton, NJ: Princeton University Press, 1994), pp. 359–401.

32   *Praktikos* 89 (Guillaumont, pp. 680–689; Sinkewicz, pp. 111–112), as noted earlier; Evagrius attributes it to "Our wise teacher," i.e., Gregory Nazianzen, while the source text attributes it to Plato.

33   See Sorabji, *Emotion and Peace of Mind*, pp. 395–397.

34   See Konstantinovsky, *Evagrius Ponticus*, pp. 27–76.

35   The second volume in his basic monastic trilogy was the *Gnōstikos*, edition and French translation by Antoine and Claire Guillaumont, *Évagre le Pontique: Le Gnostique*, SC 356 (Paris: Cerf, 1989); see Stewart, "Evagrius Ponticus on Monastic Pedagogy," pp. 254–271. On Evagrius's exegesis of the Psalms and their role in contemplation, see Luke Dysinger, *Psalmody and Prayer in the Writings of Evagrius Ponticus* (Oxford: Oxford University Press, 2006).

36 See Columba Stewart, "Imageless Prayer and the Theological Vision of Evagrius Ponticus," *Journal of Early Christian Studies*, Vol. 9 (2001), pp. 173–204; Corrigan, *Evagrius and Gregory*, pp. 162–173; Konstantinovsky, *Evagrius Ponticus*, pp. 77–107.
37 The Greek is in *PG* 79:1165A-1200C; English trans. in Sinkewicz, *Evagrius of Pontus*, pp. 191–209. There is still no critical edition, despite—or because of—the wide circulation of the Greek text, typically under the name "Nilus." It was later included in the *Philokalia*.
38 The classic study is Hans-Veit Beyer, "Die Lichtlehre der Mönche des vierzehnten und des vierten Jahrhunderts, erörtert am Beispiel des Gregorios Sinaïtes, des Euagrios Pontikos und des Pseudo-Makarios/Symeon," *Jahrbuch der österreichischen Byzantinistik*, Vol. 31 (1981), pp. 473–512.
39 The work survives complete in Syriac, Armenian and Arabic. For the Syriac text and a modern retroversion into Greek, see Wilhelm Frankenberg (ed.), *Euagrius Ponticus*, Abhandlungen der königlichen Gesellschaft der Wissenschaften zu Göttingen, Philologisch-historische Klasse, Neue Folge 13.2 (Berlin: Weidmann, 1912), pp. 472–544. David Brakke has recently published an excellent English translation of the Syriac text in *Talking Back: A Monastic Handbook for Combating Demons*, Cistercian Studies 229 (Collegeville, MN: Cistercian Publications/Liturgical Press, 2009). See particularly Books 3, 5, and 7, *passim*, on the way that avarice, anger, and vainglory played out in Evagrius's setting.
40 Origen outlined a notion of "two creations" and the ultimate restoration of all of creation in Christ (*apokatastasis*) in *On First Principles*; Evagrius did so more definitely in his *Kephalaia Gnōstika*. Neither work survives complete in Greek, though there are complete translations in Latin and Syriac, respectively. For a thorough treatment of Evagrius's theology, see Guillaumont, *Un philosophe au désert*, pp. 337–404 and Konstantinovsky, *Evagrius Ponticus*, pp. 153–178; for an overview, see Stewart, "Imageless Prayer," pp. 174–182.
41 The condemnation of 553 was prompted by fervent devotion to the more esoteric elements of Origen's and Evagrius's thought among a monastic faction in Palestine; see Joseph Patrich, *Sabas, Leader of Palestinian Monasticism: a Comparative Study in Eastern Monasticism, Fourth to Seventh Centuries* (Washington, DC: Dumbarton Oaks, 1995), pp. 331–348. On the fate of Evagrius's works, see Guillaumont, *Un philosophe au désert*, pp. 77–95.
42 In Jerome's *Letter 133 to Ctesiphon*, where Jerome suggests that *apatheia* means that the soul is moved by "neither thought nor vice, and, I shall say simply, is [like] a stone or God" (Latin text in Isidore Hilberg, ed., *Sancti Eusebii Hieronymi Epistulae*, Vol. 3, CSEL 56 [Vienna: Tempsky, 1918], p. 246).
43 Thus, for example, the *Praktikos* circulated under Evagrius's own name; other ascetical works such as *On the Eight Thoughts* were attributed either to Evagrius or to Nilus of Ancyra, while the treatise *On Prayer* was consistently attributed to Nilus, and included in the eighteenth-century Greek *Philokalia* under that name.
44 Prominent among them was the French Jesuit and editor of the *Dictionnaire de Spiritualité*, Irénee Hausherr.
45 The best introduction to the whole textual tradition is in Guillaumont, *Un philosophe au désert*, 99–159.
46 On Evagrius's influence on Cassian, see Columba Stewart, *Cassian the Monk* (New York: Oxford University Press, 1998), *passim* and also "John Cassian's Schema of Eight Principal Faults and his Debt to Origen and Evagrius," in Cristian Badilita (ed.), *Jean Cassien entre Orient et Occident*, (Paris: Beauchesne, 2003), pp. 205–219. On *apatheia* particularly, see Mark Sheridan, "The Controversy over *apatheia*: Cassian's Sources and his Use of Them," *Studia Monastica*, Vol. 39 (1997), pp. 287–310.
47 Gregory moved pride out to become an overarching sin, added envy, and combined sadness and *accidie*. For the later western tradition, see the various essays in Newhauser, *The Garden of Evil*.

5

TEARS AND WEEPING: AN AUGUSTINIAN VIEW

PAUL J. GRIFFITHS

How should the relations among faith, rationality, and the passions be construed? I here address Augustine on one aspect of this complex question: that of how tears (*lacrimae*) and weeping (*fletus*) are depicted and understood. I limit myself mostly to the *Confessiones*, a work of Augustine's maturity composed in his early forties, in which these topics have considerable prominence. Sadness (*tristitia*), sorrow (*dolor*), and anguish (*luctus*)—all words much used by Augustine—are, for us, typically understood as emotions or affects, with tears and weeping as their public signs. This pattern of thought is not altogether alien to Augustine, but his depictions of tears and weeping suggest that he understood these not principally as outer witnesses to an inner condition, but rather as communicative judgments offered to an interlocutor or interlocutors. Approaching them in this way has implications for a broadly Augustinian understanding of the relations between reason and the passions (*passiones, affectiones*)—and, since Augustine's thought is intimate with Christian orthodoxy, indeed to a considerable extent definitive of it, also for a broadly Christian understanding of this matter.

The first extended treatment of tears and weeping in the *Confessiones* occurs in the third book,[1] where Augustine reports his mother Monnica's laments over his adherence to the Manichees and his concomitant rejection of Catholic Christianity. She cries for her son the Manichee more copiously than do most mothers for their dead (*amplius quam flent matres corporea funera*), and her tears are a mode of address to the Lord, who hears and responds to them by giving her a dream-vision in which she sees Augustine converted, baptized, standing where she stands. In weeping, she communicates to the Lord a judgment or understanding of what is the case: that her son is confused, and that his confusion has separated him from the Lord's love. Her tears are a form of prayer, which is to say of direct address to the

Faith, Rationality, and the Passions, First Edition. Edited by Sarah Coakley.
© 2012 Blackwell Publishing Ltd. Book compilation © 2012 Blackwell Publishing Ltd.

Lord. It is a prayer answered proleptically by the dream-vision,[2] and then later in reality when Augustine is baptized by Ambrose. Augustine depicts Monnica's tears in this episode not principally as an outer manifestation of an inner feeling, but rather as an understanding of a state of affairs intentionally communicated to another—in this case to the Lord. Her tears are, as well, a communication answered: she speaks to the Lord in and by them, and he responds to her.

In Book Four (4.4.9-4.7.12), Augustine describes his tear-figured response to the death of an unnamed friend. The friendship, even though not *vera amicitia* (true friendship) because it is not between Christians (neither Augustine nor his friend is at this point baptized), is intense. The two are perhaps twenty or twenty-one, and Augustine writes that their friendship was sweet to him beyond all the sweetness of his life to date (*super omnes suavitates illius vitae meae*). The friend becomes seriously ill and is baptized without his knowledge. This matter, Augustine writes, was of no *cura*, no care or concern to him; and when his friend began to get well he tried to joke with him about what had been done, only, to his puzzlement, to be rebuked by his friend, who takes the matter more seriously than Augustine had thought he would. Augustine decides that he will conceal his *motus*, the movements of his soul, from his friend until he is completely well; but the friend relapses and dies. Augustine echoes Lamentations: *dolor*, sorrow, casts shadows over his heart,[3] and he becomes to himself a great question (*factus eram mihi magna quaestio*). The only thing that comforts him is weeping: "Only weeping was delicious to me: it replaced my friend in my soul's delights" (*solus fletus erat dulcis mihi et successerat amico meo in deliciis animi*).

That tears can comfort puzzles Augustine, and he meditates on the question of why they do. Is it that our tears are a means of communicating our unhappiness to the Lord, and that they comfort because of the hope that we are heard (*quod speramus exaudire te*)? This could be true if, as we have already seen in Monnica's case, tears are a form of prayer. But for the youthful Augustine, unbaptized and without faith, tears are not prayer; rather, they are for him simple misery, a bitter thing (*res amara*), comfortable only because they distract from awareness of the friend's absence, which would be even bitterer. Tears, as the middle-aged Augustine sees it, show the youthful Augustine his true condition, which is one of unrelieved misery; but because he could not at that time understand this, he becomes attached to that very life of misery and dwells on and in it instead of upon his dead friend.[4] He becomes more unwilling to lose his tear-soaked misery than he had been to lose his dead friend: "Although I wanted it to be different, I was more unwilling to lose it [my misery] than to lose him" (*nam quamvis eam mutare vellem, nollem tamen amittere magis quam illum*). Tears are the only things that provide a temporary escape from the agony of the dead friend's absence, but when, Augustine writes, he stops crying, his soul is "weighed down with a vast weight of misery" (*onerabat me grandis sarcina miseriae*).[5]

Augustine's youthful tears for his dead friend are in part different from Monnica's for him, and in part the same. In both cases, they are knowledge-bearing judgments about the state of things. For Augustine, it is a judgment of desolation: a world with death in it but without the Lord is a place of unremitting and unremittable grief, a hopeless place in which tears communicate desolation with no one to hear. For Monnica, it is a judgment that things are out of joint, but a judgment communicated to one who hears it and responds to it with a word of hope. Monnica's tears are transparent: they can be looked through to the one they speak to. Augustine's youthful tears are opaque: their flood shows only themselves, and that is why Augustine comes to prefer them to the memory of his dead friend. Their bitterness can become, if savored for long enough, half-sweet, a tangy flavor to be rolled around the tongue, puckering the tissues of the palate.

The next major episode of crying in the *Confessiones* is in the account of the conversion in the garden (8.12.28-8.12.30). The young Augustine has, by the time this episode occurs, understood Christianity, and assented, intellectually, to its truth. But he is not yet ready to give himself to the Lord. He is held back by his old loves (*antiquae amicae meae*), especially his love for the bodily delights of sex, and he cannot yet imagine letting these old friends go and permitting their transfiguration by the love of the Lord, even though he deeply and intensely desires this. He sees clearly the weight of his misery, and this prompts an *ingentem imbrem lacrimarum*, a great tear-storm. He is with his friend Alypius, but at this point moves away from him because, it seems to him, solitude is more appropriate than company for the business of weeping (*ad negotium flendi*). He goes away, lies down under a fig-tree,[6] and abandons himself to tears. Rivers flow from his eyes, and he takes these to be an acceptable sacrificial offering to the Lord. As he weeps, he hears the voice of a child from a nearby house saying *tolle, lege* (take and read). In response, he gets up after having checked the tear-flood (*repressoque impetu lacrimarum*), goes back to where his friend Alypius is sitting, which is where he has left the codex containing Paul's letters which he had earlier been reading, and opens it at random. What he reads (Romans 13:13–14) infuses his heart with a light of assurance and removes every shadow of doubt (*omnes dubitationis tenebrae diffugerunt*). He is able to proceed from this point toward baptism, and all his tears are gone.

They return soon, as we shall see: baptism's waters do not finally remove the water of tears. The point to emphasize here is that the tears shed in the garden are, like the tears shed at the friend's death, a judgment. The judgment in both cases is one of despair: here, under the fig tree which bears no fruit and whose leaves were used to cover Adam's and Eve's nakedness, there is nothing but a desert of lament. But there is a difference between the tears shed for the dead friend and those shed for Augustine's own sins and habits, for his inability to abandon his old loves. Those former tears were not a message: Augustine did not then see that there was anyone he could communicate his despair to, and so his tears became recursive, a bitter substitute for the dead friend which, eventually and perversely, he came to savor and was unwilling to give up. But now, in the garden, he knows that there is a Lord to whom his tears can be offered, and he describes his tears exactly as a sacrifice acceptable to the Lord (*acceptabile sacrificium tuum*, echoing Psalm 50), and so the tears become, as Monnica's were, a prayer, an utterance directed to the Lord, and moreover a prayer answered. This was not possible in the case of the younger Augustine's tears shed for his dead friend. It is interesting that weeping (*fletus*) is described by Augustine as a bit of business, a negotiation (*negotium*) best done in solitude. Weeping is work: *negotium* is the opposite of *otium*, which is exactly doing nothing, a holiday from work. And the work of tears is one of communicative exchange between the one who weeps and the Lord to whom the tears are offered as prayer. Why in solitude? Theologically speaking, I expect, because of Matthew 5:6, where Jesus exhorts those who pray to do so in solitude. Also, perhaps, because tears are a peculiarly intimate form of communicative exchange, better given in privacy, like a caress. And yet again, because the late-antique man would likely have found weeping—especially his own—an embarrassment.

Following his account of the tears in the garden, Augustine mentions (without describing) his baptism, and shortly thereafter describes the death of Monnica. The treatment of tears at and after his mother's funeral (9.11.27-9.13.37) is the most complex and nuanced of any in the *Confessiones*, and in thinking it through it is important to keep in mind that these are post-baptismal tears.

Monnica dies at the age of 56, when Augustine is 33; and immediately upon her death, a great grief, he writes, flows into his heart and threatens to flow out from there into his eyes in the form of tears. By a violent effort of the soul (*violento animi imperio*) he restrains the tears, drying (*usque ad siccitatem*) his eyes by an effort of will. His son, Adeodatus, does cry, and is rebuked for doing so. There is the implication of struggle: Augustine wants to cry and at the same time would prefer not to. He would prefer not to, he writes, because weeping at funerals might be taken to imply that death is miserable or that it issues in extinction, and these are judgments Christians should not make. Notice, once again, that tears are understood to be a form of judgment or understanding: they are, Augustine implies, appropriate when what they respond to is indeed lamentable; but since death, on a Christian understanding, is not, funerary tears are inappropriate. Were they to be shed, they would be a sign of Christian immaturity, like Adeodatus' weeping (Adeodatus would have been sixteen or seventeen at the time). That, at least, is how the mature Augustine first represents his youthful self's initial reluctance to weep at his mother's death. The understanding present in that reluctance is soon shown to be erroneous.

Augustine is still puzzled at the intensity of his grief. If it is not grief at his mother's extinction, or at the unhappiness of her post-mortem condition, what is he grieving? It is, he writes, the loss of the sweet pleasure (more affect-language) of the habit (*consuetudo*) of living with her and talking to her. That habit was powerful, and to have it suddenly broken is painful. In an attempt to cover up his grief, to make firmer and more reliable his mind's restraint of it, he discourses to his friends upon the meaning of death. Offering these discourses—and it is not hard to imagine what their Polonius-like character might have been—soothes him, offers balm to his anguish. His friends listen to him with no sense that he is suffering (*sine sense doloris me*)—and indeed, for a while, as he discourses, he does not suffer. But then, in typically Augustinian fashion, he begins to reproach himself for the mildness of his feeling, his *affectus*. His grief has bowed to his will, and even that fact grieves him; and as it does, his first grief returns in flood, even in paroxysm. At that, he becomes unhappy that he is so moved with grief for his mother's death: he now sorrows for his sorrow, just as he had earlier grieved for his lack of grief. The disturbance or turbulence of sorrow has become multi-layered. Still, he does not cry, even though he wants to; and although he asks the Lord to take his sorrow away, this does not happen. Augustine comments that his sorrow provides a lesson in the power of habit, and that the Lord does not remove it exactly in order to drive that lesson home. The habit in question is, again, that of living happily with his mother.

Monnica's body is taken out for burial, and Augustine and his companions accompany it tearless (*imus redimus sine lacrimis*), even when the interment is done. Throughout the day, however, he finds himself oppressed with a hidden (*occultus*, here meaning not made outwardly manifest) suffering and disturbance of mind. Still hoping that his sorrow might be taken from him, he decides to take a bath, with the thought that this might expel the grief from his soul (*anxietatem pellat ex animo*). He offers etymological speculation on the meaning of the Greek word for "bath" (*balanion*) in order to explain this, a typical instance of the imbrication of his metaphysics with his understanding of language. The bath does not wash away his grief; but now he is alone, and he permits memories of his mother to return to him and press upon him. In doing so, he writes, he finally sets free or liberates the tears he had kept bottled up (*dimisi lacrimas quas continebam*), and their flow becomes a pillow for his heart. Once again, he cries in solitude, as a mode of address to the Lord: his tears, or at least his depiction of them, are a mode of address directly to the Lord. The tears heal his wound, his *vulnus*—that is, the wound of his separation from his mother, the shattering of that habit. The wound in question is a *humanum*, a human thing, part of the human condition; and tears, he now sees, are an element in the appropriate response to that wound, its salve or balm.

In shedding tears, Augustine cries for all flesh and all fleshly wounds, and in giving an account of his solitary weeping for his mother's death, he provides an account of what tears mean for Christians. This is worth quoting in full:

> I wept freely before you [that is, before the Lord] for her and about her, for myself and about myself. I let out the tears I had held in so that they might flow as much as they wanted, supporting my heart. It rested on them because your ears were there, not those of some man offering an arrogant interpretation of my weeping. And now, O Lord, I confess to you in written words which anyone who wishes may read and interpret as he wishes; if he discovers any sin in the fact that I wept for my mother for a small part of an hour, that mother who had died before my eyes and had for many years wept for me that I might live before yours, he should not deride me but should rather, if he has any love, himself weep before you, the father of all the brothers of your Christ, for my sins.[7]

Tears have an audience: they are communicative, and in thinking about what they communicate it is important to think about their audience. Augustine here distinguishes a critical human audience, Stoic or Platonist in tendency,[8] whose members might interpret his tears arrogantly, as a sign of weakness or childishness. This is a tendency he is himself subject to, as his conflict about whether he should cry for his mother shows. But such hearers are not the real audience for Christian tears. That, rather, is the Lord: as Augustine strikingly puts it, his ears are in our tears (*ibi erant aures tuas*), and that is why tears provide a support for our hearts, our *cordes*. The play with eyes and ears in the passage is remarkable: our eyes weep; Monnica has died before Augustine's eyes; she has spent a good portion of her life weeping with her eyes for him so that he might live before (in the sight of) the Lord's eyes. And ears hear: the Lord's ears are present in the tears the eyes weep, and that fact both provides comfort and shows the tears to be appropriate as understandings of the way things are; the ears of the arrogant, by contrast, mishear and take tears to be sin or childishness.

The Lord listens to our tears and knows them for what they are, which is a form of confession. In the passage just quoted, Augustine draws closely together the act of weeping with the act of writing about weeping, and subsumes them both under the rubric of confession, which also provides the title for the work in which these episodes of weeping are described. Weeping is an appropriate, perhaps the most appropriate, response to an accurate, fully Christian, discernment of what things are like for us, and Augustine takes this interpretation up in Book Ten, just a few hundred words after the passage just quoted. There (10.1.1-10.4.5) weeping is assimilated to confession: both are means by which sinners open themselves more fully to the Lord, and in that way become more intimate with him. In weeping, as in confessing, we show that we understand what we are and what the world is. Not to weep would be to show that we misconstrue both; in restraining our tears we distance ourselves from the Lord.

Augustine's depictions of tears and weeping in the *Confessiones* are complex: he judges that both the presence of suffering-grief-anguish and its absence may be problematic, and that it is possible to respond affectively to affect—to grieve the absence or presence of grief, for example. He is consistent in his view that tears involve understandings, and that judgments as to whether or not the tears are in particular cases desirable cannot be separated from judgments about the understandings they involve. He is consistent, also, in the view that tears communicate understandings to others. And, lastly, he is consistent in depicting tears as responsive to an ascetical discipline of the passions: he can undertake, with struggle, not to cry even when moved by grief, just as he can undertake to yield to tears. And habits (*consuetudines*, usually) of greater or lesser persistence can be formed by one discipline or the other. What Augustine writes about tears in the *Confessiones* is in accord with the broader picture of the intellective and emotive (or, better, motile) aspects of human life in his work as a whole.

The fundamental or governing metaphor in Augustine's thought about the mental life, a metaphor that ties together its rational, appetitive, and affective aspects, is that of motion. The soul, the *animus*, moves toward or away from the things it finds in its environment; and its movements are both embodied and habituated. That is, the movements of the soul typically find a bodily correlate, as in Augustine's tears at the death of his childhood friend, or those shed in response to Monnica's death. These movements therefore do not occur simply as mental events, and they are typically habitual in the sense that they do not occur in punctual form as separate and unrelated responses to stimuli. The weight (*pondus*) of an affective or appetitive or rational habit—Augustine uses this trope of weight a good deal—is accumulated over time in such a way as to move us with an often-irresistible force toward or away from this or that. The grieving movement of Augustine's soul toward the absence of his mother was weighted in this sense, as was that toward the absence of his dead friend. The difference in the two cases is that the former's tears address only the one who weeps them— which is why the tears in that case become an object of independent fascination—while the latter's tears address themselves to and find comfort in the Lord.

Tears of either sort, like any other action, can become habits. Habits accumulate weight; weight produces movement; and the movements of the soul are, collectively, what constitute the soul's life. The moving force of all these movements of the soul is most often labeled by Augustine with one of the words from his extensive and nuanced vocabulary of love: *amor* and *dilectio* are the most frequent. We are weighted by our habituated loves, and in those loves, woven together with them, is the knotted thread of desire and will:

what we love is what we want, and what we want is what we love. The appetitive and the affective are so tightly linked in Augustine's thought that separating them is effectively impossible. The movements of our soul are all, to somewhat different degrees, movements of love and will and desire all at once. The love-will-desire of solipsistic tears wants, finally, nothing; that of confessional tears wants the Lord.

The movements of the soul, these habituated love-wills, generally (but not always) have a phenomenal feel. That is, they generally seem like something to their subjects, those who undergo them. But Augustine is not very interested in this: it is not possible, I think, to derive from his work a phenomenology of affect or appetite, interested though he is in giving an account of their importance. He is in this respect more interested in the categorial or grammatical than in the phenomenological. He wants to know how to think about appetite and affect, but not to provide an artist's depiction of their flavor. In his depictions of tears in the *Confessiones*, he uses strong language for the movements of the soul involved in grief, as for the bodily movements involved in crying; but his language has to do with motion and desire and end, not with the shades and particularities of feeling, finely etched. Augustine is neither Proust nor Henry James.

For Augustine, tears cannot be separated from the judgments and understandings in intimacy with which they occur. He writes elsewhere that nonhuman animals cannot have passions, if these are understood as habituated love-wills.[9] He thinks they cannot because they lack reason. Your dog is certainly, in Augustinian terms, an appetitive being: he is moved by appetites toward or away from things. But these amount neither to desires nor to passions (in Latin, they are not *desiderium* and not *passiones*) because they bear no relation to the intellect's capacity to discern and judge what is good. Such relations may be complex and conflicted, as we have seen in Augustine's account of his responses to his mother's death. But the in-principle absence of such a relation means also the absence of passions. Passions are, for Augustine, rational or irrational (most often a complex mix of both); they can never be arational. And this is why, we might say (though Augustine so far as I know does not), nonhuman animals do not cry: tears, being rational or irrational but never arational, cannot belong to them.[10]

A particular movement of the soul, understood as a passion, may then be separated from reason in the sense of being intimate with a false understanding of what there is, and therefore active in opposition to true understandings. It may also be in accord with reason, and when it is it involves or is concomitant with a love of the good, which is also a love of the Lord. Our ordinary condition, in Augustine's view, is, with respect to the passions, one of fluidity, malleability, instability, motility, and ductility. Our passions, when they are active in opposition to love and therefore to the Lord, are a flood that tends toward nothing—which is the only possible direction in which they can tend, given a standard Augustinian account of evil as absence and lack.[11] But we may also, to the extent that our passions resound to the Lord's love for us, be moved toward the solidity and eternity of union with the Lord.

A rather different way to put the same point is to say that each of us (save only Jesus and Mary, according to Catholic doctrine) is inevitably subject to *passiones contra rationem*, and that this is true whether *ratio* is taken in the universal-objective sense to mean what it is rational (and therefore good) to want, or in the phenomenological-subjective sense, to mean what it seems rational to me at the moment to want. If our passions are irrational in the first sense but not the second, then we will have misidentified and misprized the good, as Augustine did when he cried for his dead friend. If in the second sense, then we will be in a condition of conflict apparent to us, as Augustine was about the death of his mother; in this condition it will seem to us that we are in disharmony with ourselves, and this is so whether or not we have rightly identified and prized what we ought to want. Our task, as Augustine sees it, a task we cannot accomplish without grace, is to order our passions so that they are in harmony with reason in both senses—that is, so that our habituated love-will draws us toward what is good for us, and at the same time so that we want what is good for us. When we are in this condition, we will often cry, and bitterly, in confessing what is lamentable about ourselves and the damaged world.

Tears do not have to be understood as Augustine, and with him most of the premodern Christian tradition, understands them. They might be understood as a purely physiological phenomenon, occurring in response to stimuli and carrying with them no claim about the way things are; those who hold such a view might think of tears as produced by or evidence of some inner condition of sadness, or they might think of them as productive of such feelings;[12] in either case it would be beside the point to ask of those who cry what their tears show about how they understand the world, or to criticize those who weep for doing so wrongly. Or, tears might be understood as indeed making a cognitive claim, but a false one that should not be taken seriously by anyone interested in the truth. Those who think this are likely to discipline their tears toward removal, as Augustine tried at first to do in his response to Monnica's death.[13] Augustine's understanding of tears is in important respects different from these views. For him, it is common to all those who cry that they understand the world or themselves or both to be in some respects lamentable. That understanding is accurate, but by itself insufficient; tears shed on such an understanding bring false comfort and thus further damage to those who shed them. Such tears end, as did Augustine's weeping for his dead friend, by diminishing those who shed them and diverting attention from what is wrong with the world to the act of weeping itself. Those tears are opaque, but they do not need to be disciplined out of existence. They need, in order to be made transparent, to become communicative as an instrument of confession. When that happens, they contribute to the world's transfiguration. This understanding of tears, as is typical of the Christian tradition in dealing with what we might call emotions and their signs, at once embraces and redirects them by catechesis.

NOTES

1 (3.11.19-3.12.21). I refer to the *Confessiones* according to the standard tripartite sectional division. I have used the text given by J. J. O'Donnell in the first volume of his three-volume edition and commentary: *Augustine: Confessions* (Oxford: Clarendon Press, 1992). I also draw heavily upon the commentary given in volumes 2 and 3, which is extraordinarily valuable.

2 Augustine also depicts his mother's tears at his deceitful abandonment of her at Carthage as a form of prayer to the Lord—only this time as one ignored (5.8.15).

3 *propterea maestum factum est cor nostrum; ideo contenebrati sunt oculi nostri*, Lamentations 5:17 (Vulgate).

4 The form of Augustine's understanding of unregenerate tears is formally the same as his understanding of sin in Book Two (2.3.5-2.10.18). Just as sin, an absence masquerading as a presence, is there depicted as becoming a matter of interest in its own right, so also for tears here in Book Four.

5 It is interesting that these sections of Book Four are the only parts of the *Confessiones* that Augustine saw fit to comment on negatively in his *Retractationes*. There (2.6.2) he writes that his earlier statement that the only reason he wanted to continue living was that if he died the last remnant of his friend would also have died should be understood as *declamatio levis*, superficial rhetoric, rather than *gravis confessio*, serious confession. Well, yes; but this is already evident in the *Confessiones*, where it is clear that this opinion belongs to the Augustine of 376 (or so) and is not endorsed by the Augustine of 397 (or so). The Augustine of 427 (or so) is insufficiently sensitive to the temporally layered rhetoric of his own work of thirty years before. Here, as is usually the case for authors, the author is not the best reader or interpreter of his own text.

6 *sub quadam fici arbore*, echoing John 1:47–48 (Jesus to Nathanael), and with Matthew 21:19 (the fig tree) and Genesis 3:1–7 (fig leaves) in the background. For Augustine, the fig tree is the place of the flesh, of the *conditio carnis* where the shadow of death falls heavy and our words bear no fruit. There, tears are better than words. See, for a useful collection of passages from Augustine on this topic, O'Donnell, *Confessions*, Vol. 3, pp. 57–58.

7 I translate from the Latin of 9.13.33, given in O'Donnell, *Confessions*, Vol. 1, p. 117.

8 Plotinus claims that the rational person does not grieve: "Even if the death of friends and relations causes grief, it does not grieve him but only that in him which has no intelligence, and he will not allow the distresses of this to move him." From *Enneads* 1.4.4, in *Plotinus: Porphyry on Plotinus, Ennead 1*, trans. A. H. Armstrong, Loeb Classical Library, Vol. 440 (Cambridge, MA: Harvard University Press, 1966), p. 185.

9 For this denial, see *De civitate dei* 8.16-17. For useful discussion, see Anastasia Scrutton, "Emotion in Augustine of Hippo and Thomas Aquinas: A Way Foward for the Im/passibility Debate?" *International Journal of Systematic Theology*, Vol. 7, no. 2 (2005), pp. 169–177.

10 Not much hinges, I think, upon whether in fact any nonhuman animals do cry. The point of importance is not the cognitive capacities of dolphins or chimpanzees; it is, rather, that tears are inseparably intimate with understandings and desires at a level of complexity which means that all crying creatures are reflexive knowers. If dolphins or chimpanzees did cry, this would be true of them too.

11 On the tendency *ad nihilum*, see Paul J. Griffiths, "Self-Annihilation or Damnation? A Disputable Question in Christian Eschatology," in *Liberal Faith: Essays in Honor of Philip Quinn*, ed. Paul J. Weithman (Notre Dame, IN: University of Notre Dame Press, 2008), pp. 83–117.

12 A summary statement of this view may be found in chapter 24 of William James's *Psychology: Briefer Course*, first published in 1892 as a condensed version of his *Principles of Psychology*.

13 See the quotation from Plotinus in note 8 above.

6

THE NON-ARISTOTELIAN CHARACTER OF AQUINAS'S ETHICS: AQUINAS ON THE PASSIONS

ELEONORE STUMP

It has become a commonplace to see Aquinas as Aristotelian in his philosophy.[1] This is particularly the case as regards his ethics. Scholars discussing Aquinas's ethics typically understand it as largely Aristotelian, though with some differences accounted for by the differences in worldview between Aristotle and Aquinas. T. I. Irwin, for example, summarizes his discussion of moral virtue in Aquinas's thought this way:

> [Aquinas's] account of moral virtue emphasizes the aspect of Aristotle's account that connects virtue with correct election. Aquinas has not only Aristotle's reasons, but also some reasons of his own, for emphasizing this feature of the virtues. . . . Aquinas' claims about action and freedom agree with Aristotle's claim that correct election is the mark of moral virtue.[2]

Ralph McInerny highlights what he sees as the Aristotelianism of Aquinas's ethics in the *Summa theologiae* this way:

> The dominant voice in these questions is that of Aristotle. . . . It is fair to say that these discussions would have been unthinkable apart from the influence of Aristotle, particularly, though by no means exclusively, of his *Nicomachean Ethics*.[3]

Anthony Kenny explains Aquinas's attempt to weave the beatitudes into his discussion of what Kenny takes to be fundamentally an Aristotelian ethics by saying,

Faith, Rationality, and the Passions, First Edition. Edited by Sarah Coakley.
© 2012 Blackwell Publishing Ltd. Book compilation © 2012 Blackwell Publishing Ltd.

The endeavor to bring together the evangelical and the Nicomachean texts can hardly be regarded as successful. . . . What is remarkable about this rapprochement is not that it is done successfully but that it is done at all. Moreover, it is noteworthy that the Christian texts are distorted to fit the Aristotelian context, rather than the other way around.[4]

Taking Aquinas's ethics as fundamentally Aristotelian has become almost scholarly dogma by now, and there is some reason for it. Aquinas's ethics is a virtue ethics, centered around a list of the virtues that includes some which, at least on the surface, appear to be identical to those on Aristotle's list: wisdom, justice, courage, and temperance.

On the Aristotelian ethics that many scholars suppose Aquinas accepts, a moral virtue is a habit which is acquired through practice and which disposes the will to act in accordance with reason in varying circumstances. Given this strong connection between virtue and reason, the passions are at best an ancillary to moral virtue and at worst an obstacle to it. As Irwin interprets what he takes to be Aquinas's Aristotelian view of the passions,

Passions are constituents of a virtue in so far as they are subject to reason and moved by reason.[5]

Adopting a similar view, Peter King says,

Aquinas holds *contra* Hume, that reason is and ought to be the ruler of the passions; since the passions *can* be controlled by reason they *should* be controlled by reason . . .[6]

For those who equate passion with emotion,[7] it can seem as if such an Aristotelianism in ethics mandates an alienation from emotion and grounds human moral excellence in reason alone. Because they understand Aristotelianism in this way, some people are repelled by what strikes them as inhuman in such an ethics; but there are certainly others who have an opposite reaction. For some contemporary thinkers, the Aristotelian focus on reason and the apparently concomitant rejection of a significant role for emotion is necessary for any ethics able to guide human life. So, for example, in a recent *New York Times* article on Catholic ethical and political stances,[8] the influential Princeton scholar Robert George is quoted as praising an Aristotelian ethics of this sort, which he attributes to Aquinas. For George, "moral philosophy . . . is a contest between . . . Aristotle and . . . David Hume."[9] On George's view, an ethics such as that of Hume, which centers ethics in the passions, can never give us an objective ethics. George thinks that we should reject the passion-centered ethics of Hume in favor of a reason-centered Aristotelian approach of the sort he thinks he finds in Aquinas. For George, the Aristotelian ethics of Aquinas is preferable to that of Hume because, on George's view, Aquinas's Aristotelian ethics grounds all virtue, all moral excellence, in reason. "In a well-ordered soul," George says, "reason's got the whip hand over emotion."[10]

Whatever the truth of this view may be as regards Aristotle's own ethics, it is certainly false, in its central claims, as regards the ethics of Aquinas; and some opposition to it has already begun to find a voice in the scholarly literature. So, for example, Jean Porter says

[There is] a . . . tendency among Aquinas scholars, . . . misleading and . . . prevalent, . . . to read Aquinas as if he not only baptized Aristotle, but is himself little more than Aristotle baptized.[11]

But I would make the point more strongly. Aquinas recognizes the Aristotelian virtues, but he thinks that they are not real virtues. In fact, Aquinas goes so far as to maintain that the passions—or the suitably formulated intellectual and volitional analogues to the passions—are not only the foundation of any real ethical life but also the flowering of what is best in it.[12]

Aquinas's Ethics is Not Aristotelian

To understand what Aquinas's position on the passions and their role in the ethical life actually is, it helps to begin by setting aside the view that Aquinas holds an Aristotelian virtue ethics.

As Aquinas rightly sees it, each of the dispositions on Aristotle's list—wisdom, justice, courage, and temperance—is meant to be both a virtue and an acquired characteristic. That is, a person gets an Aristotelian virtue or moral excellence by practicing it, by doing acts of the sort that yield the disposition of the virtue when those acts have been done often enough. Furthermore, each Aristotelian virtue is an intrinsic characteristic, a property that can be gotten and preserved by an individual acting by himself as an agent in his own right. The problem with thinking of Aquinas's ethics as Aristotelian is that none of these things true of the items on Aristotle's list of the virtues is true of the things Aquinas takes to be real virtues.

Speaking of Aquinas's virtue theory, Robert Pasnau and Christopher Shields define virtue for Aquinas this way:

A virtue is a *habitus* [a disposition] that informs a reason-governed power in such a way as to perfect the activity of that power.[13]

This is perhaps an acceptable definition of an Aristotelian virtue, but it is not Aquinas's definition of what he takes to be a virtue.

Aquinas himself affirms Augustine's definition of a virtue:

A virtue is a good quality of the mind by which one lives righteously, of which no one can make bad use, and which God works in us without us.[14]

This is manifestly an un-Aristotelian definition, not least because it is impossible to acquire for oneself by practice a disposition that God works in a person without that person[15] (though, Aquinas thinks, without in any way precluding the freedom of that person's will[16]). Commenting on this definition, Aquinas says,

> This definition comprises perfectly the whole formula of virtue.[17]

Aquinas recognizes that the Aristotelian virtues, acquired through practice of the acts correlated with a virtue, do not fit this definition because of its last clause: "which God works in us without us." He says,

> acquired virtue, to which these words do not apply, is not of the same species as infused virtue.[18]

And so acquired virtues are not habits that contain, as he says, the whole formula of virtue, as the infused virtues do.

Whatever benefits the Aristotelian virtues, with their source in human reason, might have for their possessor, on Aquinas's views, a person who has only the Aristotelian virtues is not yet in accord with the true moral good, whose measure is the divine law. He says,

> human virtue directed to the good which is governed according to the rule of human reason can be caused by human acts . . . But virtue which directs a person to good as governed by the divine law, and not by human reason, cannot be caused by human acts, the principle of which is reason, but is produced in us by the divine operation alone. That is why Augustine in giving the definition of such virtue inserts the words "which God works in us without us."[19]

In discussing the thesis of the unity of the virtues, Aquinas maintains that the thesis does not hold of the Aristotelian virtues but does hold of the infused virtues. Explaining this distinction, he says,

> Moral virtue may be considered either in its perfect or in its imperfect state. An imperfect moral virtue, temperance for instance or fortitude, is nothing but an inclination in us to do some kind of good deed, whether such inclination be in us by nature or by habituation. If we take the moral virtues in this way, they are not connected. . . . But perfect moral virtue is a habit that inclines us to do a good deed well; and if we take moral virtues in this way, we must say that they are connected. . . . [20]

And a little later in the same question he says,

> if a person exercises himself by good deeds in regard to one matter, but not in regard to another, for instance by behaving well in matters of anger but not in matters of concupiscence, he will indeed acquire a certain habit of restraining his anger; but this habit will lack the formula of virtue . . . [21]

Finally, Aquinas is emphatic that there can be no moral virtue at all without the infused virtue of love. He says,

It is written: "He who does not love abides in death" (I John 3:14). Now the spiritual life is perfected by the virtues, since it is by them that we live rightly, as Augustine states (*De libero arbitrio* ii). Therefore, the virtues cannot be without love.[22]

He considers the following objection to this view of his:

moral virtues can be acquired by means of human acts . . . whereas love cannot be had otherwise than by infusion . . . Therefore it is possible to have the other virtues without love.[23]

In response to this objection, he says nothing more than this: "This argument holds good of moral virtue in the sense of acquired virtue."[24]

From his point of view, then, the claim that the acquired virtues can be had without the infused virtue of love is no objection to his claim that no virtues can be had without infused virtue of love. And this conclusion can be true only if, in his view, the acquired virtues are not real virtues at all.

In fact, on Aquinas's account, it is possible to have all of the acquired virtues and still not be a moral person. A person in mortal sin is a person whose moral condition is bad enough that his soul is in peril; but, for Aquinas, a person could have all the acquired virtues and still have mortal sin. That is why he says,

Mortal sin is incompatible with divinely infused virtue. . . . But an act of sin, even mortal sin, is compatible with humanly acquired virtue.[25]

This conclusion is, of course, what one might have expected given Aquinas's position on the unity of the virtues thesis.

In another question, Aquinas asks whether it is possible to have the infused virtue of love without also having the moral virtues; and, in response, he says (again, as one would expect from his position on the unity of the virtues thesis),

All the moral virtues are infused simultaneously together with love.[26]

If this is true, Aquinas goes on to ask, why, then, do some people who have the infused virtue of love still have difficulty with some acts of moral virtue, contrary to Aristotle's claim that a person with a virtue does easily the acts correlated with that virtue? In reply, Aquinas explains that what is at issue for Aristotle is only the acquired virtues; but these are not the real virtues. For this reason, it is true that the acquired virtues are not part of what is infused when all the moral virtues are infused together with love. And Aristotle's claim about the acts associated with a virtue is not true with regard to the real (that is, the infused) moral virtues; it is true only of the acquired virtues.[27]

There are many other places one might cite, but these are sufficient, it seems to me, to show that Aquinas's account of the virtues is not

Aristotelian. Although Aquinas certainly recognizes a role for reason in the ethical life, the virtues around which his ethics is based are the virtues infused by God.

Aquinas's Three-Layered Theory of Moral Dispositions

To understand Aquinas's own theory of ethics, it is important to see that he recognizes three kinds of things that can be considered moral dispositions: the Aristotelian or acquired virtues, the infused virtues, *and* the gifts of the Holy Spirit.[28] The list of the things that are dispositions acquired by practice includes Aristotle's main four: wisdom, justice, courage, and temperance. The list of the infused virtues includes some that have the same names as the acquired virtues and some that do not, most notably the theological virtues of faith, hope, and love. Although there is some apparent overlap between these two lists and the list of the gifts of the Holy Spirit, the gifts are radically different from both the acquired and the infused virtues, because, in Aquinas's view, the gifts are a product of an on-going relationship between a human person and the third person of the Trinity, the Holy Spirit, which somehow is within that human person. There are seven gifts of the Holy Spirit: *pietas,* courage, fear of the Lord, wisdom, understanding, counsel, and knowledge.

As I have been at pains to illustrate above, for Aquinas, the infused virtues are the real virtues and are necessary for the moral life. Nonetheless, on Aquinas's account, the heart of the moral life lies in the gifts of the Holy Spirit. It is not possible, on his view, to have one's rational faculties of intellect and will be in a good state without the indwelling Holy Spirit; and when a person does have the indwelling Holy Spirit, that person also has the gifts that the Holy Spirit brings with it. Without the gifts of the Holy Spirit, Aquinas thinks, it is not possible to be a moral person or to be in union with a perfectly good God.[29]

Aquinas gives a relatively clear explanation of the function of the gifts. They are something like enzymes for the theological virtues, and especially the theological virtue of love, which is the *sine qua non* of the whole ethical life. An enzyme can bind with one active ingredient of a biochemical reaction and, altered in form and function by that binding, it can interact with another substrate to catalyze a reaction which would go very imperfectly without the enzyme. In the same way, for Aquinas, the gifts of the Holy Spirit have the effect of anchoring the infused theological virtues more deeply in a person's psyche and enabling them to have their desired effect there. The gifts of the Holy Spirit as-it-were cement the infused virtues into the psyche.[30]

Nonetheless, even with so much clarification of their function, it is not immediately apparent what the gifts of the Holy Spirit are, on Aquinas's account. In this connection, it is worth noticing that, although each of the four main Aristotelian or acquired virtues have analogues among the infused virtues, each also has a correlate among the gifts of the Holy Spirit. The list of the gifts includes courage and wisdom, each of which is on the Aristotelian list; and the other two on that list, justice and temperance, also have correlates among the gifts, although under different names. Turned into gifts, as Aquinas himself makes clear, temperance becomes fear of the Lord, and justice becomes *pietas*.[31]

To begin to see what the gifts of the Holy Spirit are and something of the way in which Aquinas's ethical theory is meant to work, take, for example, courage. On Aquinas's theory, courage can be considered as an Aristotelian virtue, as an infused virtue, or as a gift of the Holy Spirit. Courage as an Aristotelian virtue is a disposition which an agent acquires for himself and which facilitates reason's governing that agent in such a way as to make him a good citizen of an earthly community.[32] Considered in this way, courage can fail to be a moral disposition; and it can be had even by those who are not moral people. Courage considered as an infused virtue is a disposition which is infused into a person by God and which makes that person suitable for the community of heaven.[33] Considered in this way, courage is a real virtue, but it is not courage in its full form. For courage in its full form, one needs courage as a gift of the Holy Spirit. Considered as a gift, however, courage is very different even from courage as an infused virtue. Taken as a gift, courage manifests itself in a disposition to act on the settled conviction that one is united to God now and will be united to God in heaven when one dies.[34]

Considered as a gift, courage, like the rest of the gifts, stems from relationship with God, whose indwelling Holy Spirit manifests itself first in a human person's enhanced openness to God in love. By filling a person with joy in love with God, Aquinas says, the Holy Spirit protects people against two kinds of evils, which might otherwise make them give way to fear:

> [it protects them] first against the evil which disturbs peace, since peace is disturbed by adversities. But with regard to adversities the Holy Spirit perfects [us] through patience, which enables [us] to bear adversities patiently. . . . Second, [it protects them] against the evil which arrests joy, namely, the wait for what is loved. To this evil, the Spirit opposes long-suffering, which is not broken by the waiting.[35]

The gift of courage in the face of adversity is thus one result stemming from the indwelling Holy Spirit.

The Second-Personal in Aquinas's Ethics

With this much clarification, we are in a better position to understand the nature of the gifts. For Aquinas, salvation from sin and the moral excellence that is part of it require the gifts of the Holy Spirit. So, for example, he says,

Of all the gifts, wisdom seems to be the highest, and fear the lowest. Now each of these is necessary for salvation. . . . Therefore the other gifts that are placed between these are also necessary for salvation.[36]

But the gifts of the Holy Spirit are not states that are wholly intrinsic to a person, and they cannot be described adequately in either first-personal or third-personal terms. Rather, as the very name suggests, the gifts of the Holy Spirit are second-personal in character.

Recently, attention has been focused on the second-personal because of the outpouring of research on autistic spectrum disorder in children, which has an impairment in the capacities for second-personal connection at its root. This research has made philosophers as well as psychologists and neuroscientists more reflective about the fact that human beings are social animals and that they are designed for what philosophers now call "mind-reading" or "social cognition." We can think of mind-reading or social cognition as a non-propositional knowledge of persons gained through second-personal experience.[37] Such knowledge is an achievement of the operation of a set of cognitive capacities that share many features with perception: they are direct, immediate, intuitive in character, and basically reliable. The deliverances of these cognitive capacities give one person, Jerome, an understanding of the mind of another person, Paula. In particular, these cognitive capacities enable Jerome to know in a direct and intuitive way *what* Paula is doing, to *what end* Paula is doing it, and with what *emotion or affect* she is doing it.[38]

For Aquinas, it is open to every human person to have a second-personal connection with God; and, because of this connection, it is possible for there to be as-it-were mind-reading or social cognition between a human person and God too. A human person can know God's presence and something of God's mind in a direct and intuitive way that is in some respects like the mind-reading between human persons.[39] On Aquinas's view,

There is one general way by which God is in all things by essence, power, and presence, [namely,] as a cause in the effects participating in his goodness. But in addition to this way there is a special way [in which God is in a thing by essence, power, and presence] which is appropriate for a rational creature, in whom God is said to be as the thing known is in the knower and the beloved is in the lover. . . . In this special way, God is not only said to be in a rational creature but even to dwell in that creature. . . . [40]

On Aquinas's reading, the gifts of the Holy Spirit are an outgrowth and a manifestation of a second-personal connection to God. Every gift of the Holy Spirit has its source in God's indwelling in a human person; and, in addition to its other functions, it results in a person's being attentive to God and apt to follow the inner promptings of God. Speaking of the gifts, Aquinas says,

These perfections are called 'gifts', not only because they are infused by God, but also because by them a person is disposed to become amenable to the divine inspiration. . . . [41]

And a little later he says,

the gifts are perfections of a human being, whereby he is disposed so as to be amenable to the promptings of God.[42]

In fact, for Aquinas, the Holy Spirit fills a person with a sense of the love of God and his nearness, so that joy is one of the principal effects of the Holy Spirit.[43] Aquinas says,

the ultimate perfection, by which a person is made perfect inwardly, is joy, which stems from the presence of what is loved. Whoever has the love of God, however, already has what he loves, as is said in 1 John 4:16: "whoever abides in the love of God abides in God, and God abides in him." And joy wells up from this.[44]

When [Paul] says "the Lord is near," he points out the cause of joy, because a person rejoices at the nearness of his friend.[45]

On Aquinas's view, a second-personal connection of love between two human persons enables them to grow in what Aquinas calls connaturality with each other. So, for example, if Paula and Jerome love each other and are united to each other, then Paula and Jerome will tend to become more like each other.[46] Their judgments and intuitions about things will become similar too. For Aquinas, a second-personal connection between a person Paula and God will have the same sort of effect. It is possible also to have connaturality with God.

If Paula has a second-personal connection with God, then Paula will grow in connaturality with God. Connected to God in this way, Paula's intuitions and judgments will naturally grow to be more like those of God; and her second-personal connection to God will enable her to interact in some mind-reading sort of way with God, too. On Aquinas's view, because of his commitment to the unity of the virtues thesis, which encompasses also the gifts of the Holy Spirit, this is the optimal ethical condition for a human person. In this condition, Paula will not need to try to reason things out as regards ethics. She will be disposed to think and act in morally appropriate ways because of her connection to God, not because of her reliance on reason. And her second-personal interaction with God will allow her judgments to be informed by God's judgments and God's will.

So, for example, in explaining wisdom as one of the gifts of the Holy Spirit (rather than as an infused or an acquired virtue),[47] Aquinas connects wisdom as a gift with the will. He says,

wisdom denotes a certain rectitude of judgment according to the eternal law. Now rectitude of judgment is twofold: first, on account of perfect use of reason, secondly, on account of a certain connaturality with the matter about which one has to judge. . . . Now sympathy or connaturality for divine things is the result of love, which unites us to God . . . Consequently wisdom which is a gift has its cause in the will, and this cause is love . . . [48]

The idea that the heart of ethics is second-personal has most recently been called to the attention of philosophers by Stephen Darwall,[49] though in the past it has often been associated with Levinas. But, as these brief remarks show, an emphasis on the second-personal is central to Aquinas's ethics, too. For Aquinas, however, unlike Levinas or Darwall, God is one of the relata; to be a moral person is a matter of having a right second-personal relationship to God. The gifts of the Holy Spirit are ethical excellences that are second-personal in character too. They stem from the Holy Spirit's indwelling in a human person, Jerome, having a second-personal connection with Jerome, and thereby enabling Jerome to have a mind-reading connection with God. For Aquinas, true, second-personal moral excellences arise when the second-personal connection between God and a human person has produced in that human person a kind of connaturality with God.

Passion: Sense Appetite and Intellect

With this much understanding of the three-layered character of Aquinas's theory of ethics, we are in a position to understand better the role of the passions in Aquinas's ethics. That is because there is also a certain three-layered character to Aquinas's account of the passions. As will be readily apparent, here, too, there is overlap among his lists.

For Aquinas, the fundamental passion, that is, the passion that underlies the others, is love; and the principal passions, that is, the passions that are the source of the others, are joy and sadness, hope and fear.[50] But Aquinas actually has three different lists of the passions or analogues to the passions. Love and joy are on all three lists; and sadness, hope, and fear are represented on two.[51]

It is helpful to begin with the lowest level of Aquinas's three-layered lore of the passions, namely, with "passion" taken in its most basic sense.[52] Here it is helpful to review very briefly Aquinas's theory of the mechanisms of human cognition and the relation of the passions to the cognitive capacities involved.[53]

Aquinas is part of the Aristotelian tradition that supposes there to be two different appetites in human beings, the sensory and the intellective. Each of these is a power whose outputs are desires. The sensory appetite produces desires on the basis of information coming into the mind from the senses—the smell of baking bread, the sight of fresh blood. A person can be absorbed in a book while he is smelling bread baking, without taking any notice of what he is smelling. If he feels hungry in that condition, before he recognizes that what he is smelling is bread baking, then his hungriness, his desire for bread, is a motion only of the sensory appetite and constitutes a passion. A desire for bread which is produced just by the smell of bread baking is a passion in the most basic sense of "passion."

So understood in its most basic sense as a motion of the sensory appetite, a passion is a response on the part of the sensory appetite to the direct and intuitive input from the senses. Nonetheless, even such a lowest-level passion is able to influence the intellect. It can make things seem good that would not have seemed good to the intellect without the influence of that passion. When it acts in this way, a passion is detrimental to the moral life. On the other hand, such a passion can also work together with the intellect subsequent to a deliverance of the intellect. In those circumstances, the passion can stimulate a person to pursue what is really good with more fervor. In cases of this kind, a passion enhances the moral life.

So if a passion is taken in this lowest level sense, it is in its own nature neither good nor bad. Its moral character is derivative from its connection to reason, in a way characteristic of Aristotelian ethics, as Aristotelian ethics is commonly understood.

But, for Aquinas, passion can also be understood in an extended sense. In this sense, a passion is not in the sensory appetite but rather in the intellective appetite. The intellective appetite produces desires on the basis of all the information coming into the mind. This appetite is what Aquinas understands as the will; and it is responsive to all the deliverances of the intellect (including those deliverances based on the intellect's connection to the senses), rather than to the deliverances of the senses alone. When a person recognizes that what he is smelling is bread and when in those circumstances, all things considered, he wants to get and eat what he recognizes as bread, the desire in question is in the intellective appetite or will, not in the sensory appetite (or at least not in the sensory appetite alone).

A passion in the basic sense is a desire aimed at the good as the good is perceived by the senses. When the good is perceived by the intellect and stimulates the intellective appetite or will, the resulting desire has something in common with a passion in its most basic sense, even though it lacks the tie to the senses. In the intellective appetite, the desire is not so much a bodily feeling prompted by a perception as it is a conative attitude prompted by the mind's understanding.[54] So, for example, although in its most basic sense love is a passion in the sensitive appetite, there is a different sense of love in which love stems from deliverances of the intellect and is an expression of the intellective appetite.

As an expression of the intellective appetite and its interaction with the intellect, love is also a passion or, more strictly, an analogue to the passions. So understood, love—and also the other passions such as joy, hope, and the rest—are, on Aquinas's view, the formal part of passion without the material part, that is, without the part which is tied to the body, namely, the senses and the sensitive appetite.[55] Passions in this analogous or extended sense are the second layer in Aquinas's three-layered lore of the passions. Considered in this extended sense, some of the things on Aquinas's list of the passions can be had even by an impassible God. God has no passions in the basic sense of "passion" in virtue of having no body and thus no senses. But, on Aquinas's view, God does have love and joy, for example.[56]

It is important to see in this connection that two of the infused virtues have the same names as two of the primary passions: love and hope. Taken as the formal part of passion without the material part, then, love, which is the foundational passion in the sensory appetite, and hope, which is one of the principal passions, can also be dispositions in the intellective appetite infused into a person by God. As infused virtues in the intellective appetite, love and hope are not morally neutral. They are always good. In fact, as I explained above, on Aquinas's account, love as an infused virtue is essential to all the real moral virtues; and, without love, no real moral virtue at all is possible. Furthermore, since Aquinas accepts the unity of the virtues thesis— not for the acquired virtues but for the infused virtues—all moral excellence, all virtue, is present at once as soon as love is infused.[57]

But this is not yet the end of the story. There is still the third layer to Aquinas's lore of the passions. Just as the virtues have analogues in the *gifts* of the Holy Spirit, so the passions also have analogues in the *fruits* of the Holy Spirit. There are twelve fruits of the Holy Spirit: love, joy, peace, patience, long-suffering, goodness, benignity, meekness, fidelity, modesty, continence, and chastity. The first two items on this list, love and joy, are, of course, also on the list of the primary passions and their intellective correlates. As Aquinas explains the first five fruits of the Holy Spirit, they are in fact all consequences of shared love between a human person and God. The remaining seven have to do, one way or another, with the love of one's neighbor understood as beloved of God or with suitable love of oneself and one's body.[58]

Like the gifts of the Holy Spirit, and unlike the passions in their most basic sense, all the fruits of the Holy Spirit are second-personal in character. Aquinas explains them as the emotional condition of someone who is connected in love with God. He says this about the first three fruits of the Holy Spirit—love, joy, and peace:

> [God] himself is love. Hence it is written (Rom.v.5): The love of God is poured forth in our hearts by the Holy Spirit who is given to us. The necessary result of this love is joy, because every lover rejoices at being united to the beloved. Now love has always the actual presence of God whom it loves. So the consequence of this love is joy. And the perfection of joy is peace . . . because our desires rest altogether in [God].[59]

For Aquinas, then, the contribution of the fruits of the Holy Spirit to the moral life is not a matter of the passions being governed by reason, any more than it is in the case of the gifts of the Holy Spirit. Rather, the fruits of the Holy Spirit are a matter of having emotions, spiritual analogues to the passions, transformed in second-personal connection to God. This is a far cry from Robert George's view of Aquinas as basing the moral life in reason's having the whip hand over emotion.

Conclusion

So here is where things stand. It may be true that for Aristotle the moral life is a matter of living in accordance with reason and disciplining the passions so that at best they help an agent live in accordance with reason. But things are very different when it comes to Aquinas's theory of the ethical life. For Aquinas, there are passions, in an analogous or extended sense, which are infused by God into the intellective appetite or which are the fruits of the Holy Spirit and stem from second-personal connection to God. These passions or analogues to the passions are foundational to all virtue and to the whole of the ethical life. On Aquinas's view, no moral virtue is possible without all the gifts and fruits of the Holy Spirit, and any moral virtue requires all of them.

What makes Aquinas's focus on the passions in his three-layered account different from Hume's focus on the passions in his ethical theory has entirely to do with relationship, with the second-personal. Hume recognizes that human beings are capable of a kind of mind-reading of one another. He says,

> The minds of men are mirrors to one another, not only because they reflect each others' emotions, but also because those rays of passion, sentiments, and opinions may often be reverberated.[60]

And that is why Hume says of himself,

> A cheerful countenance infuses a sensible complacency and serenity in my mind, as an angry or sullen one throws a sudden damp upon me.[61]

Nonetheless, for Hume, a passion is just an intrinsic characteristic of an agent, which the agent has in himself alone as the individual he is. By contrast, from Aquinas's point of view, the gifts and the fruits of the Holy Spirit are not intrinsic characteristics but relational ones. The gifts stem from second-personal connection to God, from second-personal interaction in as-it-were mind-reading with God; and the fruits are the emotions that result from this second personal connection. What differentiates Aquinas from Hume, then, is not that Aquinas privileges reason while Hume privileges passion in the ethical life. Rather, it is that the emotions Aquinas highlights as essential to the ethical life have to do with relationship to God. Understood as the infused virtues of hope and love, or as the fruits of the Holy Spirit, the flowering of second-personal connection with a personal God, passion in its analogous sense is for Aquinas the touchstone of all morality.

NOTES

1 For a review of the disputes over the connection between Aristotle and Aquinas in the history of Thomism, see, for example, Mark Jordan, "The Alleged Aristotelianism of Thomas Aquinas," in *The Gilson Lectures on Thomas Aquinas*, ed. James Reilly (Toronto: Pontifical Institute of Mediaeval Studies, 2008), pp. 73–106.

2 See, for example, T. I. Irwin's treatment of virtue in Aquinas's thought in Irwin's *The Development of Ethics: A Historical and Critical Study* (Oxford: Oxford University Press, 2007), Vol. 1, p. 544 [footnotes omitted in quotation].

3 Ralph McInerny, *The Question of Christian Ethics* (Washington, DC: Catholic University of America Press, 1993), pp. 25–26.

4 Anthony Kenny, "Aquinas on Aristotelian Happiness," in *Aquinas's Moral Theory*, eds. Scott MacDonald and Eleonore Stump (Ithaca, NY: Cornell University Press, 1999), pp. 15–27.

5 Irwin, "Development of Ethics," p. 522.

6 Peter King, "Aquinas on the Passions," in *Aquinas's Moral Theory*, eds. Scott MacDonald and Eleonore Stump (Ithaca, NY: Cornell University Press, 1999), p. 126.

7 There is some reason for rejecting this equation if "passion" is taken in its most basic sense. In contemporary discussion of the emotions, an emotion is typically held to have cognitive content. For Aquinas, as I explain below, a passion taken in its strictest sense is an act of the sensitive appetite when that appetite is responding to deliverances from the senses alone. In order to have the cognitive content of the sort typically thought to be at issue in an emotion, what is needed is some deliverance from the intellect, rather than the senses. On the other hand, a passion in its extended or analogous senses, explained below, can have cognitive content; and so, depending on the account of emotion given, a passion in this extended sense might well be the same as an emotion.

8 *The New York Times Magazine*, December 20, 2009, pp. 24–29.

9 Ibid., p. 27.

10 Ibid., p. 27.

11 Jean Porter, "Right Reason and the Love of God: The Parameters of Aquinas' Moral Theology," in *The Theology of Thomas Aquinas*, eds. Rik van Nieuwenhove and Joseph Wawrykow (Notre Dame, IN: University of Notre Dame Press, 2005), pp. 167–191. See also her essay "Virtues and Vices," in *The Oxford Handbook of Aquinas*, eds. Brian Davies and Eleonore Stump (Oxford: Oxford University Press, 2011).

12 For a thorough and persuasive argument that Aquinas's ethics is not Aristotelian but in fact takes the second-personal as foundational for ethics, see Andrew Pinsent, "Gifts and Fruits," in *The Oxford Handbook of Aquinas*. See also his "Joint Attention and the Second-Personal Foundation of Aquinas's Virtue Ethics," PhD diss., St Louis University, 2009; and his review of Robert Miner's *Thomas Aquinas on the Passions, Notre Dame Philosophical Reviews* (February 2010).

13 Robert Pasnau and Christopher Shields, *The Philosophy of Aquinas* (Boulder, CO: Westview Press, 2004), p. 229.

14 ST I-II q. 55, a. 4. In this chapter, with a very few alterations, I am using the translation of the Fathers of the Dominican English Province, (Westminster, MD: Christian Classics, 1981), because it has become standard and because there are few cases in which I think I could improve on it substantially. There are some quotations where I have altered the Dominican translation in minor ways (as in the quotation to which this footnote is appended) or even significantly (as in the quotation to which the designation for footnote 15 is appended); but I have left those alterations generally unmarked, thereby erring on the side of giving more credit than is due to the Dominican translation.

15 For detailed discussion of the way in which, on Aquinas's views, God does so, see chapter 13, on grace and free will, in my *Aquinas* (London: Routledge, 2003).

16 For a discussion of the way in which such a claim can be made consistently, see chapter 13 in my *Aquinas*.

17 ST I-II q. 55, a. 4.

18 ST I-II q. 63, a. 4 s.c.; cf. also, for example, *Quaestiones disputatae de virtutibus in communi* q. un, aa. 9-10 and ST I-II q. 55, a. 4.
19 ST I-II q. 63, a. 2.
20 ST I-II q. 65, a. 1.
21 ST I-II q. 65, a. 1 ad 1.
22 ST I-II q. 65, a. 2 s.c.
23 ST I-II q. 65, a. 2 obj.2.
24 ST I-II q. 65, a. 2 ad 2.
25 See, for example, ST I-II q. 63, a. 2 ad 2.
26 ST I-II q. 65, a. 3.
27 ST I-II q. 65, a. 3 ad 2.
28 There is another story to be told about the way in which the gifts of the Holy Spirit are mediated by the sacraments, but this subject is outside the bounds of this chapter.
29 See, for example, ST I-II q. 68, a. 2.
30 See, for example, ST I-II q. 68, a. 2 ad 2.
31 See, for example, ST II-II q. 19 and q. 121, a. 1.
32 See, for example, ST I-II q. 63, a. 4.
33 For the general discussion, see *Quaestiones disputatae de virtutibus in communi* q. un. a. 9 and *Quaestiones disputatae de virtutibus cardinalibus*, q. un. a. 2. Cf. also ST II-II q. 124, a. 2 ad 1, and q. 123, a. 5, 6, and 7 and q. 140, a. 1.
34 See, for example, ST II-II q. 139, a. 1.
35 Aquinas, *In Gal* 5.6. There is an English translation of this work: *Commentary on Saint Paul's Epistle to the Galatians by St. Thomas Aquinas*, trans. F. R. Larcher and Richard Murphy (Albany, NY: Magi Books, 1966). Although I have preferred to use my own translations, I found the Larcher and Murphy translation helpful, and the citations for this work are given both to the Latin and to the Larcher and Murphy translation. For this passage, see Larcher and Murphy, p. 180. Cf. also, *In Gal* 5.6 (Larcher and Murphy, p. 179) and *In Heb* 12.2.
36 ST I-II q. 68, a. 2 s.c.
37 For a discussion of the knowledge of persons, see Chapter 4 in my *Wandering in Darkness: Narrative and the Problem of Suffering* (Oxford: Oxford University Press, 2010).
38 For a summary of some of the literature on this subject and its significance for understanding second-personal interaction, see Chapter 4 of my *Wandering in Darkness.*
39 For a detailed argument for this claim, see my "Eternity, Simplicity, and Presence," in *The Science of Being as Being: Metaphysical Investigations*, ed. Gregory T. Doolan (Washington, DC: Catholic University of America Press, 2011). See also my "Simplicity," in *The Oxford Handbook of Aquinas*, eds. Brian Davies and Eleonore Stump (Oxford: Oxford University Press, 2011).
40 ST I q. 43, a. 3.
41 ST I-II q. 68, a. 1.
42 ST I-II q. 68, a. 2.
43 See, for example, *In Rom* 5.1.
44 *In Gal* 5.6; Larcher and Murphy, pp. 179–180.
45 *In Phil* 4.1. For an English translation, see *Commentary on Saint Paul's First Letter to the Thessalonians and the Letter to the Philippians by St. Thomas Aquinas*, trans. F. R. Larcher and Michael Duffy (Albany, NY: Magi Books, 1969), p. 113.
46 See, in this connection, ST I-II q. 27, a. 3 and q. 28, a. 1.
47 The question of ST at issue is on wisdom as a gift. The first article asks whether wisdom should be numbered among the gifts of the Holy Spirit, and Aquinas, of course, answers in the affirmative.
48 ST II-II q. 45, a. 2.
49 Stephen Darwall, *The Second-Person Standpoint: Morality, Respect, and Accountability* (Cambridge, MA: Harvard University Press, 2006).
50 See, for example, ST I-II q. 25, a. 4.
51 There are intellective analogues for the basic passions of sadness, fear, and hope; and hope, of course, is also on the list of the infused virtues. Depending on how one understands fear as a gift of the Holy Spirit, it may be that fear should also be reckoned as on three lists, one of which is the gifts. In this chapter, I have separated the three-layered account of ethics—acquired virtues, infused virtues, and gifts of the Holy Spirit—from the

three-layered lore of the passions—passions in the most basic sense, passions in their intel-lective analogues, and fruits of the Holy Spirit. As these brief remarks about fear show, however, there are also connections between these two sets of three lists. Nonetheless, in the interest of brevity, I am leaving these connections to one side here.

52 For the basic Thomistic lore of the passions, see Robert Miner, *Thomas Aquinas on the Passions* (Cambridge: Cambridge University Press, 2009).
53 For the basic Thomistic lore on the mechanisms of cognition, see chapter 8 in my *Aquinas* (London: Routledge, 2003).
54 See, for example, ST I-II q. 26, a. 1.
55 See, for example, ST I q. 20, a. 1 ad 2.
56 See, for example, ST I q. 20, a. 1.
57 See ST I-II q. 65.
58 See, for example, ST I-II q. 70, a. 3.
59 ST I-II q. 70, a. 3.
60 Hume, *Treatise on Human Nature*, Book 2, Pt. 2, section 5. I am indebted to Annette Baier for this reference. As she herself makes clear, Hume's philosophy emphasizes the impor-tance of what he calls "sympathy" for all of ethics.
61 Hume, *Treatise of Human Nature*, Book 2, Pt. 1, section 11. I am grateful to Annette Baier for this reference.

7

SKEPTICAL DETACHMENT OR LOVING SUBMISSION TO THE GOOD? REASON, FAITH, AND THE PASSIONS IN DESCARTES

JOHN COTTINGHAM

The Myth of Cartesian Independence

The standard view of Descartes among contemporary analytic philosophers sees him above all as an epistemologist, obsessed with the threat of skepticism, and as a rationalist (in the broad sense), deploying the weapons of pure rational argument to establish the foundations of knowledge. Fairly characteristic of the standard view is the comment of Alistair MacIntyre, in his latest book, which describes Descartes as claiming that "anyone who follows [his] procedure . . . arguing . . . through the Cogito [and] the arguments for the existence of God . . . will have defeated the sceptic."[1]

Building up the foundations of all knowledge from scratch seems a very tough undertaking for those wishing (as Descartes did)[2] to defend the cause of religion, and most philosophers now think it is hopelessly over-ambitious. MacIntyre sums up the typical verdict when he says: "Everything turns on the *arguments* for the existence of God and those arguments fail."[3] But there is another, and I think more fruitful, way of reading Descartes, as less of an obsessive epistemologist and more of what we might call a rational intuitionist. Yes, he was a champion of reason, and of the mind's innate power to apprehend clearly perceived truths; but his reaching for those truths was not conducted in quite the epistemic vacuum that the skepticism-driven reading of his work suggests. On the contrary, if we look beneath the surface we can see his stance as having more in common with the "faith seeking understanding" tradition, reflecting the ideas of some of his patristic and medieval

Faith, Rationality, and the Passions, First Edition. Edited by Sarah Coakley.
© 2012 Blackwell Publishing Ltd. Book compilation © 2012 Blackwell Publishing Ltd.

mentors, whose presence, I shall argue, can be clearly felt at some of the most crucial stages of the *Meditations*.

The idea that *all* human knowledge should or can be rebuilt from the bottom up is in any case a fantasy—and one that Descartes himself would surely have rejected. First, even in the extremities of doubt in the First Meditation, the meditator clearly has to rely on a stable domain of ideas and meanings which are not of his making, and whose structure as reliable guides to the truth he has to take on trust—or else no systematic doubt, no reflection, no meditation would be possible in the first place. Science (*scientia*) may need to be reconstructed; but the mind's fundamental power of intuiting or cognizing basic truths and their logical connections—what Descartes called *cognitio*—is, and must be, taken for granted.[4] Secondly, Descartes implicitly believes from the outset that the source of this reliable cognitive power of the mind must be the divine creator, source of all truth. Even when the method of doubt appears to extend as far as questioning God, and substituting the nightmare scenario of demonic deception, the meditator immediately draws back, and almost by automatic reflex acknowledges his maker: "I will suppose that not God, *who is supremely good and the source of truth*, but rather some malicious demon . . . is bent on deceiving me."[5] As for the demon, like Satan he retreats as soon as he is confronted: when I focus on the sum of two plus three, says Descartes, I spontaneously declare that however powerful and vicious he is, he could not make it now true that the answer is more or less than five.[6] The entire project of the *Meditations* in effect presupposes faith in the reliability of the mind's fundamental semantic and logical intuitions, which only a theistic worldview can properly underpin. As it is phrased in the interview Descartes gave to the young Dutchman Frans Burman in 1648, "a reliable mind was God's gift to me."[7]

Reaching God: Demonstrative Proof or Direct Encounter?

Properly understood, then, Descartes's philosophy is far from subscribing to the delusion of pure, presuppositionless inquiry by an isolated and wholly autonomous meditator; on the contrary, it effectively presupposes from the outset our complete cognitive dependence on God. Yet in that case, what are we to say of the famous Cartesian "proofs" for God's existence—the "trademark" argument in the Third Meditation (that the content of my idea of God shows it must have been placed in me by God),[8] and the Fifth Meditation argument that God's existence is inseparable from his essence? Are these not presented by Descartes as self-standing, purely rational arguments—exercises of reason supposed to be entirely independent of any presuppositions of faith?

If by faith is meant acceptance of certain revealed truths, for example regarding the Incarnation, or the Trinity, then certainly Descartes thought the philosopher should steer clear of them and leave them to the theologians.[9] Indeed, his famous rule—accept only what is clear and distinct —might seem to put such mysteries entirely off limits for the Cartesian meditator. But in fact Descartes insisted that there was another source of clarity and transparency besides the natural light of reason. In the Second Set of Replies to the *Meditations*, he articulates the idea of a "double source" of clarity or transparency (*duplex claritas sive perspicuitas*), one coming from the natural light, the other from divine grace.[10] The latter, the *lumen supernaturale*,[11] gives rise, no less than the natural light, to the irresistible assent of the intellect. The key passage for understanding Descartes's views about this comes in the Fourth Meditation, where Descartes declares true human freedom to reside not in the maintaining of some detached critical stance, but in spontaneous submission to the light. From a great light in the intellect there comes a great inclination of the will; and this assent, says Descartes, can be produced *either* by "clearly perceived reasons of truth and goodness" (the natural light) *or* by a "divinely produced disposition of my thought" (the supernatural light).[12]

We have to remember here that Descartes, in writing about God, was steeped in a meditative and contemplative tradition, stretching from Augustine (in his *Confessions*), through Anselm (in the *Proslogion*), to Bonaventure (in his *Journey of the Mind towards God*), a tradition that intermingles philosophical reasoning with humble praise and worship.[13] The two elements may seem incompatible to the modern analytic mind, but they coexist happily in the tradition. It is noticeable, for example, (though to modern readers perhaps baffling) that Anselm actually *addresses* God, humbly prays to him, at the very moment he is about to embark on trying to prove his existence by deploying the famous ontological argument: "I will not attempt, Lord, to reach your height, for my understanding falls so far short of it. But I desire to understand your truth just a little, the truth that my heart believes and loves."[14]

Anselm here recapitulates Augustine, for whom God can never be brought wholly within the grasp of our human comprehension, for that would be the best indication that what was so grasped was not God: *[Deus] non est, si comprehendisti*—if you claim to have grasped him, what you have grasped is not God.[15] Thus, for Anselm, God is precisely *not* the "greatest conceivable being" (as the account commonly found in undergraduate essays inaccurately, if understandably, puts it); on the contrary, he always recedes beyond the horizon of our thinking—he is that "than which nothing greater can be thought." In similar fashion, Descartes stresses in many of his writings how far the human mind falls short in its grasp of the infinite. We should, he warns, not so much try to grasp the perfections of God as surrender to them—*non tam capere quam capi*.[16] And in a passage at the end of the Third Meditation, whose style and tone is such that it could easily have come from Augustine or Anselm, Descartes expresses the longing "to gaze at, wonder and adore the beauty of this immense light, so far as the eye of my darkened intellect can bear it."[17] This is hardly the tone of the dispassionate analytic philosopher, engaged for purely instrumental reasons on the epistemic project of validating the edifice of knowledge. Rather, it is the voice of the worshiper, one for whom philosophy would make no sense without the divine source of truth and goodness that irradiates it from start to finish.

Admittedly, the passage just quoted comes at the *end* of Descartes's reasoning to support God's existence in the Third Meditation, whereas Anselm is prepared to pray, and to adore, before even embarking on his own reasoning. But Descartes's acknowledging of his creator's existence actually hinges on a very basic and straightforward intuition. To be sure, he does take some time to elaborate his reasoning in the Third Meditation[18] (just as, for that matter, Anselm does for his own very different reasoning in the *Proslogion*); but the rational intuition involved can be compressed down to a single nugget of cognition, which Descartes encapsulated in his earlier writings by means of a tag that deserves to be much better known: *Sum, ergo Deus est*— "I am, therefore God exists."[19]

The key to this is Descartes's awareness of his own creaturely imperfection, which plays a pivotal role in his reaching for God. "How could I understand that I . . . lacked something, and that I was not wholly perfect, unless there were in me some idea of a more perfect being which enabled me to recognize my own defects by comparison?" (The phrasing, incidentally, echoes very closely that of Bonaventure four centuries earlier.)[20] My awareness of my weakness and finitude carries with it, for Descartes, an implicit and immediate sense of something other than, and infinitely beyond, myself, which necessarily eludes my mental grasp. This crucial point is very aptly seized on by Emmanuel Levinas in his account of the *Meditations*. On Levinas's view (as neatly summarized by Hilary Putnam):

> what Descartes is reporting is not a step in a deductive reasoning, but a profound religious experience, an experience which might be described as the experience of a *fissure*, of a confrontation with something that disrupted all his categories. On this reading, Descartes is not so much proving something as *acknowledging* something, acknowledging a Reality that he could not have constructed, a Reality which proves its own existence by the very fact that its presence in my mind turns out to be a phenomenological impossibility.[21]

What the Levinas reading in effect succeeds in uncovering, I think, is a luminous paradox at the heart of the Cartesian cognition of God. On the one hand the Cartesian programme cannot proceed unless the meditator has a "clear and distinct" idea of God—the need for such clarity and distinctness is the chief slogan of Cartesian philosophy, the very hallmark of the system. But on the other hand, it is crucial to the apprehension of that idea of God as authentic that it exceeds the complete grasp of the human mind, that it cannot be fully encompassed by my finite intellect. If this is right, then

Descartes's line of thought about God, not just in his version of the ontological argument, but also in the earlier so-called "Trademark argument" of the Third Meditation, hinges in one crucial respect on a very similar mode of reflection to that we find in Anselm's, namely reflection on what happens when the finite creature attempts to confront its infinite creator—when, as Anselm put it, the "wretched mind" is "stirred up to contemplation of God."[22]

To avoid any possible confusion, I am not of course suggesting that Descartes's Third Meditation argument is a kind of ontological argument: the formal presentations of the arguments of the Third and Fifth Meditations are quite different—the former (in both its phases) hinging on considerations about causality, the latter depending on analysis of essences (and the geometrical analogy with a triangle). But the question of how Descartes came to weld such seemingly quite distinct types of argument together into the basic structure of his metaphysics deserves to be asked more than it is. No commentator, to my knowledge, has ever provided a really satisfactory explanation of why the meditator addresses the question of God's existence twice—and indeed many students may well go away from the standard lecture course on the *Meditations* feeling that Descartes may have been afflicted by the "two leaky bucket" syndrome (nervously deploying the Fifth Meditation reasoning because of residual suspicions that that of the Third Meditation may not have been watertight). But once we begin to think along the lines suggested by Levinas, I would argue that we can begin to see that the two pieces of reasoning, for all their formal differences, are informed by essentially the same movement of thought—the reflective finite mind's direct confrontation with something that infinitely transcends it.

In one of the best recent studies of the *Meditations,* John Carriero seems to me to go a fair way to discerning the true character of Descartes's approach, when he contrasts Descartes's position on the cognition of God with that of Aquinas. For Aquinas, whose famous "five ways" infer God as the mysterious "something" behind the observed features of the cosmos, our knowledge of God is oblique; only by divine grace, as for the blessed in heaven, is one enabled to have a more direct cognition of him.[23] Descartes, by contrast, is, as Carriero puts it, "launching an argument for the existence of God in the midst of a cognitive situation that he takes to resemble the beatific vision."[24] In contrast to the obliqueness which in the Thomist account applies to our cognitive relation to God, the Cartesian meditator has a cognitive access to God which is much more direct: the idea of God "confers access to a subject-matter so that [the meditator] may *recognize* its truths and understand *why* they hold."[25] Yet if Levinas's analysis is right, we can push this even further. "Cognitive access" is no longer a matter of simply reflecting on an idea; it becomes, as its name implies, *access*—what Gilbert Ryle would have called a "success" verb.[26] Just like another "success-verb," and one which Descartes himself uses in connection with our knowledge of God, it is a mental "attaining" (*attingere*) or "touching" (*toucher*)—a touching of something which, like a mountain, is hugely beyond my power to encompass, but which my mind can truly reach.[27]

The Role of the Passions

The language of adoration with which Descartes concludes the Third Meditation, as he "gazes at, wonders at, and adores the beauty of this immense light" (*intueri, admirari, adorare*), involves a remarkable fusing of cognitive intuition with an outpouring of passion. Wonder, *l'admiration*, is one of the important passions discussed by Descartes in his last published work, *Les Passions de l'âme* (1649). So should we say that the passions have an accepted place in the Cartesian journey towards God, alongside the elements of reason and faith which (as I hope has begun to emerge) are already intertwined in his meditations?

The answer is a complicated but I think fascinating one. In line with the Platonic and Augustinian method of *aversio*, leading the mind away from the senses, Descartes aims in the *Meditations* to deliver the mind from the confusion and obscurity arising from the corporeal part of our nature, so that the *lumen naturale*, the light of our pure intellectual intuition, can disclose the truth about ourselves and God. Given this Platonic orientation, the privileging of pure intellect, one might have expected Descartes to shun the passions as a source of sin and error, since, like the senses, they depend on our corporeal nature. The Cartesian recipe for escaping error is "avoid what is obscure and confused";[28] and any cognition derived from the passions is characteristically obscure and confused, compared with the transparent light of rational intuition. So just as the senses can distort our perception of the truth (making us judge that the moon is as large as the sun, for example, when mathematical reason tells us, correctly, that it is far, far smaller),[29] so the passions can distort our perception of the good. This indeed is the direction Descartes himself seems to want to take in many of his ethical writings, as when he writes to Princess Elizabeth:

> Often passion makes us believe certain things to be much better and more desirable than they are; then, when we have taken much trouble to acquire them, and in the process lost the chance of possessing other more genuine goods, possession of them brings home to us their defects; and thence arise dissatisfaction, regret and remorse. And so the true function of reason is to examine the just value of all the goods whose acquisition seems to depend in some way on our conduct, so that we never fail to devote all our efforts to trying to secure those which are in fact the more desirable.[30]

Yet alongside this (very traditional) view of the suspect nature of the passions, there is another strand in Descartes which (to borrow a theological term) I would venture to call *incarnational*. In discussing the relation between mind and body, Descartes insists that we are *not* incorporeal creatures like angels, pure minds inhabiting the machine of the body; on the contrary, we are very closely intermingled with it to form a true unity—what he called *verus homo* (or in French *le vrai homme*), the genuine human-being.[31] Our human nature, an integral compound of spirit and matter, was given us by God; and its operation, says Descartes, is in principle designed to benefit us. Our sensory, imaginative and passional apparatus furnishes us, not, to be sure, with clear and distinct truths, but with powerfully motivating signals that alert us to what is beneficial or harmful for the mind-body composite. This apparatus, Descartes frequently points out, operates, like all God's creation, in accordance with *uniform and immutable principles*; and the inevitable result of this is that it is bound to lead us astray from time to time (as when sugar continues to taste good to the seriously obese person, or when the dropsical patient continues to feel a raging thirst). But the system as a whole (feelings of hunger and thirst, passions of fear and love) directs us to what is *generally and in the long run* beneficial to us embodied creatures, and so "there is absolutely nothing to be found there that does not bear witness to the power and goodness of God."[32]

This theodicy of the passions, for it is nothing less than that, leads Descartes in a different direction both from his predecessor Augustine, who often connects our passional nature with the fall, and also from his early-modern contemporary Blaise Pascal, who issues a severe indictment of the senses, imagination and passions as contaminated by their inherent corporeal involvement.[33] Descartes, by contrast, has a far more optimistic view. Let us take, by way of illustration, the biblical story of the Fall.[34] What happened to Eve was, in the words of Genesis (3:6), that she saw the tree was "good for food and pleasant to the eye." On the Cartesian analysis there would be nothing wrong with that in itself: the sensory and passional faculties did indeed alert her to something genuinely attractive and nutritious; but because she focused exclusively on that, she was led to suppose that tasting the apple was (to borrow Descartes's phrase) "more desirable than it really was"—in comparison with the far greater good of obedience to God. The conclusion to be drawn from this type of case as regards the Cartesian assessment of the passions is consistent with the more moderate line found in St Thomas: the passions are neither good nor bad in themselves, but need to be put to the service of the good.[35]

This, of course, is exactly what happens in the scenario described at the end of the Third Meditation. The passion of wonder reinforces and supports the rational contemplation of the "immense light," source of all goodness and truth. The passional part of our nature, provided it is harnessed to the service of the good, conduces to our fulfilment (an idea whose roots go right back to Plato, with the notion in the *Republic* that the spirited part of our nature can serve as a valued auxiliary of reason).[36]

But how *do* we harness the passions? One of the effects of the Fall, as Augustine pointed out, is infirmity of the will.[37] In Cartesian terms, the weakness of our nature means we are unable always to keep focused on the good and the true, and this allows scope for us to be led astray by lesser or specious goods. Yet Descartes stresses that since our human nature is given us by God, it operates regularly and consistently; and this gives us the opportunity to retrain and re-programme it. Descartes's scientific theories of conditioned responses, and his psychological inquiries into how events in childhood can set up powerful associations which remain dormant in adult life, but which can later be investigated and modified[38]—all this, when properly studied, offers us humans the chance to *manage* our passions, so as to make sure they operate in the service of the good.

This optimistic vision contrasts with Pascal's view of the wretchedness of man, and our need for divine redemption; set against this, Descartes's more independent stance can seem to prefigure the arrogance of the modern technological age, which aims to take salvation wholly into our own hands, through manipulating our physiology and psychology to whatever ends we decide to pursue. Descartes clearly shared something of this vision: the new science, as he announced in the *Discourse*, would give us mastery of the natural world and of the conditions for our own health and welfare.[39] But we need to remember that this ambitious programme still remains at the service of the theistic worldview that shines out so clearly in the *Meditations*. Descartes would never have subscribed to the modern Nietzschean fantasy that we choose our own ends; for in his view these are already laid down for us by the light of reason—perceived via the faculty of clear and direct intuition of goodness and truth, which is bestowed on us as the gift of God. The passions, themselves part of the divine gift of our embodied or incarnate nature, can play a part here, as reinforcers and motivators, but only against a background where our reason glimpses what faith has never really doubted: the eternal source of truth and goodness on which every moment of our existence depends. Finite and weak though our creaturely nature may be, we can be sure, as Descartes resoundingly declares, that it contains "absolutely nothing that does not bear witness to the power and goodness of God."[40]

NOTES

1 Alasdair MacIntyre, *God, Philosophy, Universities: A Selective History of the Catholic Philosophical Tradition* (London: Continuum, 2009), p. 116.
2 See for example Descartes's letter to Mersenne of 25 November 1630, AT I p. 181: CSMK p. 29. In this paper, "AT" refers to the standard Franco-Latin edition of Descartes by C. Adam and P. Tannery, *Œuvres de Descartes* (12 volumes, revised edition, Paris: Vrin/CNRS, 1964–1976); "CSM" refers to the English translation by J. Cottingham, R. Stoothoff and D. Murdoch, *The Philosophical Writings of Descartes, Volumes I and II* (Cambridge: Cambridge University Press, 1985), and "CSMK" to Vol. III, *The Correspondence*, by the same translators plus A. Kenny (Cambridge: Cambridge University Press, 1991).

3   MacIntyre, loc. cit., emphasis supplied.
4   *Cognitio* is an important quasi-technical term in Descartes, often employed to convey a direct and isolated mental apprehension which does not require being evidenced, or deduced from other propositions. For *cognitio* versus *scientia*, see Descartes, *Meditations on First Philosophy* [*Meditationes de prima philosophia*, 1641], Second Replies, AT VII p. 141: CSM II p. 101 (and my footnote in CSM ad loc.).
5   *Meditations*, First Meditation, AT VII p. 22: CSM II p. 15, emphasis supplied.
6   *Meditations*, Third Meditation, AT VII p. 25: CSM II p. 25.
7   *"Non me fallit ingenium, quia illud a Deo rectum accepi"* ("My mind does not deceive me, since a reliable mind was God's gift to me." [or "since I received it in good shape from God"]). *Descartes's Conversation with Burman* [1648], AT V p. 148: CSMK p. 334. In arguing for Descartes's indebtedness to the "faith seeking understanding" tradition, I would not wish to deny there are important divergences from his predecessors. The trust which is presupposed from the outset of the *Meditations* is of a fairly austere variety, relating to the reliability of our (God-given) cognitive faculties, whereas a more comprehensive kind of submission is found in Augustine or Anselm. I shall however go on to argue in Section 2 that there are passages in Descartes where the tone is much closer to one of humble submission than is commonly recognized.
8   AT VII p. 51: CSM II p. 35.
9   See *Conversation with Burman*, AT V p. 159: CSMK p. 342.
10 AT VII pp. 147–8: CSM II p. 105.
11 Second Replies, AT VII p. 148, line 27: CSM II p. 106.
12 AT VII p. 58 lines 1–2: CSM II p. 40. See further J. Cottingham, *Cartesian Reflections* (Oxford: Oxford University Press, 2008), p. 228. I have drawn on material from this collection of papers in developing several of the other themes broached in the present chapter, and the reader is referred in particular to Part V of the volume in question for more detailed treatments of the various ways in which God occupies a central role in Descartes's philosophy.
13 Augustine of Hippo, *Confessiones* [397–401]; Anselm of Canterbury, *Proslogion* [1077–1078]; Bonaventure, *Itinerarium mentis in Deum* [1259].
14 *Proslogion*, Chapters 1 and 2.
15 *"Quid ergo dicamus, fratres, de deo? si enim quod vis dicere, si cepisti, non est deus: si comprehendere potuisti, aliud pro deo comprehendisti. si quasi comprehendere potuisti, cogitatione tua te decepisti. hoc ergo non est, si comprehendisti: si autem hoc est, non comprehendisti."* ("What then shall we say, brothers, of God? Whatever you say, if you have grasped it, that is not God. For if you have been able to grasp it, what you have grasped is something other than God. If you have been capable in any way of grasping him in your thought, then by your thought you have deceived yourself. So if you have grasped him, it is not God, and if it is God, you have not grasped him.") Augustine, *Sermones* [early 5th cent] 52:16.
16 *Meditations*, First Replies, AT VII p. 114: CSM II p. 82. Compare the letter to Mersenne of 27 May 1630: "I say that I know [that God is the author of everything, including the eternal truths], not that I conceive it or grasp it; because it is possible to know that God is infinite and all powerful although our soul, being finite, cannot grasp or conceive him. In the same way we can touch a mountain with our hands but we cannot put them around it as we could put them around a tree or something else not too large for them. To grasp something is to embrace it in one's thought; to know something it is sufficient to touch it with one's thought." Letter to Mersenne of 27 May 1630, AT I p. 151: CSMK p. 25.
17 *"immensi hujus luminis pulchritudinem, quantum caligantis ingenii mei acies ferre poterit, intueri, admirari, adorare."* Third Meditation, final paragraph.
18 Nor should anything I say here be taken to imply that this elaboration is not worth detailed analytic scrutiny—something I have offered elsewhere. See Cottingham, *Descartes* (Oxford: Blackwell, 1986), pp. 48–57.
19 *Rules for the Direction of Our Native Intelligence* (*Regulae ad directionem ingenii, c.* 1628], AT X p. 421: CSM I p. 46.
20 *"Qua ratione intelligerem me dubitare, me cupere, hoc est, aliquid mihi deesse, & me non esse omnino perfectum, si nulla idea entis perfectioris in me esset, ex cujus comparatione defectus meos agnoscerem?"* (Third Meditation, AT VII p. 46: CSM II p. 31.) Cf. Bonaventure: *"Quomodo sciret intellectus hoc esse ens defectivum et incompletum, si nulla haberet cognitionem entis absque omni defectu?"* (*Itinerarium*, Part III, §3).

21 The wording here is not that of Levinas himself but comes from the admirable discussion by Hilary Putnam, in his "Levinas and Judaism," in *The Cambridge Companion to Levinas*, eds. S. Critchley and R. Bernasconi (Cambridge: Cambridge University Press, 1986), pp. 33–70, at p. 42. The relevant Levinas text is *Ethique et infini* [1982], trans. as *Ethics and Infinity* (Pittsburgh, PA: Duquesne University Press, 1985), pp. 91ff. In Descartes's words, "the entire luminous power of the argument depends on the fact that this ability to have within us the idea of God could not belong to our intellect if the intellect were simply a finite entity (as indeed it is) and did not have God as its cause." *Meditations*, First Replies, AT VII p. 105: CSM II p. 77.

22 Anselm *Proslogion*, Chapter 1. I have elsewhere called this interpretation of what Descartes's meditator is doing the "cognitive confrontation" view ("The Desecularization of Descartes," typescript).

23 Thomas Aquinas, *Summa theologiae* [1266-73], Ia, q. 12, a. 5.

24 John Carriero, *Between Two Worlds* (Princeton, NJ: Princeton University Press, 2009), p. 181.

25 Carriero, *Two Worlds*, p. 213.

26 Gilbert Ryle, *The Concept of Mind* [1949] (London: Penguin, 1988), pp. 143–147.

27 The Latin term *attingere* is used in my relation to the existence and perfections of God in the Fifth Meditation (AT VII p. 51: CSM II p. 350; the verb is a compound of *tangere*, to touch. *Toucher de la pensée* ("touching in thought"), and the image of the mountain, is in the letter to Mersenne of 2 May 1630 (AT I p. 152: CSMK p. 25), cited in my translation of the Third Meditation at CSM II p. 32 (AT VII p. 46), and quoted above, note 16. See also Carriero, *Two Worlds*, pp. 176–177.

28 Compare Fourth Meditation, final paragraph.

29 Third Meditation, AT VII p. 39: CSM II p. 27.

30 Letter of 1 September 1645 (AT IV pp. 284-5: CSMK p. 264). Descartes goes on to say that the passions often "represent the goods to which they tend with greater splendour than they deserve and they make us imagine pleasure to be much greater before we possess them than our subsequent experiences show them to be." The letter concludes with the observation that "the true function of reason in the conduct of life is to examine and consider without passion the value of all the perfections, both of the body and of the soul, which can be acquired by our conduct, so that since we are commonly obliged to deprive ourselves of some good in order to acquire others, we shall always choose the better."

31 See letter to Regius of January 1642 (AT III p. 493: CSMK p. 206) for the contrast between an angel and a genuine human (*verus homo*); cf. *Discourse*, Part Five, AT VI p. 59: CSM I p. 141 (*vrai homme*).

32 Sixth Meditation, (AT VII p. 87: CSM II p. 60).

33 For the war between imagination and reason, see Blaise Pascal, *Pensées* [1670], ed. L. Lafuma (Paris: Seuil, 1962), no. 44. Cf. William D. Wood, "Axiology, Self-Deception and Moral Wrongdoing in Blaise Pascal's Pensées," *Journal of Religious Ethics*, Vol. 37, no. 2 (2009), pp. 355–384.

34 I take this as a convenient illustration, but it is not so employed by Descartes himself.

35 Thomas Aquinas, *Quaestiones disputatae de malo* [1266-72], 3, 9, ad 15.

36 Plato, *Republic* [c. 375 BC], 439d–440d.

37 Augustine, *De correptione et gratia* [426], Chapter 11.

38 For an exploration of these themes in Descartes, see J. Cottingham, *Philosophy and the Good Life: Reason and the Passions in Greek, Cartesian and Psychoanalytic Ethics* (Cambridge: Cambridge University Press, 1998), Chapter 3.

39 Descartes, *Discourse on the Method* [*Discours de la méthode*, 1637], part vi (AT VI p. 62: CSM pp. 142–143).

40 See note 32, above. I am indebted to Katia Saporiti and other participants at an April 2010 workshop on *Ideas in Early Modern Philosophy* at the University of Zurich for helpful discussion.

8

HUME *VERSUS* KANT: FAITH, REASON, AND FEELING

JOHN MILBANK

We live in a period where the humanist consensus is being challenged both by naturalisms and by more militant forms of faith. In the face of this circumstance, Jürgen Habermas proposes that we need to reinstate a firm Kantian distinction between what belongs to discursive reason on the one hand, and to ineffable faith on the other.[1] Discursive reason should recognise that it operates within strict limits and therefore is not competent to pronounce against either metaphysically naturalist or religious positions. Both must be allowed to speak in their own voices in the public domain (and one should welcome Habermas's step beyond Rawls in saying this) and yet—problematically from the point of view of democratic inclusion—official constitutional debate and decision-making must be conducted within the terms of "neutral" discourse. The latter is notably an emotion-free discourse, following Kant's views about the moral law. For despite the contortions that Kant went through in relation to the role of feeling with respect to the ethical, this played for him either a negative role as the feeling of the emptily sublime ushering us into the presence of the moral law, or a subordinate role in terms of our "feeling" that the moral should be harmonised with the sensorily pleasurable and the emotionally satisfying.[2]

Arguably, however, Habermas's "solution" merely reiterates the "agnosticism" of twentieth-century "public doctrine" and so begs the question that this agnosticism is the very thing that is coming under pressure. Quentin Meillassoux's diagnosis is here far more plausible. "Agnosticism" is breaking down for two reasons.[3]

First, intellectual: the terms of "transcendentalist" neutrality have been deconstructed within both Analytic and Continental philosophy, and

Faith, Rationality, and the Passions, First Edition. Edited by Sarah Coakley.
© 2012 Blackwell Publishing Ltd. Book compilation © 2012 Blackwell Publishing Ltd.

therefore "post-metaphysical" philosophy is collapsing—ironically because it has been exposed as the very consummation of the metaphysical as a supposedly autonomous discourse about being, inevitably mutated into a foundational epistemology. It no longer seems plausible that there is a "correlation" between the way our minds work and the way that reality is insofar as it appears to us. Instead, philosophy (again both Analytic and Continental) is proposing full-blooded accounts of nature which incorporate (with various degrees of reduction) an account of the human mind. Kantian anthropocentrism and finitism now appears, with good reason, to be unscientific and indeed to revert to the pre-Copernican. Conversely, if one wishes to defend the spiritual character of mind, it is not possible to appeal to some supposedly "given" transcendental circumstances. One needs instead a speculatively metaphysical account of the reality of mind and soul.

Hence if naturalism and religion are squeezing out the agnostic middle, this is not because the bounds of reason are being transgressed; it is rather because reason (with good reasons) no longer tends to credit such bounds. Reason is being once more infinitised—but from two opposite directions.[4] This does not at all mean, however, that such bold speculative programmes can be fully justified from a rational point of view. To the contrary, their best practitioners admit that a certain stance of "faith" is involved.

Secondly: sociological. Speculative metaphysics is not a leisurely pastime—to the contrary, it is directly linked to people's pragmatic need to direct their life by certain definite beliefs about reality. Hence metaphysically agnostic philosophy has allowed religious extremism to fill a certain void. Moreover, simply formal discursive conditions for politics and formal respect for rights do not deal with the fact that certain substantive choices and views have necessarily to prevail. Hence if one restricts reason to the formal and insists that it operates only within knowable boundaries, one will encourage entirely irrational and purely emotive political movements to take centre-stage, even though they are playing by the rules. This is what the Nazis did; Weimar was thoroughly "Kantian" and Habermas repeats the error of Weimar even though he imagines that his philosophy guards against any repetition of totalitarianism.

Indeed, any sharp separation of reason and faith is dangerous for a politics that is "liberal" in the sense of constitutional. It implies that faith at its core is "non-rational" and beyond the reach of any sort of argument, while also implying that reason cannot really have a say on issues of crucial substantive preference. But in reality reason and faith are always intertwined in a beneficial way, even if this is hard to formulate theoretically. Reason has to make certain assumptions and trust in the reasonableness of the real—as indeed Kant himself acknowledged. Faith has continuously to think through the coherence of its own intuitions in a process that often modifies those intuitions themselves. So if critical faith has to become a more reflective mode of feeling, then reason has always to some degree to feel its ways forward. What it at first seeks to know, it already knows obscurely, as Plato taught in the *Meno*—which is to say that it feels it, Plato says through the reach of *eros*.

Here the idea that if there are no absolute foundations then argument between different positions is precluded is pragmatically absurd. All arguments short of tautology have to assume an area of given agreement and to win an argument usually means (following Socrates) that one shows someone that something he imagines he thinks contradicts something which he more profoundly thinks. Outside a horizon of shared faith no arguments would get off the ground and shared faith means something like "common feeling."

The Kantian agnostic notion of public space is feeling-neutral, yet this is not the only "enlightened" model to hand. Both the Scottish and the Italian Enlightenments saw the public sphere as primarily one of "sympathy."[5] Often this just meant imaginative projection or animal instinct and this predominantly Stoic perspective tended to neglect questions of teleology or of shared "ends." But in the case of David Hume, in the long-term wake of Benjamin Whichcote through the Earl of Shaftesbury, "sympathy" at times seems to be a self-grounding end in itself, and the sympathetic links between people to be something that reason alone cannot really grasp. While we are to "sympathise" with public "utility," the "public" is itself only composed through the reciprocal bonds of sympathy, which are irreducible to any mere "original instincts of the human mind," or, in other words, any projected egoism.[6] Hence Hume's human "sympathy" remains (extraordinarily enough) a kind of "occult" sympathy, in continuity with the inscrutable binding powers within nature: "the coherence and apparent sympathy in all the parts of this world."[7] (By historical derivation "sympathy" in Platonic, Stoic and Hermetic thought meant the secret power that binds together the cosmos, the body and human society.)

One can link this with the entire character of Hume's philosophy and suggest that our current situation is "Humean" and not Kantian, both in critical and sociological terms.

Critically, Hume, unlike Kant, attempted a full-blooded "experimentalist" account of human nature and the human mind. This means that he was prepared to account for human thinking in terms of pre-human natural processes. At the same time, he was prepared to think nominalism, with which much of modern science had long been linked, through to its very limits.

However, the second enterprise clashes with the first in his thought. To explain human nature scientifically he must do so in terms of "atomic" individual substances and efficient causality. Yet Hume shows that nominalism is as fatal for individual substance as it is for universals and real relations, for efficient causation as it is for formal, teleological and material causes. In this way he turns Ockham's minimising rationalist instrument against Aristotle against even Ockham's legacy itself. Hence he says that there are, rationally speaking, only bundles of qualities and no "substance," and that any inherent "link" between cause and effect is just as occult and merely nominal as scholastic ideas of specific form.

Given this circumstance, Hume has been read three ways: 1. as a positivist, who reduces science to observation of constant conjuncture; 2. as someone implicitly calling for a Kantian transcendentalist solution; 3. as someone so ultra-modern that he indicates a new "nocturnal," proto-Romantic entry to a traditional realist metaphysics of some sort or other. On this last view, it is as if Hume knocked over all the furniture inside the Western intellectual house and then exited into the sunlight through a front door marked "reason" with a triumphantly complacent sceptical smirk on his face. But then, when no one was looking, he sneaked round to the back where the garden lay in shadows, and was conducted by a Jacobite servant through a backdoor marked "feeling" and then proceeded to put back in place at least some of the furniture he had earlier abused.[8] In fact, for this account, Hume rescues modern scientific rationality only through linking it once more (albeit obscurely) to a traditional metaphysic by ascribing a new disclosive role to "feeling."

The first two views assume that Hume was only a sceptical rationalist. The third claims that he advanced beyond scepticism in the name of feeling and the view that feeling not reason (reason being but a variant of feeling) is what *truly* discloses to us the real.

Any unbiased reading of Hume suggests strongly that the third reading is the correct one.[9] The positivist reading is false because Hume is clear that even constant conjuncture is something ineffably experienced and established according to habitual imagination and not something rationally known: empirical linkage is for him extra-rational. It is emotionally sensed and not *merely* "imagined," precisely because the imagination performs a mysterious work in excess of rational probability by assuming that an absolutely novel instance will fall into the same "historical" sequence of cause and effect as instances have been taken to so fall in the past; thus we "feel" the link of cause and effect and do not merely "speculate" that what is constantly conjoined might be in some way connected.[10]

It is of course this sense of a "connection" that Kant elaborated into a rational *a priori*, and yet the Kantian "reading" of Hume is also false because there is simply no warrant to suppose that the biases of our mind are anything other than natural, or that the phenomena we know are not the things themselves—as they explicitly are for Hume. "Correlationism" in Kant between rational category and sensory information remains a mode of pre-established harmony and it takes little intellectual effort to see the unsophisticated core of Kant's (astonishing) surface sophistication: it is only his own variant on a speculative monadology that allows an absolute gulf between phenomena and noumena which paradoxically permits the "banishing" of claims to know both finite and infinite spirit.[11]

Hume, by contrast, never denies the full ontological ("noumenal" as well as "phenomenal") reality of causation, substance, personal identity or the soul[12]: he doubts them all, but in the end finds a new way to affirm them. In a Baconian tradition he sees knowledge as to do with experience and making, but insists (after Socratic-Platonic example, as he indicates)[13] that what we most experience and make is ourselves. Even though he takes it that we are but part of natural causation,[14] he says that the best clue to the nature of the latter lies within our own self-experience. But within ourselves the experience of our own consecutive causal action is a matter of feeling, habit and imagination. One might say that we are led according to a consistent pattern to "make ourselves up."

In one place in the *Treatise* Hume indicates quite clearly that we have to assume that causality in nature is something analogous to this human process: "I do not ascribe to the will that unintelligible necessity which is suppos'd to lie in matter. But I ascribe to matter, that intelligible quality, call it necessity or not, which the most rigorous orthodoxy must or does allow to belong to the will. I change nothing, therefore, in the receiv'd systems with regard to the will, but only with regard to material objects."[15] In other words, Hume insists in an "intellectualist" manner that the will never exercises pure "free choice" but is always in some fashion "compelled." Yet this cannot be to reduce the will to the determination of efficient causality, because he has already deconstructed the latter. So even though he is arguing for a naturalistic account of willing, it is still in terms of our experience of willing that we must try to decipher causality and not vice-versa. Therefore he is a revisionist *not* with respect to orthodox psychology, but with respect to the philosophy of nature: in nature herself there must reside something analogous to "will." It follows that the primacy of feeling in Hume entails also a species of vitalism, as the *Dialogues Concerning Natural Religion* also indicate.[16]

This therefore reverses not only his scepticism as regards causation, but also as regards constitutive relation. Reason can only make sense of individual items that are shifting and unstable but utterly isolated and in no way intrinsically connected with anything else. The same must be true, rationally speaking, of our "impressions"; yet we "feel" certain unshakeable links between them in various ways. The feeling of association that sustains the link between cause and effect in our experience of thoughts then leads to a legitimate projection of intrinsic association also into the world of things, since we are otherwise unable to make sense of our experience of causality and the way in which its constant conjoining of elements seems to involve an emotive coinherence that is in excess of rational inference, as already explained.[17] Hence while the denial of internal relation lies at the heart of Hume's thought insofar as it is a merely rational empiricism, a certain "internal" (or rather "constitutive") relation returns within his thought insofar as it is an extra-sceptical empiricism of feeling that even points us back towards a metaphysical realism in the broad sense of affirming a structure to objective reality that is independent of our perceptions.[18] Significant in this respect is the fact that Hume declares that the crucial difference between mere fictions, apparitions, dreams and reality is nothing other than the strength of feeling we have in the face of the real, despite the fact that every experience of the real is only conveyed by a series of impressions that we *imaginatively* put together.[19] It is as if Hume is saying that reality is simply a very convincing and continuous story that frames all other stories. A story that we have to take to be true, like Vico's *vera narratio*.[20]

Hume, then, claims that all thought is feeling and that reason is tempered feeling; that we must trust our feelings and that there may be something "like" feeling already in pre-human nature. This concurs with the fact that he affirms and does not at all deny "design" in nature, while seeing this as far more immanent that did the Paleyite approach.[21] Clearly Hume broke with rationalism by empirically observing that reflection cannot seriously separate itself from habit and that even the most basic assumed stabilities (substance, the self, causation) depend upon habit and not upon sheer intuited "givenness." But he also began to break with empiricism by allowing (albeit in a highly reserved fashion) that, in being slaves to habit, human beings must acknowledge the workings of a natural power that *exceeds* our capacity to observe it.[22]

This is why Jacobi argued that Hume was effectively showing that all reason requires faith and why Maine de Biran and then Félix Ravaisson developed Humean insights regarding causality and potency in a more specifically vitalist direction, which eventually led to the diverse yet kindred philosophies of Bergson and Blondel.[23] Nature is a matter of sedimented habits and not laws; on this assumption it became possible for Ravaisson to reconcile Hume with Aristotle and restore a "classical" metaphysics in terms of the view that all reality is a matter of mutually affective (passive and active) response in which habit is both degeneration (as identical repetition) and elevation (as non-identical repetition). Ravaisson (who was close to Schelling in certain respects) in effect brought Jacobi and Biran's Humeanism together by suggesting that one can only explain how habit is fundamental even though it must be established, or why there is "a habit of contracting habits," by invoking theological notions of grace within cosmology itself. This is because it is *theology* that, in terms of grace, thinks the paradox of "a habit at the origin." Thus for Aquinas grace was a "supernaturally infused habit" or *aliquod habituale donum* (ST I.II q. 109, a. 9, resp.; 110 a. 2 resp.) and he subverted Aristotle by proclaiming that our only genuinely good, uncontaminated virtue in terms not only of charity but also of perfectly authentic justice and prudence, involves, under grace, the seeming impossibility of a habit that can "suddenly" begin and, just as suddenly, be lost. Ravaisson, citing however not Aquinas but Fénelon, deploys this model to conclude that, if all temporal, evolutionary being is habitual, then its deepest character must be that of "grace," which implies for him at once both "gift" and "beauty."[24]

With respect to Aristotelian metaphysics, there are certain indications in Hume that one can, after all, "feel" the operation of formal and final as well as of efficient causality.[25] This is a logical development of his view that efficiency has to do with a repeated pattern. For if there is a pattern, then there is a substantively constituting form and if there is a groundless passion then it must at least "presume" a teleological direction in order for it to be operative. Indeed, since it is our sympathies that attune us to natural reality, and since the teleological establishment of the community of sympathy is irreducible to interest, instinct or projected egoism, then it would appear that (as Gilles Deleuze argued in 1952) Hume thought that nature teleologically fulfilled itself in the human *civitas*.[26]

Moreover, Hume effectively re-establishes "substance" in terms of the view that infinite divisibility is not really thinkable for the feeling intellect and therefore should not be taken as real. There is no endorsement of an atomism here, much less any exaltation of "difference" as Deleuze argues, even though Deleuze well indicates how Hume in the end makes relation (rather than difference) ontologically fundamental, since we only think at all and only make sense of the world in terms of constitutive relations, even though pure reason must conclude to a strict nominalism that recognises only "external" ones.[27] Instead of endorsing an ontological atomism, Hume is indicating, rather like Aristotle, how in any *genus*, in order for it to be a *genus*, we have to suppose ultimate stable constituents—as, for example, geometry *must* presuppose indivisible points and lines, even though this indivisibility is not rationally thinkable and must even be rationally negated.[28]

Within the "third" hybridly Jacobian/Biranian—and I claim genuinely Humean—perspective, one can see how "feeling" operates as the crucial third term in two respects. First, between matter in motion and mind that experiences "meanings." It is not that mind "represents" an external world; it is rather that natural habits in us turn reflective, more intense and more adaptable. In a footnote to the second page of the *Treatise*, Hume actually *rejects* Lockean "ideas" and his favoured term "impression" for patterned or structured cognitive content implies an initial agnosticism as to the origins of these impressions.[29] They are neither sense impressions nor representations, even though they are assumed to be (somehow) of sensory origin. They are rather more like "phenomena" in Husserl's sense, though without his subjectivism, since they are not sharply distinguished from external "objects." (Indeed it was the influence of Hume which allowed Husserl to break with neo-Kantianism).

In this context, Jerry Fodor's neo-positivist use of Hume to support a "representationalism" of the brain is completely erroneous and shamelessly deploys only the first part of the *Treatise*.[30] For Hume is *not* a sceptic about metaphysics and a dogmatician about morals. Instead he is a sceptic concerning reason in both domains, but a trusting affirmer of feeling and "sympathy" in both domains also. Sympathy retains for him both Stoic and Platonic connotations and we fail to note that he was an "academic sceptic" like Cicero—which means a sceptic *of the Platonic school*. A kind of incredibly apophatic Platonist one might almost say.[31] Hence in his account of philosophies, which is clearly *in order of merit*, Hume put scepticism at the top followed by Platonism and then Stoicism with Epicureanism at the bottom.[32] Like Vico and Doria in Naples, he incorporates elements of Hobbes and so of Epicurus, but finally rejects this mode of materialism as "uncivil"—as too linked with a selfish individualism.[33]

This academic scepticism has its political equivalent in his "speculative Toryism" and support for the ancient if not the modern House of Stuart. Hume thought that human society only exists through the ability of monarchic or aristocratic families to combine particular with general sympathy—otherwise the range of human sympathy is too restricted to accommodate justice.[34] Hence Hume, unlike Locke, Rousseau or Kant, considers that the core of political society is a matter of substantive feeling—no mere formality could ever at bottom move human beings to collective action. It follows that a Humean repose to Habermas would include the point that political order depends always less on any formal procedure than on a "political class" however constituted or to whatever degree dispersed—that is, a class of people able to link their personal destinies with the destiny of the whole of their society: local, national or global. In this way Hume, in a no doubt over-Stoic fashion, still retains an antique virtue-perspective upon the political which Kant abandons.

Feeling is in the second place a middle term between reason and faith. Hume, the defender of Church establishment, took it that the unity of interest between monarch and people has to have sacred sanction if people are really to feel its force.[35] Likewise, in his ethics, the comparison of promise as fiction to transubstantiation as fiction (he actually says that the latter is a *more* rational notion as less "warped" by the exigencies of perpetual public interest) is not meant merely sceptically.[36] Rather, by carrying the sceptical critique of religion in a proto-Nietzschean fashion through also to ethics and to aspects of our belief in cause and substantial unity, Hume is at once chastening our all-too human assumptions and yet at the same time indicating how religion as "natural" is in continuity with the rest of human natural and cultural existence. It secures our sense of the diversity, unity, order and mystery of life in terms of the polytheistic, the monotheistic, the extra-humanly designed and the apophatic—all of which aspects of religiosity Hume explicitly affirms.[37]

It follows from this that the Humean view that what binds us together is shared sympathy cannot possibly make any easy discriminations (*à la* Habermas) between what belongs to the realm of reason and what belongs to the realm of faith. For just as, in some sense, political society at its core must always be monarchic/aristocratic, so, also, religion must always be established: in Europe we disallow public bloody sacrifice and we tend to ban Scientological offers of high cost chemical salvation not simply because we are "enlightened," but because at bottom our mode of "enlightenment" still retains a Christian colouring.

If the risk then seems to appear that fanaticism could win through the democratic process if the latter is not "transcendentally" bound to the formal use of reason, then one needs to reflect further. First, how could one ever legislate for this without in reality suppressing freedom of speech, and forever excluding those perfectly rational voices who do not accept the Kantian terms of settlement? Secondly, and more crucially, I have already pointed out how formalism gives substantive claims the licence to be unreasonable and unaccountable, even though something substantial *always* rules in the end. In this way Habermas encourages rather than guards against a problematic positivity. Faith placed behind an unpassable sublime barrier is encouraged to be dangerous faith—as much to be fanaticism as to be a Wittgensteinian fideism or an Iris Murdoch-style agnosticism, and for just the same reason.

Habermas speaks much of the possibility of the "translation" of religious insights into sheerly secular terms. But if this means into the norms governing fair communicative discourse, this translation must always mean the loss of substantive content as well as of religiosity. And it remains patronising to religious people to say that the only humanly "shareable" aspect of their truths must be a non-religious one. Moreover, this perspective is fundamentally naive and shallow. It is simply not the case that people of other faiths or of none can only embrace the insights of, say, Judaism in a purely non-religious guise. This disallows the fact that they might well allow certain intimations of transcendence to be involved in their act of partial appropriation.

For to define reason quite apart from faith is to place it also quite apart from feeling; only so can it be self-enclosed within a realm of procedural norms or structural framework for apprehension. If, by contrast, we allow that discursiveness is always inextricably bound up with emotions and is never merely austere (Habermas cleaves all too closely to Weber here), then it becomes easier to see how there can be *partial* degrees of assent as to religious perspectives, for example, in terms of the feeling that "the good" is rather more than a mere human fiction.

Of course the kind of Humean perspective which I am suggesting can favour naturalism as much as it can favour religion. The habituated and the vital might be sheerly immanent, somehow not requiring grace. This means that, if transcendentalism is both false and dangerous, we must now accept that the public space is one of a clash of rival metaphysics and not of polite agnostic neutrality. We live now in the era of Dawkins versus Ratzinger, not of agnostics and clerics equally savouring the novels of Iris Murdoch.

However, this does not condemn us to a future of unmediated violence, and I have already offered arguments as to why the return of metaphysics can temper violence on the side of religion. But the reason for optimism is more primarily because the shared horizon of feeling with its inherent fluidity permits of many substantive shared outlooks and actually *less* fosters conflict than a situation where we will endlessly debate whether formal barriers between faith and reason have been transgressed or not.[38] In the face of the arrival in the West of Islam we now see far more clearly how our shared modern Western ethos is both a development of a Christian ethos and a radical departure from it. The horror of Muslim critics of the West is often a horror at all these aspects, in particular at the religiously iconic and liturgical, the secular pictorial and theatrical, and the debasement of the latter as the modern society of the spectacle.

To these sociological considerations one can add psychological ones. In certain ways naturalism is less problematic for religion than is transcendentalism. For the *a priori* categories of understanding can in principle be psychologised with the advance of brain science—especially if they have been *already* pragmatised, as by Rawls or Habermas.[39] The norms of communicative action can be reduced to evolutionary purposiveness. All that holds out against this is freedom: the freedom of human discourse to construct the language that denies even the force of the evidence that the human person is pre-determined; the freedom of the "last experimenter" upon the human brain whose own decision to experiment can never be neurologically explained without an infinite series of experiments being carried out. These arguments defending freedom are valid, but all they defend is a freedom to experiment or a bare freedom to refuse the force of the evidence (the freedom of the crank which nonetheless oddly validates his crankiness) without any practical upshot that would incarnate freedom itself as something that makes a difference in the "real" realm of matter in motion.

Therefore no truly substantive freedom, linked to the reality of a wide range of human emotional and ethical categories is thereby established. This is because rationalism, of which transcendentalism is a mode, is unable to attribute any teleology to the will other than bare self-assertion. No choosing, outside the range of formal reason, can be defined by that reason as anything other than mere choosing. Thus in relation to neural science all it can do is to indicate a bare and contentless transcendence of the brain by a supposed human mind. As to both formal and instrumental reasons themselves, precisely because they can be publicly and exhaustively expressed in linguistic structures, they are somewhat subject to a reductionist view as regards consciousness, because we could imagine all instrumental and co-operative uses of reason as taking place unconsciously. It is at this point that the quasi-transcendental status of governing pragmatic norms (like Habermas's rules for a perfect speech community, or Rawls's "neutral" principles of justice derived from the supposition of the "veil of ignorance") slides back towards mere empirical generalisation, in such a way that they no longer protect the dignity of human freedom as such and become instead utilitarian accounts of how to coordinate the clash of inevitably differing animal perspectives. Hence within the bounds of mere rationalism one can propose, with more or less plausibility, that consciousness is sheer epiphenomenon or even, in some sense, illusion.

But if instead we speak more naturalistically of "feelings" in Hume's sense as always accompanying "impressions" and supplying them with their relative weight and significance, then we do not have any "bare consciousness" with which one could possibly dispense. For when emotion is brought into consideration, consciousness can no longer be seen as an accidental accompaniment to representation (as though a camera was superfluously self-aware) but is always a "modification of consciousness" in such a way that its *qualia* belong to a "language" (external as well as internal) that is entirely incommensurable with the vocabulary of firing neurons. Even the bare experience of consciousness is thus incommensurable,[40] but in the case of feelings one has more than an irreducible spectator, but rather an entire irreducible realm of "actors" who are emotionally-inflected states of mind giving rise to an entire evaluative register of human discourse.

So far was Hume from pointing in the direction of the reduction of mind to brain that he actually says that purely physical explanations of feelings should *only* be invoked when these feelings are pathological.[41] This means that he sustained not only the soul, but also a certain teleology of the soul. Even though he could give no rational defence of subjective unity, his affirmation of this inexplicable unity in terms of feeling involves far more of a narrative and teleological register than the Cartesian or the Kantian model of self-awareness.[42] Indeed for Hume we "make ourselves up" as fictions, but since he denies the reality of any purely self-sustained will, it therefore follows that for him we are obscurely compelled within our very own fictioning towards certain ends, such that we are also passively "made up." Nor is freedom here quite denied, because will is for Hume but a more intense manifestation of the adaptability of natural habit which at bottom he appears to see as a kind of spontaneity.[43]

Feelings, for Hume, are in some sense trustworthy: we can distil true from false feeling through long processes of experience, comparison, interacting and rational analysis—which is yet itself for Hume but a further feeling about feeling, since he sees ideas as merely reflectively-doubled impressions, intensifying their crucially accompanying emotions.[44] And as trustworthy, we can say, they are therefore not reducible to brain-processes. But this does not mean that they are "yet more interior" than the brain itself. To the contrary, since feelings are for Hume prior to identity—identity being a kind of patterning of feelings—they at first impinge from "without," or rather they impinge as our insertion within the very stream of things.

This observation then concurs with the views of modern philosophers who rightly deny that we think only with our brains and not with our bodies and indeed the whole natural and social environment within which we are set.[45] For to imagine, with Fodor, that we think only with our brains, is to remain the victim of the Lockean "mirror of nature." It is to think of the brain as a repository of representing ideas or "evidences" of things, just as Locke thought of the mind as "taking pictures" of things rather in the way that the eye reflected visible realities. But this is oddly to "anthropomorphise" the brain which is only a physical organ! All the brain does is encode signals from the senses and the body in neurological connections. Hence the reason why researchers discover that there is never any perfectly predictable one-to-one correlation between thoughts and observably firing neurons and that the networks of neurons seem spontaneously to re-order themselves in parallel to thoughts, is that what goes on in the brain is *not* the only nor even the prime material instantiation of thinking. For if thoughts as feelings and reflected feelings are in any sense real, the brain can only be the *occasion* for the arising of these things which we should more properly say are caused by our entire insertion in our environment and our active reception of this environment—just as every physical reality constitutes a "prehensive" active reception of its temporal antecedents and spatial surroundings.[46] Because neither the brain nor the mind primarily "mirrors," we can see how the crucial aspect of thought is to do with "feeling" other realities in such a way that one is both responding to them and asserting oneself in relation to them. Thought is reciprocal—it establishes a real relation, precisely because it is a species of feeling.

And far from this being an "irrational" conclusion, it is in fact what alone saves metaphysical realism and a realist basis for science. For in terms of pure reason it is impossible, as Hume saw, to understand why there are regular links within nature and hence one will tend to become sceptical about their reality. Moreover, the reduction of the mind to brain-processes must invite scepticism as to whether the brain truly mirrors anything objective, and scepticism as to the very existence of reason itself or the rationality of reality, once reason has been so denatured that one no longer considers it to be a spiritual category.

It is perfectly possible and indeed more logical for naturalism to entertain the view that we do not think merely with our brains but also with our bodies and with our environment. However, if consciousness somehow "reaches out to things" in this rather Aristotelian way, then does one not have to speak of some sort of "spiritual exchange" between action and response taking place, however rooted this may be in materiality? Is not me thinking the tree as the tree where the tree is, also me being really moved by the tree in an ontological dimension of emotion in which the tree is situated alongside myself? Would not this be the precondition of the idea that meaning is "out there" in things, as John McDowell has suggested?[47] Otherwise one would have to espouse the "direct realism" of the Franciscan Peter John Olivi as revived by Thomas Reid: but this involves (as is clear in Reid's case) a vicious mode of correlationism that necessitates some sort of pre-established harmony. Actually Hume is curiously nearer to Aristotle, as Ravaisson eventually (in effect) realised: his "feelings" which seem to migrate from things in order to shape "selves" can, not implausibly, be seen to play in a more affective mode the rational role of Aristotelian *species* which, for the Stagirite, is abstracted from the hylomorphic compound to become pure form within human cognition.

This defence of the "outwardness" of cognition and meaning in terms of the priority of feeling can also readily concur with the advocacy of panpsychism by various recent analytic philosophers.[48] If things besides ourselves belong within the space of meaning, then, in order to avoid idealism, this must be because something already approximating to mutual feeling (without necessarily being fully conscious as we experience consciousness) exists within the physical world and is indeed its most primary ontological characteristic—responsible for shaping the sedimented habits that then constitute the regular shape of the universe.

In the light of these considerations, one can see how the clash of naturalistic and religious visions is a clash that is somewhat capable of mediation—if a sheerly reductive naturalism is critically avoided.

For myself, nevertheless, I think that habit as fundamental is only explicable (if there be any such thing as "explanation") as grace, and that for this reason the grace of eternal life which we receive again through Christ—a supernatural infused habit as Aquinas puts it—is, although superadded, paradoxically the most fundamental ontological reality in the universe: the undying force of life itself. Again, for me, this force must be transcendent and not just immanent, because otherwise one is always forced to choose between the ultimacy of reason, which leads to a Promethean idealism concerning human cognition (with all its political dangers), or else the ultimacy of matter, which is what reason supposedly reasons "about"—which leads to the nihilistic denial of the reality of reason (again with politically disastrous consequences). By contrast, the invocation of the transcendent, triune God allows one to think of *reason itself as unknown and yet real*—that is of an infinite reason in which we faintly participate.[49] In this way the appearances of both matter and reason are saved and kept in play.

The same is true of the will as a desiring emotion: it too is infinitised as unknown and participated. For Trinitarian doctrine the Holy Spirit as pure desire is in one respect the desire of the Father for the *Logos*, for the rationally desirable. Yet in another respect it is equally the yearning of the *Logos* for the sustained obscurity of the Paternal source, for all the infinite completeness of the expression of this source in itself as the Son. The *Logos* is infinite form, infinite pattern, infinite habituated order, yet it only arises as the still desiring expression of the Paternal source of all being. For this source gives birth to the *Logos* through the simultaneous outflowing of the Holy Spirit as desire which is the breath of the Father or the Womb of the Word as Son. So if desire is both desire *for* habitual order and the expression *of* habitual order, it is also true that reason exists only as the infinite expression of desire and that desire is somehow unexhausted within this process which it constantly renews through its surplus of searching delight. This is why the Holy Spirit constitutes a third person within the Trinity and why the Spirit as "the spirit of wisdom" can be seen in some sense especially to express the divine essence as Wisdom which is the wisdom specifically of love.[50] In some such manner as this one might try to give a Trinitarian grounding in terms of a certain "primacy of the Spirit" to a Humean primacy of feeling—which is not at all the same as a primacy of the will. Indeed, since feeling is always for this outlook a kind of intelligencing "recognition," the primacy of feeling belongs with intellectualism, not with voluntarism.

Trinitarian doctrine in this way saves both matter and reason, just as the doctrine of integral grace or of creation as being for the sake of deification elucidates the primacy of habit.[51] The same view that there is no reason without grace also remotely suggests how even in God reason is a matter of reciprocal interaction both initially and finally led by a desire that, in some sense, "obscurely finds its way."

In this fashion I would propose that Christian doctrine makes metaphysical sense of finite reason as a mode of feeling. But conversely, since we participate in the triune life and are what we are paradoxically through the supplement of grace, orthodoxy requires that we understand the universe in vitalist and panpsychic terms (as intimated by Maximus's created *logoi* doctrine and Augustine's similar doctrine of created *rationes seminales*) precisely because the natural is ontologically inseparable from the lure of the supernatural. Ockham's theology, by contrast, within whose lineage Kant's philosophy still falls (as André de Muralt has explained),[52] by requiring a sharp separation of reason from will, as of reason from faith, and nature from grace, ensured the corralling of nature and reason in the sterile hall of mirrors which is the epistemological universe of representation. This is constituted precisely through the banishment of the mediating but ineffable third, which is feeling.

But the strange thing is, it was only after this banishment that theology and philosophy started fully to see that feeling, along with imagination, creativity and dynamic habit had always secretly played this crucial role. It was ironically precisely certain men of the Enlightenment, not always so pronouncedly Christian in their outlook, but remaining in the traditions of Italian civic humanism, who began obliquely to see this because they were already worried—in a proto-Romantic fashion—about both the non-civil consequences of nominalist materialism and the both absolutist and individualising political consequences of theological voluntarism which had engendered at once theories of absolute sovereignty and of indefeasible individual rights.

For this reason *a certain Enlightenment* (and indeed the most sophisticated and crucial one; the one that engendered political economy)—however ultimately unsatisfactory for Christians—was already concerned to restore that supra-political space which had been "the Church" under the new name of "civil society." And its goal of binding together in "sympathy" was at least a distorted echo of the earlier binding-together in charity (eschewing any merely unilateral gesture). Once one has grasped this double point one can then see that Habermas's alternative between the modern secular and the postmodern "freely theocratic,"[53] is not an exclusive one after all, even for genuinely modern times. For the idea of a "community of feeling," extended to include even the natural world, is both a Christian and a post-Christian one. Indeed it is our most crucial European legacy, which we must now both defend and elaborate.

NOTES

1 Jürgen Habermas, *Between Naturalism and Religion: Philosophical Essays*, trans. Ciaran Cronin, (Cambridge: Polity Press, 2009).

2 For my own understanding of Kant at this point, see John Milbank, *Being Reconciled: Ontology and Pardon* (London: Routledge, 2003), pp. 1–25.

3 Quentin Meillassoux, *After Finitude*, trans. Ray Brassier (London: Continuum, 2008).

4 For a much fuller account of this development, see John Milbank, "From the Mystery of Reason to the Mediation of Habit" in *The Grandeur of Reason*, ed. Conor Cunningham (London: SCM Press, 2010).

5 See Luigino Bruni and Stefano Zamagni, *Civil Economy: Efficiency, Equity, Public Happiness* (Oxford and Bern: Peter Lang, 2007), pp. 77–122. It is true, however, as Bruni and Zamagni argue, that the Scots lagged behind Neapolitans like Antonio Genovesi (directly influenced by Vico) who developed a "civil" not a "political" economy, such that the market lay *fully inside* civil society and therefore contract could still be a matter of mutual sympathy and one *might* (contra Adam Smith) care about the personal well-being of one's butcher and he about yours. In either case these thinkers deployed Epicurean and Jansenist themes (from Boisguilbert) of how order can be distilled from human selfishness and evil (Smith's "hidden hand"), but in either case also this was qualified by a humanist concern with disinterestedly binding sentiment and deliberate teleological orientation. However, the Neapolitans admitted the latter into the market in a way that the Scots failed to do. Thus Hume bequeathed to Smith too strong a division between "natural" and "artificial" justice, and because of the supposed limited reach of sympathy attributed too much to the liberal individualist contractualism of the latter. All the same, Hume's invocation of the role of aristocratic identification of familial with general societal interests, his attribution of acceptance of private property to the force of inherited association, his ideas of emotional attachment to the artificial, plus his more general interweaving of the affective and the fictional in his account of cognition means that this division is arguably somewhat more qualified for him than it is for Smith. One should also mention here that Hume's appeal to "utility" was not as yet that of Bentham, but rather meant something more like the "convenient and fitting," following the Horatian and Ciceronian coupling *utile et dulce*.

6 David Hume, *A Treatise of Human Nature* (Oxford: Oxford University Press, 1978), III, XII, vi, p. 619 and pp. 618–621.

7 David Hume, *Dialogues Concerning Natural Religion* (New York: Hafner, 1948), XII, p. 86. See also VI, p. 42.

8 We know that when he was in France, Hume was regarded as a Crypto-Jacobite and even occasionally crypto-Papist opponent of Voltaire's "whiggish" view of English history in favour of a defence of the Catholic deep past (including Thomas More) and the Stuart recent past; that Catholic apologists sometimes returned the compliment of Hume's covert deployment of the Catholic sceptics; and finally that Hume's political thought continued to inspire the thought of the traditionalists in France up to and beyond the French Revolution. This all casts serious doubt upon Alasdair MacIntyre's ascription to Hume of an "Anglicising subversion." See Lawrence L. Bongie, *David Hume: Prophet of the Counter-Revolution* (Oxford: Oxford University Press, 1965) and Alasdair MacIntyre, *Whose Justice: Which Rationality?* (London: Duckworth, 1988), pp. 281–299. MacIntyre's reading of Hume is accurately criticised by Donald W. Livingston: see subsequent footnote. It may well be that Hume is in a certain fashion *nearer* to Aristotle than is Francis Hutcheson, whereas MacIntyre has this the other way round.

9   A variant of such a reading (which I can do little more than hint at in this short article) is upheld by the greatest living Hume scholar, Donald W. Livingston, who has made the sadly rare attempt to read all of Hume's works (including the historical ones) together in the round. In his two crucial studies of the Scottish philosopher, Livingston validly compares him to Vico, insofar as both thinkers point out, and draw back from, the existential and political consequences of living according to pure reason and suggest that, by contrast, the emotions and the imagination may have an irreducible role in the discerning of truth. See Donald W. Livingston, *Hume's Philosophy of Common Life* (Chicago, IL: University of Chicago Press, 1984) and *Philosophical Melancholy and Delirium: Hume's Pathology of Philosophy* (Chicago, IL: University of Chicago Press, 1998).

10 I hope that this paragraph now answers Stephen Mulhall's question to me when I gave an earlier version of this chapter in Cambridge as to why feeling tends to be always blended with the imagination in Hume. See Hume, *Treatise*, I, I, v, pp. 12–13: "cohesion" amongst ideas "is a kind of ATTRACTION, which in the mental world will be found to have as extraordinary effects as in the natural . . . ." Hume is *not* doing "epistemology" but experimental science of mind which renders his perspective upon knowing both naturalistic and ontological. Just like "sympathy," "attraction" is to be found in nature as well as in the human mind. "Cohesion" being inscrutable for Hume, it is not the case that the "constant conjuncture" of two objects causes us to engender the notion of cause and effect by virtue of probability, since this cannot apply to the absolutely unanticipated instance. Rather we *imagine* a union of ideas according to an impulse which is a "principle of association" or else "certain relations" which are naturally given and cannot be comprehended, since they are the unknowable *ground* of all human comprehension. Jacobi was right to see that Hume undermined all "foundationalism." See *Treatise*, I, III, vi–vii, pp. 90–98 and also xii, p. 134: we only "transfer the past to the future" by "habit" and it is habit which informs "the first impulse of the imagination." Later Hume affirms that human reason is but heightened animal instinct and that our assumption of temporal consistency, although it is the very foundation of our "reason," is the work of an instinctual power that thinks in excess of the rational evidence. This instinct is a "habit" that is "nothing but one of the principles of nature and derives all its force from that origin" (I, II, xvi, p. 179). It follows then that though the cause and effect relation is only something that we "make up," that this very making up is the work of a natural causal power which is a kind of habitual flow, not a law-governed efficiency.

11 See John Milbank, *The Word Made Strange* (Oxford: Blackwell, 1997), pp. 7–35.

12 I disagree with Edward Caird that Hume's prime target is the *imago dei* in human beings. Caird bases this claim on the view that Hume attacks deductive reasoning as linked to notions of direct spiritual insight and the notion of reason as a divine spark. It is true that Hume adopts the model of Baconian inductive reason, but he also subverts it by (a) saying that the empirical knowledge of other things depends upon "Socratic" self-knowledge and (b) saying that our self-experience is of fathomless processes. Therefore reason is not *reduced* to feeling; rather, reason as the instrument of nominalist reduction is humiliated and feeling gets elevated. In terms now of feeling, the idea of insight as direct intuition is sustained and if anything extended. Moreover, in the *Dialogues Concerning Natural Religion* Hume is prepared equivalently to re-conceptualise *God*, following Plotinus, as supra-intellectual. See note 23 below and Edward Caird, *The Mind of God and the Works of Man* (Cambridge: Cambridge University Press, 1987), pp. 69–130.

13 Hume sees his relationship to Bacon as like that of Socrates to Thales: see Hume, *Treatise*, Introduction, pp. xvi–xvii.

14 Hume, *Treatise*, I, IV, v, p. 248: "motion . . . is the cause of thought and perception."

15 Hume, *Treatise*, II, III, ii, p. 410.

16 Hume, *Dialogues*, VI, p. 42. Hume's alter ego Philo (as he surely is, by and large—and note the Platonic name!) is happy to entertain the notion that the world is like "an animal or organized body" and seems "actuated with a like principle of life and motion" which is a kind of world-soul.

17 See note 10 above.

18 I prefer the term "constitutive" to the term "internal" relation, because the former implies a relation that enters into the very substance of a thing (and is not therefore merely accidental and "external") without implying that its *relata* can be logically deduced from the nature of the thing after the fashion of idealism. For if there is *no* element of external contingency in

a relation, then all relations are in the end internal to the one monad of all reality and relationality is after all abolished.

19 Hume, *Treatise*, Appendix, pp. 623–629; 629: "An idea assented to *feels* different from a fictitious idea, that the fancy alone presents to us"; I, III, viii, pp. 98–106; I, IV, ii, pp. 193–218.

20 Indeed Hume's historicism is more thoroughgoing than Hegel or Marx's because he denies that there is any reality beneath established habitual fiction—whether composed by nature or by humanity. In terms of human history there can therefore be no social order outside a continued allegiance to such fictions.

21 Hume, *Dialogues*, VI–VIII, pp. 42–56; XII, p. 94.

22 Clare Carlisle and Mark Sinclair well describe this sequence regarding habit that passes from Cartesian rationalist scepticism through empiricist scepticism to conclude in affirmed vitalism. However, they fail to allow that the inklings of the third "ontological" move are already there in Hume. See their "Editor's Introduction" to Félix Ravaisson, *Of Habit*, trans. C. Carlisle and M. Sinclair (London: Continuum, 2008), p. 7 and also their "Editor's Commentary," pp. 111–112. They do however rightly say though that Hume already tried to explain association of ideas by habit and not vice versa, such that he was closer to Ravaisson than the latter realised. Ravaisson underrated the degree to which, via Biran, he was developing a Humean lineage. See also Alberto Toscano, *The Theatre of Production* (London: Palgrave MacMillan, 2006), pp. 114–116. Toscano also denies that Hume begins to ontologise habit and sees him as concerned only with the observed "principle" of habit and not with its ontogenesis. This reading is contradicted by Livingston's demonstration that Hume's fundamental thinking is "historical" or genetic in character, rather than merely psychological or proto-transcendentalist. Hume thinks that we can "compare" a present to a past sensation and on this basis establish "ideas" because the past sensation only survives at all by always already being contained within the idea: in other words because we remember it in "narrative connection" with a present sensation. Although this is to historicise the content of habit and not habit as such, the refusal of the primacy of "presentist" association (in contrast with nearly all non-Humean empiricisms) means that habit is self-referring and deliriously abyssal: habits which arise historically are only accounted for by the habit of habit in general. This implies the ultimacy of a genetic account and the constitution of human beings through habit rather than the idea that habits reside "inside us." So however apophatic Hume is about ontogenesis, he still gestures towards it. See Livingston, *Hume's Philosophy of Common Life*, pp. 91–105. Arguably Toscano misreads Deleuze when the latter affirms that there is no "geneticism" in Hume: for Deleuze seems to line this up with psychologism and so an account of human genesis that would either be merely "internal" or cultural in character and therefore *not* an ontogenesis. Since Deleuze clearly himself favours the latter and yet also identifies with Hume's "empiricism" (while refusing the usual psychologising readings of the Scottish philosopher), one has to read his saying "Genesis must refer to the principles, it is merely the particular character of a principle" to mean that there can be no "rationalistic" genealogy (not even a Nietzschean one should be the implication) that would seek to ground the obscure "principles" which in Hume constitute relations. However, these principles *only* act historically. An ontology of habit that goes "all the way down" is also an abyssal historicism. See Gilles Deleuze, *Empiricism and Subjectivity*, trans. Constantin V. Boundas (New York: Columbia University Press, 1991). Hume's "historicism" (which is not constrained to any determined metanarrative as with Hegel or even Nietzsche) also casts a different light upon his distinction of fact from value. For if all thought is for him a matter of historically-constituted feeling, according to an unfathomable process (whose effects we can merely observe), then *all thought* is a kind of valuation, even though it still registers realities. (One can note here that for Hume, unlike Locke, primary qualities are as subjective as secondary ones and yet both can still be taken to be in some sense extra-subjective also: see Hume, *Dialogues*, I, IV, iv, pp. 225–231.) Thus factual discourse differs from evaluative discourse for Hume only in terms of a diversity of feeling. In the one case of the observation of facts we *feel* objective difference and distance, whereas in the case of ethical and aesthetic valuation we feel both a more intense connection and yet a greater uncertainty as to what in the object occasions in us the sentiment. Yet that this is a matter of objective relating of ourselves to "outness" is not by Hume, as by later positivists, denied.

23 Friedrich Heinrich Jacobi, "David Hume on Faith" 1787, 253–3a38 and Preface to the 1799 version, pp. 537–590; Maine de Biran, *Essai sur les fondements de la psychologie, Oeuvres*

complètes, Vol. 7, ed. F. C. T. Moore (Paris: J. Vrin, 2001), pp. 161–168; *Influence de l'habitude sur le faculté de penser* (Paris: L'Harmattan, 2006). Maine de Biran deployed Hume's scepticism against Locke and Condillac's empiricist "way of ideas" and followed Hume in the view that we only have an "internal" clue to notions of cause and power as operating in nature. However, he attributed to Hume a complete scepticism as to the existence of a mysterious "principle" of force within us and explained this in terms of the neglect of the centrality of touch in favour of the centrality of vision in the philosophies of Locke, Berkeley and Hume (in contrast, of course, to Aristotle). However, he is clear about the way in which Hume himself invites an ontologisation of habit: I would simply argue, along with Deleuze and others, that he underrated the beginning of this move in Hume himself. Biran, however, illustrates very well in *Influence* the logical sequence which I am advocating: 1. One tries to explain thinking in terms of motion; 2. We discover that the causality of motion cannot be thought; 3. Therefore the closest we get to understanding it is through our immediate experience of mental motion as habit; 4. In consequence, in order to avoid scepticism, we are speculatively justified in projecting habit onto nature as the pre-legal reality of causality and so in developing a vitalist ontology. In *Influence* Biran refuses any mere associationism or physicalism as inadequate to explain why sensation and action become "unconscious" as habit and why the interruption of habitual sensing and acting is emotionally distressing. He rather accounts for this in terms of "a secret activity" that belongs to "the principle of life" and that results in a sort of sympathetic fusion or "equilibrium" of a sensing organ with the object sensed. As I argue in this article, the ontologisation of sympathy is also at times hinted at by Hume.

24 Ravaisson, *Of Habit*; see also Milbank, "From the Mystery of Reason to the Priority of Habit."
25 Hume, *Dialogues*, VIII, pp. 54–55. Arguing against Cleanthes's "extrinsicist" notion of design, which was typical of theo-mechanistic physics, Philo notably says: "It is vain . . . to insist upon the uses of the parts in animals or vegetables and their curious adjustment to each other. I would fain know how an animal could subsist unless its parts were so adjusted? Do we not find that it immediately perishes whenever this adjustment ceases, and that its matter, corrupting, tries some new form? It happens indeed that the parts of the world are so well adjusted that some regular form immediately lays claim to this corrupted matter; and if it were not so, could the world subsist?" Earlier Philo has speculated that the world appears to us as if there were some kind of stabilising principle that balances and stays the work of an anarchic "actuating force." Thus alongside a kind of *élan vital*, Hume seems to argue for the notion of a formative power at work in each substantial thing that is in excess of materiality: "Let us contemplate the matter a little, and we shall see that this adjustment if attained by matter of a seeming stability in the forms, with a real and perpetual revolution or motion of parts, affords a plausible, if not a true, solution of the difficulty" [i.e. the appearance of "design" in nature]. So against the barbarism of Newtonian theology (though in deliberate keeping with Newton's admission of the working of unknown "active principles") Hume, in a "neo-Renaissance" fashion, hints at a kind of vitalised Aristotelian ontology after all. In terms of reason indeed, as the *Treatise* argues, we cannot make sense of hylomorphism, yet we cannot really *imagine the stability that we see* (in nature) without this supposition: nature appears to have an occult attraction for certain patterns into which it typically falls. Likewise in Part VII (pp. 47–51) Philo invokes the finality at work in biological generation as a model for the whole world taken as a kind of "animal" (*Gaia* as we might now say, following James Lovelock—who adopted the term at the suggestion on the novelist William Golding) against Cleanthes's argument for an extrinsic finality. For more on final causality, see XII, pp. 82, 84–86. While refusing the mere external imposition of design, Hume still affirms God as the ultimate designer on the basis of something like the view that, since reason belongs to nature, God must be eminently rational as well as eminently generative in the biological sense. He invokes both Malebranche and Plotinus in the course of a truly remarkable—and remarkably theologically orthodox—refutation of an idolised God who is a mere infinitisation of human reasoning power: II, p. 15; III, pp. 29–30. Hence for Hume, if, by virtue of naturalism one must see biological generation as governing thought—against Cleanthes Philo says it would be more natural to think of the first principle as an unconscious animal than as a knowing God—by virtue of his scepticism he has to give a certain cautious epistemological primacy to knowing over generation, since knowing is (a) the generative process into which we have the most insight and (b) the one

which, within our own experience most achieves a spontaneity of origination. So the *most* concession to naturalism that Hume's scepticism will allow is not at all an Epicurean or even a Stoic immanentism, but rather an explicitly *neoplatonic* view that God lies absolutely as much beyond intellect as he does beyond matter, reinforced by Hume's citation in the voice of Demea (whose mysticism Philo avowedly *shares*: *Dialogues* X, p. 67) of the spiritualist Malebranche's view that God is just as much eminently matter as he is eminently mind. (One can also note here that in the doctrine of the Trinity, thought and generation absolutely *coincide*.) Thus Hume always affirms transcendence and never merely immanence, just as Philo defends against Cleanthes the (Thomistic) doctrine of the divine *simplicity* by denying that God entertains "plans" separate from his own being (*Dialogues* IV, p. 32). It is partly for these reasons that one should also question the idea that Hume is abandoning the notion of the *imago dei* rather than redefining it (see note 12 above). His reported declaration to a French host that he had never met an atheist must be linked with his view in the *Dialogues* that everyone must naturally suppose that there is some sort of vital, driving force behind the entire universe and that we must assume that this is somewhat like the different processes found *within* the universe—processes which also obscurely resemble each other. Both vertical and horizontal analogies are therefore affirmed by Hume. In this light he would appear to regard the "atheist" more as a minimal theist who is extremely cautious about these analogies and thereby becomes indistinguishable from a very apophatic theologian. The theist, by contrast, insists more on the likeness, but he can only do so by *faith* (as Hume stresses) because feelings vary according to degrees of intensity that cannot be strictly measured. As Frédéric Brahami argues, Hume sees this instability of feeling as a far better way of explaining how human thought shifts and develops than that provided by the Lockean representationalist model, which cannot account for how the mind is so readily able to move from the presence of one image to that of another, nor why we habitually link diverse things beyond any scope of reason. One can then argue that Hume sees the dominance of analogy in theological discourse, with its undecidability between "atheism" and "theism" as an especially acute manifestation of the indeterminacy of feeling. Because we have at once to affirm and to deny the likeness of the intra-cosmic to the trans-cosmic we can never confidently know "just how like" or "just how unlike" the Creation is to the Creator. It may perhaps be this communicated circumstance which creates an hermeneutic undecidability for the reader as between Hume's religious scepticism on the one hand and a both apophatic and fideistic piety on the other. See Frédéric Brahami, *Le Travail du scepticisme: Montaigne, Bayle, Hume* (Paris: Presses universitaires de France, 2001), pp. 167–234.
26 Deleuze, *Empiricism and Subjectivity*, pp. 123–133.
27 Deleuze, *Empiricism and Subjectivity*, pp. 66ff., 91, 98ff., 100–101.
28 Hume, *Treatise*, I, II, i–v, pp. 26–66.
29 Hume, *Treatise*, I, I, i, p. 2 footnote 1; I, III, x, p. 106. Edward Caird rightly insists on this point. See *The Mind of God and the Works of Man, loc. cit.*
30 Jerry Fodor, *Hume Variations* (Oxford: Oxford University Press, 2003).
31 Besides Hume's citing of Plotinus in the *Dialogues*, his use of the Platonic-Ciceronian dialogue form and his speaking through the mouth of "Philo," one can cite his approving mention of the Origenist, Platonist, Freemason and Catholic covert, his fellow Scot, the Chevalier Andrew Michael Ramsey in a footnote to *The Natural History of Religion*. See *Dialogues* and *Natural History of Religion* (Oxford: Oxford University Press, 1993), *The Natural History of Religion*, note 1, pp. 190–193. Hume's citation of Ramsey's description of the immorality of a "positivist," voluntarist theology has been taken as merely ironic. Yet this seems surely over-simplistic, because in the *Dialogues* Hume abundantly shows himself aware of how something like Ramsey's Origenism could lay claim to being a far more ancient and authentic mode of religiosity. He became friends with Ramsey during his Paris sojourn.
32 David Hume, *Essays Moral, Political and Literary* (Indianapolis, IN: Liberty Fund, 1987), XV, XVI, XVII, XVIII, "The Epicruean," "The Stoic," "The Platonist," "The Sceptic," pp. 138–180.
33 Although he breaks important new ground in his systematic comparison of the Edinburgh and Neapolitan Enlightenments, and specifically between Hume and Vico, John Robertson wrongly half-assimilates Vico to Hume's supposedly more explicit Epicureanism, instead of somewhat assimilating Hume to Vico's clearly more explicit Platonism. Even though Vico incorporates elements of the French Augustinian synthesis of Augustine with Epicurus

(notably in his vision of feral fallen man), both his theology and his ontology are more Platonic-humanist than Jansenist or semi-Jansenist. See John Robertson, *The Case for Enlightenment: Scotland and Naples 1680–1760* (Cambridge: Cambridge University Press, 2005). And even though Hume can appear to take the opposite side to Vico in the great debate over Pierre Bayle's question about a possible society of atheists, his grounding of the ethical in feeling and imagination tends to approximate it to the religious, which Hume also (like Vico) grounds in feeling and imagination. Moreover, most of his polemic is directed against the idea of any *necessary* connection between religion and ethical goodness—the point being to discriminate between forms of religion, not to recommend a virtuous atheism. See David Hume, *The Natural History of Religion.*

34 Hume, *Treatise*, III, II, vii–x, pp. 534–567.
35 Hume, *Essays*, VII, VIII and XI, "Whether the British Government inclines more to absolute monarchy or to a republic," "Of parties in general" and "Of the Parties of Great Britain," pp. 47–72.
36 Hume, *Treatise*, III, II, v, pp. 524–525.
37 *The Natural History of Religion, passim*. Religion, for Hume, secures our sense of the diversity, unity, order and mystery of life in terms of the polytheistic, the monotheistic, the extra-humanly designed and the apophatic. He argues that the ancient gods were little more than modern Scottish fairies, and in either case he contends that the recognition of such preter-natural beings may be a perfectly rational acknowledgement of hidden psychic forces within nature. Polytheism has the ethical value of sustaining both social tolerance and bravery, as we can more easily imitate the heroism of the gods than the ineffability of "God." The order of the universe, however, demands monotheistic assent and morally speaking monotheism better sustains political unity. Yet pure monotheism, which is philosophical, is at variance with human capacities, and therefore must be qualified by the mediation of angels, daemons, saints and sacraments. These, in turn, when they over-proliferate, become super-stitiously absurd and thus one gets an event like the Reformation. Not only does this idea of the flux and reflux of polytheism seem akin to Vico's *corso* and *ricorso* between imagination and reason in human religious and social history, it also suggests a kind of Catholic or perhaps Episcopalian balance between the monotheistic and the polytheistic. Hume rejected both Papal superstition as proceeding from an excess of melancholy, and Protestant enthu-siasm as stemming from an excess of commercial success and material well-being (antici-pating Weber here). Yet Part XI of the *Dialogues* implies clearly a still Augustinian and Baylean bias towards the "Catholic" (in Humean terms) primacy of *melancholia* in the face of overwhelming natural suffering and human iniquity. Although Philo defends traditional religion in terms of its mysticism and ontological-cosmological arguments against modern debased attempts to see God as a supreme but extrinsic and ontic designing influence, he still denies against Demea that the "proofs for God's existence" emphatically point to God rather than to a self-designing nature. So if we "feel" the superiority of human habits and aims and suspect their elevation beyond analogous forces in nature, it is finally a certain melancholic *refusal* of nature and search for salvation which causes us to embrace the mysticism and affirm the proofs. As he is clearly represented, Philo is more sceptical than the apophatic Demea only because he is also more *fideistic*. So true religion for Hume is a melancholy seeking refuge in the *abstract sublime*, which nonetheless pulls back from Catho-lic superstition in the direction of the *beauty* of this-worldly sympathy and yet then restrains in turn the self-congratulating yearning towards enthusiasm. If this sounds like Anglican-ism, then there is no *entirely* conclusive reason to deny that Hume also thought it was orthodox Christianity. (With respect to miracles, the point is that there is never any con-vincing *reason* to affirm them.) Indeed the only explicit Christian doctrine which Hume denied on grounds of faith as well as reason was that of eternal damnation—objecting that fear of this does nothing to elevate human virtue and that it implies a contempt of the divine person. For this reason he seems to endorse his friend the Chevalier Ramsay's Origenism. See note 31 above.
38 Just as, for Hume, human beings as creatures of feeling do not really know quite how atheistic or theistic they are, so also they never really know how far they exist in the domain of esoteric faith and how far in that of exoteric reason.
39 On the relationship between transcendentalism and pragmatism in both Habermas and Karl-Otto Apel, see Jean-Marc Ferry, *Philosophie de la communication I* (Paris: Cerf, 1994). For

a scintillating account of the way in which John Rawls' pragmatising of Kant's transcendentalism creates fatal problems for his account of justice, see Michael Sandel, *Liberalism and the Limits of Justice* (Cambridge: Cambridge University Press, 1983), pp. 15–65.

40 As is rightly argued by Colin McGinn in his book *The Mysterious Flame: Conscious Minds in a Material World* (New York: Basic Books, 1999).

41 Hume, *Treatise*, I, II, v, pp. 60–61. Hume declares that he has normally refrained from describing the operation of thought in physiological terms. This is clearly because he sees the mind—as a faculty of the soul—as irreducible to the physiological: it is a spiritual power which interacts with the body by means of intermediate vitalistic "animal spirits." Thus he says here that "as the mind is endowed with a power of exciting any idea it pleases; whenever it despatches the [animal] spirits into that reach of the brain, in which the idea is placed; these spirits always excite the idea, when they run precisely into the proper traces, and rummage that cell, which belongs to the idea." It is only *mistakes* that arise from sheerly physiological influences: "the animal spirits, falling into contiguous traces, present other related ideas in lieu of that which the mind first desir'd to survey."

42 Hume, *Treatise*, I, I, vi, p. 261: "our identity with regard to the passions serves to corroborate that with regard to the imagination, by making our distant perceptions influence each other, and by giving us a present concern for our past or future pains or pleasures." Hume has just—like Plato—compared the human psyche to a "republic" containing several members who are synchronically-speaking *hierarchically* arranged in "reciprocal ties" and diachronically-speaking connected by sequences of cause and effect. The self is thus both a drama and a narrative and its only substantial identity lies in this continuity, not, as for Locke, in any "punctuality." And see again Livingston, *Hume's Philosophy of the Common Life*, pp. 91–111.

43 Hume, *Treatise*, II, III, i–iii, pp. 399–418.

44 Hume, *Treatise*, I, I, i, pp. 1–7. Hume was perhaps the first person to use the term "emotion" besides the more traditional terms "feeling" and "passion." However, little seems to hang upon this new usage. Soon, however, "emotion" in other Scottish thinkers, beginning with Thomas Brown, came to imply something definitely caused by physical "motions" such that the resultant "feelings" could not be taken to offer any clues whatsoever about reality. [See Thomas Dixon, *From Passions to Emotions* (Cambridge: Cambridge University Press, 2003), pp. 98–134.] This constitutes an enormous shift towards a radical subjectivism that took firm root in the nineteenth century and arguably renders even the eighteenth century "ancient" and in ultimate continuity with the preceding millennia by comparison. For in that century "sympathy" was still seen as disclosive of the states of being of other persons and even of natural realities: both things remain true for Hume. In the eighteenth century the passions still *mediated*, and hence the association of passion with the externality of *music* was absolutely crucial: "what passions cannot music raise and quell?" asks John Dryden in his Ode for St Cecilia that was set to music by many, including of course both Purcell and Handel. Arguably, music itself is denatured when it becomes regarded merely as a physical and mechanical arouser of "emotions" in the later Romantic period. This may be one clue to our fascination with "early music": in it we uncannily "hear" and so experience an older "participatory" ontology (in Owen Barfield's sense of an intrinsic link between meaning and objectivity, humanity and nature). Compare, for example, Carette's Baroque sonata "On the Pleasures of Solitude" which, despite its subject-matter, remains part of a *dance*, with Mahler's Late Romantic piece "Blue Flower" which, even though it is ostensibly referential, sounds both sentimental and solipsistic.

45 See Alva Noë, *Out of our Heads* (New York: Hill and Wang, 2009); Andy Clark, *Supersizing the Mind* (Oxford: Oxford University Press, 2008); Michael Tye, *Consciousness Revisited* (Cambridge, MA: MIT Press, 2009).

46 Alfred North Whitehead, *Process and Reality* (New York: Free Press, 1978), pp. 19–20.

47 John McDowell, *Mind and World* (Cambridge, MA: Harvard University Press, 1994), pp. 108–126. McDowell refuses however to make the ontological moves which would accommodate his insights about meaning in terms of allowing an ontology of nature in excess of the conclusions of natural science.

48 See David Skrbina, *Panpsychism and the West* (Cambridge, MA: MIT Press, 2005), pp. 249–269.

49 See Milbank, "From the Mystery of Reason."

50 See John Milbank, "Sophiology and Theurgy: the new Theological horizon" in *Encounter Between Eastern Orthodoxy and Radical Orthodoxy*, eds. Adrian Pabst and Christoph Schneider (London: Ashgate, 2009), pp. 45–85.

51 See John Milbank, *The Suspended Middle: Henri de Lubac and the Debate Concerning the Supernatural* (Grand Rapids/London: Eerdmans/SCM, 2005/2006).

52 André de Muralt, "Kant, le dernier occamien: une nouvelle définition de la philosophie moderne," *Revue de Mataphysique et de Morale*, Vol. 80 (1975), pp. 32–53.

53 See Vladimir Soloviev, *The Philosophical Principles of Integral Knowledge*, trans. Valeria Z. Nollan (Grand Rapids, MI: Eerdmans, 2008), pp. 53–54. Soloviev explained that "free theocracy" means that "The Church as such does not interfere in governmental and economic matters, but provides for the government and district council [!] a higher purpose and absolute norm for their activities."

9

KANT, THE PASSIONS, AND THE STRUCTURE OF MORAL MOTIVATION

JOHN HARE

This chapter is about Kant's view of the passions, which is, simply put, that he is against them. To use an Aristotelian phrase, passions are, for Kant, "named together with the bad."[1] He is typical here of a long tradition.[2] But I should say at once that the term "passions" is misleading if we are talking about Kant's theory of emotion, or feeling, or desire more generally. He has a very specific meaning for the term "passion," and part of the difficulty in comparing his view with, for example, Aristotle's, is that the usage of the term is not the same in the two authors, in particular because in Aristotle only *some* of the *pathe* (often translated "passions") are named together with the bad (e.g., spite, shamelessness and envy). First I want to lay out how Kant uses the terms "feeling," "inclination," "affect," and "passion." This will require looking at texts in the *Metaphysics of Morals*, *Religion within the Bounds of Mere Reason*, *Anthropology*, and *Lectures on Education*. Then I will discuss a famous passage in the *Groundwork* about sympathetic inclination, and that will enable me to propose two ways in which Kant thinks feelings and inclinations enter into moral judgment, and two ways in which this can go wrong. I will end with a paragraph defending Kant's view, but a full defense would take a much longer project.[3]

Feeling, Inclination, Affect, and Passion

I will start with the *Metaphysics of Morals* since this sets out most clearly the relations Kant sees between these four terms, "feeling," "inclination," "affect," and "passion."[4] Affects and passions, he says, are essentially different from each other.

Faith, Rationality, and the Passions, First Edition. Edited by Sarah Coakley.
© 2012 Blackwell Publishing Ltd. Book compilation © 2012 Blackwell Publishing Ltd.

Affects belong to feeling insofar as, preceding reflection, it makes this impossible or more difficult. . . . It even has one good thing about it: that this tempest quickly subsides. Accordingly a propensity to an affect (e.g. anger) does not enter into kinship with vice so readily as does a passion. A passion is a sensible desire that has become a lasting inclination (e.g. hatred, as opposed to anger).[5]

Desires can come and go, but when they become settled habits of mind, Kant calls them inclinations.[6] He continues,

The calm with which one gives oneself up to a passion permits reflection and allows the mind to form principles upon it and so, if inclination lights upon something contrary to the law, to brood upon it, to get it rooted deeply, and so to take up what is evil (as something premeditated) into its maxim.[7]

We have in this passage a table of relations: as affect is to feeling so passion is to inclination. When feelings are resistant to reason or reflection, or even make it impossible, Kant calls them "affects." When this resistance to reason is true of inclinations, he calls them "passions."[8] Affects are characterized by turbulence, but passions can be calm, and are then all the more deadly because they allow reflective formation of an immoral maxim, or life-policy.[9]

Note that Kant does not imply, and I will suggest that at his best he denies, that inclinations are in themselves opposed to reason or reflection. He acknowledges in *Religion within the Bounds of Mere Reason*[10] that it is tempting to locate the ground of evil "in the sensuous nature of the human being, and in the natural inclinations originating from it."[11] But he denies this, on the grounds that evil is imputable to us and the natural inclinations are not. Rather "the difference, whether the human being is good or evil, must not lie in the difference between the incentives that he incorporates into his maxim (not in the material of the maxim) but in their subordination (in the form of the maxim): which of the two he makes the condition of the other."[12] Inclinations are not in themselves the ground of evil, but what is evil is incorporating them into a maxim in a way that subordinates everything else to them. Evil, as imputable, has to be chosen, and the choice is the incorporation into a maxim. But an inclination can be incorporated in two fundamentally different ways, or, as Kant also puts it, the matter of the maxim can be given two fundamentally different forms. We can tell ourselves to pursue the satisfaction of the inclination and take any means necessary. In this case the indexing of the inclination to me, making it *my* inclination, is a necessary salient feature. Or, we can tell ourselves only to pursue the satisfaction of the inclination if this is consistent with duty, if the maxim can be willed as a universal law. In this case, the indexing of the inclination to me is not salient, since anyone can will that a person with this inclination should act to satisfy it. The same inclination can serve as the matter of the maxim in both cases, but the form is different. Kant says that in the first case I am under the evil maxim and in the second under the good maxim. We are born under the evil maxim, and it requires a revolution of the will, which we cannot accomplish entirely by our own devices, to reverse the order of incentives. Kant, in this set of ideas, is recapitulating Luther in *The Bondage of the Will*, who says that the source of evil,

> is not in the flesh, in the sense of the lower and grosser affections, but in the highest and most excellent powers of man, in which righteousness, godliness, and knowledge and reverence of God, should reign— that is in reason and will, and so in the very power of 'free-will', in the very seed of uprightness, the most excellent thing in man.[13]

Kant uses the term "passion" in his discussion in *Religion* of the three grades of evil, suggesting that passions are above or beyond inclinations. He says,

> Above inclination there is, finally, still another level of the faculty of desire, *passion* (not emotional agitation [perhaps this is affect], for this belongs to the feeling of pleasure and aversion), or an inclination that excludes mastery over oneself.[14]

The three grades of evil are frailty, impurity, and depravity. Depravity is where we adopt maxims contrary to the original predisposition to good, which is innate in us. Kant thinks, again like Luther, that there is an innate and imputable depravity in human beings, though he also thinks this propensity is not essential to us, in that we can be fully human and overcome it. In this way the propensity to evil is unlike the predisposition to good, or the seed of goodness, which *is* essential to us. So we are born under the evil maxim that subordinates duty to happiness. But this is not the same as the lower grades of evil that can coexist with the revolution of the will by which we come under the good maxim that subordinates happiness to duty. As in Luther, we can be *simul justus et peccator*, at the same time justified and sinner. Kant takes himself to be interpreting Paul in Romans 7 and (unlike some commentators, but like Luther) he takes Paul to be describing his state after conversion. Frailty is where an inclination is subjectively stronger than the good, which is "an irresistible incentive objectively, but is subjectively the weaker (in comparison with inclination) whenever the maxim is to be followed." So here is an inclination, or habitual desire, which wins repeatedly in the civil war, but is not yet taken up into a maxim of living contrary to the moral law. The frail person may be under a purely good maxim, but this does not have the right force to produce good action. I will suggest at the end of this chapter that Kant could, though he does not in this passage, appeal to the notion of respect here, which is a feeling occasioned by consciousness of the moral law. The frail person is deficient in respect.

Frailty is different from impurity, where "although the maxim is good with respect to its object and perhaps even powerful enough in practice, it is not purely moral, i.e. it has not adopted the law *alone* as its *sufficient* incentive."[15] For Kant, desire is always present for human action.[16] The presence of desire, or (in its habitual form) inclination, is therefore not what prevents an action from being morally permissible. But when the will is moved by the law as the only sufficient incentive, the desire or inclination is taken up into the maxim as matter formed by the subordination of happiness to duty. With impurity, by contrast, even if the choice to do what conforms with the law prevails, "it needs still other incentives beside it in order to determine the power of choice for what duty requires." This is different from depravity, because there is no decision in principle to make duty subordinate to happiness. But impurity is different also from frailty because the commitment to the good needs a supplement from inclination that is more than just respect for the law.[17] Kant describes what is presumably a relatively benign case of impurity in *Metaphysics of Morals*[18] where he says we should cultivate sympathetic feelings and, for this reason, we should not avoid places (like poorhouses and hospitals) where we will find poor and sick people, because sympathy is one of the "impulses nature has implanted in us to do what the thought of duty alone might not accomplish."[19]

Kant gives us examples of what he means by passions later in *Religion*, where he discusses the role of society in the origin of evil, and in its solution. He says,

> It is not the instigation of nature that arouses what should properly be called the *passions*, which wreak such great devastation in his originally good predisposition. . . . Envy, addiction to power, avarice, and the malignant inclinations associated with these, assail his nature, which on its own is undemanding (*an sich genügsame*), *as soon as he is among human beings*.[20]

The passions here are malignant inclinations occasioned by our contact with and our dependence upon other people, which, as social beings, we cannot do without.

Kant also draws the distinction between affects and passions in the *Anthropology*, and again ties passion to inclination and affect to feeling. He says,

> Inclination that can be conquered only with difficulty or not at all by the subject's reason is *passion*. On the other hand, the feeling of a pleasure or displeasure in the subject's present state that does not let him rise to *reflection* (the representation by means of reason as to whether he should give himself up to it or refuse it) is *affect*.

With respect to affects, Kant accepts the Stoic principle of apathy, that the wise person must never be in a state of affect,[21] because affect makes us (more or less) blind. A couple of examples will help us understand this point. Fear is a feeling but not yet an affect, but a panic attack (*Schreck*) is an affect, preventing us for the moment from seeing our situation as reason would present it to us. Similarly hilarity (*Fröhlichkeit*) is a feeling but not yet an affect, but when it becomes convulsive it is an affect, causing us for the moment to lose rational control. But Kant is not completely steadfast in his endorsement of the elimination of affect, because he allows in the *Anthropology* two cases where reason itself *produces* affect. For example, "courage as affect (consequently belonging in one respect to sensibility) can also be aroused by reason."[22] Kant imagines that we do something worthy of honor, and do not allow ourselves to be intimidated by taunts and derisive ridicule of it, and (I conjecture) he thinks this may require a temporary feeling, which I will call (though Kant does not) "bravura," that is like an affect because it has the same phenomenal character of independence from reason, even though reason arouses it. There is a parallel passage in the *Metaphysics of Morals*,[23] where he talks about "an aesthetic of morals," in which "the feelings that accompany the constraining power of the moral law (e.g. disgust, horror, etc., which make moral aversion sensible) make its efficacy felt." A second example in the *Anthropology* is when "he who thoughtfully and with a scrutinizing eye pursues the order of nature in its great variety falls into *astonishment* at a wisdom he did not expect: an admiration from which he cannot tear himself away. . . . However, such an *affect* is stimulated only by reason."[24]

Passion, on the other hand, is described as "inclination that prevents reason from comparing it with the sum of all inclinations in respect to a certain choice."[25] Unlike affect, passion is not a temporary tumult, but allows the reflective adoption of a maxim contrary to practical reason. Kant accepts the Stoic principle that wisdom admits of no passions at all.[26] Again an example will help. Kant thinks that ambition (*Ehrbegierde*, literally the desire for honor) is an inclination whose direction is approved by reason, but it is properly accompanied by all sorts of other desires, for example the desire to be loved by others, and for the maintenance of financial security. But when ambition becomes a passion, it is blind to these other ends, and it overlooks completely the risk of being hated by others, or impoverished through the required expenditure. Nevertheless, Kant thinks that we never lose the predisposition to good, and so some receptiveness to the moral call, however sunk in vice we become. So even in the passion, a person will feel the call of freedom, and will groan in his chains, but he cannot break away from them "because they have already grown together with his limbs."[27]

I will close this section of my chapter with a couple of passages from Kant's *Lectures on Education*. He says,[28] "the first step towards the formation of a good character is to put our passions on one side. We must take care that our desires and inclinations do not become passions, by learning to go without those things that are denied to us." Here he is explicit that not all desires and inclinations are passions, but we have to control them so that those which have the potential to become passions do not in fact do so. This requires, as the Stoics said, that we "bear and forbear." Earlier he gives an example of what controlling a desire or feeling is like. He describes with admiration how the Swiss venture along the narrowest paths with perfect confidence, and leap over chasms.

> Most people, however, fear some imaginary danger of falling, and this fear actually paralyses their limbs, so that for them such a proceeding would be really fraught with danger. This fear generally grows with age, and is chiefly found in those men who work much with their heads.

The way to avoid this is to allow children to climb, run and jump, of their own accord putting their strength to the proof. They will learn by experience when there is danger and when there is not, and their fear will not be out of control; it will not be, as he says in the *Anthropology*, an affect. Another example is anger. Children have to learn how to control it, and Kant suggests that it should not be the parent's goal to *thwart* the child (because the child's inward rage will be all the stronger, even if he does not show it). On the other hand, if the children can get whatever they want by making a fuss, this increases the incentive to rage. So the parents should give the children what they want, if there is no important reason to the contrary, and if there is such a reason, it should not be given, and the parent should not then back down.[29] Anger, when it becomes a controlling desire for revenge, has become a passion.

The general point I want to make here is that Kant has an account of desires and inclinations which are not in themselves opposed to reason, and which can be and should be harnessed by reason. When desires and inclinations *are* opposed to reason, he calls them passions, and he is against them.

Inclination and Duty

There is a passage in the *Groundwork* that is often held to be inconsistent with this account. But I think Barbara Herman has been successful in her exegesis of the passage, and it does not have this implication.[30] Kant describes persons "of so sympathetic a temper that, without any further motive of vanity or self-interest, they find an inner pleasure in spreading happiness around them."[31] But such an action,

> however right and amiable it might be, has still no genuinely moral worth. It stands on the same footing as [action from] the other inclinations—for example, the inclination for honor, which if fortunate to hit on something beneficial and right and consequently honorable, deserves praise and encouragement, but not esteem; for its maxim lacks moral content, namely, the performance of such actions, not from inclination, but *from duty*.

When I teach this passage, I often find that my students object. Action from duty, for example visiting a patient in hospital, seems less attractive, less desirable than doing that same thing out of love for the patient. If Kant's point were that the sense of duty is more reliable than sympathy, we could again object, on empirical grounds. People who find an inner pleasure in spreading happiness around them can be *more* stable than those acting only from conscientiousness. My students' unease grows with the second stage of the example, where Kant imagines this same "friend of man" so overcome by sorrow that he is no longer moved by the needs of others. Kant continues, "Suppose that, when no longer moved by any inclination, he tears himself out of this deadly insensibility and does the action without any inclination for the sake of duty alone; then for the first time his action has its genuine moral worth." Richard Henson responds, "Surely the most obvious way of generalizing from this remark yields the doctrine that only when one acts from duty alone—'without *any* inclination'—does [the] act have moral worth."[32] But this doctrine seems wrong.

Herman explains this passage by denying this implication. She points out that it is the *same person* in both stages of the example. He is a man of sympathetic temper who normally helps others because he is stirred by their need but sometimes, when he is in depression and his affective life has gone grey, he helps them because that is what duty requires. We do not need to suppose that his character changes. He is still a sympathetic kind of person, but in the new circumstances (of depression) the inclinations are not there to get him to act. Of *him* it was true that when he had the inclination, he did not act from duty. But there is no implication that for *others* the motive of duty requires the absence of inclination. Kant's point is just that there is a particular kind of worth, which should occasion esteem. Sympathetic inclinations have a different kind of worth, which occasions praise and encouragement, but not esteem. The maxim of the person who acts from duty has moral content, and so moral worth, and the action of the "friend of man" does not. What is this moral content? The maxim of the act of helping has to be willed under the Categorical Imperative procedure, as a universal law. Herman mentions an example to show that merely helping is not going to be enough. "Suppose I see someone struggling, late at night, with a heavy burden at the backdoor of the Museum of Fine Arts. . . . The class of actions that follows from the inclination to help others is not a subset of the class of right or dutiful actions."[33] In terms of the Third Formula of the Categorical Imperative in the *Groundwork*,[34] the Formula of the End-in-Itself, we could put the point this way. I am required to share the ends of those affected by my actions, and so make them my ends, but only if those ends are morally permitted. Kant can be understood as translating the Lutheran doctrine of sanctification this way: We grow towards being the kind of person who is not without inclinations, for we would cease to be human, but whose inclinations are in line with duty.

One small revision of Herman's account is necessary. She puts her point in terms of over-determination (replying to Henson). But it is better not to think about the usual case as one where inclination and the moral incentive are two rival determining factors, of which only the second is necessary and sufficient for moral worth.[35] It is tempting to think of incentives or motives acting mechanically, pushing and pulling like rival physical forces. But the rational motive is precisely not that kind of cause. Kant often uses the metaphor of form and matter, from Aristotle. The Categorical Imperative procedure, for example in its First Formula that requires that a maxim can be willed as universal law, gives us the form. But the matter of morality, which goes under that form, is standardly provided by desire and inclination, though Kant wants to preserve the possibility of duty motivating all by itself. I desire to borrow money without paying it back, and so I propose to myself the maxim of a false promise. But this matter resists the form, or is recalcitrant to it. In Aristotle, form is standardly not something separable from matter, but it is the specifying activity of a kind of living thing, and is the cause (in Aristotle's sense) of the development of the matter of the organism.[36] Matter does not exist on its own (except perhaps as prime matter, but that is for a different discussion), and neither does form (except in the case of God and the intelligences), but they exist together within material substance. This is important for Aristotle because he wants unity in the definition of substance, and he achieves this by saying that the matter is potentially just what the form is actually. The fact that there is material cause as well as formal cause does not mean that the substance is "over-determined." We cannot simply read forward the details of Aristotle's account into Kant's metaphor, but in the present context they fit. The choice against a false promise is a choice against an action in the world for an end in the world in a situation that arises in the world, and it is this conjunction of particulars that is recalcitrant to the morally good form.[37] There is no such thing as the material incentive being practical all by itself. It has to be taken up into a maxim either under the morally good form or its opposite, which subordinates duty to inclination. In the usual case, if there were no desire or inclination there would be no processing under the Categorical Imperative, which serves as a limiting condition.[38] When we do process the inclination, we acquire an "interest," in the sense of "a connection of pleasure with the capacity for desire that the understanding judges to hold as a general rule."[39] An interest is a settled pattern of affection and rational endorsement, and is thus a pattern of what Aristotle calls "deliberative desire," where "the reasoning affirms what the desire pursues."[40]

The objection may be raised that there is also the *unusual* case in which Kant says the person "is no longer moved by any inclination."[41] But even here, there is something the person is moved by, namely the person's respect for the moral law, and this respect still has to be incorporated into a maxim, if it is to result in a free action. There is no such thing as the matter even in this case being sufficient for an action. I will say more about respect in the following section. If an inclination were to be sufficient in the sense that it could lead to action without the motive of duty, this would have to be because the agent is under the evil maxim that subordinates duty to inclination.

The Structure of Moral Motivation

Having laid the groundwork, we can now go on to describe the ways in which Kant thinks desires and feelings enter into moral judgment, and the ways in which this can go wrong. Some of this will be obvious from what I have already said. I will be responding here to an important paper by Karl Ameriks, who locates Kant's theory of moral motivation against the background of two debates within contemporary Anglo-American metaethics.[42] The debates are between "internalists" (who hold that motivation is internal to moral belief or moral judgment) and "externalists" (who hold that it is external), and between "realists" (who hold that moral judgment is about moral properties that are really there in the world independently of volition or desire) and "expressivists" (who hold that it is an expression of volition or desire).[43] Since there are many varieties under each of these labels, and since these are two of the most difficult topics in moral philosophy, it is not sensible in this chapter to try to lay out all the options. I will proceed by discussing the two positions within these debates that Ameriks wants to deny that Kant holds. The first position is "motive internalism," the position that "believing that something ought to be is tantamount to (i.e., has 'internal' to it) being committed to trying to bring it into being." Ameriks quotes a statement of this view from Michael Smith: "If someone judges that it is right that she does X, then, *ceteris paribus*, she is motivated to X."[44] Note that this is an internalism about moral judgment. Kant does not use "judgment" in exactly this sense, but I am going to defend the claim that he is an internalist about ethical "propositions" when these play the role in life that he is most interested in showing they can play. But what matters is not the label, whether Kant is a kind of internalist, but to give a convincing account of what Kant in fact thinks about the relation between judgment (in Smith's sense) and motivation. The second position that Ameriks wants to deny that Kant occupies is the "constructivist" position that "the validity of our judgment must be basically the effect rather than the cause of the relevant feeling" or (a different form of constructivism) that moral principles are constructed out of the "very idea of having a 'practical identity' at all, and these roots are what lead to, rather than presuppose, the rationalist Kantian perspective."[45]

Ameriks lays out four stages that Kant thinks an agent goes through, with the fourth being the action itself, and I am going to add a fifth at the beginning, which is a supplement rather than a revision to Ameriks's account because he simply starts later in the process. My first stage is where the agent feels a desire or inclination for something. Usually, as I have said already, action starts with desire or inclination, and this does not differentiate a moral agent from any other kind of agent. The same would be true even if an agent had no interest in morality, but only in prudence (in making herself happy). The difference in a moral agent is that she is concerned with whether the maxim that prescribes satisfying this desire can be willed as a universal law. The second stage is applying the test of the categorical imperative. This is an intellectual procedure, a testing for one of two different kinds of consistency. This is not yet an act of willing. It would be possible for a person to determine that a maxim could be willed as universal law without thereby *willing* it as universal law.[46] But in humans, though not in rational beings as such, the apprehension of a maxim that can be willed as a universal law creates in us a third stage, what Kant calls "respect." Respect is a feeling, but it is unique in that it is occasioned only by the presentation by reason of the pure practical law.[47] This feeling is not the ground of morality, but is a consequence of our apprehension of the moral law. But there is, so-to-speak, a feedback mechanism, because the feeling of respect "promotes the influence of the law on the will."[48]

This is a problematic moment for Kant, because he cannot allow causal influences from the phenomenal realm on the noumenal. He tries to mitigate the difficulty by saying that all we feel is the dislodgement of an obstacle, not a direct influence on the will. The obstacle is our self-love, and so our attachment to the satisfaction of our inclinations as a sum, and the obstacle is removed by the lowering of our sense of the worth of this satisfaction in comparison with the worth of the moral law. Kant calls this our "humiliation," and says that the effect we perceive is negative. But rather like a pair of scales, where lowering one scale raises the other, the lowering of "the pretensions to self-esteem on the sensuous side is an elevation of the moral, i.e. practical, esteem for the law on the intellectual side."[49] Respect is thus like the feeling of the sublime, which also starts from a negative moment (e.g., a sense of one's smallness) and ends with a comparative sense of the higher worth of something inside oneself. We can say that because of this positive effect, or elevation, "respect for the law is not the drive to morality; it is morality itself, regarded subjectively as a drive, inasmuch as pure practical reason, by rejecting all the rival claims of self-love, gives authority and absolute sovereignty to the law."[50]

Since respect "promotes the influence of the law on the will," we can assume that the willing of the morally good action comes after the respect has had this influence. This, then, is the fourth stage, the willing of the morally good maxim as the agent's own maxim, as a maxim *for her*. Kant talks about willing that the law be *my* law, which is what it means for the law to be *practical*. The respect is taken up, or incorporated, into the agent's maxim.[51] Note that there is still a gap between the adopting of a maxim and

the action itself. I do not mean merely that there may be external impediments to the action (if the bus is late, for example), but that there may still
be internal impediments to an action *with moral worth*. We still have to make
room for what Kant calls impurity, "where although the maxim is good with
respect to its object and perhaps even powerful enough in practice, it is not
purely moral, i.e. it has not adopted the law *alone* as its *sufficient* incentive."[52]
We can see how to make room for impurity if we can suppose, as is strongly
suggested by Kant's language of "elevating" and "lowering" and "promoting the influence," that respect comes in *degrees*. There may be enough
respect for a person to adopt a maxim that is good in terms of its object, but
not enough so that it would lead to action if this incentive were to be all
alone. (As argued earlier, this does not mean that the morally worthy action
has to be *in fact* without any other incentive, but that the moral incentive
would be enough even if it *were to be* alone.) If there is enough respect, then
there will not be impurity, and the resulting action (the fifth and final stage)
will have moral worth strictly speaking.

If this account is correct, what is the implication about whether Kant is or
is not some kind of internalist? It will be helpful to describe a small piece of
twentieth-century Anglo-American Kant-exegesis here, and ask whether it
contains an insight worth preserving. John Austin coined the term "descriptive fallacy," and said that Kant had already discovered it.

> It has come to be commonly held that many utterances which look like
> statements are either not intended at all, or only intended in part, to
> record or impart straightforward information about the facts: for
> example, "ethical propositions" are perhaps intended, solely or partly,
> to evince emotion or to prescribe conduct or to influence it in special
> ways. Here too KANT was among the pioneers.[53]

No doubt Austin had in mind passages like Kant's famous introduction to
the formula of universal law in the *Groundwork* (in H. J. Paton's translation),
as "the formula containing the only proposition that can be a categorical
imperative."[54] In Anglo-American moral philosophy, the alternative that
ethical propositions are intended to express emotion had been taken by the
emotivists, A. J. Ayer in *Language, Truth and Logic*, and more systematically
Charles Stevenson in *Ethics and Language* (who also emphasized the role of
moral language as a social instrument of persuasion). On Stevenson's
account, normative judgments express attitudes and invite others to share
these attitudes. R. M. Hare (who called his view "universal prescriptivism")
took Austin's other alternative, that these "propositions" are intended to
prescribe conduct. He reports that a key step in the development of his view
was when H. J. Paton drew to his attention "the essential similarity between
Stevenson's 'attitudes' and Kant's maxims."[55] Contrary to Stevenson,
however, Hare wanted to preserve the prescriptive force of these "propositions" without sacrificing their rationality. His *Language of Morals* can be

understood as a restatement of a rational ethics in the Kantian mold, acknowledging the recent developments in the philosophy of language associated with Austin and the "ordinary language" school.[56]

I want to suggest that there is an insight here about the relation between ethical propositions and motivation that is worth preserving, and that fits the texts of Kant, though it is not required by them. Going back to the five stages I have just described from Kant, the connection between the proposition and motivation will depend on where the proposition comes in the stages. I said I would defend the claim that Kant is a kind of internalist. I will put this, as Ameriks does (quoting Smith) in terms of judgment, though, as I said earlier, Kant does not use the term "judgment" in quite this way. The first thing to say is that there could be judgments at *any* of the stages: the judgment that I am feeling the initial inclination (or, differently, the judgment that expresses such an inclination), the judgment that a maxim passes the Categorical Imperative test, the judgment that I am feeling respect (or, differently, the judgment that expresses this respect), the judgment that I am willing (or the judgment that expresses a willing), and the judgment that I am acting. But the judgment at the fourth stage is particularly important if we are interested in ethical propositions being *practical*. Kant says that the moral law, which is the objective determining ground of the morally good will, "must at the same time be the exclusive and subjectively sufficient motive of action if the latter is to fulfill not merely the letter of the law but also its spirit."[57] The motive is what actually moves the person to action, though as a reason rather than as a cause. Willing is causing, but unlike all other kinds of causing (except, perhaps, transcendental apperception), it is free. It is a plausible interpretation that an ethical proposition at the fourth stage, where there is enough respect so that an action with pure moral worth results, has an internal relation, on Kant's view, to the motive, and it has this because, as a first-person imperative, it expresses the already-present will.[58] If the moral law can be related to the will in *this* way, then it can be practical. Kant says: "The pure understanding (which in such a case is called reason) is practical through the mere representation of a law."[59] One merit of the five-stage account is that we can see how the very same form of words, or the very same representation, could, at *other* stages, not be practical (for example, at the second stage, where an amoralist could determine that a maxim could be willed as a universal law). The possibility of the amoralist is supposed to be the main objection to internalism. The difficulty is mitigated if we can see that an amoralist is perfectly possible, as long as she is not attributed a moral judgment at the fourth stage, with full respect for the law. But no-one ever supposed the amoralist does *that*. It is exactly this role for an ethical proposition whose possibility Kant is especially interested to defend.

This interpretation of what it means for an ethical proposition to be practical is not the only possible interpretation. One could suppose instead, for example, that an ethical proposition is entertained in its completeness by the intellect and it becomes practical when there is a subsequent and independent act of will. But this interpretation is hard to sustain, if we treat the ethical proposition as a maxim, and grant that the maxim has an "internal relation" to the motive, and the motive is what is actually moving the agent as a reason for action.[60] Surely it is more natural to take the moral maxim as a command that the will addresses to itself, or, less metaphorically, that the person in her willing addresses to herself.[61]

We can now see two ways in which our affective lives are involved in Kant's account of the good will, and two ways in which our affective lives could be an obstacle. The first way is that feelings and desires usually provide most of the material for the maxim that is eventually willed. The difference between a morally good maxim and a morally impermissible one is not that only the first takes its matter from our affective lives. But the matter contributed by a good person's affections (in the broad sense) is receptive to the form that morality provides, and the maxim that incorporates them can be willed as universal law. So one way our affective lives can be an obstacle is, as Kant puts it in the *Lectures on Education*, when the desires and inclinations have become passions, and so in themselves resistant to reason, or to the form that morality provides. The second way our affective lives are involved in good willing is that when we have determined that the matter can take the required form, we human beings still need something in our affective life to get us to the corresponding willing. We need, that is, respect, and (if I am right) *enough* respect so that the moral incentive can be sufficient (even if, as is usually the case, not in fact alone). Again I am speculating, because Kant does not put it in exactly this way, but I think he thinks that all humans, however depraved, have *some* respect for the moral law. This is guaranteed by their predisposition to the good. But not all humans have enough respect to will a maxim that is good in its object, or even if they do this, enough respect so that the moral incentive is sufficient. So the second way our affective lives can be an obstacle is if we have deficient respect, or (though I have only briefly discussed these) the other moral feelings that come under "an aesthetic of morals."

I want to end with a brief paragraph in defense of this complex view of our affective lives. Kant does not think, at least at the time of the Second Critique and later, that he can justify the claim that we are under the moral law. He simply starts from what he calls "the fact of reason" that we are so bound. But if we are under the moral law, and so under the obligation to treat every human being as an end and no-one merely as a means, we can see why emotions, or desires, or affections, or passions in the broad non-Kantian sense have to be kept limited in their authority over us. We have to have some way of knowing that they have not turned into what Kant calls affects or passions. To use a humble analogy, the affections give us goals to pursue, and this is like driving in a car to some destination. Usually there will not be much point in driving if we are not trying to get somewhere. But we need to make sure that our driving to this destination is consistent with the goals of the other drivers on the road. We have to check in our rearview mirrors, stay a safe distance behind the vehicles in front, and so on. This is because our getting to our destination is no more important (from what Henry Sidgwick called "the point of view of the universe") than their getting to theirs. The other drivers count morally the same as we do. Some philosophers have denied that it makes sense to talk about the point of view of the universe, or that even if it does make sense, it is inconsistent with human agency. I am not going to try here to refute this view. But if we start, like Kant, from the fact of reason, we can see that the affections do not in themselves carry the necessary limitation or constraint. Some of them are in themselves hostile to such constraint (Kant calls them "affects" and "passions"), and others are not. But even the ones that are not need the supplement that before we act on them, we consider the well-being of all those affected by what we propose to do, and we count all those people equally. Only this consideration will give what Kant calls "moral content" to the maxim of our action, and so give the action moral worth.[62] This paragraph will not persuade anyone who does not already agree that we have moral obligations of a Kantian kind. But it would be too large a task for the present chapter to try to say more.

NOTES

1   The phrase is from Aristotle's *Nicomachean Ethics*, II, 6, 1107a10.

2   I will mention just three examples. Gregory Nazianzen, *Verses*, bk. 1, 10, "Formerly he was not counted among the wise, but rather was a servant of exceedingly shameful pleasures; later, he was possessed by a longing for the good, and…suddenly he was seen getting the better of the passions," *Patrologia Graeca*, ed. J. P. Migne (Paris: Garnier, 1857–1866), Vol. 35. Erasmus, *The Handbook of the Militant Christian*, 18th rule, "If, when passion stirs us to commit sin, we recall how loathsome, abominable, and detestable sin is, this will help to counteract the temptation," *The Essential Erasmus*, trans. John P. Dolan (New York: Mentor-Omega Books, 1964), p. 81. He mentions, in a list of the passions very similar to Kant's, ambition, envy, gluttony, lust, avarice, pride and haughtiness. A source closer to Kant himself is Rousseau, who talks of conquering our passions by acting on the terms of the general will, in "Political Economy," *Oeuvres* 3: 364–365.

3   There is a substantial recent literature defending Kant's view or a Kantian view of the emotions. I would mention especially Nancy Sherman, in a series of articles, particularly "The Place of Emotions in Kantian Morality," in *Identity, Character, and Morality: Essays in Moral Psychology*, eds. Owen Flanagan and Amelie Rorty (Cambridge, MA: MIT Press, 1990); Barbara Herman, *The Practice of Moral Judgment* (Cambridge: Harvard University Press, 1993); Marcia Baron, *Kantian Ethics Almost without Apology* (Ithaca, NY: Cornell University Press, 1995); G. Felicitas Munzel, *Kant's Conception of Moral Character* (Chicago, IL: University of Chicago Press, 1999); Robert Louden, *Kant's Impure Ethics* (Oxford: Oxford University Press, 2000); Patrick Frierson, *Freedom and Anthropology in Kant's Moral Philosophy* (Cambridge: Cambridge University Press, 2003); and Jeanine Grenberg, *Kant and the Ethics of Humility* (Cambridge: Cambridge University Press, 2005). The details of the Kant-exegesis in these texts varies, but a common thread, which I want to endorse, is the complaint that the secondary literature has often mischaracterized the opposition Kant draws (e.g. at *Groundwork of the Metaphysics of Morals* 4, p. 400) between reason and inclination as one of exclusion rather than control. I have not used the term "emotion" in this paper, because Kant does not. His closest term is perhaps *rührung* (e.g. *Critique of Judgment* 5,

pp. 273f). The term "emotion" in its current sense is a nineteenth-century invention. See Thomas Dixon, *From Passions to Emotions: The Creation of a Secular Psychological Category* (Cambridge: Cambridge University Press, 2003).

4 The difference between feeling and desire is that the faculty of desire is the faculty of choice ("Desire is the self-determination of a subject's power through the representation of something in the future as an effect of this representation. Habitual sensible desire is called inclination," *Anthropology* 7: 251). Feeling does not, *qua* feeling, have representational content. Desire is connected to feeling because it is standardly (though not always) aimed at the feeling of pleasure and avoiding the feeling of pain. But not all pleasure is conversely connected with desire. See also *Metaphysics of Morals* 6, pp. 212–213.

5 6, p. 408.

6 I will not, in what follows, observe this distinction between "desire" and "inclination," unless it is necessary for the argument, and Kant does not always observe it.

7 Kant's distinction between affect, as brief, and passion, as lasting, is not present in his earlier lectures on Anthropology (e.g. the 1776 Friedlander notes, 25, pp. 589–591, 612). See Frierson, op. cit., p. 180.

8 A fuller treatment would also look at Kant's discussion of the affect of enthusiasm, *Critique of Judgment* 5, pp. 272–275, where he likewise distinguishes between the affect and the related passion, fanaticism, saying that the affect is an unbridled and temporary madness, but the passion is a deep-seated mania.

9 I have not mentioned here the class of "asthenic affects," a term which Kant takes from John Brown (*Anthropology* 7, p. 256), and which are characterized not by turbulence but sedation. See Maria Borges, "Physiology and the Controlling of Affects in Kant's Philosophy," *Kantian Review*, Vol. 13, no. 2 (2008), pp. 46–66. She emphasizes Kant's acknowledgement of the physiological basis of affect, both "asthenic" and "sthenic," and the corresponding need for physical rather than merely mental therapy. For example, Kant says that when a man in a rage comes into the room, it is best to sit him down before trying to reason with him (Ibid. 7, p. 252), "because the comfort of sitting is a relaxation which does not really conform to the menacing gesticulations and screaming while one is standing." She also holds that Kant's view about the need for a cultivation of proper feeling only applies to three specific contexts (moderating one's shyness, using sympathy in the right contexts, and the moral feelings such as respect); but while these are indeed his examples, I do not think he means to confine the point to these examples.

10 6, p. 35.

11 He betrays that he is himself tempted in this way, in the *Metaphysics of Morals* (e.g. 6, pp. 384–385, "Since the basis of great crimes is merely the force of inclinations that weaken reason," though this does not *imply* that all inclinations do so. See also 6, pp. 380 and 394.).

12 6, p. 36.

13 Martin Luther, *The Bondage of the Will* (New York: Fleming H. Revell Co., 1957), p. 280.

14 6, p. 29.

15 6, p. 30.

16 *Critique of Practical Reason* 5, p. 9, "The faculty of *desire* is the faculty such a being has of causing through its ideas, the reality of the objects of these ideas," and 5, p. 34, "Now it is indeed undeniable that every volition must also have an object and hence a matter; but the matter is not, just because of this, the determining ground and condition of the maxim."

17 It is hard to reconcile Kant's view here with his rigorism at 6, p. 22. Perhaps Kant means that there is, even for the impure agent, only one maxim, good with respect to its object, but the maxim does not collect together all the agent's incentives for action.

18 6, p. 457.

19 See Sherman, op. cit., pp. 158–159.

20 6, p. 93. For Allen Wood, *Kant's Ethical Theory* (Cambridge: Cambridge University Press, 1999), our propensity to evil is equivalent and reducible to unsocial sociability, but see Jeanine Grenberg, "Social Dimensions of Kant's Conception of Radical Evil," in *Kant's Anatomy of Evil*, eds. Sharon Anderson-Gold and Pablo Muchnik (Cambridge: Cambridge University Press, 2009). Grenberg argues convincingly that the propensity to evil is something previous not only to social engagement but to any empirical exercise of freedom.

21 7, p. 253.

22   7, p. 257.
23   6, p. 406.
24   *Anthropology*, 7, p. 261, emphasis on "affect" added.
25   7, p. 265.
26   7, p. 271.
27   7, p. 267.
28   Chapter VI, section 93.
29   Chapter II, section 55.
30   Herman, op. cit., pp. 4–22.
31   *Groundwork* 4, p. 398.
32   Richard Henson, "What Kant Might Have Said: Moral Worth and the Over-determination of Dutiful Action," *Philosophical Review*, Vol. 88 (1979), p. 45.
33   Herman, op. cit., pp. 4–5.
34   4, p. 430.
35   Marcia Baron, "Overdetermined Actions and Imperfect Duties," in *Moralische Motivation*, pp. 23–37, also argues that Kant does not have a notion of over-determined actions. But this is because she thinks that with perfect duties, duty has to be the only decisive motive and that imperfect duties (despite what Kant says) are not done from duty at all. On imperfect duties, I agree with Allen Wood, *Kant's Ethical Thought* (Cambridge: Cambridge University Press, 1999), p. 44, "The 'necessity' of duty…consists solely in the fact that duty involves *rational* constraint on our actions." This includes imperfect as well as perfect duties. On perfect duties, we can agree that duty is the decisive motive without that preventing the presence of an incentive from inclination.
36   I give a brief account of one version of Aristotle's doctrine of form and matter in John Hare, *God and Morality* (Oxford: Blackwell, 2007), pp. 21–23, but for a full account see Montgomery Furth, *Substance, Form and Psyche: an Aristotelian Metaphysics* (Cambridge: Cambridge University Press, 1988).
37   I am paraphrasing from Frierson, op. cit., pp. 98–99.
38   Herman, op. cit., pp. 15 and 31–32.
39   *Metaphysics of Morals*, 6, p. 212. See Jeanine Grenberg, *Kant and the Virtue of Humility*, pp. 814f.
40   *Nicomachean Ethics* VI, 2, 1139a 24–26.
41   *Gl* 4, p. 398.
42   Karl Ameriks, "Kant and Motivational Externalism," in *Moralische Motivation*, eds. H. Klemme, M. Kühn and D. Schönecker (Hamburg: Felix Meiner, 2006), pp. 3–22. See also Ameriks, *Kant and the Historical Turn* (Oxford: Oxford University Press, 2006), Chapter 4.
43   I have defended a view called "prescriptive realism" which combines realism and expressivism. See John Hare, "Prescriptive Realism," in *Realism and Religion*, eds. Andrew Moore and Michael Scott (Aldershot, Hampshire: Ashgate, 2007), pp. 83–101.
44   Ameriks, op. cit., p. 14. The quotation is from Michael Smith, *The Moral Problem* (Oxford: Blackwell, 1994), p. 12.
45   Ameriks, op. cit. p. 2. He is talking in the first case about Humean empiricists, and in the second case about Christine Korsgaard, *Creating the Kingdom of Ends* (Cambridge: Cambridge University Press, 1996), and *The Sources of Normativity* (Cambridge: Cambridge University Press, 1996). In another paper, "On Schneewind and Kant's Method in Ethics," *Ideas y Valores*, Vol. 102 (December 1996), p. 48, Ameriks discusses the form of constructivism that holds that moral value is constructed from a procedure of practical reasoning, rather than desire. Both Humean and Korsgaardian forms of constructivism are a denial of what Korsgaard calls "substantive moral realism." See Korsgaard, *Sources*, pp. 4–5.
46   Ameriks suggests that the second stage is a perception of value. I do not mind putting it this way, and I have in fact put it this way myself; see "Prescriptive Realism," *op. cit*. G. E. Moore makes a similar distinction between perceiving a value, the affective response, and then the judgment that is an endorsement of that response. See John Hare, *God's Call* (Grand Rapids, MI: Eerdmans, 2001), pp. 3–6. For the present chapter the important point is that the third of these, or Ameriks's third stage (my fourth), is a judgment that is itself prescriptive, an expression of a volition that has taken up the affective response into endorsement. In separating out the second stage, I am assuming that the perception or recognition of universalizability is conceptually separable from commitment to the moral life.

47   Kant says that respect applies to persons only, never to things (*Critique of Practical Reason* 5, p. 76), and is thus different from admiration. I respect the example of a humble plain man, in whom I perceive righteousness in a higher degree than I am conscious of in myself. But he also says (5, p. 78) that the respect that we have for such a person is really for the law, which his example holds before us.

48   KpV 5, p. 75.

49   KpV 5, p. 79.

50   KpV 5, p. 76. Kant's treatment of respect is a valiant attempt to say what happens at the junction of the noumenal and the phenomenal, but (like Descartes's treatment of the pineal gland) it merely postpones the conceptual difficulties.

51   See *Religion* 6, p. 23, freedom "cannot be determined to an action through any incentive *except so far as the human being has incorporated it into his maxim.*"

52   *Religion* 6, p. 30.

53   John Austin, *How to Do Things with Words* (Oxford: Oxford University Press, 1965), p. 3. The capitalization "KANT" is in the original.

54   Gl 4, p. 420.

55   R. M. Hare, "A Philosophical Autobiography," *Utilitas*, Vol. 14, no. 3 (2002), p. 287.

56   See John Hare, *God and Morality: a Philosophical History* (Oxford: Blackwell, 2007), Chapter 4.

57   KpV 5, p. 72.

58   A first-person imperative is an imperative addressed by an agent to herself, often rendered in English by "*Let me* do x." In some inflected languages (like Greek and Latin) there is a separate form of the imperative for first-, second- and third-person imperatives.

59   KpV 5, p. 55.

60   Herman, op. cit., pp. 10–12.

61   In a fuller treatment I would discuss the point that the moral agent, according to Kant, both recognizes the obligation as God's command, and makes it her own command. But this is not the topic of the present paper. See *God's Call*, Chapter 3.

62   Gl 4, p. 398.

10

"THE MONSTROUS CENTAUR"? JOSEPH DE MAISTRE ON REASON, PASSION, AND VIOLENCE

DOUGLAS HEDLEY

The entire earth, perpetually steeped in blood, is nothing but an immense altar on which every living thing must be immolated without end, without restraint, without respite, until the consummation of the world, until the extinction of evil, until the death of death. (Maistre, *Les Soirées de Saint-Pétersbourg*, translated as *St Petersbourg Dialogues*, trans. R. A. Lebrun [Montreal, 1993], 217)

These are the famous words of Joseph de Maistre: the "friend of the executioner" (Stendahl).[1] This is the thinker described as "a fierce absolutist, a furious theocrat, an intransigent legitimist, apostle of a monstrous trinity composed of Pope, King and Hangman, always and everywhere the champion of the hardest, narrowest and most inflexible dogmatism, a dark figure out of the Middle Ages, part learned doctor, part inquisitor, part executioner" (Emile Faguet).[2] Joseph-Marie, Comte de Maistre (1753–1821) was a Savoy diplomat of French stock in the service of the Kingdom of Sardinia as ambassador to Russia (1803–1817) and in Turin (1817–1821). A trenchant critic of the French Revolution, he viewed it as the apotheosis of the atheism and philosophical empiricism of the Enlightenment. For Maistre, the core of Enlightenment ideology was the denial of God, the view of morality as essentially secular and the belief in the inevitability of progress. Unfortunately, his savage critique of Enlightenment optimism has been misinterpreted as the avowal of violence and irrationalism. Isaiah Berlin saw Maistre as a harbinger of the "Fascist inner passion."[3] Maistre develops in his *Soirées de St Pétersbourg* Platonic dialogue a theodicy which is, at the same time, a theory of redemption: evil reveals God's plan for mankind, which is the

Faith, Rationality, and the Passions, First Edition. Edited by Sarah Coakley.
© 2012 Blackwell Publishing Ltd. Book compilation © 2012 Blackwell Publishing Ltd.

expiation of guilt through vicarious suffering—represented by the shedding of blood in sacrifice, and more remotely in execution and war. Yet this is not the whole theory: "Y a-t-il quelque chose de plus certain que cette proposition: tout a été fait par et pour l'intelligence?"[4] ("Is there anything more certain than the proposition that everything has been made by and for intelligence?")[5] It strikes me that any philosopher who proposes that the universe is grounded *in and for reason* is a very unlikely precursor of the Fascist "vision." Indeed, it may be more accurate to view Maistre as a prophet of the paradoxical cruelty of "secular" ideologies.

We can dispose of the proto fascist label easily. Yet Maistre remains, many would suggest, a morally questionable figure. Does he not rejoice in suffering, draconian punishment and violence? Is he not the embodiment of a grotesque militarism that is such a shameful legacy of the Christian tradition? If that challenge is correct, then the famed eloquence of Maistre's pen is put to the service of a cruel philosophy. My answer is twofold. Firstly, the challenge confuses the descriptive with the normative. Maistre is describing the violence of the world as it appears to him. His perception may be false, but that is quite different from advocating such suffering and violence! Secondly, his theology is that of a lamb in wolf's clothing. For all his sombre pronouncements, Maistre, like F. D. Maurice in England, or his own venerated Origen, is robustly universalist. Here he departs from the mainstream of Western theology in the wake of Augustine's doctrine of grace and its influence in those grim theories of double predestination that emanated from the African doctor.

Voltaire and the Ambivalence of Violence

Maistre is deeply opposed to Voltaire's claim that "Certainement qui est en droit de vous rendre absurde est en droit de vous rendre injuste." ("Whoever can make you accept absurdity, can make you commit injustice.")[6] Voltaire presented Christianity as not just false but immoral. Through his *Candide*, Voltaire is the thinker most associated with the critique of theodicy. His *Traité sur la Tolérance à l'occasion de la mort de Jean Calas* of 1763 is a critique of iniquity perpetrated in the name of religion, inspired by the persecution and execution of the French Protestant Jean Calas by the Toulouse magistrature, the last man to be executed on the wheel in France on the trumped-up charge of murdering his son (in all likelihood it was a suicide). Voltaire's moving and scathing critique of the cruelty inflicted upon Calas became celebrated throughout Europe and thirty-nine of Voltaire's works were placed upon the Index. One gains a sense of the more intransigent and polemical side of Maistre's nature in his remarks about the doubtful innocence of Calas. Yet it is perhaps helpful to view his metaphysics of punishment in the context of the controversy raised by Voltaire.

Maistre's interest in punishment is philosophical, not pathological. Generally a philosophical justification of punishment is either retributive (e.g. Kant or Hegel) or consequentialist (e.g. Hobbes or Rousseau): either punishment redresses an intrinsic wrong or produces favorable results for society at large (e.g., protection from violence, theft or dishonesty). Many of Maistre's Enlightenment "opponents" maintain that the "just desert" of retributive punishment is either atavistic (i.e., revenge) or illusory (because metaphysically impossible). Some, like Foucault, may claim that punishment merely reflects the desire to exert power over others.[7] Both the ultra-liberal and the Foucauldian positions rest upon the anti-Platonic view that there are no objective values. For both the liberals and Foucault, punishment is just a human institution, not a natural fact—and it could theoretically be dispensed with. For Maistre, punishment is not an arbitrary fact about human society but reflects a spiritual law of punishment. Warfare and punishment are indexes of mankind's duality: man is, for Maistre, "the monstrous centaur."[8]

I think that this Platonic dimension of Maistre's thought can be seen in his emphasis upon the mirroring of eternal justice upon earth, however obliquely. The executioner represents order amidst disorder. For all the horror of his acts, they are not—*pace* Foucault—the expression of brute power. Let us consider the notorious executioner passage. It is remarkable in its imaginative engagement with the person of the executioner, as well as his ambivalent status in society:

> In outward appearance he is made like us; he is born like us. But he is an extraordinary being, and for him to be brought into existence as a member of the human family a particular decree was required, a FIAT of creative power.[9]

What does Maistre imply with the allusion to the "Fiat Lux" of the Vulgate? In the creation story of Genesis, God creates heaven and earth and light and darkness, and the light is good. Maistre suggests that the executioner is an organ of Divine justice: "There is then in the temporal sphere a divine and visible law for the punishment of crime. This law, as stable as the society it upholds, has been executed invariably since the beginning of time. Evil exists on the earth and acts constantly, and by a necessary consequence it must constantly be repressed by punishment."[10] Rather than akin to the *bellum omnium contra omnes* of Hobbes, Maistre's perspective is quite the opposite: resolutely providentialist. For Hobbes sovereignty is grounded in the pressing need to combat the chaotic violence of man's natural state. For Maistre, the existence of society at all presupposes the victory of *justice*, however imperfectly realised, over sheer power. The institution of capital punishment is a shadow of the eternal and immutable divine law that lies at the basis of human association and society. Whereas the God of Hobbes is at best a *Deus absconditus*, for the Platonist Maistre God is the transcendent source of earthly and temporal justice and order. In the words of Dante:

> La gloria di colui che tutto move
> per l'universo penetra e risplende
> in una parte più e meno altrove.[11]

Maistre avers that we must turn our eyes to the invisible world as the explanation of the visible, "tenons nos yeux fixes sur ce monde invisible qui expliquera tout."[12] Even when considering the person of the executioner, Maistre sees him as part of a broader providential scheme, notwithstanding the horror of his work:

> Consider how he is viewed by pubic opinion, and try to conceive, if you can, how he could ignore this opinion or confront it! Scarcely have the authorities assigned his dwelling, scarcely has he taken possession of it, when other men move their houses elsewhere so they no longer have to see his. In the midst of this seclusion and in this kind of vacuum formed around him, he lives alone with his female and his offspring, who acquaint him with the human voice. Without them he would hear nothing but groans. . . .
>
> Is this a man? Yes. God receives him in his shrines and allows him to pray. He is not a criminal, and yet no tongue would consent to say, for example that he is virtuous, that he is an honest man, that he is admirable, etc. No moral praise seems appropriate for him, since this supposes relationships with human beings, and he has none.
>
> And yet all greatness, all power, all subordination rests on the executioner.[13]

Maistre is speculating about the *anomalous* status of the executioner. He stands without relation to other creatures. Moral categories seem subverted. While necessary for the well-being of the state, the executioner is regarded with a mixture of anxiety and awe by his fellows. Yet this uncanny figure is presented psychologically from a very human perspective. Maistre depicts the literally dreadful loneliness of the executioner's role. The executioner is an organ of justice and yet isolated from human contact: only his own family "acquaint him with the human voice." In this short passage, sometimes cited by critics as evidence for Maistre's sadism, we find a remarkable empathy for the human being performing this grim task.

Maistre uses the thought-experiment of an extra-terrestrial visiting the world presented with the two kinds of men allowed to kill: the soldier and the executioner. Given that the former kills honest and good men and the latter kills criminals, the visitor will doubtless be surprised to discover the esteem exhibited for the warrior and the ignominy of the executioner.[14] "Il est défendu de tuer; tout meurtrier est puni, à moins qu'il n'ait tué en grande compagnie, et au son des trompettes." ("It is forbidden to kill; therefore all murderers are punished unless they kill in large numbers and to the sound of trumpets.")[15] Maistre uses the example of war to attack materialistic theories of human behavior such as "God is always on the side of the big battalions." On the contrary, here laws of physical force are often quite impotent: "C'est l'imagination qui gagne et qui perd les batailles." ("It is imagination that wins or loses battles.")[16] In such passages Maistre is attacking the crude mechanical anthropology employed by prominent philosophes like La Mettrie or D'Alembert. The violence of warfare is grounded in man's (ambivalent) spiritual nature and resists mechanical explanation. Moreover, notwithstanding its real horrors, war generates much that is positive for human life: it is a dreadful "scourge" and yet "the *real* fruits of human nature—arts, sciences, great enterprises, noble ideas, manly virtues—are due especially to the art of war."[17]

Closely linked to this doctrine is his resolute innatism or "original notions common to all men, without which they would not be men."[18] Through these innate ideas men can interpret the visible world as the symbolic juncture between the temporal and the divine. I was lately told a tale of a small terrier in rural England, one that was uncommonly fond of a cat in the same household. When the cat died, the tiny dog went into the garden, dug up the corpse of the cat, dragged it through the cat flap and licked it clean for the owner, who found his cat thus "resurrected" when he arose the next morning. The dog's devotion to his feline companion is startling and touching, but one is reminded of Vico's thoughts about the uniqueness of burials for human beings.[19] Maistre makes a rather similar point when he describes an execution with his dog and he describes the very different world of the dog. He and the dog have the same phenomenal experiences but dwell in different worlds. The dog can sense the crowd or the action of the guillotine but has no conceptual or symbolic *awareness* of the cessation of a human life or the execution of justice; these are ideas and symbols beyond his ken.[20] The dog and his master have different perceptions of the world, different inputs. Bradley claims that Maistre "was among the first . . . to thematize how power . . . is based not merely on coercion but also, and even more fundamentally, on the symbolic, on custom, representation, and belief."[21] This emphasis upon the figurative is essential for Maistre: the physical world is a set of signs or Divine language: all things are suffused by the Divine and the whole cosmos points back to its creator. God is not a superfluous addition to the world, but the transcendent and sustaining source of its meaning. Thus even the horrors of war or execution are not strictly "natural." The distinctly human sense of cruelty and disorder in warfare and the terror of violent punishment presuppose a realm of transcendent meaning utterly removed from the sensorium of the brute. War and punishment fill the heart with dreadful awe and terror—yet not because mankind is thereby unveiled a wolf unto itself ("homo homini lupus est" in Hobbes's invocation of the adage of Plautus in his *De cive* of 1651), but precisely, as Seneca said, because man is a thing sacred to man ("homo sacra res homini").[22]

Religion and Sacrifice

In Maistre's political and social reflections, the Age of Enlightenment is depicted as an age of violent crisis. The seventeenth century represents, by contrast, a period of relative tranquility—the age of stability based upon a culture of willing Christian self-sacrifice. That stable epoch is ravaged and destroyed by the eighteenth century—an age of abstraction, of individualistic, critical reason, corroding the traditions of past centuries without replacing them. Within the framework of Maistre's thought the recent age of secular destruction, with the unleashing of the passions under the violent impulses of the selfish part of the soul, was the age when "the holy laws of humanity were struck down, innocent blood covering the scaffolds that covered France; men frying and powdering bloody heads, and even the mouths of women stained with human blood."[23] Far from glorifying violence, Maistre is producing an unflinching protocol of its baneful presence in the world. According to Maistre, it is not religion that is the cause of conflict but rather mankind's fallen nature, and sacrifice is the attempt to stem it. Suffering is purgative as well as punitive. Humanity's fallen nature can be expiated only by sacrifice, which is *vicaria anima*, a substitute soul. Maistre sees instances of this practice throughout the heathen world. Ancient pagans did not sacrifice wild or useless animals. But

> the most precious for their utility were chosen, the most gentle, the most innocent, the ones closest to man by their instincts and habits [. . .] the most human victims, if one may express oneself in this way. Before Christ a sacrificial victim was anthropomorphic. After Christ, the paradigmatically human is the willing self-sacrifice. Christianity is distinctive because for it sacrifice is ethical, as self-renunciation. The Christian aims to be Christ-like in self abnegation: "under the empire of this divine law, the just man (who never believes himself to be such) nevertheless tries to come up to his model through suffering. He examines himself, he purifies himself, he works on himself with efforts that seem to surpass humanity to obtain finally the grace of being able to return what has not be stolen."[24]

One might fruitfully consider Glaucon's claim in Plato's *Republic* that the righteous man will be humiliated and tortured, bound, blinded and crucified:

> They will say that the just man, as we have pictured him, will be scourged, tortured, and imprisoned, his eyes will be put out, and after enduring every humiliation he will be crucified, and learn at last that one should want not to be, but to seem just.[25]

Kant shares this perception of suffering: "the sublimity and inner worth of the command is the more manifest in a duty, the fewer are the subjective causes for obeying it and the more there are against. . . ."[26] Thus virtue "reveals itself most splendidly in suffering."[27] In the *Religion* Kant is explicit:

> The emergence from the corrupted disposition into the good is in itself already sacrifice (as "the death of the old man" "the crucifying of the

flesh") and the entrance into a long train of life's ills which the new human being undertakes in the disposition of the Son of God.[28]

Maistre is much less coy than Kant about the theological dimension of his philosophy of suffering, of *régénération dans le sang*. And Maistre is more inclined to provoke and shock. But the ethics of both philosophers is shaped by an anthropology of emotions in an asymmetrical, even agonistic, relationship with reason.

Reason and Passions

A modern adherent of the Enlightenment tradition, Simon Blackburn in his book *Ruling Passions*, attacks the rationalist tradition from Plato to Kant. I wish to argue that Maistre represents an even more radical version of Blackburn's rationalist target than Kant. My aim is to argue that, far from being an irrationalist, Maistre resembles an extreme instance of rationalism. This, I further claim, can be traced to Maistre's particular devotion to the thought of the great Alexandrian divine Origen.

Blackburn thinks the problem with the rationalist model of agency lies precisely in placing desires, impulses, and appetites into an asymmetrical relationship with reason. In particular, he concentrates on Kant's idea of the noumenal self by using an analogy of a ship. Blackburn expounds his own Humean view of the individual as like a ship manned by many different crew members. Each member of the crew represents a distinct influence within the self. The running of the ship means cooperation. However, conflicts are inevitable. As a decision needs to be made, the members of the crew argue:

> After one voice has prevailed, various things may happen to the losers: they may be thrown overboard and lost altogether, or more likely they may remain silenced just for the occasion, or they may remain sullen and mutinous, or they may continue to have at least some affect on the ship's course.[29]

For Blackburn, this Humean model presents rationality as just another member of the crew. Rationality has a distinct purpose, perhaps most aptly conveyed in the simile as the lookout of the crow's-nest. Reason's task is to examine the external world and describe it to the rest of the crew. In this fashion, reason facilitates deliberation about the best course to take. The ship will run smoothly only if all the sundry members of the crew work without too much conflict and turmoil, or with swift resolution of conflict. However, if there are members of the crew in perpetual strife, the ship will not function adequately.

Kant does not deny the influence of Humean desires, impulses, and appetites. The Kantian ship is also manned by a variety of crew members in a similar situation to the Humean ship. However, this crew sails under the masterful eye of reason as its captain. For Kant, reason is its own determining agent. It is not influenced or determined by any other factor. Thus, the captain of Kant's ship does not engage with the fractious crew. Indeed, reason has the final authority in any decision; thus the captain is capable of ending any turmoil between crew members simply by stepping in. This is not to say that because a human being possesses reason there is never internal conflict. Sometimes one does not use one's reason as one should, or at all. Thus one is left with a "wanton ship" without an ultimate authority to guide it. Additionally, one should note that Kant felt that all rational, free agents shared the same rational mind. Thus, for Kant, the captain of every ship would be exactly the same, even if every person does not "employ" their captain in the same way.

Blackburn's key objection to Kant's view of decision making is that it places too much emphasis on reason as the "captain." By placing reason in a position of total authority over all other aspects of the self, Kant makes every other aspect of the individual an object of deliberation—an object for reason.

> Making desires the *object* of deliberation, rather than features of the person determining the selection and weighing of external features, inevitably leads to postulating an inner deliberator. This is a noumenal, transcendental, self whose relationship to desire is uncannily like my relationship to the world, yet mysteriously unlike it in not itself needing second-order desires to drive it.[30]

Blackburn explains that viewing desires as objects causes desires to appear arbitrary, or even absurd. Yet, as Blackburn avers, these desires are just as integral parts of the self as reason, if not more so. By separating desires from the "rational self" Kant alienates a tremendous portion of the self. In my view Maistre is a thinker very much in the tradition that Blackburn sees as the rationalistic Platonic-Kantian model. Indeed, it is radicalised and reinforced by his Origenism. On Maistre's view the self is alienated from its own core. Duplicity is an unavoidable dimension of the human condition, a state known to the ancient pagans:

> Plato tells us that in contemplating himself, he does not know if he sees a monster more duplicitous and more evil than Typhon, or rather a moral, gentle, and benevolent being who partakes in the nature of divinity. He adds that man, so torn in opposite directions, cannot act well or live happily without reducing to servitude that power of the soul in which evil resides, and without setting free that which is the home and the agent of virtue. This is precisely the Christian doctrine, and one could not confess more clearly the doctrine of original sin.[31]

The violence and suffering of the world must be understood from the perspective of the divided self: man is "the monstrous centaur," part steeped in violence and terrible crimes, and yet capable of love and compassion. Any society, like Revolutionary France and its totalitarian descendents in twentieth-century Europe, that loses the sense of mankind's divided being and its violent passions, will be apt to unleash terrible suffering.

Origen Redivivus

Maistre's theory of sacrifice—*Régénération dans le sang*—presupposes a traditional dichotomy of the rational self and its passions and the objectivity of morality. Commentators sometimes refer to his Augustinianism, but Maistre is strangely reticent about the African doctor and enthusiastic about the Alexandrian divine, Origen (185–254), the doctor of universal salvation, whose speculations about the cosmic process through which all things descended from an initial unity in God and the process that produces a final return to unity. This is Origen's treatise *On Principles*, which develops the idea of restitution of all to the divine source (*apokatastasis panton, restitutio universalis*). This universalistic doctrine is the opposite of double predestination and Augustine's grim doctrine of the *massa damnata*. Let us reflect again upon the famous lines about the earth as an altar:

> The entire earth, perpetually steeped in blood, is nothing but an immense altar on which every living thing must be immolated without end, without restraint, without respite, until the consummation of the world, until the extinction of evil, until the death of death.[32]

The reference to the "consummation of the world, until the extinction of evil, until the death of death" is an allusion to the *apokatastasis panton*. Like Descartes, Maistre was trained by the Jesuits and developed a loathing for the Augustinian Jansenists, whom he saw as proto-Protestants or *philosophes*. Maistre presents an Origenist vision of a fallen mankind: "every man as man is subject to all the misfortunes of humanity: the law is general, so it is not unjust. To claim a man's rank or virtues should exempt him from the actions of an iniquitous [. . .] tribunal is precisely the same as wanting such honours to exempt him from apoplexy, for example or even death."[33] It is original sin, viewed as cosmic fall, that determines the existence of suffering, death and evil. But all mankind is suffering and will be redeemed through Christ: "the blood that was shed on the calvary was not only useful to men, but to the angels, to the stars, and all other created beings."[34]

Maistre sees Empiricism, i.e. a sensualistic epistemology, as the core error of the French Enlightenment. For Maistre this means an unacceptable rejection of the classic Platonic-Aristotelian-Christian identification of the rational self or soul as the divine component of a composite human being and its replacement with a naturalistic theory of human cognition and action.

"Know Thyself" for Plato, Aristotle or the Christian humanists like Justin, Clement or Origen, meant "Know thy Divine self." The "odious Hume," as Maistre calls him, and the celebrated authors of the radical French Enlightenment, were engaged in the attempt to dismantle this tenet. It should be noted that this construal of the Delphic Oracle is not triumphalistic in Maistre. It has its epistemic dimension: he admired and supported the innatism of the Cambridge Platonists against Locke. But it is the basis of terrible tension in human nature that requires expiation through sacrifice:

> [Man] *gravitates* [. . .] toward the regions of light. No beaver, no swallow, no bee wants to know more than its predecessors. All beings are calm in the place they occupy. All are degraded, but they do not know it; man alone has the feeling of it, and that feeling is at once the proof of his grandeur and of his misery, of his sublime rights and of his incredible degradation. In the state to which he is reduced, he does not even have the sad happiness of ignoring himself: he must contemplate himself without cease, and he cannot contemplate himself without blushing; his very greatness humiliates him, since the lights that elevate him toward the angels serve only to show him the abominable tendencies within him that degrade him toward the beast. He looks in the depths of his being for some healthy part without being able to find it: evil has soiled everything, *and man entire is nothing but a malady.*[35]

But Maistre avoids the Manichaean tendency of Augustine. Thus Origen rejects not only the literal narrative of the Fall of Adam and Eve in the garden, but also the Augustinian idea of a collective fall in Adam. Grace must not impede freedom and God cannot be confused with any arbitrary power. Quoting Origen, Maistre states,

> Those who have adopted it, do not think the words of the apostle *the flesh lusts against the spirit* (Galatians 5:17) should be taken to mean the flesh properly speaking, but to this soul, which is really *the soul of the flesh*: for, they say, we have two souls, the one good and heavenly, the other inferior and terrestrial: it is of the latter that it has been said *that its works are manifest*, and we believe that this soul of the flesh resides in the blood.[36]

Maistre insists that evil is tied to human free will but it is also through free will that mankind returns to God. Mankind is like a "tree that an invisible hand is pruning, often to its benefit."[37] The cosmic and historic process of return to primeval unity is really a divine education of mankind. Faced with the question, why is human life marked by so much inequality and suffering, Maistre wishes to claim, like Origen, that God is not to blame for evils and injustice by appeal to a fall of each soul into the world: "it is man who is charged with slaughtering man."[38] The apparently pathological interest in violence and suffering in Maistre is linked to his Origenistic desire to avoid a tyrannical deity who has preordained misery in his inscrutable will. The suffering of humanity is the price to be paid for preserving an arena of genuine freedom: such is the *loi d'amour* ("law of love") that entails the making inward of sacrifice, the ethical submission to goodness and spirit.[39] Here is the liberal humanist theologian in Maistre, so indebted to Origen. Ironically, the Maistre who was identified by Isaiah Berlin as the political theorist at the origins of modern irrationalism emphasises the dark and cruel dimension of human experience *in order to avoid* an irrationalist and voluntarist theology that rests upon the twin doctrines of human depravity and inscrutable and arbitrary divine will.

NOTES

1 Isaiah Berlin, *The Hedgehog and the Fox: an essay on Tolstoy's views of history* (New York: Simon and Schuster, 1953), p. 66. Cf. Émile Faguet, *Politiques et moralistes du dix-neuvieme siècle* (Paris: Boivin, 1899), p. 1.
2 Berlin, "Introduction," in Joseph de Maistre *Considerations on France* (Cambridge, 1994), p. xi.
3 Berlin, *Freedom and Its Betrayal: Six Enemies of Human Liberty*, ed. Henry Hardy (Princeton, NJ: Princeton University Press, 2002), p. 153.
4 Maistre, *St Petersburg Dialogues*, p. 383.
5 Ibid.
6 Voltaire, *Questions sur les Miracles* (1765), ed. Louis Moland, *Oeuvres complètes de Voltaire* (Paris: Garnier, 1877–85), Vol. 25, pp. 357–450.
7 Michel Foucault *Discipline and Punish: the Birth of the Prison* (London: Penguin, 1977), p. 23 (on the idea of the "technology of power").
8 Ibid., p. 36.
9 Maistre, *St Petersburg*, p. 19.
10 Maistre, *St Petersburg*, p. 20.
11 "The glory of Him who moves all things penetrates the universe and shines in one part more and in another less." Dante's *The Divine Comedy*, 3 *Paradiso* (Oxford University Press, 1939), p. 19.
12 Maistre, *Les Soirées de Saint-Pétersbourg*, p. 661.
13 Maistre, *St Petersburg*, p. 19.
14 Maistre, *Les Soirées de Saint-Pétersbourg*, p. 650.
15 Voltaire, *Questions sur l'Encyclopédie*, "Rights" (London, 1771).
16 Maistre, *Les Soirées de Saint-Pétersbourg*, p. 665.
17 Maistre, *Considerations*, p. 29.
18 *St Petersburg*, p. 234.
19 Vico, *The New Science*, trans. D. Marsh (Harmondsworth: Penguin, 1999), §130.
20 Maistre, *St Petersburg*, p. 131.
21 Owen Bradley, *A Modern Maistre: The Social and Political Thought of Joseph de Maistre* (Lincoln, NE: University of Nebraska Press, 1999), p. 91.
22 Seneca, *Epistulae morales ad Lucilium* XCV, p. 33.
23 Maistre, *Elucidation on Sacrifices*, in *St Petersburg*, p. 371.
24 Maistre, *Dialogues*, pp. 381–382.
25 Plato, *The Republic*, trans. D. Lee (Harmondsworth: Penguin, 1987), p. 49 (362a).
26 Immanuel Kant, *The Moral Law*, ed. H. J. Paton (London: Hutchinson, 1981), p. 88.
27 Immanuel Kant, *Critique of Practical Reason*, V 156, ed. Mary Gregor (Cambridge: Cambridge University Press, 2004), p. 129.
28 Immanuel Kant, *Religion within the Bounds of Mere Reason* 6:74, trans. Allen Wood and George di Giovanni (Cambridge: Cambridge University Press, 1998), p. 90.
29 Simon Blackburn, *Ruling Passions* (Oxford: Clarendon Press, 1998), p. 245.
30 Ibid., p. 255.
31 Maistre, *St Petersburg*, p. 38.

32   Ibid., p. 217.
33   Ibid., p. 16.
34   Maistre, *Elucidation on Sacrifices*, p. 382.
35   Ibid., p. 43.
36   Maistre, *St Petersburg*, p. 355.
37   Maistre, *Considerations*, p. 28.
38   Maistre, *St Petersburg*, p. 217.
39   Ibid., p. 371.

11

KIERKEGAARD ON FAITH, REASON, AND PASSION

MEROLD WESTPHAL

Religious faith is often criticized (patronized, ridiculed, rejected) in the name of reason as being irrational, or at least insufficiently rational. Sometimes this is because the beliefs ingredient in faith do not qualify as knowledge in some philosophically defined ideal sense which calls itself reason. At other times it is because religion is seen as too much a matter of emotion, of feeling. The two are easily combined: faith is irrational because it rests on feeling rather than knowledge.

In *Fear and Trembling*, Kierkegaard challenges this double critique as a misunderstanding of all three elements: faith, reason, and emotion.[1]

Faith

The first challenge is to what we might call the "Platonic" view of faith, the notion that it is the failed attempt to be knowledge in some philosophically defined ideal sense. Thus, for Plato, true knowledge is to be found in mathematics and that moral and metaphysical intuition of the forms that is even purer, less discursive, and less tied to images. It is represented by the upper "half" of the divided line (*episteme, noesis, dianoia*) and by the world of sunshine outside the dank darkness of the cave. *Pistis* is the upper "half" of the lower "half" of the divided line and occurs in the cave. It is normally translated as "opinion" to signify that it falls short of knowledge. At best it may include correct beliefs, but having them is like being a blind person who just happens to have found the right road.[2]

Unfortunately *pistis* is also the New Testament word for faith, which has opened the door in modernity for treating faith as a failed attempt at knowledge whose ideal is mathematics, or natural science (mathematical physics or evolutionary biology), or some more generic foundationalist

Faith, Rationality, and the Passions, First Edition. Edited by Sarah Coakley.
© 2012 Blackwell Publishing Ltd. Book compilation © 2012 Blackwell Publishing Ltd.

model, or, in the case of Hegel, an anti-foundationalist, holist account of absolute knowing.

For Kierkegaard this is completely to misunderstand the sort of language game in which religious faith, at least in its biblical form, occurs. To criticize it for not being knowledge in the mode of mathematics, or natural science, or speculative metaphysics is like criticizing a football team for not serving aces. In response to such a critique, the football players might quote one of Kierkegaard's pseudonyms: "It is just as you say, and the amazing thing is that you think that it is an objection."[3]

What, then, is faith for Kierkegaard, and what is the language game to which it belongs? Different pseudonyms give us different accounts. Anti-Climacus describes faith as the opposite of despair and gives the following formula for faith: "in relating itself to itself and in willing to be itself the self rests transparently in the power that established it."[4] For Christian faith, which is Kierkegaard's concern, this power is the Christian God, and what is at issue is relational and not epistemic, at least not obviously or primarily epistemic. It is a matter of being rightly related to oneself and to God. The suggestion is that these two relations are interdependent, but there is no suggestion that knowledge in some philosophically ideal sense is either necessary or even helpful to such faith.

Johannes Climacus defines truth as subjectivity this way: "*An objective uncertainty, held fast through appropriation with the most passionate inwardness, is the truth*, the highest truth there is for an *existing* individual." Then he adds that "the definition of truth stated above is a paraphrasing of faith. Without risk, no faith. Faith is the contradiction between the infinite passion of inwardness and the objective uncertainty."[5] We shall return to the passionate character of faith.

But let us focus on *Fear and Trembling*. Although Johannes de Silentio doesn't give us a neat formula, we can easily enough formulate one from his retelling of the story of Abraham's near sacrifice of Isaac in Genesis 22. Faith is trusting in the promises of God and obeying the commandments of God. The focus, of course, is on Abraham's obedience, first to the command to sacrifice Isaac, and then, at the last minute, to desist. But Kierkegaard calls our attention to the fact that Abraham's obedience is grounded in his trust in God's promises. "By faith Abraham emigrated from the land of his fathers and became an alien in the promised land. . . . By faith Abraham received the promise that in his seed all the generations of the earth would be blessed."[6]

The crucial issue is relational. The concern of Abraham's faith is to be and to remain in a right relation with God. There is no question that beliefs are involved here.[7] For Abraham the crucial belief is that there is a God who has given certain promises and commands. But this presupposes that God speaks, which in turn means that this God is truly personal; for the ability to perform speech acts would seem to be a necessary condition, possibly even a sufficient condition, of personhood. We do well to remember that for the Abrahamic monotheisms, the emphasis is not only on the oneness of God but on the personal character of God; for Judaism, Christianity, and Islam worship a God who speaks, unless they have sold their soul to some extra-scriptural philosophy.[8] So the basic belief is not trivial, but precisely because of it faith must be understood as an I-Thou relation and not a failed attempt at some philosophical ideal of knowledge. It is a subject-subject relation, not a subject-object relation, and it is not self-evident that one can rightly trust the promises of God and obey the commands of God only if one has based this relation on Knowledge as defined by some extra-biblical philosophy.[9] That would involve the kind of spiritual elitism that Kierkegaard finds so odious in Hegel, who holds that philosophy provides the only truly adequate knowledge of God and that "Religion is for everyone. It is not philosophy, which is not for everyone."[10]

Of course, one can reflect on the epistemic status of the beliefs ingredient in faith, but one must remember two things. First, it would be more than a little weird to assume that these beliefs can or should have the form of our beliefs in mathematics, natural science, or speculative metaphysics. *Prima facie* our knowledge of other human persons would provide the best analogy and clue, and it does not have these forms. Second, to engage in distanciated reflection is to abstract from the fullness of faith. We need to avoid confusing the abstract, doxastic dimension of faith with its core concern of being rightly related to a personal God and thereby to oneself. The demons have the right, monotheistic metaphysics, we are told (James 2:19), but they do not have faith.

Reason

Kierkegaard himself engages in such epistemic reflection. In so doing he challenges the assumption, typical of enlightened modernity, that reason in its autonomy has any rightful hegemony over faith, that the beliefs ingredient in faith require certification by reason. We need to be clear here about the meaning of our terms. For Kierkegaard, faith is a response to revelation, to the speech acts by which one has been addressed by God, and reason, in its most general sense, is the activity of human thought independent of divine revelation.

Thus, for example, in *Philosophical Fragments* Johannes Climacus argues that Christian faith rests on revelation and not on recollection, the assumption that unaided human thought has the ability to discover or at least to recognize the truth, in this instance about God. In *Postscript* he calls attention to the epistemic and existential risk involved in basing one's life on beliefs that are "objectively uncertain," incapable of the intuitive or discursive infallibility required and often promised by certain philosophical ideals of knowing. In other words, epistemic reflection calls attention to the distinctiveness of the beliefs ingredient in faith and exposes the dogmatism of the assumption that reason has a rightful hegemony over faith, either to dismiss it as irrational or to require it to be reinterpreted by the canons of reason.[11] It's a bit like requiring astronomy and biology to justify themselves without the benefit of telescopes and microscopes.

The emphasis on the heterogeneity of faith and reason is especially strong in *Fear and Trembling*. In a Kantian tone of voice Kierkegaard describes human understanding as the "stockbroker of finitude." But beyond Kant, who emphasizes the *incapacity* of unaided human thought to grasp the divine as infinite, unconditioned, and eternal, Kierkegaard emphasizes the *incompatibility* of the worldview of reason with the worldview of faith.[12] He repeatedly uses three terms to express this conflict. *Vis-à-vis* reason as merely human understanding, faith will necessarily be seen as paradox,[13] as absurd,[14] and as madness.[15] These are relational, not intrinsic qualities.

There is a double relativity to this "irrationality" which needs emphasis. On the one hand, faith is not presented as intrinsically absurd but as bound to be seen as such from the standpoint of autonomous reason, which has left divine revelation out of account. To dismiss faith as "irrational" because it fails to conform to reason is to beg the questions of what ultimately makes sense and of what legitimate sources of knowledge are. It is to confuse the fact that faith will affirm what reason cannot confirm with the normative superiority of reason. As before, faith says to reason, "It is just as you say, and the amazing thing is that you think that it is an objection."[16]

On the other hand, the paradoxical madness of faith, relative, as just noted, to "worldly understanding" and "human calculation,"[17] is also relative to the awesome transcendence of its "object," the God who speaks on God's own terms. Here Kierkegaard sounds more than a little like Rudolf Otto.[18] God is the *mysterium* precisely by being the *tremendum*.[19] Thus faith "shudders" and is "shattered" and "repelled" by its encounter with the "terror" ("terrible," "terrifying"), the *"horror religiosis,"* the "dreadful."[20] The God of biblical faith is not tame enough to fit without remainder into the horizons of the finite world of human speech and thought, the logos in terms of which reason defines itself.[21]

Kierkegaard also challenges modernity's assumption that reason is ahistorically universal. He might have illustrated the historical particularity of "reason" with reference to the project of "religion within the limits of reason alone."[22] In the seventeenth century, one of the most powerful versions of this project was Spinoza's; in the eighteenth century, Kant's; and in the nineteenth century, Hegel's. But the project runs aground here. Each of these is fundamentally incompatible with the other two. Reason shows itself to be anything but univocal and universal. Lessing's hope to find a universal religion of reason that would transcend the differences between Judaism, Christianity, and Islam[23] showed itself to be wishful thinking when reason's denominations turned out to be as different from each other as Judaism, Christianity, and Islam.

But Kierkegaard wants to show that the particularity of reason is not simply a matter of personal differences but of historical embeddedness. *Fear and Trembling* opens with a reference to "our age," and throughout the text with reference to matters aesthetic, ethical, and religious Kierkegaard calls attention to prevailing assumptions that differ from those of earlier ages. These are not just the superstitions that enlightened reason promises to dispel, but the very beliefs on which it prides itself. Thus, for example, while earlier ages thought that faith, like doubt and love, were tasks of a lifetime, never fully achieved, the present age proudly asserts that it has gone further than faith to the scientific system of philosophy.[24]

In other words, what calls itself reason turns out to be ideology, the self-defining and self-legitimizing discourse of a contemporary culture. Instead of being universal and necessary, it turns out to be both particular and contingent by virtue of the world it both reflects and ratifies. Having appeared on the literary scene in 1843, the same year as Marx, Kierkegaard suggests a non-materialist version of ideology critique.[25] It deflates the proud claims of Reason by showing it to be human, all too human.

An especially important way in which the present age is a particular culture rather than universal, pure reason is that it "has crossed out passion in order to serve science."[26] By "science" Kierkegaard clearly means detached, disinterested objectivity (both as a goal and a putative achievement). His reference is to the Hegelian system, though in our day reason's challenge to faith is more likely to be made in the name of the natural or social sciences than of speculative metaphysics.

Passion

This brings us to our third theme, passion, which links our first two, faith and reason. Kierkegaard makes the following claims: that "the essentially human is passion,"[27] that "faith is a passion,"[28] that faith is a "prodigious" and "supreme" passion,[29] and that "faith is the highest passion in a person."[30] The emotions he associates most closely with Abraham's faith are fear, trembling, distress, and anxiety.[31] By contrast, reason, in its scientific mode, is the attempt to become dispassionate. Like the ancient Stoics, but for different reasons, it wants to extirpate passion, to become apathetic, making *apatheia* the horizon of all human life.[32]

Here Kierkegaard anticipates his sustained contrast in *Two Ages* (a lengthy review of a current novel) between the present age as one of spiritless reflection and the revolutionary age as one of passion;[33] he complains that "what our generation lacks is not reflection but passion."[34] In an earlier draft he complained about his own age "whose insipid rationality has pumped all passion out of life."[35]

What is of interest to us here is that faith, so far from being inferior to reason by virtue of its passionate character, is precisely in this respect superior, more genuinely human. Reason without passion is as incomplete as reason without revelation. For religious questions and the closely related questions of ethics are about who we are and what we can and should do with our lives; and these questions deserve our passionate concern. Kierkegaard thinks it a vice, not a virtue, to try to become dispassionate about one's own existence.

Fear and Trembling does not help us very much in seeing how this might be true. Kierkegaard does not give us the phenomenology of passion that we would like.[36] He seems to think we can fill that in for ourselves. As we attempt to do so, we can perhaps find some help in the "cognitive-evaluative" or "cognitive-intentional" understanding of the emotions that has gained widespread acceptance in recent philosophical discussion.[37] Although ordinary language doesn't distinguish between passions, emotions, and feelings, clarity might be served if we do so as follows.

(1) To begin we can say that to have a passion for something is to care deeply about it.[38] To say of someone that he has a passion for, say, fly fishing, is not merely to say that he enjoys it. We enjoy many things that are not important enough to us to generate a passion. To have a passion for fly fishing is to care about it so deeply that it becomes part of one's identity. Faith is a passion when we care deeply enough about our God relation that it becomes part of our identity; and faith becomes a "supreme" or "highest" passion when the God relation is the most important part of our identity.

(2) Our next thesis is that a passion is a disposition to have emotions such as grief, fear, love, joy, hope, anger, gratitude, hatred, envy, jealousy, pity, guilt, compassion, wonder, reverence, awe in the presence of certain beliefs.[39] Thus if I have a passion for fly fishing I may feel anger if I believe someone has stolen my rod and flies; I may feel envy if I believe someone has better equipment than mine or has a summer cottage I can't afford near a great stream; and I may feel gratitude if I believe someone has recovered the stolen rod and flies or invited me to spend time at that cottage.

(3) In speaking of feeling anger, or envy, or gratitude I have acknowledged that emotions include feelings. The most natural way to speak about what anger is is to speak about what it feels like to be angry.[40] This feeling might be in part a bodily sensation such as a knot in the stomach or a felt increase in the pulse rate or breathing rate. Thus it can be what philosophers sometimes call "raw feels," like a tickle or an itch or an ache. This dimension of emotions can be described as non-cognitive and, in that sense, irrational.[41]

(4) But emotions cannot be reduced to these "kinetic and affective" aspects.[42] As already indicated, they presuppose two other elements, a caring about something and a believing that something is the case. Only if, for example, I care about fly fishing and believe that you have been helpful to me (in this regard) will I feel gratitude toward you (in this regard).[43]

(5) Emotions, then, can be seen as complex wholes with three distinct aspects: caring, believing, and feeling.[44] The feeling component may be non-cognitive, but the emotion as a whole is not. It can be described as "rational," an exercise of human reason, in three ways. First, it is intentional. It is about something or someone in a way that "raw feels" are not. I am angry at him, grateful to her, and so forth. Second, it has the form of a judgment, an evaluative judgment. It is a seeing as, a construal, an interpretation of something or someone with respect to what concerns me or what I care about. Third, because of its link to factual beliefs, it is subject to rational critique and, at least to some degree, to rational modification. If I am reminded that I lent my fishing equipment to my cousin and he did not steal it, my anger will be assuaged (unless it has some deeper, hidden motivating belief). In this sense emotions can be shown to be justified or unjustified.

(6) There is another sense in which the complex whole that is an emotion can be subject to rational evaluation, though this is likely to be more problematic. Whether or not my emotion is justified depends in part on whether the factual beliefs ingredient in it are true. But it also depends on whether what I care about, and in the case of a passion, what I care about so deeply that it becomes part of my identity, is worth caring about.[45]

Some things are worth caring about because they provide a pleasure sufficiently free from negative factors (for me or for others, including the environment) that cancel out this good. In a eudaimonistic framework, Nussbaum sees things as worth caring about in terms of their contribution to our flourishing, which, in an Aristotelian manner, is not equated with pleasure. In either case, what is worthwhile may be person-relative or culture-relative. But in the latter case there may be aspects of human flourishing distinctive of the human as such and thus worth caring about for everyone (as fly fishing obviously is not).

Biblical religion makes such a claim for the God relation. Whether such a claim is justified depends on whether there is a God, what this God may be like, and who we are. Such metaphysical matters are controversial and open to debate. But just as it would be sheer dogmatism to assume that reason, in the sense of human thought without the benefit of divine revelation, has an a priori privilege over faith, in the sense of human thought informed by divine revelation, so it would be question-begging to discredit faith because it is a passion that gives rise to a rich and complex emotional life before God, including fear, guilt, grief (sorrow for sin), love, joy, gratitude, compassion, wonder, reverence, and awe. For if the biblical picture of God is right, such emotions are in principle well-justified value judgments and fundamental to human flourishing.

The opponent might respond that it is all right for well founded beliefs to give rise to emotions; the problem is that in religion it is emotions that give rise to beliefs, and this is irrational. Here we meet Plato again and his fear that the "lower" parts of the soul (appetitive and spirited) will rule the "higher" part. But this seems to presuppose that emotions are merely affective, feelings in the sense of raw feels. If, however, emotions are complexly cognitive, they may be well founded judgments, and there is no obvious reason why they should not play a role in the life of belief. The task is to sort out the good ones from the bad ones. The fact that this is no easy task is no good reason to dismiss the emotions wholesale.

That our emotions and the passions that give rise to them are neither good nor bad *per se* is Aristotelian. Thus, for example, the rational task is to learn how to be angry "with the right person, to the right extent, at the right time, for the right reason, and in the right way." This is not easy, but it is "rare, praiseworthy, and noble."[46] It is within this horizon that Roberts can point out that some virtues, like compassion and gratitude, are dispositions to the emotions whose name they bear,[47] and Nussbaum can argue that emotions have a proper role to play in moral reasoning.[48]

Kierkegaard seems to presuppose something like this analysis of our affective life and to extend it from the moral to the religious life. Religious life has gone astray, to be sure, when it rests on bad emotions or nourishes them. But this is just as true of secular life, and the politics of resentment, for example, is not an aid to personal flourishing or to the common pursuit of the common good. In neither case is the problem with emotion and passion as such.

So, in sum, Kierkegaard argues that when we pay sufficient attention to what faith, and reason, and emotion really are, we will not be in a position to say that faith is irrational because it rests on feeling rather than knowledge.

NOTES

1 By "Kierkegaard" I shall mean the actual author who gave us various ideas to think about, whether pseudonymously or not. I am honoring his request not to attribute to him the views of his pseudonyms, since, in any case, our interest is not in what the historical Kierkegaard thought but what we might think. In the present context, recognizing a single source for the various pseudonyms is helpful in reading them intertextually.

2 Plato, *Republic*, 506c. It would seem that Plato had been reading Gettier.

3 PF p. 52. The following sigla will be used for the works of Kierkegaard. All volumes are from *Kierkegaard's Writings*, published by Princeton University Press and translated by Howard V. Hong and Edna H. Hong.

  CUP *Concluding Unscientific Postscript to* Philosophical Fragments, 1992.
  FT   *Fear and Trembling/Repetition*, 1983.
  PF   *Philosophical Fragments/Johannes Climacus*, 1985.
  SUD *The Sickness Unto Death*, 1980.

4 SUD p. 49; cf. pp. 14, 30, 82, 131.

5 CUP I, pp. 203–204. Some rationalist ideals of what counts as knowledge have certainty built in, while empiricist ideals tend to be fallibilist. But for Kierkegaard faith is not just siding with empiricist fallibilism, which all too easily can play the Platonic game of assigning faith to the cave as either wholly unverifiable/unfalsifiable or not rising to the level of verification that scientific knowledge requires. Again the issue is relational, this time the relation of the self to its beliefs about God and the world. The emphasis falls on the "how" of believing, not on the "what."

6   FT p. 17.

7   In *Sickness* the most central beliefs are that God (not nature, nor society, at least not ulti-
    mately) is the power that has established the self and that God offers forgiveness of sins,
    the various forms of misrelation to God and to self. In short, the beliefs are in God as Creator
    and Redeemer. In *Postscript* the central belief concerns the Incarnation, that the eternal God
    has become a particular human being and that our relation to God is mediated through
    this divine human being.

8   On God as a performer of speech acts, see Nicholas Wolterstorff, *Divine Discourse: Philo-
    sophical Reflections on the Claim that God Speaks* (New York: Cambridge University Press,
    1995) and my review, "On Reading God the Author," *Religious Studies*, Vol. 37 (2001),
    pp. 271–291.

9   This does not preclude the possibility that the relation is between human communities and
    a personal God. But in *Fear and Trembling* the emphasis is on the individual so as to empha-
    size that God is the middle term between the individual and both the church and the state,
    and not the other way around. Kierkegaard's "attack upon Christendom" is already at
    work in *Fear and Trembling*. In *Concluding Unscientific Postscript* Johannes Climacus bases a
    sustained case for spiritual egalitarianism on the notion that faith does not require the kind
    of knowledge philosophy sometimes requires, eliminating all risk and grounding one's
    security on one's own cognitive powers.

10 G. W. F. Hegel, *Lectures on the Philosophy of Religion. One-Volume Edition. The Lectures of 1827*,
    ed. Peter C. Hodgson (Oxford: Clarendon Press, 2006), p. 106.

11 With regard to specific themes of Christian belief, Lessing is an example of the first strategy,
    Kant and Hegel of the second.

12 Thus in *Postscript* Johannes Climacus insists that Christian faith is not merely beyond but
    more specifically "against the understanding" (CUP I, pp. 565–566). We are dealing with
    what Paul Ricoeur calls a "conflict of interpretations," a radical conflict because the sources
    and norms of interpretation are different, not just the results.

13 FT pp. 33, 48–49, 51–53, 55–56, 62–66, 85, 88.

14 FT pp. 34–37, 40, 46–51, 56, 59.

15 FT pp. 17, 23, 76–77. Silentio calls faith a divine madness, referring to Plato, who speaks of
    "the superiority of heaven-sent madness over man-made sanity" (*Phaedrus*, 244d).

16 PF p. 52.

17 FT pp. 17, 36.

18 See Rudolf Otto, *The Idea of the Holy*, trans. John W. Harvey (New York: Oxford University
    Press, 1958).

19 Jean-Luc Marion's notion of the saturated phenomenon is also relevant here, with its notion
    of revelation as in excess of our ability to comprehend. See "The Saturated Phenomenon,"
    in *The Visible and the Revealed*, trans. Christina M. Gschwandtner and others (New York:
    Fordham University Press, 2008); *Being Given*, trans. Jeffrey L. Kosky (Stanford, CA: Stan-
    ford University Press, 2002), Book IV; and *In Excess: Studies of Saturated Phenomena*, trans.
    Robin Horner and Vincent Berraud (New York: Fordham University Press, 2002).

20 FT pp. 9, 33, 61, 72, 77–78, 114.

21 FT pp. 46–47.

22 This is indeed the name of a project undertaken by many and not just of a book by Kant.

23 In *Nathan der Weise*.

24 FT pp. 5–7, 121–23. The satire against "going further" runs throughout the text, but in these
    passages it is the bookends between which the entire text is placed. The system in question,
    of course, is the Hegelian system.

25 I have developed this theme in *Kierkegaard's Critique of Reason and Society* (Macon, GA:
    Mercer University Press, 1987). Paul Ricoeur lists Marx, Nietzsche, and Freud as the
    "masters of suspicion," in *Freud and Philosophy: An Essay on Interpretation*, trans. Denis
    Savage (New Haven, CT: Yale University Press, 1970), p. 32. But Kierkegaard is equally a
    master of the hermeneutics of suspicion that detects particular self-interests hiding behind
    alleged universal objectivity and suggests that this hiddenness is not ignorance but self-
    deception (FT p. 121).

26 FT p. 7. In this spirit, Charles Taylor writes, "Modern enlightened culture is very theory-
    oriented. We tend to live in our heads, trusting our disengaged understandings.... We can't
    accept that part of being good is opening ourselves to certain feelings." *A Secular Age*
    (Cambridge, MA: Harvard University Press, 2007), p. 555.

27 FT p. 121.
28 FT p. 67.
29 FT p. 23.
30 FT p. 122.
31 In *Christian Discourses*, Kierkegaard presents faith as the overcoming of various anxieties that the "heathen" have. The emphasis in *Fear and Trembling* on God as the *Tremendum* is not the whole story. "Anxiety" is the rendering in the earlier translation of *Christian Discourses* by Walter Lowrie (Princeton, NJ: Princeton University Press, 1971). In the later translation by the Hongs (Princeton, NJ: Princeton University Press, 1997), it is the "cares" of the pagans from which faith is free. But this can be misleading, for faith cares passionately about the relation to God.
32 See Martha Nussbaum, *The Therapy of Desire: Theory and Practice in Hellenistic Ethics* (Princeton, NJ: Princeton University Press, 1994), pp. 9–10.
33 Note the implication that reason is ideology, that the revolutionary conception of reason and the contemporary view of reason as systematic, speculative science represent two quite different modes of social self-legitimation.
34 FT p. 42n. In *Postscript* this becomes the complaint that what the System lacks is not objectivity but subjectivity, the "infinite, personal, passionate interest" in one's own existence (CUP 1, pp. 29, 33, 55).
35 FT p. 257. The Preface to *Sickness Unto Death* contrasts the "earnestness" of the "ethical aspect of Christianity" that is concerned with upbuilding with the "scholarly distance" that is a "scienticity and scholarliness that is 'indifferent'" and is "a kind of inhuman curiosity" (SUD p. 5).
36 In addition to faith he identifies, randomly, other sites where passion appears: infinite resignation (FT p. 42n), the willingness to distinguish, with Socrates, what one knows from what one doesn't know (FT p. 42n), irony and humor (FT p. 51), repentance (FT pp. 99, 102), and love (FT pp. 121). He links passion with the understanding of faith as the task of a lifetime, always unfinished (FT pp. 7, 121–23). He links passion with the leap as opposed to mediation, his shorthand, borrowed from Lessing and Hegel, for the realm of objective uncertainty where I have to decide what to do or believe without the guarantees that some impersonal reason will make my decision for me (FT p. 42n).
37 I shall be drawing especially on the "neo-Stoic" view as developed by Martha Nussbaum historically in *The Therapy of Desire* and systematically in *Upheavals of Thought: The Intelligence of the Emotions* (Cambridge: Cambridge University Press, 2001). The quoted phrases to describe the theory are from the latter. See also A. Kenny, *Action, Emotion and Will* (London: Routledge, 1963); G. Pitcher, "Emotion," in *Mind*, Vol. 74 (1965), pp. 326–346; R. C. Solomon, *The Passions* (New York: Doubleday, 1976); and R. C. Roberts, *Spiritual Emotions: A Psychology of Christian Virtues* (Grand Rapids, MI: Eerdmans, 2007) and "Existence, Emotion and Character: Classical Themes in Kierkegaard," in *Cambridge Companion to Kierkegaard*, eds. Alastair Hannay and Gordon Marino (Cambridge: Cambridge University Press, 1998), pp. 177–206.
38 Harry Frankfurt's "The Importance of What We Care About" is therefore important for any account of faith as a passion. See *The Importance of What We Care About* (Cambridge: Cambridge University Press, 1998), pp. 80–94.
39 This list is drawn from Nussbaum, *Upheavals*, pp. 24, 54, 297 ff.
40 I'm obviously alluding to Thomas Nagel, "What is it like to be a bat?" in *Mortal Questions* (Cambridge: Cambridge University Press, 1979), pp. 165–180. Nussbaum argues that we cannot assume that there is a single feeling, in this sense, that is uniformly found in each emotion.
41 C. Stephen Evans points out that feelings in this sense are not what Kierkegaard means by passion and that a person whose life is governed by such "momentary feelings" or "involuntary urges" is pretty much what Frankfurt (see note 38) calls a "wanton." *Kierkegaard: An Introduction* (Cambridge: Cambridge University Press, 2009), pp. 21–22. Frankfurt's notion of a wanton and Kierkegaard's notion of the aesthetic stage or sphere of existence are at least first cousins.
42 Nussbaum, *Upheavals*, p. 44.
43 Frankfurt calls attention to the fact that sometimes we care about things because we believe they are important (as opposed to their becoming important because we care about them,

like fly fishing), and Nussbaum notes that these beliefs can be culture-relative. Frankfurt, *Importance*, pp. 92–93 and Nussbaum, *Therapy*, pp. 38–39.

44 I am deliberately speaking rather loosely, not trying to settle debates that do not directly concern my argument. Thus, Nussbaum raises the question whether the beliefs are constituent parts, necessary conditions, or sufficient conditions of emotions. They can hardly be sufficient conditions, since lacking the caring element the beliefs would not give rise to emotions. Rather than choose between the other options, I am content to say with her, rather vaguely, "Emotions…involve judgments [or beliefs] about important things." *Upheavals*, pp. 19, 34. Nor am I trying to settle the debate over whether we should speak of beliefs or belief-like states that involve construals on the ground that the former are involuntary and the latter somewhat voluntary. I am inclined to see all beliefs as construals, most of which, if not all, are a messy mix of voluntary and involuntary. See Robert C. Roberts, *Emotions: An Essay in Aid of Moral Psychology* (New York: Cambridge University Press, 2003).

45 Unless I am a positivist, I will not think that my judgments about what is worth caring about are themselves merely expressions of emotions.

46 Aristotle, *Nicomachean Ethics*, 1109a, 27–29.

47 Roberts, *Spiritual Emotions*, especially Chapter 2.

48 Nussbaum, *Upheavals*, p. 3.

12

REVOLTING PASSIONS

THOMAS DIXON

Whatever happened to the passions? The *pathe, passiones,* or passions of the soul were a major mental category for thinkers from the ancient Greeks to the early moderns, until the "emotions" came into existence in the nineteenth century. The new science of psychology took over many ancient categories wholesale. The senses and the intellect, the memory and the will were all preserved. But the passions and affections—although they persisted, and persist to this day, in some contexts—were never studied by the exponents of evolution and neuroscience. Instead they were displaced by the "emotions," whose place as a psychological category was cemented through its adoption by eminent scientific figures including Charles Darwin and William James.[1]

The predominant scholarly attitude towards the emotions in recent decades has been one of loving restoration. Long maligned by moralists and theologians as irrational and harmful, so the story goes, it has fallen to modern philosophers, neuroscientists and psychologists in recent years to retrieve the emotions from centuries of neglect and abuse and to restore their intellectual lustre. The standard view now is that emotions are cognitive states which constitute intelligent appraisals of the world. They are neither mere feelings, nor obstacles to reason. The cognitive nature of emotions is used to argue not only against a strong dichotomy between reason and emotion, but also in favour of the relevance of our emotions to ethical decisions. Our pro-emotional revisionism has also extended to rereading canonical works in the history of ideas in search of precursors for the modern orthodoxy about the close interconnection between thinking and feeling.

There is a danger that this modern surge of approval for the emotions will obscure our view of the real nature of both secular and religious traditions of thought about these subjects. Looking carefully at the history of our categories can alert us to important differences between a mental typology

Faith, Rationality, and the Passions, First Edition. Edited by Sarah Coakley.
© 2012 Blackwell Publishing Ltd. Book compilation © 2012 Blackwell Publishing Ltd.

which differentiates between "appetites," "passions," "affections," and "sentiments" and one which invokes a much more homogenous category of "emotions." In pre-modern and early modern texts, to assert an opposition between reason and the passions was not the same as asserting an opposition between reason and our modern-day "emotions." Nor was it the same as the strict separation made between the intellect and the emotions by nineteenth-century psychologists. The most obvious loss in the transition from theories about the long-established "passions" to distinctively modern theories of "emotions" was the sense of pathology that had accumulated in the former but which was excised from the latter. In what follows I investigate each of these issues a little further, focussing especially on the moral, theological, political and aesthetic reasons that have been put forward historically for fearing a revolt of the passions.[2]

I

In one of his *Epistulae Morales ad Lucilium*, Seneca wrote: "Show me a man who isn't a slave; one is a slave to sex, another to money, another to ambition; all are slaves to hope or fear." True philosophy, Seneca told his young friend the trainee Stoic Lucilius, was a medicine that could heal the mind, by dispelling fear, rooting out empty desires and reining in the passions.[3] Nearly four centuries later, in *The Free Choice of the Will*, St Augustine wrote similarly about the pernicious power of the passions:

> Passion [*libido*] lords it over the mind, dragging it about, poor and needy, in different directions, stripped of its wealth and virtue. . . . And all the while, the cruel tyranny of evil desire holds sway, disrupting the entire soul and life of man by various and conflicting surges of passion; here by fear, there by anxiety; here by anxiety, there by empty and spurious delights; here by torment over the loss of a loved object, there by a burning desire to acquire something not possessed. . . . On every possible side the mind is shrivelled by greed, wasted away by sensuality, a slave to ambition inflated by pride, tortured by envy, deadened by sloth, kept in turmoil by obstinacy, and distressed by its condition of subjection. And so with other countless impulses that surround and plague the rule of passion.[4]

This seems like a textbook assertion of that opposition between reason and emotion that modern scholars have been at such pains to disclaim, expressing as much distrust of our emotional side as did Seneca. But elsewhere Augustine wrote explicitly against the Stoics:

> Even if *apatheia* is merely a state in which one neither trembles from fear nor suffers from sorrow, it is still a state to guard against in this life if we want to live as human beings should, in the sense of living according to

God's will. . . . And as for those few who, with a vanity which is even more frightful than it is infrequent, pride themselves on being neither raised nor roused nor bent nor bowed by any emotion [*affectus*] whatsoever—well, they have rather lost all humanity than won true peace.[5]

At first reading, one might suppose that in the first passage Augustine is arguing that our emotions are dangerous, and in the second that they are to be cherished as part of a life of full humanity lived according to God's will. But such a reading, employing the modern English-language category of the "emotions," cannot capture Augustine's intent since he knew no such category (despite the use of the term in modern translations of his work). We cannot expect to find in Augustine (or any other pre-modern author) any attitude towards the "emotions." Augustine was suspicious of those movements of the appetite that he considered misdirected *passiones, perturbationes, libidines* or even, in Stoic vein, *morbos*; but he took a more positive stance towards higher movements of the will given milder designations such as *motus, affectus, affectiones* or simply *voluntates*, acts of will.[6]

A similar set of distinctions between appetites, perturbations and passions on the one hand, and higher affections on the other, can be discerned in Aquinas. His adoption of the Aristotelian philosophical categories reinforced a sense of the passivity and, hence, inferiority, of the *passiones*.[7] Aquinas made an important distinction, however, between the passions and other movements of the will:

> The words "love", "desire" and so on are used in two senses. Sometimes they mean passions [*passiones*], with some arousal in the soul. This is what the words are generally taken to mean, and such passions exist solely at the level of sense appetite. But they can be used to denote simple attraction [*affectus*], without passion [*passio*] or perturbation [*concitatio*] of the soul, and such acts are acts of will [*actus voluntatis*]. And in this sense the words apply to angels and to God.[8]

For Aquinas, then, as for Augustine, the realm of the lower passions did not exhaust the affective capacities of the soul. They were complemented by other states which carried a higher spiritual value—namely godly affections without any associated arousal or perturbation of the soul.[9]

The term "passions" has, of course, had a very wide range of meanings both before and after the composition of the *Summa Theologiae*, some more positive than others. When invoked neither as a word of warning nor as a neutral designation for a broad range of movements of the soul, the term "passion" has had important and positive roles in moral and theological discourse. The "passion" of Christ has always been pivotal to Christian teaching, and has been the basis for ideas about the purgative, educative and redemptive role of suffering, whether physical or spiritual, in the Christian life, and about the positive value of ascetic discipline and the mortification of the flesh. There have also been positive roles envisaged for the calmer and more other-regarding of the passions by moralists and preachers through the centuries and celebrations of the power of religious art and sacred music to command violent but holy passions, as in John Dryden's "Song for St Cecilia's Day" (1687), which exclaims "What passion cannot music raise and quell!"[10]

Nonetheless, the most frequent purpose of moralists, both secular and religious, when it came to discoursing on the passions in medieval and early modern Europe, was to warn and arm against them. A wide range of metaphors was deployed to suggest their malign power. Passions were sins, diseases, natural disasters, wild animals, demons, tyrants or rebels. When not pictured naturalistically as gales, eruptions, storms or earthquakes, passions were personified as advocates of vice, or as a rowdy and ungoverned mob clamouring to have their wicked way. The mind seemed to mirror society, comprised of its potentially rebellious lower orders (ungoverned appetites and passions), its well-ordered middling sorts (domestic affections, moral sentiments, sympathy), and its ruling elites (reason and the will). For political theorists, controlling the passions and controlling the people were spoken of in the same breath.[11] In his *Reflections on the Revolution in France* (1790), Edmund Burke argued that the role of government was to satisfy the need "not only that the passions of individuals should be subjected, but that even in the mass and body as well as in the individuals, the inclinations of men should frequently be thwarted, their will controlled, and their passions brought into subjection."[12]

Religious writers took a similar view. Isaac Watts's judgement in the 1720s was a typical one when he warned that "Ungoverned passions break all the bonds of human society and peace, and would change the tribes of mankind into brutal herds, or make the world a mere wilderness of savages." Watts wrote that he would not "give up the devout Christian to all wandering fooleries of warm and ungoverned passion." But neither did Watts want to see morality and religion become merely a "matter of speculation or cold reasoning."[13] For him, as for many others in the eighteenth century, a subduing of passion was to be combined with a cultivation of appropriate affections, conceived as a combination of feeling with thinking. Jonathan Edwards wrote in his *Treatise Concerning Religious Affections* (1746): "Holy affections are not heat without light, but evermore arise from some information of the understanding, some spiritual instruction that the mind receives, some light or actual knowledge."[14]

Francis Hutcheson captured well the eighteenth-century penchant for a rational and yet affectionate moral philosophy. He wrote, in the 1742 third edition of his *Essay on the Nature and Conduct of the Passions and Affections*, that the "temper which we esteem in the highest degree" was that "universal calm good-will or benevolence, where it is the leading affection of the soul, so as to limit or restrain all other affections, appetites, or passions." When such calm good-will and benevolent restraint prevailed, Hutcheson wrote, then we could approve, albeit to a lower degree, "every particular kind of affection or passion, which is not inconsistent with these higher and nobler dispositions." Our innate moral sense, he thought, showed this "calm extensive affection to be the highest perfection of our nature; what we may see to be the end or design of such a structure, and consequently what is required of us by the Author of our nature."[15]

Here then we have a sketch of what had become a standard view in moral philosophy by the eighteenth century, and one which persisted into the nineteenth. To live according to one's highest nature was to live as a rational animal, with libidinous passions subdued and godly and sympathetic affections cultivated (by reason, by the will, by habit). This twofold moral axiom—subdue passion, cultivate affection—assumed a division between reason and the passions. A governed and rational passion, properly educated and smartly dressed, could be deemed to have won the approval of the will and intellect, and to have gained entry into polite society in the form of sympathy, affection or sentiment. Thinkers who subscribed to some version of this standard view undoubtedly evoked a distinction between reason and the passions, but—and this is the key point—mental states we might today consider "emotions" were to be found on both sides of that divide. Consequently, statements by pre-modern theologians and their early-modern successors about either the terrible tyranny of the passions or the value of moral sentiments and religious affections cannot be taken as evidence of any generalised attitude to the "emotions."

II

It was against the backdrop of this widespread secular and religious consensus that reason ought to govern the passions that David Hume's famous dictum looked so striking: "Reason is, and ought only to be the slave of the passions."[16] In these few words, Hume signalled not only the humbling of reason, now given a lowly place as just one among the crowd of common passions, but also his rejection of the standard psychological model in which the mind was comprised of the capacities and movements of two great faculties, namely the will and the intellect. For Hume, instead, mental life was reduced to a series of impressions and feelings, strung together like beads on an unobservable necklace. Hume was one of the first writers in the English language to refer to "emotions" in something like the modern psychological sense. In this he may have been inspired by Descartes's recommendation of the term *émotions*. Other early users of the category were also Scottish, including Adam Smith, Lord Kames, and the Edinburgh moral philosopher Thomas Brown. Brown's hugely popular *Lectures on the Philosophy of the Human Mind* (1820) did more than any other work to fix the "emotions" in the nineteenth-century mind.[17]

The word "emotion" had previously signified any sort of commotion or disturbance (among the people, of the body, or in the mind). During the eighteenth century it became a more common term, sometimes used simply as a stylistic variant for "passion," "affection" or "feeling," but sometimes in a way that was deliberately contrasted with those older terms. Hume and Smith both used the term "emotions" quite freely and generally unsystematically to designate "movements" or "agitations" of the mind. In this sense, for Hume, an "emotion" could be something "which attends a passion."[18] Among those who made a clear distinction between "passions" and "emotions," Lord Kames stipulated that passions involved desires but that emotions did not, while the dissenting physician and philosopher Thomas Cogan was among those who thought that the term "emotions" should be used to refer to the outward bodily effects of inward passions of the mind.[19] Thomas Brown can be credited with laying the groundwork for a new paradigm, securing the place of the emotions as a modern psychological category, and bringing an end to some decades of terminological dispute.[20] Brown, like Hume before him, set aside the traditional faculty psychology espoused both by the scholastics and by his predecessors in the "Common Sense" school, instead reducing all mental phenomena to a series of states, conceived as basic psychological atoms, and divided into just three categories: sensations, thoughts, and emotions.

Brown's *Lectures* went through twenty editions between 1820 and 1860 and exercised a considerable influence on philosophical and psychological writers on both sides of the Atlantic. Brown's admirers included Thomas Chalmers and John Stuart Mill, and his category of the "emotions" was taken up by the pioneers of neurological and evolutionary approaches to the mind, including Alexander Bain, Herbert Spencer, Charles Darwin and William James. In 1874 Yale President Noah Porter wrote: "The influence of Brown's terminology and of his methods and conclusions has been potent in the formation and consolidation of the Associational Psychology—represented by J. Mill, J. S. Mill, Alexander Bain, and Herbert Spencer."[21] William James recalled, when delivering his Gifford Lectures in Edinburgh, that he had spent his youth "immersed in Dugald Stewart and Thomas Brown," whose works had inspired "juvenile emotions of reverence" that he had not yet outgrown.[22] The "emotions" served the purposes of a self-consciously secularising group of psychological thinkers. Through Darwin's *The Expression of the Emotions in Man and Animals* (1872) and William James's "What is an Emotion?" (1884) this new category became the property of the fledgling science of psychology. The "emotions" thus had a scientific cachet lacked by the "passions," and none of the latter term's theological and moral connotations. Unlike terms such as "passions," "lusts," "desires" and "affections," the term "emotions" never appeared in an English translation of the Bible.

Aside from inhabiting the more sterile semantic field appropriate to a scientific category, what else was different about the "emotions"? It was clear from the outset that this was a very capacious category. Previous distinctions between appetites, passions, affections and sentiments were gradually forgotten. Members of all of these older categories could now be found masquerading as emotions. Brown himself acknowledged that in creating a new category to replace what had previously been considered as various "active powers of the mind," he had "formed one great comprehensive class of our emotions."[23] Writing several decades later, the Scottish philosophical psychologist Alexander Bain also made clear the huge expanse of psychic territory that was being annexed under the new flag: "Emotion is the name here used to comprehend all that is understood by feelings, states of feeling, pleasures, pains, passions, sentiments, affections."[24]

While passions and affections had been generally defined as movements of the soul (specifically of the will and, in some cases, of the intellect too), the emotions were, from the outset, understood as basic mental feelings independent of any powers or faculties of the soul, which now disappeared. These were also feelings which were very strictly separated from the intellectual states. The new "emotions" paradigm therefore created a starker opposition between intellect and feeling than had existed in earlier systems of thought, and a contrast in which a much wider set of mental states was on the "feeling" side of the divide. Two-volume psychology textbooks of the late nineteenth century reinforced the division between intellect and emotion by allocating them one volume each.[25] Their separability was also evident in psychiatric debates about a condition known as "moral insanity" or "emotional insanity" in which the intellect remained intact but the emotions were disordered.[26] Finally, William James inscribed this same distinction onto the human body by treating cognition as cerebral and emotion as visceral. Emotions for James were nothing more than our awareness of bodily, visceral changes.

While the opposition between reason and the passions had been complex and mitigated, partly by the potentially rational nature of the passions, and especially by the existence of enlightened and reasonable affections, there was no such subtlety here. The intellect and the emotions were, from their nineteenth-century psychological conception onwards, deeply divided. It was this divide, more than the ancient opposition between reason and the passions, that had to be bridged by those scholars who sought, in the later twentieth century, to cross over to the other side to rescue our forgotten feelings. It is also here, in the nineteenth-century creation of the "emotions," that we find one place to mark a caesura, albeit a rather belated one, between the pre-modern and the distinctively modern in the history of thinking about feelings.

III

In 1895 a man with distinctively modern thoughts about his feelings, Oscar Wilde, was imprisoned for committing acts of "gross indecency." His sentence of two years imprisonment with hard labour, a secular mortification of his criminal flesh, forced him to rethink his sexual desires in a language appropriate to his new institutionalised existence. In July 1896 he petitioned the Home Secretary for early release, writing that he feared it would not be long before he entirely lost his mind. The petition was declined. In it Wilde wrote of himself, with we can only guess what motives, as the victim of a form of moral insanity:

> The petitioner is now keenly conscious of the fact that while the three years preceding his arrest were from the intellectual point of view the most brilliant years of his life . . . still that during that entire time he was suffering from the most horrible form of erotomania, which made him forget his wife and children, his high social position in London and Paris, his European distinction as an artist, the honour of his name and family, his very humanity itself, and left him the helpless prey of the most revolting passions, and of a gang of people who for their own profit ministered to them, and then drove him to his hideous ruin.[27]

This complex passage, in which several moral and medical ways of thinking are combined, gives some clues as to what happened to the passions after the arrival of the emotions. The first thing to note is that they still existed. However, once the scientific psychology of the emotions had emerged, to speak of the "passions" was to adopt a register of emphatic and somewhat archaic moralism. Wilde employed in this petition a view of the passions similar to those of Seneca and Augustine with which we started. He presented himself as the "helpless prey" of these moral predators, which operated in consort with an unscrupulous "gang of people." The passions, the blackmailers and the rent boys conspired together to undo him. Wilde's description of the passions as "revolting" depicted them simultaneously as disgusting and rebellious. Alongside the established mode of personifying the passions, however, was a distinctively modern and medicalised view: that this gruesome gang of passions amounted to a disease; that Wilde had been "suffering from the most horrible form of erotomania."

New concepts of "emotion" lacked the sense both of pathology and of suffering that had been so strongly embodied in the language of "passion" and its many cognate terms in theology, philosophy and medicine. In the "passions," passivity, pathology and suffering had all combined. It is thus no surprise that they had long been a medical as well as a moral category. Both "passion" and "affection" were used as terms for disease in the early modern period, as in phrases such as "hysteric passion" or "febrile affection." Passions were conceived as both causes and symptoms of organic disease, and as diseases themselves. In Erasmus Darwin's *Zoonomia* (1794–6), for instance, a wide range of passions, including grief and anger, were treated as examples of "Diseases of Volition" and as varieties of temporary insanity.[28] From the point of view of the history of medicine, the passions were not replaced by "emotions" but by the whole panoply of manias and phobias which were brought into being by the techniques and theories of modern psychiatry. One answer, then, to the question of what happened to the passions is that they were incarcerated en masse in Victorian lunatic asylums and prisons.

While inside Reading Gaol, as well as writing of his revolting passions, Oscar Wilde reflected on philosophy, art and emotion. In the spiritual autobiography which would ultimately be published as *De Profundis* he wrote that, while he had previously thought that the true self should be realised through pleasure he now believed that it could only be through pain, and that sorrow, "being the supreme emotion of which man is capable, is at once the type and test of all great art." He attributed to Wordsworth the idea that the true aim of the poet was "to contemplate the spectacle of life with appropriate emotions." In fact this was a dictum of Walter Pater's, which Wilde now adapted to his circumstances. Imprisoned, he felt "dead to all emotions except those of anguish and despair," and was prey now not to the passions of erotomania but to "the first and most prominent emotion produced by modern prison life—the emotion of terror."[29]

This ethos of "appropriate emotions" found a more definitive and analytic expression in the *Principia Ethica* (1903) of G. E. Moore. Like Wilde, Moore could still employ the old language of the "passions" when in moralistic mode. In order to illustrate his view of the nature of the good, for example, Moore started by explaining the nature of evil, taking as his two instances "cruelty and lasciviousness." "That these are great intrinsic evils we may, I think, easily assure ourselves," he wrote, "by imagining the state of a man, whose mind is solely occupied by either of these passions, in their worst form." Moore went on to explain that right action often involved the "suppression of some evil impulse," which accounted for the plausibility of the view that "virtue *consists* in the control of passion by reason."[30] However his was an ethos of emotion rather than of either reason or passion. The whole moral register was different. While phrases such as "evil passions" or "criminal passions" had previously been commonplace, and even occurred in the writings of Wilde and Moore, no-one wrote about "evil emotions." Moore's ethical ideas show how both the "Moral Sense" and the Platonic ethical traditions could find a central place for emotions. It was, then, not just the passions but also the moral sentiments and aesthetic affections that could be rethought under the guise of "emotions," conceived either as an innate moral compass or as the very goal of life.

Thomas Brown was a pioneer in thinking not only about "emotions" in general but about the "moral emotions" in particular. Following in the Humean tradition of asserting the supremacy of feeling over reason in the moral realm, Brown suggested a modification of the moral sense tradition in terms of "moral emotions." Moral approval was, for Brown, a matter of feeling, not of reasoning. "To say that an action excites in us this feeling," he wrote, "and to say, that it appears to us right, or virtuous, or conformable to duty, are to say precisely the same thing." It was a brute fact about our minds that "in certain circumstances, we are susceptible of moral emotions." The universality and objectivity of morality was justified, on this model, as on Hutcheson's, by the identical constitution of all human minds, which revealed the intentions of the Deity.[31]

A secularised version of this same idea was to be found in Charles Darwin's moral thought. In one of his early private notebooks, Darwin had already invoked common descent as an idea that could shed a whole new light on the moral economy: "Our descent, then, is the origin of our evil passions!! The Devil under form of Baboon is our grandfather!"[32] In the *Descent of Man* (1871), Darwin turned his attention to those higher instincts of sympathy and love which comprised the "moral sense." Darwin's naturalised and inherited moral sense, like Brown's divinely devised moral emotions, guaranteed universal moral standards. But the Darwinian moral sense had its origins not in the mind of God but in the contingencies of the natural and social history of our species, which could have been quite different:

> If, for instance, to take an extreme case, men were reared under precisely the same conditions as hive-bees, there can hardly be a doubt that our unmarried females would, like the worker-bees, think it a sacred duty to kill their brothers, and mothers would strive to kill their fertile daughters; and no one would think of interfering.[33]

For G. E. Moore too, it was emotion rather than reason that had the key role in directing the moral life. Following on from his thought that cruelty and lasciviousness were evil passions which were bad in themselves, Moore suggested that an idea of particular evils to be avoided was usually accompanied by a "strong moral emotion" directing us away from evils and towards moral duties.[34]

Moore's *Principia Ethica* became known as the "Bloomsbury Bible" not for its more or less conventional ideas about the capacity of moral emotions to reinforce our sense of duty, however, but for its gospel of hedonistic aestheticism. In the final chapter of the book, Moore set out his vision of the good life and of those things that were good in themselves. The latter were said to be the emotions felt in response to beauty and to human friendship. These were not merely put forward as the favoured mental states of refined late-Victorian students, artists and intellectuals but were grandly asserted to constitute "*all* the greatest, and *by far* the greatest, goods we can imagine." The appreciation of beauty was the highest good of all. Such appreciation, Moore stipulated, should not be

> merely a bare cognition of what is beautiful in the object, but also some kind of feeling or emotion. It is not sufficient that a man should merely see the beautiful qualities in a picture and know that they are beautiful, in order that we may give his state of mind the highest praise.[35]

In short, in order to deserve the highest praise, "he should have an appropriate emotion towards the beautiful qualities which he cognises." For G. E. Moore, in one of the defining transitional texts between Victorianism and Modernism, the proper end of life was neither rationality nor good character, neither the knowledge nor the love of God, neither the greatest happiness of the greatest number nor the general good of society. The goal of life was the experience of appropriate aesthetic emotions.

IV

While we might assume that it does nothing to the physical structure of a piece of matter to categorise it as a salt rather than a metal, nor to the physiology, or even the mental experience, of an animal, if we categorise it as a mammal rather than a fish, we cannot make such an assumption about our psychological categories. In this case, the nature of the thing studied (our mental life) is changed by the theoretical instruments used to investigate and explain it.[36] It surely makes a difference, for instance, to our experience and understanding of ourselves, whether we think of our anger as being produced by our inner demons or by our inner baboon; of our love as the movement of a soul or the firing of neurons; of our conscience as an inherited emotion or the voice of God; of our frustration and despair as signs of sin and the Fall or of suppressed and unconscious desires. Theories of passions and emotions take their place within larger histories of psychological models and languages, which in turn reflect their social and institutional contexts. The death of the passions in the nineteenth century coincided with aggressive secularisation; with widespread state incarceration of criminals and lunatics; and with the granting of the vote to increasing numbers of the working classes. We might accordingly try to answer the psychological question of what happened to the passions in social and institutional terms: they died with God; they were locked up; they got the vote. And in the twentieth and twenty-first centuries, the personification of feeling states continues but in new terms. Instead of thinking about our passions as unruly subjects to be governed or as dangerous enemies to be driven out, we treat our emotions as corporate employees to be managed and psychotherapeutic patients to be counselled and understood. The histories of our social lives, our language, and our self-understanding proceed together.

Current psychological theories of emotions may be new, but they are not entirely detached from their histories. Recent work in the philosophy of emotion has shown signs of rediscovering some ancient ideas. Contemporary philosophers of emotion tend to divide into two broad camps: the cognitivists, who favour the view that emotions are a form of appraisal or judgement, and the non-cognitivists, who take their lead from neuroscientific accounts of emotion. Among cognitivists, Robert Solomon and Martha Nussbaum have been influential in promoting the neo-Stoic idea that emotions are judgements rather than mere feelings or epiphenomena of bodily processes. While the ancient Stoics taught that all passions were mistaken judgements (the relevant mistake generally being the valuing of external goods such as health and prosperity), the neo-Stoics have promoted the idea that emotions are judgements while denying that they are necessarily mistaken ones. In the field of neuroscience, Antonio Damasio and Joseph LeDoux have proposed new ways of thinking about the emotions as hard-wired appraisal mechanisms in the brain. This line of research has also resulted in the suggestion that there are two distinct emotional pathways in the brain, one for basic emotions or "affect programmes" and another more cognitive and complex route for secondary emotions. It seems that neuroscience, as well as the history of ideas, can suggest ways we might create subdivisions within Thomas Brown's over-inclusive category of the "emotions."[37]

The main casualty in the creation of secular, scientific, and sterilised psychologies of the emotions has been that strong sense of cognitive, moral and even medical pathology which was prominent in both Stoic and Christian traditions of thought about the passions. Psychoanalytic theories have had more success than other strands of secular psychology in describing the disordered and chaotic state of the human mind. But even then, that disordered condition of the mind which used to be thought of as universal tends now to be recognised only in those in need of psychiatric or psychotherapeutic treatment rather than in everyone; in patients rather than in passions. But even here the wisdom of the Stoics has not been entirely forgotten. Martha Nussbaum looks at the world today with the weary but penetrating gaze of a modern Stoic. What do we see, she asks, when we look around ourselves at our friends and colleagues?

Do we see calm rational people, whose beliefs about value are for the most part well based and sound? No. We see people rushing frenetically about after money, after fame, after gastronomic luxuries, after passionate love—people convinced by the culture itself, by the stories on which they are brought up, that such things have far more value than in fact they have. Everywhere we see victims of false social advertising: people convinced in their hearts that they cannot possibly live without their hoards of money, their imported delicacies, their social standing, their lovers— although these beliefs result from teaching and may have little relation to the real truth about worth. Do we, then, see a healthy rational society, whose shared beliefs can be trusted as material for a true account of the good life? No. We see a sick society, a society whose sick teachings about love and sex turn half of its members into possessions, both deified and hated, the other half into sadistic keepers, tormented by anxiety; a society that slaughters thousands, using ever more ingeniously devastating engines of war, in order to escape its gnawing fear of vulnerability. We see a society, above all, whose every enterprise is poisoned by the fear of death, a fear that will not let its members taste any stable human joy, but turns them into the grovelling slaves of corrupt religious teachers.[38]

Unfeeling apathy may be no more desirable a goal than the chaotic world of anxieties and desires conjured up by Nussbaum, but at the same time as rethinking our recent affection for the emotions we might also question our antipathy to *apatheia*. The task of the apprentice Stoic today—a latter-day Lucilius—would be to articulate and live out an ideal of calm philosophical detachment in the midst of computerised consumerised chaos, but without losing all humanity. Should we be offering the requisite mental training for such a task? Or is there no reason left to resist our revolting passions?

NOTES

 1 Charles Darwin, *The Expression of the Emotions in Man and Animals* (London: Murray, 1872); William James, "What Is an Emotion?," *Mind*, Vol. 9 (1884), pp. 188–205. The ideas that form the background to the present chapter are developed and documented in two previous publications: Thomas Dixon, *From Passions to Emotions: The Creation of a Secular Psychological Category* (Cambridge: Cambridge University Press, 2003); idem "Patients and Passions: Languages of Medicine and Emotion, 1789–1850," in Fay Bound Alberti (ed.), *Medicine, Emotion and Disease, 1700–1950* (Basingstoke: Palgrave Macmillan, 2006), pp. 22–52.
 2 Several of these historical and philosophical issues are brought into focus by Stephen Mulhall.
 3 Seneca, *Letters from a Stoic* selected and translated with an introduction by Robin Campbell (London: Penguin, 1969), Letter xlvii, p. 95; see also Letters xl and lxxxviii. On the therapeutics of the passions in ancient philosophy, see Pierre Hadot, *Philosophy as a Way of Life: Spiritual Exercises from Socrates to Foucault*, trans. M. Chase (Oxford: Blackwell, 1995); Richard Sorabji, *Emotion and Peace of Mind: From Stoic Agitation to Christian Temptation* (Oxford: Oxford University Press, 2000); Martha C. Nussbaum, *The Therapy of Desire: Theory and Practice in Hellenistic Ethics*, new edition (Princeton, NJ: Princeton University Press, 2009).
 4 Augustine, *The Free Choice of the Will*, trans. R. Russell, in *The Fathers of the Church*, Vol. LIX (Washington, DC: Catholic University of America Press, 1968), pp. 93–94.
 5 Augustine, *The City of God*, trans. G. Walsh and G. Monahan, in *The Fathers of the Church*, Vols. XIII-XV (Washington, DC: Catholic University of America Press, 1952), XIV.9.
 6 Dixon, *Passions to Emotions*, chap. 2, esp. pp. 39–48.
 7 Ibid. For alternative and more detailed readings of Aquinas on the passions of the soul see also Robert C. Miner, *Thomas Aquinas on the Passions: A Study of Summa Theologiae 1a2ae 22–48* (Cambridge: Cambridge University Press, 2009); Diana Fritz Cates, *Aquinas on the Emotions: A Religious-Ethical Inquiry* (Washington, DC: Georgetown University Press, 2009); Nicholas E. Lombardo, *The Logic of Desire: Aquinas on Emotion* (Washington, DC: Catholic University of America Press, 2010).
 8 Thomas Aquinas, *Summa Theologiae*, trans. Dominican Fathers (London: Blackfriars, 1964–81), Ia, q. 82, a. 5, ad 1.
 9 In both Augustine and Aquinas the key Latin terms are not used in an entirely consistent way, and the distinction between passions and affections that I am suggesting is not worked out by them systematically. However there is considerable textual support for the basic interpretation suggested here: see Dixon, *Passions to Emotions*, pp. 39–48.
10 I am grateful to Douglas Hedley and David Martin for pointing out some of these more positive roles for the passions.
11 Dixon, "Patients and Passions"; Roy Porter, *A Social History of Madness: Stories of the Insane* (London: Phoenix, 1996), pp. 39–59. A recent edited collection looks at a wide range of roles for the passions (and emotions) in the history of political thought: Rebecca Kingston and Leonard Ferry (eds.), *Bringing the Passions Back In: The Emotions in Political Philosophy* (Vancouver: University of British Columbia Press, 2008).

12   Edmund Burke, *Reflections on the French Revolution, and Other Essays* (London: Dent, 1910), p. 57.

13   Isaac Watts, *The Doctrine of the Passions Explained and Improved* (Coventry: Luckman, n.d.), p. v; *Discourses on the Love of God, and its Influence on all the Passions* (London: Oswald and Buckland, 1746), p. xi. Both works were first published in 1729.

14   Jonathan Edwards, *A Treatise Concerning Religious Affections*, J. Smith (ed.) (New Haven, CT: Yale University Press, 1959), p. 266. First published 1746.

15   Francis Hutcheson, *An Essay on the Nature and Conduct of the Passions and Affections, with Illustrations on the Moral Sense*, third edition, introduction by Paul McReynolds (Gainesville, FL: Scholars' Facsimiles & Reprints, 1969), p. xvi. First published London, 1742.

16   David Hume, *A Treatise of Human Nature*, L. Selby-Bigge and P. Nidditch (eds.) (Oxford: Clarendon, 1978), p. 415. First published 1739–40. See also Dixon, *From Passions to Emotions*, pp. 104–109.

17   Dixon, *From Passions to Emotions*, pp. 109–127; idem (ed.), *Thomas Brown: Selected Philosophical Writings* (Exeter: Imprint Academic, 2010).

18   Hume, *Treatise of Human Nature*, p. 419.

19   On Kames, see Adela Pinch, *Strange Fits of Passion: Epistemologies of Emotion, Hume to Austen* (Stanford, CA: Stanford University Press, 1996), pp. 4–6, 49–50. Cogan, who received his MD from Leyden for a dissertation on the passions, wrote three books on the subject, which were widely cited in the first half of the nineteenth century: Thomas Cogan, *An Ethical Treatise on the Passions* (Bath: Hazard and Binns, 1807); *A Philosophical Treatise on the Passions* (Bath: S. Hazard, 1802); *Theological Disquisitions; or an Enquiry into those Principles of Religion, which are Most Influential in Directing and Regulating the Passions and Affections of the Mind* (Bath: Hazard and Binns, 1812).

20   Dixon, *From Passions to Emotions*, pp. 130–131.

21   Noah Porter, "Philosophy in Great Britain and America: A Supplementary Sketch," in Friedrich Ueberweg (ed.), *History of Philosophy from Thales to the Present Time*, Vol. II. *History of Modern Philosophy* (London: Hodder and Stoughton, 1874), pp. 349–460, quotation at p. 410.

22   William James, *The Varieties of Religious Experience: A Study in Human Nature. Being the Gifford Lectures on Natural Religion Delivered at Edinburgh in 1901–1902* (London: Longmans, Green, and Co., 1902), p. 2.

23   Thomas Brown, *Lectures on the Philosophy of the Human Mind* (Edinburgh: Tait, 1828), Lecture 73, p. 485.

24   Alexander Bain, *The Emotions and the Will* (London: Parker, 1859), p. 3.

25   Alexander Bain, *The Senses and the Intellect* (London: Parker, 1855) and *The Emotions and the Will* (London: Parker, 1859); James McCosh, *Psychology: The Cognitive Powers* (London: Macmillan, 1886) and *Psychology: The Motive Powers* (London: Macmillan, 1887); James Mark Baldwin, *Handbook of Psychology I: The Senses and the Intellect; II: Feeling and Will* (London: Macmillan, 1891); James Sully, *The Human Mind: A Textbook of Psychology* (London: Longmans, Green, and Co., 1892).

26   Richard Hunter and Ida Macalpine (eds.), *Three Hundred Years of Psychiatry, 1535–1860: A History Presented in Selected English Texts* (London: Oxford University Press, 1963), pp. 836–842; Vieda Skultans, *Madness and Morals: Ideas on Insanity in the Nineteenth Century* (London: Routledge and Kegan Paul, 1975), chapter 6; idem, *English Madness: Ideas on Insanity 1580–1890* (London: Routledge and Kegan Paul, 1979), pp. 65–68.

27   Merlin Holland and Rupert Hart-Davis (eds.), *The Complete Letters of Oscar Wilde* (London: Fourth Estate, 2000), p. 656. See also Ellis Hanson, "Wilde's Exquisite Pain," in J. Bristow (ed.), *Wilde Writings: Contextual Conditions* (Toronto and Buffalo: University of Toronto Press in association with the UCLA Center for Seventeenth- and Eighteenth-Century Studies and the William Andrews Clark Memorial Library, 2003), pp. 101–123; Thomas Dixon, *The Invention of Altruism: Making Moral Meanings in Victorian Britain* (Oxford: Oxford University Press for the British Academy, 2008), pp. 333–343.

28   Erasmus Darwin, *Zoonomia, or the Laws of Organic Life* (London: Johnson, 1794–6), 2 vols, Vol. 1, section XXXIV.

29   Oscar Wilde, *The Complete Works of Oscar Wilde, Volume 2. De Profundis: "Epistola in Carcere Et Vinculis,"* edited with an introduction and notes by Ian Small (Oxford: Oxford University Press, 2005), pp. 105, 109, 316, 324; the last two quotations are from letters to Robbie Ross and to a daily newspaper, respectively.

30 G. E. Moore, *Principia Ethica*, Revised edition. Edited and with an introduction by Thomas Baldwin (Cambridge: Cambridge University Press, 1993), pp. 257–258, 267. First published 1903.

31 Thomas Brown, *Lectures on the Philosophy of the Human Mind* (Edinburgh: Tait, 1828), Lecture 74, pp. 493–494.

32 Paul H. Barrett *et al.* (eds.), *Charles Darwin's Notebooks, 1836–1844: Geology, Transmutation of Species, Metaphysical Enquiries* (Cambridge: Cambridge University Press, 1987), pp. 549–550.

33 Charles Darwin, *The Descent of Man, and Selection in Relation to Sex*, second edition, revised and augmented (London: John Murray, 1882), pp. 98–99. First published 1871. See also Dixon, *Invention of Altruism*, pp. 129–180.

34 Moore, *Principia Ethica*, pp. 266–267.

35 Ibid., p. 238.

36 This idea was suggested by comments made at the Cambridge Symposium by Peter Goldie, about the reflexivity of psychological categories. See also Roger Smith, "The History of Psychological Categories," *Studies in History and Philosophy of Biological and Biomedical Sciences*, Vol. 36 (2005), pp. 55–94; idem, *Being Human: Historical Knowledge and the Creation of Human Nature* (Manchester: Manchester University Press, 2007); Ian Hacking, *The Social Construction of What?* (Cambridge, MA: Harvard University Press, 1999); Muhammad Ali Khalidi, "Interactive Kinds," *British Journal for the Philosophy of Science*, Vol. 61 (2010), pp. 335–60.

37 Two particularly helpful collections of recent work in the philosophy of emotions are Anthony Hatzimoysis (ed.), *Philosophy and the Emotions* (Cambridge: Cambridge University Press, 2003) and Peter Goldie (ed.), *The Oxford Handbook of Philosophy of Emotion* (Oxford: Oxford University Press, 2010).

38 Nussbaum, *The Therapy of Desire*, p. 103.

13

WITTGENSTEIN ON FAITH, RATIONALITY, AND THE PASSIONS

STEPHEN MULHALL

Wittgenstein's actual impact in the philosophy of religion has been more a function of the work of those inspired by him than of his own remarks on this topic (which are exiguous and fragmentary in the extreme, often mediated through the recollections and annotations of others, and so hard to interpret with any confidence).[1] Wittgensteinian philosophers of religion anyway took their primary inspiration not from his writings on religion (most of which were not published until after much canonically Wittgensteinian work in the field had been done),[2] but from his later approach to philosophy in general, as manifest in the *Philosophical Investigations*.[3] And their work has been burdened virtually from its outset by the charge of fideism. This charge originated with Kai Nielsen, who argued that assumptions common to a range of Wittgensteinian authors entailed an unacceptable immunization of religious belief against rational criticism (just as theological fideists hold that religious belief is grounded on faith rather than reason). Repeated and fervent attempts on the part of those authors to rebut the charge have never succeeded in removing it from this intellectual scene;[4] so in the argument that follows I cannot avoid engaging with that charge, if only to clear the ground for a more productive discussion of the real bearing of Wittgenstein's actual reflections on that theme. After that ground-clearing, I propose to divide my attention more or less evenly between the two key sources we have for Wittgenstein's own views. Accordingly, the second part of this article will look at one exemplary issue arising from the 1938 lecture material—that of the indispensability of pictures in religious speech, thought and life; and the third part will focus on a limited sample of the remarks about the Christian religion in *Culture and Value*, since a number of those remarks explicitly

Faith, Rationality, and the Passions, First Edition. Edited by Sarah Coakley.
© 2012 Blackwell Publishing Ltd. Book compilation © 2012 Blackwell Publishing Ltd.

address the question of how religious faith relates to reason (in the form of wisdom or the speculative intellect) and to the passions.

Fideism and the Veil of Grammar

In his original article, Kai Nielsen specifies the unacceptable core of Wittgensteinian Fideism as follows:

> There is no Archimedean point in terms of which a philosopher (or for that matter anyone else) can relevantly criticize whole modes of discourse or, what comes to the same thing, ways of life, for each mode of discourse has its own specific criteria of rationality/irrationality, intelligibility/unintelligibility and reality/unreality. (WF, p. 22)

Nielsen emphasizes that this unacceptable conclusion results from attempts by Wittgensteinian philosophers to elaborate certain, possibly insightful strands of Wittgenstein's thought in ways that Wittgenstein himself might not have endorsed; but he also asserts that these elaborations are perfectly natural developments of claims that Wittgenstein did make, and that the conclusion they license is patently absurd. The strands of thought he has in mind are as follows: i) to imagine a language is to imagine a form of life [cf. PI, § 19]; ii) what must be accepted—the given—are forms of life [cf. PI, § 226]; iii) ordinary language is in order as it stands [cf. PI, § 98, citing TLP 5.5563]; iv) philosophy must in no way interfere with the actual use of language, but can in the end only describe it [cf. PI, § 124]. One can hardly deny that Wittgenstein makes these claims, or something like them. The key question is: to what extent does a proper understanding of them license a species of fideism in the philosophy of religion?

It is worth emphasizing that these four claims are not restricted to the field of religion; their range of application is perfectly general, including all aspects of our ordinary lives with words. By contrast, their intended audience *is* restricted: they are primarily addressed to philosophers, forming part of Wittgenstein's various attempts to articulate his sense of what philosophy—with its particular cares and commitments—can and cannot do with respect to our ordinary lives with words. Two points follow immediately. First, if the consequence of applying these claims with respect to religious belief is a species of fideism, then a parallel conclusion must follow from their application to any other mode of discourse. If Wittgenstein is a fideist about religion, that will not be because of any view he holds about religious faith in particular, but rather because he adopts what amounts to a fideist stance with respect to human language and forms of life in general—an entirely global substitution of faith for reason. Second, Nielsen's assumption that the apparent restrictions Wittgenstein places upon the critical activities of philosophers must also apply more generally is potentially misleading. It is legitimate, but trivially so, if it means that the "restrictions" apply not just to those who profess to be academic philosophers, but to anyone with a genuinely philosophical interest in our language and forms of life; but it is mistaken if it means that those "restrictions" apply to everyone, regardless of whether their critical interest in our language and forms of life is genuinely philosophical.

What does Wittgenstein take to be distinctive of a philosophical interest in things? What is the typical character of a philosophical question or problem? According to the discussion of philosophical method in §§89–133 of the *Investigations* (from which two of Nielsen's four strands of Wittgensteinian thought are taken), a philosopher is interested in the essence of things; she is driven by an urge to comprehend not the facts of nature but rather the basis or essence of everything empirical—the space of possibilities within which what happens to be the case locates itself. A philosophical question is thus one to which the acquisition of further empirical knowledge is irrelevant: the philosopher does not seek new knowledge in order to alleviate ignorance; she seeks understanding in order to relieve a sense of confusion about what she already knows. And whereas traditional philosophers tend to conceive of the essence of things as hidden from view, hence as having to be revealed, say by penetrating the veil of mere appearance, Wittgenstein suggests instead that essence finds expression in grammar—in the kinds of statement that we make about the relevant phenomenon. In short, our philosophical inquiries into essence can and must take the form of grammatical investigations; the essence of things can be rendered surveyable simply by a rearrangement of what any speaker always already knows—how to use words, what to say when.

Wittgenstein's view seems to be that the kinds of statement we make about a phenomenon, and the kinds of statement we do not make, display the kind of phenomenon it is; if we clarify the criteria we employ for counting something as a phenomenon of the relevant kind, we thereby clarify that without which such a phenomenon would not be the kind of thing it is. What we judge that it does (not) make sense to say about something makes manifest its essential possibilities, the kinds of features it must possess if it is to count as the kind of thing it is, as well as those features it may possess (and the kinds of variation of feature to which it might intelligibly be subject) without ceasing to count as that kind of thing. To know this is, in effect, to grasp our concept of that thing; and what more might there be to knowing the essence of a thing than that?

But might not the essence of the thing nevertheless differ from our concept of it, so that its true, underlying nature is not manifest in, but rather hidden by, the grammar of our discourse about it? If so, grammar is simply one more veil of appearance that philosophical inquiry must, in principle, be willing to penetrate. But to conceive of grammar as an (at least potentially) concealing veil involves conceiving of it as a false or otherwise misleading representation of what is really the case; and that in turn involves conceiving of it as being in the business of representation (as if modes of discourse were theories). But if a grammatical investigation displays what it makes sense to say about something (what it is for any talk about something to count as, to be, talk about that kind of thing), then the grammar thereby made manifest is not itself a kind of talk about that thing, and so cannot be saying anything false or otherwise misleading about it—any more than it can be saying something true.

Grammar, one might say, articulates a logical space of possibilities within which something of the relevant kind will occupy some particular location or other; it articulates the terms in which that kind of thing can intelligibly be represented (truly or falsely). But if one regards those terms as themselves representations of something, one is attempting to conceive of a mode of discourse as if it were a particular discursive act—to think of this logical space as itself the occupant of a particular location in a larger space of possibilities, as if grammar itself were a deployment of grammar, and clarifications of meaning were descriptions of reality. It amounts to viewing the distinction between sense and nonsense as if it were a species of the distinction between truth and falsehood.

This is one way of recounting the grammar of Wittgenstein's concept of grammar, as understood by the canonical Wittgensteinian philosophers Nielsen targets. And the point of recalling it is not to demonstrate that the highly controversial conception of philosophy it engenders is right, but to clarify what the consequences of adopting it really are. First, Wittgenstein's methodological advice is directed primarily to those with a distinctively philosophical interest in the essence of things, and a distinctively philosophical tendency to imagine that our modes of discourse with respect to those things stands in need of a certain kind of rational justification (because they presupposed a mode of correspondence to reality that they might not possess). It is only to those in the grip of such a picture of grammar as a kind of representation that Wittgenstein's methodological remarks are worth making.

Second, although those remarks appear to restrict philosophy to the task of describing grammar (as opposed to explaining, hypothesizing or theorizing about an essence of things that grammar might veil), they do not in fact impose a restriction of any kind. For if, as Wittgenstein claims, evaluations in terms of truth or falsity are not amongst the kinds of judgements to which we subject articulations of grammar, then there is no intelligibly specifiable task of the kind philosophers take themselves to be envisaging when they suggest that grammar might veil essence from our sight, and so nothing that we are prevented from doing, or even from attempting to do, when observing Wittgenstein's methodological advice. That advice is, strictly speaking, not a recommendation or a command, but a reminder—a reminder that what we are tempted to picture as a limitation (beyond which there is something specific that we cannot do) is in fact a limit (an acknowledgement that nothing, neither a possible task nor an impossible task, has thus far been specified). One might say: there is no larger philosophical space of the relevant kind within which Wittgenstein's conception of the subject locates itself, and hence no alternative conception to which one might oppose it. Accordingly, properly understanding his remarks means realizing that they are in a certain sense self-subverting—that their apparently prohibitive intention is in fact nothing of the kind, and leaves everything precisely as it was for those who wish to criticize any given mode of discourse or form of life.

In the specific case of religious practices and ways of life, it is not just that one can wield the full range of internally-acknowledged ways of criticizing specific elements, as well as specific versions, of that way of life (modes of criticism embodied in such notions as "superstition" and "heresy"). There is also a wide range of what one might call external modes of criticism, including ones that question the legitimacy of religious ways of life as such. Nothing Wittgenstein claims about the grammar of "grammar" prohibits someone from finding religious belief to encourage immorality, political and social discrimination, cultural primitivism and barbarism, to name but a few of the more familiar objections to which religions are heir.

Nietzsche is a particularly interesting example here. His genealogical analysis of Christianity is an attempt to characterize the essence of that mode of religious belief—where essence here is understood exactly as Wittgenstein proposes in PI §§ 89–133: as a matter of the function or structure of the phenomenon under consideration, taken not as a doctrinal system on which a set of practices is founded but as a mode of speaking, thinking and living—a way of making sense of things as a whole. When Nietzsche characterizes that form of human life as inherently ascetic, hence as a sadomasochistic mode of life-denial, he aims to provide a criticism of the point or purpose of the Christian religious enterprise as such (together with its secular variants and offshoots). And nothing Wittgenstein says about the essentially descriptive nature of philosophy provides any reason for believing that religious forms of life, taken as a whole, cannot coherently be criticized in such terms.

Nielsen's critical characterization of Wittgensteinian philosophy of religion as fideistic implies that it regards religious forms of life as founded on faith rather than reason, hence as immune to any kind of rational criticism, because their intelligibility depends on criteria internal to those forms of life, and essentially distinct from those governing other modes of discourse. In fact, Wittgenstein's general philosophical principles (if they deserve so grand a title) suggest only that one apparently coherent kind of rational evaluation of modes of discourse is really empty; there is no obvious sense to be made of such criticism at the level of forms of life taken as a whole. But if there is no conceptual space for such exercises of reason, then there is no space that might be occupied by faith as opposed to reason, either in general or in the specific case of religious forms of life. And since "external" critiques of the kinds mentioned above plainly make sense both to religious believers and to others, we have no reason to believe that either the intelligibility or the rationality of religious belief must be settled in terms that are determined by religious believers, and essentially distinct from the terms appropriate to other forms of life. Nietzsche's criticism, for example, aims rather to subvert the terms of religious self-understanding, as well as the central concepts of modern, non-religious ethics.

What *is* (trivially) required of such "external" critiques is that they be comprehensible as critiques of the particular forms of religious life that they purport to target: in other words, we must be able to make sense of them as criticisms of this specific phenomenon. But whether any such critique does so is not settleable a priori—as if grammar determines in advance which forms of criticism of religion are licit and which are not. It can only be settled in our actual judgements, from case to case, of actually-constructed criticism, and as the example of Nietzsche shows, such cases might as easily compel us to revise our hitherto-settled overall sense of what religion can and does mean as they might confirm it.

Faith, Pictures, and Philosophy

It is commonly assumed that Wittgenstein's view of religious belief amounts to a species of expressivism, one which claims—as one standard commentary puts it[5]—that "talk of God is in some manner expressive of feelings, attitudes and emotions" (IWPR, p. 67). This claim is usually presented as if entailed by the kind of account Wittgenstein offers of various religious beliefs in his 1938 lectures—as, for example, when he suggests that a belief in the Last Judgement may be better understood, not as a speculative hypothesis about a future event but rather as a picture playing a certain role in the life of the believer (one of admonition, so that the idea of himself as under judgement pervasively shapes the way in which he lives). Generalizing from such specific accounts, commentators conclude that for Wittgenstein religious discourse as a whole does not have a straightforwardly object-naming, fact-depicting character, but rather deploys an array of pictures and stories designed to have a particular psychological-cum-moral practical force. Hence, for Wittgenstein, religion is best understood as "an aid to conduct, a collection of pictures which serve to reinforce a distinctive morality, 'rules of life dressed up in pictures'" (IWPR, p. 71).

This generalization emerges from a very meagre diet of examples, to the specific details of which very little attention has been given—for example, the quoted phrase "rules of life dressed up in pictures" comes from Wittgenstein's discussion of Bunyan's *Pilgrim's Progress* (CV, p. 34), and hence is specifically responsive to the language of an allegorical tale with religious designs on us rather than to the language of the Gospels, or of religious liturgy. It also manages to conflate feelings, emotions and attitudes, and assumes that if something has expressive force it cannot have cognitive content as well. But we can set such difficulties of detail aside for present purposes, for they will be pertinent in evaluating Wittgenstein's position only if the very idea of a religious belief as involving the use of a picture commits one to a form of expressivism that embodies such difficulties—the kind we have just seen being attributed to him. And in my view, it does not.

One might, of course, define the genus of expressivist accounts of a given type of language use in very broad terms: for example, it may suffice for an account of religious utterances to be an expressivist one if that account identifies an internal relation between the utterance and the domain of will and action (as opposed to its aspiring merely to describe a putative state of affairs).[6] But the charge of expressivism as levelled above carries a greater weight of implication, and hence invokes a stronger or more substantial species of that genus, for it attributes to Wittgenstein the view that pictures are essentially dispensable discursive ornaments. The relevant attitude or feeling might be powerfully or dramatically expressed by utilizing them, but it could also in principle be expressed in other ways, so the identity of the relevant attitudes must be given independently of those modes of expression. This is why commentators attracted to this interpretation of Wittgenstein think of him as offering a moral interpretation of religion—that is, an interpretation of religion as morality dressed up in pictures: the pictures are mere clothing, and the core of the phenomenon they cloak is ethical (i.e., having to do with principles of conduct or ways of living), hence articulable in non-religious terms. This kind of expressivism thus amounts to a species of reductionism about religion (and may invite or embody further reductionist impulses, insofar as it appears to attribute mere practical force—as opposed to intellectual content—to moral rules, and thereby to sign up to non-cognitivist or even emotivist interpretations of ethics).

But Wittgenstein explicitly denies that the pictures he claims to find in religious discourse function as dispensable ornaments; a picture is in use, but it is not used in order to express an attitude or feeling that might be perfectly adequately expressed in some other way. In the third of his lectures on religious belief, he imagines a friend of his who, before going on a long and dangerous journey, says to him: "we might see one another after death." One of his long-suffering students suggests that, if Wittgenstein is right to regard this as another example of the use of a picture, his friend's remark should be understood as expressive of a certain attitude, to which Wittgenstein responds: "No, it isn't the same as saying 'I'm very fond of you'—and it may not be the same as saying anything else. It says what it says . . . Of certain pictures we say that they might just as well be replaced by another. [In other cases], the whole *weight* may be in the picture" (LC, pp. 71–72).

What, however, might it mean for the whole weight to be in the picture? What are the kinds of case in which religious believers employ a picture about which one might want to say that "the whole weight is in the picture"?

Cora Diamond has discussed this matter in a fascinating essay, and provided an illuminating example of just such a case by examining one way in which anthropomorphic ways of speaking of God might present themselves as indispensable, and so as not adequately replaceable by—for example—an inherently impersonal concept of the Divine[7]. She picks up the Judaeo-Christian idea of God as having revealed himself, in deed and word (those of his prophets and, in the Christian case, those of Christ himself), and as having thereby made it possible for his hearers to speak and act in response to this unprecedented self-revelation; it is only in the terms made newly available through God's actions in history that the hearer can understand the kind of conduct truly expected of her. God is thus held to have revealed himself in such a way as to have given a transformed content to the word "God"—Diamond, following Rosenzweig, calls this the conversion of our concepts through God's self-revelation. Suppose we think of this as a picture of God as speaking to his people. In what circumstances would it be natural to say that this picture is indispensable to the religious believer concerned—or as Wittgenstein elsewhere puts it, to say that this picture lies at the basis of all her thinking?

Imagine a philosopher who wants accurately to characterize this aspect of our believer's life with words. He will note that she describes her language-game as one in which God speaks and is responded to, but he will naturally want to ask what, in her game, counts as God's having spoken—what, one might say, the criteria are that she and her fellow-believers employ in playing this language-game. From the believer's point of view, however, the very form of that question implies that we—in our ways of speaking—are the ones who in the last instance determine what counts as God's speaking, whereas it is essential to her understanding of the God of whom she speaks that her ways with religious words have a kind of openness to God's actions, an openness which means that it is not for her (or anyone other than God himself) to lay down rules for what counts as God's speaking. To do otherwise would mean arrogating to ourselves the authority to determine in advance the limits of God's capacity to reveal Himself, rather than remaining open to the ineliminable possibility that His self-revelation might show up our current ways of talking about Him to be utterly shallow or misconceived.

About such a person one might well say that the picture of God's speaking lies at the basis of all her religious thought, because it is not only central to the religious language-games that she plays but also to the way she regards or relates to those language-games—namely, not as practices in which what counts as God's speaking is ultimately subject to determination by our rules. Part of what it means for that picture to be at the basis of her thinking is, accordingly, that she will resist any philosophical description of her religious language that makes its deployment ultimately a matter of our modes of speaking rather than God's. More formally: the grammar of the concept "description of this language-game" here includes the use of the relevant picture in the description. This religious believer's practice of talking about God as speaking to her cannot be characterized in a way that does justice to its role in her life unless the characterization invokes the very picture whose use it aspires to describe.

If, however, Wittgenstein regards religious pictures as indispensable to the religious believer's ways of talking in just this manner, he is committed to denying the expressivist stance that is so often attributed to him; there is no perspective one can attain upon the use of the language we're concerned with that would allow us to characterize that use in a way that dispenses with the very picture that it embodies, and thereby to demonstrate its dispensability (its being just one optional way of dressing up a stance that might be accurately characterized without it). Consequently, we cannot here regard the business of philosophical clarification as essentially distinct from the business of employing the language about which we seek philosophical clarification. For when that language makes indispensable use of pictures, any philosopher who attempts to clarify its role cannot do so in a way that is neutral with respect to the "first-order" commitments that the use of the picture embodies, without misrepresenting that role.

Someone for whom the picture of God as speaking to us is indispensable in the sense just envisaged is someone who is committed to a particular, religiously substantial view of the relation between religious language and its subject-matter (in particular, to the view that its subject-matter is also its source, hence that its own authority as speech derives from a reality independent of it rather than from its suitability to express an attitude or feeling about that reality); and such a view hangs together with a range of other views—about language in general (in its relation to reality), about history, and hence time, and so unforeseeably on. Her way with words, and hence with this picture, thus includes certain views about matters of central philosophical concern, as well as the view that certain other ways of viewing those matters fail properly to acknowledge the nature and significance of her own religious perspective. On this way of seeing things, philosophy cannot hope to avoid taking a stand on the issues addressed by those whose ways of addressing them it might have hoped merely to characterize.

Faith, Wisdom, and Passion

In the third and final part of this chapter, I want to shift attention to some material from *Culture and Value*, and in particular to address two further misunderstandings of Wittgenstein's view about the relation between passion, reason and faith. The first of these misunderstandings finds exemplary expression in the following passage:

> [T]ime and again in Wittgenstein's later thought ... religion is a realm of *passion* rather than of intellect. Religion springs, not from the head,

not from speculative enquiries, but from our emotional lives, from the
passions. (IWPR, p. 52)

This is the Wittgenstein passage that the above sentences explicitly claim to
summarize:

> What inclines even me to believe in Christ's resurrection? I play as it were
> with the thought.—If he did not rise from the dead, then he decomposed
> in the grave like every human being. *He is dead & decomposed*. In that case
> he is a teacher, like any other & can no longer *help*; & we are once more
> orphaned & alone. And have to make do with wisdom & speculation.
> It is as though we are in a hell, where we can only dream & are shut out
> from heaven, roofed in as it were. But if I am to be REALLY redeemed,—I
> need *certainty*—not wisdom, dreams, speculation—and this certainty is
> faith. And faith is faith in what my *heart*, my *soul*, needs, not my specu-
> lative intellect. For my soul, with its passions, as it were with its flesh and
> blood, must be redeemed, not my abstract mind. Perhaps one may say:
> Only *love* can believe the Resurrection. Or: it is *love* that believes the
> Resurrection. One might say: redeeming love believes even in the Res-
> urrection; holds fast even to the Resurrection. What fights doubt is *as it
> were redemption*. Holding fast to *it* must be holding fast to this belief. So
> this means: first be redeemed & hold on tightly to your redemption (keep
> hold of your redemption)—then you will see that what you are holding
> on to is this belief. So this can only come about if you no longer support
> yourself on this earth but suspend yourself from heaven. Then *everything*
> is different and it is "no wonder" if you can then do what now you
> cannot do. (It is true that someone who is suspended looks like someone
> who is standing but the interplay of forces within him is nevertheless a
> quite different one & hence he is able to do quite different things than can
> one who stands.) (CV, p. 39)

The gulf between text and exegesis frankly beggars belief. Where the commentary presupposes that passion and intellect, heart and mind, stand in a relation
of mutual exclusion, and that the mind as such can be identified with one form
of its functioning (that of speculative enquiry), the text rather distinguishes
between wisdom and speculation, or the specifically abstract mind, on the one
hand, and on the other the heart, understood as a way of referring to the
soul—where "soul" must be understood *with* its passions, hence neither
reducible to them nor essentially distinguishable from them, any more than
one's soul can—on Wittgenstein's view—be distinguished from its flesh and
blood. If, then, faith at once engages, and concerns itself with, the soul of the
believer, it is with that believer's *embodied* soul, or more precisely, with the
believer *qua* ensouled body—just as the belief in the resurrection to which this
believer finds herself holding fast is a belief in the resurrection of Christ's
embodied reality (his overcoming of decomposition and death), and so is a

belief in her own essentially bodily resurrection. In other words, Wittgenstein makes use of the central elements of the religious picture he is attempting to comprehend in his characterization of those who deploy it. Once again, then, accurately characterizing the role of this belief in a religious person's life turns out to require that the picture it articulates (of the resurrection of the ensouled human body) be involved in the characterization itself.

Note also that, on Wittgenstein's account, the religious believer discovers or discloses her belief in the resurrection by making use of her intellect—motivated, to be sure, by a conviction that she has been redeemed, but with her understanding of what that commits her to dependent upon the exercise of her reason: more specifically, from her coming to see that redemption presupposes a redeemer, and that she cannot make sense of the idea that someone utterly dead and gone might be such a redeemer. One might think of this as a process of coming to understand what God in Christ is saying to us, how his Incarnation converts our concepts in such a way as to allow us to respond to him more fully. But one might also think of it as an example of how a believer's relation to the words they feel compelled to use is akin to the way Wittgenstein pictures our relation to a mathematical conjecture (both are akin to our relation to riddles—to forms of words whose sense is to-be-disclosed, never beyond the possibility of further conversion).[8]

But this point also suggests that a certain complexity might underlie another, all-too-familiar and seemingly all-too-simple, opposition that surfaces briefly in the passage I just quoted, and is often seen as generally informing Wittgenstein's thinking about religion (an opposition he is thought to inherit from Kierkegaard)—that between the prescriptive chill of wisdom and the passionate heat of faith. This is the second misunderstanding I want to address, to which the following two passages are relevant:

> Amongst other things Christianity says, I believe, that sound doctrines are all useless. That you have to change your *life*. (Or the *direction* of your life.)
>
> That all wisdom is cold; & that you can no more use it for setting your life to rights, than you can forge iron when it is *cold*.
>
> For a sound doctrine need not *seize* you; you can follow it, like a doctor's prescription.—But here you have to be seized & turned around by something. (I.e. this is how I understand it.) Once turned round, you must *stay* turned round.
>
> Wisdom is passionless. By contrast Kierkegaard calls faith a *passion*. (CV, p. 61)
>
> Wisdom is something cold, & to that extent foolish. (Faith, on the other hand, a passion.) We might also say: wisdom merely *conceals* life from you. (Wisdom is like cold, grey ash covering the glowing embers.) (CV, p. 64)

Three complications seem to me to surface from this conjunction of aphorisms, and I will conclude by drawing them out. First: Wittgenstein certainly associates passion with passivity, with being seized, and the wisdom of doctrine with agency, following precepts issued by an authority; but he also implies that our being seized is nothing without our being turned around, say converted—and we have already seen that for Wittgenstein conversion is as much a matter of turning around our concepts (and so our intellect) as it is the direction of our lives (each being an ineliminable aspect of the other). Second: if redirecting one's life is like reforging iron, then the passionate heat of faith is not only not necessary for the reforged iron to serve its new purpose, but is positively an obstacle to its doing so; only iron informed by the chill of sound doctrine can sustain its new orientation. Third: if wisdom is the ash that covers the glowing embers of life, then it is not the opposite or enemy of life's passionate heat but its residue—something precipitated by it, hence something into which the fuel of that vital combustion is converted. After all, if wisdom is foolishness insofar as it is cold, then its truly being itself is a matter of its maintaining an internal relation to the heat it has always already lost, that absence or recession to which its attenuated presence always accordingly points. Wisdom is thus an inevitable transfiguration of faith, its natural fate; and insofar as ash can not only preserve the heat of the embers it covers,[9] but also feed future vegetable growth even when those embers have all been converted into ash (thereby cultivating new fuel for more life), then sound doctrine also presents itself as a condition for the possibility of maintaining and renewing the vital passion of faith.

NOTES

1 They include brief remarks in the *Tractatus Logico-Philosophicus*, trans. C. K. Ogden (London: Routledge & Kegan Paul, 1922)—hereafter TLP—and the "Lecture on Religious Belief" [*Philosophical Review*, Vol. 74 (1965)]; in *Lectures and Conversations on Aesthetics, Psychology and Religious Belief* (Berkeley, CA: University of California Press, 1966), hereafter LC, which are in fact a collation of notes taken by those attending the lectures; and in *Culture and Value*, trans. P. Winch (Oxford: Basil Blackwell 1977)—hereafter CV.

2 Uncontroversial members of this canon include P. Winch, *The Idea of a Social Science* (Routledge: London, 1958); N. Malcolm, "Anselm's Ontological Arguments" [*Philosophical Review*, Vol. 69 (1960)]; reprinted in his *Knowledge and Certainty* (Englewood Cliffs, NJ: Prentice-Hall, 1963); and D. Z. Phillips, *The Concept of Prayer* (London: Routledge, 1965).

3 Ludwig Wittgenstein, *Philosophical Investigations*, trans. G. E. M. Anscombe (Oxford: Basil Blackwell, 1953)—hereafter PI.

4 Kai Nielsen's article, "Wittgensteinian Fideism" appeared in *Philosophy*, Vol. 42 (1967)—hereafter WF.

5 B. Clack, *An Introduction to Wittgenstein's Philosophy of Religion* (Edinburgh: Edinburgh University Press, 1999)—hereafter IWPR.

6 I thank John Hare for rightly forcing me to be clearer about this matter in the discussion following my conference presentation of these arguments.

7 Cora Diamond, "Wittgenstein on Religious Belief: the gulfs between us," in D. Z. Phillips and Mario Von der Ruhr (eds.), *Religion and Wittgenstein's Legacy* (Aldershot: Ashgate, 2005), pp. 99–138.

8 This too is a central theme in Diamond's work—in particular, her essay on Anselm and his ontological proof, which I would commend to your attention. See Cora Diamond, "Riddles and Anselm's Riddle," in *The Realistic Spirit* (Cambridge, MA: MIT Press, 1991), pp. 267–290.

9 As Paul Griffiths has helpfully suggested to me.

14

PSYCHOLOGY AND THE RATIONALITY OF EMOTION

GERALD L. CLORE

Questions addressed by recent psychological research on emotion include questions about how thought shapes emotion and how emotion, in turn, shapes thought. Research on emotion and cognition paints a somewhat different picture than that seen in traditional discussions of "passion" and reason. This chapter reviews several aspects of this research, concentrating specifically on three views of rationality: let us call these "Rationality as Process," "Rationality as Product," and "Rationality as Outcome." Note that for the purpose of this chapter, "rationality as process" will refer to the assumption that conscious, logical, and coherent thought serves as the basis of people's beliefs, decisions, and actions.

Rationality as Process

"Rationality" is not a concept in much current use in psychology itself. Psychologists tend to find the term ambiguous in meaning and value-laden. In common usage, being "rational" is assumed to be good, whereas saying that someone is being "irrational" or "emotional" is assumed to be bad and to lead to error. Psychological science, however, is primarily interested in understanding thought processes, rather than in passing judgment on them. Its goal is to describe how people think, rather than to prescribe how they should think. Hence, rather than studying "rational" and "irrational" thought, psychological accounts often focus on the "dual processes" of thought. Examples of the names given to such dual processes or kinds of thinking include,

Support in writing this article is acknowledged from Research Grant R01 MH 50074 from the National Institute of Mental Health, United States Public Health Service.

Faith, Rationality, and the Passions, First Edition. Edited by Sarah Coakley.
© 2012 Blackwell Publishing Ltd. Book compilation © 2012 Blackwell Publishing Ltd.

"controlled vs. automatic processing," "systematic vs. heuristic processing," or "rule based vs. associative processing." Are these just the same as "rational vs. emotional?" No, partly because they are not value-laden. Thinking in an automatic way is neither better nor worse than thinking in a controlled way. Each has a different, but equally valuable, function.

If part of the mission of this volume is to consider whether people characteristically think "rationally" or not, psychology can be quite useful. It sees people as capable of thinking logically and of appreciating the difference between logical and illogical inference. At the same time, research makes it clear that human judgment, thought, and choice are not primarily guided by the kind of controlled and deliberative processes that are implied by saying that people are rational. This fact is dictated by the high cost of deliberative thought in time and mental resources. Research shows that thinking routinely involves mental short-cuts, and that everyday inferences and reasoning are generally guided by judgment heuristics and rough rules of thumb, rather than by explicit logic. Thus, people's thought is not well characterized as being guided by "rationality as process."

A major contribution of psychology in the last forty or fifty years has been the discovery of the many ways in which human thought processes are nonrational. These discoveries do not suggest that people are "irrational," because the "nonrational" processes to which we refer generally yield quite reasonable results, as we shall see. The claim is that in general human thought is not rational in process because much of it is unconscious,[1] automatic,[2] emotional,[3] and heuristic in nature.[4] Each of these four attributes of human thought has been the subject of much controversy; but at this point in our history, one is unlikely to find much disagreement among psychologists that thought has these characteristics. My point is that human thought, decision, and action are much more routinized, automated, and unconscious than most people realize. Moreover, this conclusion is obviously as applicable to the everyday thoughts of theologians and religious practitioners as it is to other individuals.

In the 1960s, Nobel prize-winner Herbert Simon proposed the concept of "bounded rationality," and noted that emotion plays an important role in judgment and decision-making.[5] In the 1970s, Nobel prize-winner Daniel Kahneman and his colleague Amos Tversky discovered some of the judgment heuristics that people use in everyday reasoning.[6] Much to the dismay of economists guided by "rational choice" models, it has become clear that people reason using whatever short-cuts or heuristics are available. An example is the "availability heuristic," in which people use the ease with which an example of some category comes to mind as a heuristic for judging its prevalence or likelihood in the world. Thus, people may overestimate the probability of dying in a car crash, for example, if they have recently heard of someone dying in a car crash. In this way, people rely on the accessibility of thoughts and other experiences of thinking itself as clues about the world.

A generation of writers has misinterpreted the message of this work, fearing that it undermined the value of reason, the bedrock of enlightened thought. This reaction, however, was based on a conflation of Kahneman and Tversky's methods with their results. As a strategy for studying judgment heuristics, they employed logical problems that encouraged error. As a result, the whole line of work became known as research on "errors and biases." But judgment heuristics do not usually lead to error. Readers who focused on the error aspect missed the point, which was not that people are prone to error, but quite the opposite. Indeed, what is exciting about this work is the discovery that humans have developed highly adaptive modes of thought and action, including judgment heuristics and other extra-rational means, which achieve the benefits of rationality without its costs.

Nonrational modes of thought certainly can lead to error, of course, but an important question is whether they are generally beneficial or harmful. One way of approaching this question is to examine individual differences in the tendency to rely on judgment heuristics. Do people who avoid judgment heuristics fare better or worse than those who do not? A clever investigation provided an interesting answer.[7] In this study, a sample of individuals was tested repeatedly on a variety of measures from childhood through adulthood. During one wave of data collection, the investigators included a measure of heuristic thinking. The measure involved viewing a brief video about a question and answer game. One individual was seen flipping a coin to decide which of two other individuals would be assigned to the role of questioner and which to the role of answerer. The questioner was then handed a sheet of paper with several general knowledge questions to ask. Because the questions were difficult, the person assigned the role of answerer was often unsuccessful. After the video, participants were asked to make ratings of the intelligence of the two individuals. Despite having witnessed the coin toss, and hence knowing that the roles could just as easily have been reversed, they tended to see the question-asker as more intelligent than the question-answerer.

Some participants in the experiment, however, did not rely on using this common judgment heuristic. If asked, most of us would probably choose to have been in the group that resisted misleading appearances and answered correctly, rather than being a member of the group that had made the heuristic error. That choice, however, turns out to be the wrong one. Because this was a longitudinal study covering many years, the experimenters knew a great deal about each individual, and in fact, those who engaged in heuristic thinking were also the most healthy, happy, and successful. The group that answered correctly by second guessing their own inclinations consisted of individuals found to engage in self-doubt, harbor neurotic beliefs, and fare less well in life generally. The results suggest that being strictly "rational" (according to our initial definition) may not always be the preferred mode of thought. Engaging in heuristic thinking, although it occasionally leads to error, tends to be adaptive rather than undesirable. How could this be? The answer is simply that conscious, deliberative, logical thought is metabolically expensive. Like trying to dance by verbalizing each step aloud, trying to deliberate carefully about everyday inferences and choices is both inelegant and exhausting. Indeed, if we routinely thought in a systematic, conscious, controlled fashion, humans would never have survived as long as we have. Thinking and acting appear to be guided, much more than is generally realized, by the requirements of resource management.[8] In fact, some psychologists, following their colleagues in behavioral ecology,[9] have concluded that the behavior of all living things is ultimately guided by concerns about resource management, including obtaining, storing, and spending resources in the form of energy.

The behavior of fish and birds, and of mammals, including humans, for most of evolutionary history has been dominated by the need to secure food and shelter, to make alliances, and to form social arrangements that would ensure resources sufficient for survival. In humans, the brain uses twenty per cent of the glucose of the body, glucose that is primarily needed to power muscles for action. The glucose used in the brain to power thought processes is therefore precious. From that perspective, humans do not routinely think in an explicitly rational manner, because heuristic approximations are fast and efficient, and we cannot afford any more explicitly rational thought than is necessary.

Rationality and Product

Arguably more important than questions about process, however, are questions about the *products* of thought. Even if our thought processes themselves are often unconscious, automatic, emotional, and heuristic, do we nevertheless arrive at logically coherent (i.e., "rational") beliefs, decisions, and actions? On the whole, it appears that we do. Like the processes taking place in our computers, our thought processes are mostly inaccessible, but we do have access to the results of our thinking, and generally we seem to have high standards for them. When we hear others being illogical, we are critical of them and find their assertions unpersuasive. And when we hear ourselves being illogical or inconsistent, we become embarrassed and motivated to rethink our position. Thus, perhaps surprisingly, emotion actually enforces standards of reason. That is, the automatic, negative affective reaction we have to incoherence and illogic motivates rational thought. The fact that people care deeply about the logic and consistency of their own beliefs and actions can be seen in the classic social psychological phenomenon of cognitive dissonance.[10] Relevant research showed that when people act in ways that are inconsistent with their beliefs, a state of tension or cognitive dissonance is generated, which motivates them to adjust their beliefs to make them consistent with their actions—the process of dissonance reduction.

In order to bring such standards of rationality to bear on our thoughts, it is necessary to make them explicit, to think about them consciously, as when we express them verbally or publicly. The fact that we do routinely assess whether our unconscious, automatic, emotional, and heuristic processes have produced logical or illogical thoughts, decisions, and actions means that our conscious and deliberative thought is able to regulate our unconscious and automatic thought.

This process can readily be seen in the domain of moral judgment. Jonathan Haidt has examined the role of emotion in moral judgment.[11] He comes to the same conclusions about emotion and consciousness that we are proposing here. Like Hume, he proposes that moral judgment is based on emotion. Traditionally, psychologists have focused on the rational reasons that people give for their moral judgments. This tradition came from Piaget's emphasis on the stage-like development of children's reasoning, which Lawrence Kohlberg (1969) extended in his well-known studies of the development of moral reasoning.[12]

In contrast, Haidt contends that moral judgments reflect universal, evolved, moral intuitions, and that the reasons people give for their moral judgments are frequently post hoc rationalizations or attempts to make sense of their intuitions.[13] Through clever demonstrations, he shows how everyday moral reasoning is subservient to emotional and intuitive reactions. If one accepts his thesis, one is then led to ask what function might be served by the rational reasons we give for our actions? He proposes that articulating reasons helps expose incoherent moral positions, motivating one to persuade oneself or others to change perspectives, which may activate different intuitions or resolve conflicting intuitions. Part of our moral reasoning process, then, involves reconciling our intuition-based moral judgments with our automatic negative reactions to illogic. We have a strong need to make sense of our intuitive and emotional judgments. But such sense-making is typically a result, rather than a cause, of the moral judgments we make.

Thus far, we have claimed that human thought is not generally conducted deliberatively or rationally (in the sense under discussion) in any explicit way. Indeed, it would be unwise and unworkable if we did try to conduct thought in that way even most of the time. In fact, the genius of human thought is that despite its unconscious, automatic, emotional, and heuristic nature, we nevertheless generally arrive at rational, defensible conclusions. And when we do not, our emotional reactions to illogic often motivate corrective action. But in addition to rationality as logically defensible inference, economists assess the rationality of decisions and actions in terms of outcomes. People act rationally when they maximize benefits and minimize costs. And the rest of us too are likely to see self-defeating choices as irrational, regardless of how deliberative they may have been. Let us turn then to a consideration of how cognition and emotion interact to achieve rational outcomes.

Rationality as Outcome

A recent news story told of a college lacrosse player who killed a former girlfriend in a fit of rage after she rejected him. Such events appear to support traditional beliefs that emotion imperils reason, and it is surely true that action in the heat of emotion can be short-sighted, sometimes tragically so. Such extreme emotion and such extreme actions are, fortunately, quite rare. Accordingly, the model of emotion suggested by such examples, however commonly believed, is misleading. But such considerations raise the larger questions of how emotion and action are related, a topic to which we turn now.

People often assume that emotion causes behavior, but anyone who has experienced a near collision when driving knows that the feelings of fear generally arrive only afterward. We step on the brake instantly, rather than waiting for the experience of fear to tell us what to do. Such considerations imply either that emotion does not cause behavior or that some part of emotion other than conscious feelings can cause behavior. A useful account of this problem has been given by Baumeister, Vohs, DeWall and Zhang, who conclude that full blown emotion generally governs action only indirectly.[14]

Baumeister also proposes that "behavior chases emotion."[15] That is, actions are motivated by *anticipated* affect, meaning that we make one decision rather than another because we think it will work out better. To make choices, people often engage in mental simulations to anticipate how they will feel about likely outcomes. Decisions then chase (try to maximize) anticipated emotion.

Current emotions provide feedback about the consequences of particular actions in particular situations. On the basis of such experiences, we can subsequently anticipate the emotional consequences of similar actions in related situations. When contemplating such actions in the future, twinges of anticipated affect can then alter our choices to maximize positive outcomes.

The process of deciding is the attempt to find the better option among alternatives, and we depend on some minimal positive affective reaction to announce the better option when it is encountered. Indeed, people usually feel comfortable exiting the decision-making process only when thinking about an option yields more positive affect than negative affect.[16] And people tend to reconsider the options again and again when none of the alternatives elicits positive affect[17] or related experiences of cognitive fluency.[18]

Does such a process lead to a "rational" outcome? It does appear to be a process that would lead to decisions that are both coherent and satisfying. Moreover, a virtue of this account is that it allows an integration of the cognitive and affective factors that we know to be involved in decision-making without forcing one to decide whether people are rational or irrational. Good decision-makers are people who are both emotionally and intellectually intelligent in that they are attuned to the affective reactions that foreshadow productive and unproductive lines of thought and action. By focusing on feelings, they can be motivated to recast the problem or reconsider available options to avoid both self-contradictory and self-defeating choices.

As an example, the behavioral economist George Loewenstein considers people who have a hard time getting up in the morning.[19] They may set an alarm, but find it too easy to turn the alarm off and return to sleep. However, after experiencing embarrassment or other negative emotions from being late, they may be motivated to move the clock across the room when the process of setting the alarm triggers some fractional part of that embarrassment. By having the alarm across the room, they are forced to get up before turning off the alarm, rather than hoping to get up afterward—an example of intelligent action based on anticipated emotion.

In this section, then, we have pointed out that the everyday choices and decisions that we make are guided by anticipated affect. The decision process often involves a quick mental simulation in which the possible consequences of alternative actions can be imagined and assessed. The anticipated affect that arises can then guide the choosing process. In this way, people may arrive at good and rationally defensible decisions precisely because they are guided by affective considerations. Thus, although human behavior is guided largely by unconscious, automatic processes, the affective residues of conscious emotional experiences can influence and even optimize action. These affective residues of prior emotions act as rewards and punishments to alter and update the unconscious programs that then trigger behavior automatically.

Emotion Stimulates Thinking

Other recent work shows how emotion also regulates action by stimulating conscious thought. We have suggested that consciousness provides a stage for comparing unconsciously produced thought with standards of rationality. That provides one rationale for why conscious cognition might be functional, but why be conscious of emotion? What are feelings for?

One function of conscious emotion is to aid learning by drawing our attention to the most important or urgent aspects of a situation. Research indicates that a prime function of emotional arousal is to draw attention and thoughts to important (i.e., arousing) events. Some of our own current experiments examine this process. We induce arousal by having people give a short speech or put their arm in ice water for a minute or two. The anxiety of speaking and the pain of the ice water activate the amygdala and relevant hormones that consolidate into long term memories whatever is experienced at the time. That is, after a delay of several days, information that has been followed by such emotional or physiological arousal tends to be well recalled.[20] In Post-Traumatic Stress Disorder (PTSD), for example, this process works too well, and people have difficulty forgetting traumatic experiences.

Such research is relevant in the present context because it indicates that rather than contaminating thought, emotion often stimulates thought, allowing for a revision of beliefs and intentions. Indeed, if it were not for emotion, people might not think as much as they do.[21] In the emotion of regret, for example, counter-factual thinking is stimulated concerning how a different decision might have led to different and more desirable outcomes.

Art, especially literature and drama, can serve a related function. These art forms may involve mental simulations of emotionally important situations that allow for learning by feeling vicarious emotions, rather than by having to experience full-blown emotions in real time.[22] Although Aristotle held that drama promotes the venting of emotion, the emotions from drama (and other mental simulations) appear mainly to help us regulate thought by attracting our attention to the important aspects of situations. In this way, art allows wisdom to be acquired vicariously.

Cognition Shapes Emotion

A common view of emotion was evident in a recently aired public television series in the United States called, "This Emotional Life." It was an interesting series, but it was preoccupied with promoting the very standard view that "the newer, rational brain conflicts with the older, emotional brain"—a presumption now under significant scientific question. The chief evidence given for this standard model of cognition and emotion concerned the difficulty people have in exercising cognitive control over attacks of anxiety and depression. Cognition is indeed poor at that task. But it provides a misleading model of how cognition usually affects emotion.

Research by James Gross helps correct this view.[23] In a well-known experiment, he showed an emotional film and asked some people to resist expressing whatever emotion it produced. He asked others to keep their emotions from arising in the first place by trying to interpret the film in a non-emotional way. He found that whereas suppressing feelings is difficult and costly, people could more easily dampen emotion by reinterpreting events in a way that kept feelings from developing. The mentally taxing nature of emotional suppression was found to reduce people's ability to remember the film they had watched, whereas reinterpreting it did not hamper memory.

The fact that cognitive reinterpretation can change and hence dampen emotion is also evident at the neurological level.[24] In brain imaging studies, benign reinterpretations of otherwise disturbing pictures were found to successfully reduce amygdala activity. Conversely, reinterpretations aimed at increasing emotional reactions also increased amygdala activity. The amygdala is often observed in such research because it reflects emotional processing. From this kind of research, one can conclude that the regulation of emotion is more successful when it is instituted before, rather than after, an emotion occurs.[25] Perhaps this effectiveness of cognition beforehand mirrors the main role of cognition in emotion more generally, which is to shape emotion as it develops, rather than to suppress it later, as traditional views would have it.

There is a range of other research that arrives at similar answers to the questions we have posed. Cognitive therapy, for example, assumes also that emotions are products of how we think, and it aims to change problematic emotions by changing problematic thoughts.[26] Similar conclusions come from classic experiments on delay of gratification in children.[27] In one such experiment, children were given a choice between eating one marshmallow immediately and waiting until later to get two marshmallows. The results showed that children can resist temptation by thinking of the tempting marshmallow in front of them, not as a delicious sweet, but as a little white puffy cloud. Again, cognitive reinterpretations of an emotionally evocative stimulus can effectively regulate emotion and hence behavior.

This dependence of emotion on thought is also seen in major theories of emotion. We have a general theory of emotion, for example, that specifies the various kinds of perceptions and thoughts necessary to elicit each of twenty-two common emotions.[28] Thus, fear is displeasure at the prospect of an undesirable outcome, shame is disapproval of a blameworthy action of one's own, and anger is a combination of displeasure at an undesirable outcome and disapproval at the blameworthy actions of another that led to it, and so on. In this and related appraisal theories of emotion, cognition is seen as shaping, rather than as opposing, emotion.

But if cognition regulates emotion, so also does emotion regulate cognition. Part of our research, for example, concerns the influence of affect on thinking.[29] Some of this research on emotion and cognition examines how moods and emotions help regulate how we think. For example, on some tasks it may be better to attend to the forest, but on others, better to attend to the trees. That is, some problems require taking a global or big picture perspective, while others require analysis and attention to detail. It turns out that our feelings in any given moment direct our mental processes, so that in happy states, people more readily adopt a global focus, whereas in negative states, (e.g., sadness) they more readily focus on details.[30] In a similar way, positive affective reactions encourage our reliance on whatever beliefs and assumptions we already hold, whereas negative reactions tend to inhibit the use of existing beliefs and motivate a search for new information. A similar logic was evident in John Dewey's prescriptions for education when he cautioned that learning could occur only when students are confronted with problems for which their existing knowledge is inadequate.[31]

Here again, evidence suggests that rather than inevitably obstructing thought, emotion often motivates thought. Moreover, to touch base with our earlier discussion of the role of mental resources or energy in thought, our current research is showing that people think efficiently when their moods and emotional reactions activate the style of thought that fits the demands of a task. In contrast, when the abilities triggered by emotion conflict with task demands, performance requires extra metabolic energy. Ordinarily, our affective reactions help optimize our thinking to fit the tasks that we face, which helps optimize energy use. Again, rather than being in opposition to cognition, affective reactions provide useful feedback about how one is coping with events.

I have argued that the time-honored view that higher mental processes are a lid on the boiling cauldron of emotion is a poor characterization of their relationship. A review of the evidence in this section shows that whereas cognitive processes do often dampen emotional power, they do so primarily by interpreting or situating the emotional reaction, thereby constraining its meaning. Emotional control generally comes not from suppressing but from shaping or directing emotion. Moreover, this shaping and directing can also make emotion more rather than less powerful, as we see next.

Cognition and the Power of Emotion

We have been discussing the interplay between emotion and cognition and how initial affective reactions can become full blown emotions as they are directed by interpretation. The general idea is that cognition shapes low-level, primitive, affective reactions (which simply indicate that something is good or bad in some way) into more precise and elaborated emotions (e.g., sadness, anger, shame, love, and so on). Cognitive interpretations *constrain* the possible meanings of affect, signaling in what way something is good or bad and how urgent or important it is. Such cognitive constraints on affective meanings have many implications. For example, we know that someone who is afraid is looking forward to the prospect of an undesirable outcome of some kind, whereas someone who is sad is looking backward to some undesirable outcome that has already happened. But a more important implication is that the power and impact of emotions ultimately depend on the object of the emotion.[32]

When the cause or object of an affective reaction is not salient, so that the reaction has a diffuse focus, we generally refer to it as a mood. In contrast, when the cause or object of an affective reaction becomes clear, then the affective reaction develops a specific focus, and we refer to it as an emotion.[33] Before a specific emotion develops, the affective reactions that are their bases are quite malleable. Their power and impact depend on the objects that give them shape and direction. Most importantly, the intensity of any emotional reaction depends on the magnitude of the implications that appear to hang in the balance. Rulers and politicians are well aware of this principle when attempting to spark public emotion. Thus, for example, the recent American president George W. Bush, referred to the struggle against terrorism as, "A war between good and evil. . . . a war to save the world."[34] Similarly, Serbian nationalists defended their fight against the independence of ethnic Albanians of Kosovo in 2008, saying, "What the West must understand is that we are not just defending Serbia, we are defending Europe against Muslim aggression."[35]

Moral and religious leaders also frame their messages expansively in order to intensify their emotional and motivational impact. Indeed, the Christian Church developed over many years an arsenal of ultimates to fortify its prescriptions (e.g., the fate of one's immortal soul; the assertion that God will be pleased or angered, and so on). Not only does the intensity of emotion depend on the importance of the object, but also objects that are symbolic, that have uncertain implications, and that are shrouded in mystery, are sometimes even more powerful. This extra power appears to derive mainly from the fact that uncertainty about outcomes makes it difficult to shift one's attention and focus elsewhere.[36]

We have indicated that affect is some registration of goodness or badness, and that specific emotions involve cognitively-constrained affect. Emotions then involve a specific goodness or badness of a specific outcome, action, or object in a specific situation. An important implication is that the power of affect and emotion depend on how they are constrained by cognition. Let us consider such implications further.

One implication concerns psychotherapy. Much of psychotherapy involves changing unconstrained affect in the form of moods into specific emotions.[37] Moods are vague affective states that are unconstrained by any particular object and hence are unclear in their meaning. Examples include states of depression and anxiety. The goal of psychotherapy is often to help the client situate his affect, to find its object, so that the person can engage in useful, problem-focused coping, rather than in emotion-focused coping (e.g., excessive drinking, eating or sleeping), which is often counter-productive.[38] Thus, persons may be empowered once the specificity of their emotions constrains their general distress to be about something in particular.

A related benefit from the cognitive constraints on the meaning of affect can be seen in the Zen Buddhist therapy for pain. I am told by a practitioner that the treatment consists of having the person in pain focus directly on the pain, indicating in detail exactly how and where it hurts. One might think that focusing on the pain would make an injury more distressing, but it turns out that constraining the pain in this way, although it does not reduce the pain itself, greatly reduces distress by making the pain nothing more than what it is.

In contrast, certain forms of meditation, although they first involve focusing on a specific object, such as the beauty of a flower, have as their goal to experience some attribute, such as beauty or truth or love or power, in a way that is unconstrained by any specific object. The process takes practice, but since God is generally thought of as unconstrained love, beauty, and power, being able to experience these attributes without the constraint or interpretation imposed by a specific object can constitute a particular sort of religious experience.

These observations show that the power of affect depends on how cognition constrains its meaning. Just as various therapies may be enhanced by constraining the meaning of affective reactions, some religious experiences may be enhanced by unconstraining their meaning. Here again we see that cognition exercises control over emotion, not by conflict or suppression, but by shaping, situating, contextualizing, and changing its meaning.

Conclusions

In summary, in this chapter, we have made the following proposals about the current state of psychological research on "rationality" and the emotions:

(a) In terms of process, humans do not generally think rationally, to the extent that "rationality" implies arriving at beliefs, opinions, and decisions through explicit reasoning or controlled logical processing.

(b) Whereas human thought does not generally follow rational, logical processes, the unconscious, heuristic, and associative processes that we do follow nevertheless tend to lead us to defensible conclusions.

(c) People hold themselves to a high standard of coherence and rationality so that thinking explicitly about one's beliefs and defending them to others allows them to be assessed against logical standards.

(d) Contrary to popular belief, it is emotion that then enforces this rational standard, because people react negatively to their own and others' illogic, which motivates the revision of thoughts and beliefs to be more coherent and logical.

(e) An important criterion for decision and action is anticipated affect: the anticipation of whether a decision alternative will lead to a good outcome or not. But people also demand that decisions and actions be reasonable, so that they generally give reasons for what they do to ensure that their actions do not appear unreasonable. Whereas the reasons given may be consistent with the actual causes, such *post hoc* constructions are not necessarily the actual causes of decisions and actions.

(f) People do entertain reasons and mentally simulate decisions to detect whether any red flag of negative affect is raised. Finding that one's reasons are defensible is empowering, whereas finding them incoherent is aversive. In this way, emotion enforces reason.

(g) Rather than suppressing or controlling emotion, as is often supposed, the power of cognition in emotion lies in the fact that emotions are cognitively-shaped affective reactions. Thus, whereas general affective reactions signal that something is good or bad in some way, specific emotions signal what aspect of a situation is good or bad and in what way.

(h) The power and impact of emotions depend on the magnitude of their objects. Political and religious leaders often demonstrate their knowledge of this fact by couching their messages in ultimate terms so that much appears to hang in the balance. As a result emotional and motivational intensity is enhanced.

(i) Much of the power of emotion lies in how the possible meanings of affect are constrained by cognition. For example, successful therapies often constrain the meanings of affective reactions to apply to specific objects, whereas some religious practices function by unconstraining the meaning of affective reactions so that they are experienced as transcending worldly objects.

(j) The overarching message in all of these comments is that, rather than thinking—as in the celebrated parable of Plato's *Phaedrus*—of emotion and cognition as horses pulling in different directions, we should think of them as strands of a single rope, made strong by their being thoroughly intertwined.

NOTES

1 T. D. Wilson, *Strangers to Ourselves: Discovering the Adaptive Unconscious* (Cambridge, MA: Belknap/Harvard University Press, 2002).
2 J. Bargh, "The Automaticity of Everyday Life: A Manifesto," in Robert S. Wyer (ed.), *Advances in Social Cognition* (Mahwah, NJ: Lawrence Erlbaum & Associates, 1997), pp. 1–61.
3 R. Zajonc, "Feeling and Thinking: Preferences Need No Inferences," *American Psychologist*, Vol. 35 (1980), pp. 151–175.
4 A. Tversky and D. Kahneman, "Judgment Under Uncertainty: Heuristics and Biases," *Science*, Vol. 185 (1974), pp. 1124–1131.
5 H. A. Simon, "Motivational and Emotional Controls of Cognition," *Psychological Review*, Vol. 74 (1967), pp. 29–39.
6 Tversky and Kahneman, "Judgment Under Uncertainty," pp. 1124–1131.
7 J. Block and D. C. Funder, "Social Roles and Social Perception: Individual Differences in Attribution and 'Error'," *Journal of Personality and Social Psychology*, Vol. 51 (1986), pp. 1200–1207.
8 D. R. Proffitt, "Embodied Perception and the Economy of Action," *Perspectives on Psychological Science*, Vol. 1 (2006), pp. 110–122.
9 J. R. Krebs and N. B. Davies, *An Introduction to Behavioral Ecology* (Oxford: Basil Blackwell, 1981).
10 L. Festinger, *A Theory of Cognitive Dissonance* (Stanford, CA: Stanford University Press, 1957).
11 J. Haidt, "The Emotional Dog and its Rational Tail: A Social Intuitionist Approach to Moral Judgment," *Psychological Review*, Vol. 108 (2001), pp. 814–834.
12 L. Kohlberg, "Stage and Sequence: The Cognitive-Developmental Approach to Socialization" in D. A. Goslin (ed.), *Handbook of Socialization Theory and Research* (Chicago, IL: Rand McNally, 1969), pp. 347–480.
13 Haidt, "The Emotional Dog," pp. 814–834.
14 R. F. Baumeister, K. D. Vohs, N. DeWall, and L. Zhang, "How Emotion Shapes Behavior: Feedback, Anticipation, and Reflection, Rather than Direct Causation," *Personality & Social Psychology Review*, Vol. 11 (2007), pp. 167–203.

15 R. F. Baumeister, K. D. Vohs, and D. M. Tice, "Emotional Influences on Decision Making," in J. P. Forgas (ed.), *Affect in Social Thinking and Behavior* (New York: Psychology Press, 2006), pp. 143–160.

16 A. M. Isen and B. Means, "The Influence of Positive Affect on Decision-Making Strategy," *Social Cognition*, Vol. 2 (1983), pp. 18–31.

17 M. Cabanac, J. Guillaume, M. Balasko, and A. Fleury, "Pleasure in Decision-Making Situations," *BMC Psychiatry*, Vol. 2 (2002), pp. 7–15.

18 D. M. Oppenheimer, "The Secret Life of Fluency," *Trends in Cognitive Sciences*, Vol. 12 (2008), pp. 237–241.

19 G. Loewenstein, "Out of Control: Visceral Influences on Behavior," *Organizational Behavior and Human Decision Processes*, Vol. 65 (1996), pp. 272–292.

20 L. Cahill and M. T. Alkire, "Epinephrine Enhancement of Human Memory Consolidation: Interaction with Arousal at Encoding," *Neurobiology of Learning and Memory*, Vol. 79 (2003), pp. 194–198.

21 Baumeister et al., "How Emotion Shapes Behavior," pp. 167–203.

22 R. A. Mar, K. Oatley, J. Hirsh, J. dela Paz, and J. B. Peterson, "Bookworms versus Nerds: Exposure to Fiction versus Non-fiction, Divergent Associations with Social Ability, and the Simulation of Fictional Social Worlds," *Journal of Research in Personality*, Vol. 40 (2006), pp. 694–712.

23 J. J. Gross, "Emotion Regulation in Adulthood: Timing is Everything," *Current Directions in Psychological Science*, Vol. 10 (2001), pp. 214–219.

24 K. N. Ochsner, S. A. Bunge, J. J. Gross, and J. D. E. Gabrieli, "Rethinking Feelings: An fMRI Study of the Cognitive Regulation of Emotion," *Journal of Cognitive Neuroscience*, Vol. 14 (2002), pp. 1215–1229.

25 Gross, "Emotion Regulation in Adulthood," pp. 214–219.

26 A. T. Beck, *Cognitive Therapy and the Emotional Disorders* (New York: Penguin, 1979).

27 W. Mischel, Y. Shoda, and M. L. Rodriguez, "Delay of Gratification in Children," *Science*, Vol. 244 (1989), pp. 933–938.

28 A. Ortony, G. L. Clore, and A. Collins, *The Cognitive Structure of Emotions* (New York: Cambridge University Press, 1988).

29 See for example G. L. Clore and J. Huntsinger, "How Emotion Informs Judgments and Regulates Thought," *Trends in Cognitive Sciences*, Vol. 9 (2007), pp. 393–399.

30 K. Gasper and G. L. Clore, "Attending to the Big Picture: Mood and Global vs. Local Processing of Visual Information," *Psychological Science*, Vol. 13 (2002), pp. 34–40.

31 J. Dewey, *Democracy and Education: An Introduction to the Philosophy of Education* (New York: Macmillan, 1916).

32 G. L. Clore and J. R. Huntsinger, "How the Object of Affect Guides its Impact," *Emotion Review*, Vol. 1 (2009), pp. 39–54.

33 G. L. Clore and A. Ortony, "Appraisal Theories: How Cognition Shapes Affect into Emotion," in M. Lewis, J. M. Haviland-Jones, and L. F. Barrett (eds.), *Handbook of Emotions*, third edition (New York: Guilford Press, 2008), pp. 628–642.

34 President George W. Bush, 2001 Remarks to State Department Employees, http://www.sourcewatch.org/index.php?title=Evil-doers

35 K. Sengupta, "We are Defending Europe against Muslim Aggression," *The Independent*, December 7, 2007, p. 2.

36 T. D. Wilson and D. T. Gilbert, "Explaining Away: A Model of Affective Adaptation," *Perspectives on Psychological Science*, Vol. 5 (2008), pp. 370–386.

37 G. L. Clore and S. Colcombe, "The Parallel Worlds of Affective Concepts and Feelings," in J. Musch and K. C. Klauer (eds.), *The Psychology of Evaluation: Affective Processes in Cognition and Emotion* (Mahwah, NJ: Lawrence Erlbaum & Associates, 2003), pp. 335–370.

38 R. S. Lazarus, *Psychological Stress and the Coping Process* (New York: McGraw-Hill, 1966).

15

THE NEUROSCIENCE OF EMOTION AND REASONING IN SOCIAL CONTEXTS: IMPLICATIONS FOR MORAL THEOLOGY

MICHAEL L. SPEZIO

The neuroscience of emotion and moral action should be of widespread interest to the fields of moral philosophy and theology, and to anyone interested more generally in normative claims regarding practical thought. That this is true is not always clear to philosophers and theologians, and that such a claim can be made from a framework that explicitly rejects psychologism may be even less so. Yet the first of two central theses of the present chapter is that moral philosophy and theology have much to gain from engagement with neuroscience; the other is that the neuroscience of emotion and moral action provides strong evidence for the adaptive, integrative function of emotion in reasoned choice.

Moral theories that are virtue-based, or based in divine commands, or inspired by Humean concerns, or even those that reject any moral justification outside of the autonomous law of reason, have reason to attend to current neuroscientific investigations of emotion, and their sometimes surprising implications. Moral systems arguing that the virtues ground moral justification would be interested in how emotion and perception combine in deliberating and actualizing dispositions in given morally relevant contexts.[1] Those systems in which moral exemplars play a critical role in moral justification, as argued by Linda Zagzebski,[2] will want to know how current neuroscientific accounts of emotion help account for how we understand and reason about the thoughts, emotions, and intentions of other people. The same is true for

Faith, Rationality, and the Passions, First Edition. Edited by Sarah Coakley.
© 2012 Blackwell Publishing Ltd. Book compilation © 2012 Blackwell Publishing Ltd.

divine command theories, for these are often supported by accounts of the divine *person* that likely rely upon the same processes as those we use to engage the virtuous exemplar.[3] Moral theories inspired by Hume or similar instrumentalist and sentimentalist accounts will certainly want to understand how emotion is taken up by intentionality and is potentially constitutive of practical reason so as to account for how morally normative claims survive charges of relativism or skepticism.[4] Finally, and especially, for Kantian theories that ground morally normative claims by rejecting the inclinations of emotion for the universality of autonomous, law-giving reason, there is still the question of how human agents actually carry out Kantian requirements. In other words, the neuroscience of emotion and moral action may shed light on how humans actually "act only on a maxim which we could will to be a law" or how a human actually thinks "of herself as a Citizen of the Kingdom of Ends."[5] It may be, for example, that for a person 1) to learn to be an expert Kantian in moral matters, and 2) to exercise that expertise, that person must deploy certain emotional processes (including integrating emotion with other aspects of cognition, or drawing on past emotionally relevant experiences). This claim is quite plausible, and is an empirical question, albeit one that is not being actively researched at present. But the Kantian moral philosopher or theologian need not worry about the outcome, or that such a claim is simply an error emerging from psychologism. For, if emotion is involved, it need not reach normative status, despite the claims of Greene and others.[6] Yet refinements of Kantian positions would seem to be necessary in such circumstances, and so the research is of interest whatever its outcome.

For (the Neuroscience of) Emotion, Against Psychologism

In turning to an overview of the neuroscience of emotion and its relevance for decision making and moral action, it is first necessary to be explicit in rejecting psychologism. Psychologism, for present purposes, is the doctrine that normative logic and ethics/morality are subsets of descriptive, causal theories of mental processes, such as are found in psychology and neuroscience.[7] Thus, psychologism is taken to hold that psychological and neuroscientific descriptions will eventually serve as the conditions by which thought is to be judged as true or rational and by which morally relevant desires, intentions, and actions are to be judged as moral. Any argument that seeks to establish the importance of descriptive accounts of action, such as those from psychology and neuroscience, for normative accounts of action, which are the focus of moral theology and philosophy, should be clear about psychologistic sympathies. To be sure, prevailing arguments for the importance of the neuroscience of emotion and moral action, specifically for questions in moral philosophy, sometimes seem to endorse a thoroughgoing psychologism with regard to deriving standards for reason and morality, or at the very least seem unconcerned with addressing the issue.[8] There are important exceptions to this pattern,[9] but those accounts that appear to embrace psychologism are sufficiently prominent that they must be considered very seriously. The influence of these accounts is strong, and because they do not address, explicitly, psychologistic claims, influential programs ostensibly aiming at broader interdisciplinary understanding can show evidence of implicit psychologistic attachments.[10] These attachments, and any disavowals, are best brought out into the open for "civil intellectual discussion within the academic community," as is argued in an influential collection of essays linking evolutionary science and moral philosophy.[11]

The conceptual problems of psychologism are well-known and have been well-refuted, at least since the work of Gottlob Frege and Edmund Husserl.[12] However, this chapter disavows psychologism when looking to the neuroscience of emotion and moral action in interdisciplinary engagement, for two very straightforward reasons. The first is that the current methods of neuroscientific investigation into reason and moral action depend utterly on the very normative distinctions that psychologistic proponents seek to replace. In order to formulate mechanistic descriptions of decision making characterized as rational or irrational, or moral or immoral, in terms of neural activity of a specific kind, neuroscientists use and rely upon those normative categories. These categories are given to neuroscience and are not generated by it. So looking to replace, for example, the moral category of "benevolence" by a configuration of neural activations, is ill-conceived, and falls victim to the same arguments that have proven so effective in showing how problematic it is to reduce morality to maximizing happiness. Similarly, it is difficult to see what may be learned about morality from assuming a utilitarian framework as normative, and then identifying some neural activations as "rational" and others as "irrational" or biased, on the basis of their statistical association or lack of association with utilitarian judgments.[13] Mark Schroeder, in his recent defense of a Humean theory of reasons, nicely summarizes the case against such simple applications of reductionism, since they fail to answer why it is permissible to make descriptive accounts the referents of normative claims.[14]

The second reason to reject psychologism with respect to relating neuroscientific models to moral theory is that those models are dependent almost entirely upon probabilistic inference, due 1) to measurement errors stemming from influential variables whose influence is unaccounted for,[15] and 2) to measurement errors stemming from noise. Significantly, even programs that advance implicitly psychologistic agendas have issued strong warnings to non-neuroscientists about the limitations of neuroimaging data, including the measurement errors that come from assuming minimal differences between the brains of individual persons. The Neuroscience & Law Project, funded by the MacArthur Foundation, in which the leading scholars include strong proponents of psychologism, such as Michael Gazzaniga, Director of the Sage Institute of Neuroscience at the University of California Santa Barbara, is an example of such a program. The project aims at clearly psychologistic outcomes, such as using brain scanning to determine whether human freedom exists. Still, one of the primary publications of the project makes clear why this goal is a distant one. Their list of "key concepts that legal thinkers should know" includes a warning against thinking that any one person's brain can be adequately understood using a brain image derived from averaging across a group of people: "Do not assume that the scan of any individual is necessarily representative of any group. Do not assume that the averaged scan of any group will necessarily be representative of any individual."[16] One simply cannot, on the basis of neuroscientific research, make the kind of strong, normative claims to which psychologism aspires.

The relevance of the neuroscience of emotion and moral action, then, for relating faith, rationality, and the passions, is not due to psychologism in any of its forms. Rather, one simply needs to recognize that moral philosophies and theologies entail implicit *empirical* claims about how emotion relates to reasoning, and that not all of these claims are yet supported by rigorous research. Some implicit claims suggest that emotion is critical to reasoning, and some suggest that it is separate from or antithetical to reason. Some of these claims, if overturned, will require rethinking and refashioning the justifying arguments for morally normative systems. What follows is a brief introduction to the empirical work, showing that there is mounting evidence in favor of considering emotion as constitutive of, and not separate from, the reasoning and decision making that people do about their own values and the preferences and values of others.

Phineas Gage and the Affect of Reason

Perhaps the most well-known and certainly most celebrated paradigm supporting the association of emotion with reasoning is the case of Phineas Gage. Simon Blackburn, in his Humean ethical analysis entitled *Ruling Passions: A Theory of Practical Reasoning*, draws heavily on the Gage paradigm.[17] Antonio Damasio, in his landmark inquiry into the relation between emotion and decision-making, *Descartes' Error*,[18] summarized Gage's story and drew several implications from it based on the then-recent anatomical reevaluations carried out by Hanna Damasio and coworkers.[19] I am here following retellings by Damasio et al., Macmillan, and others, of the original case studies by Harlow.[20]

Gage was a railroad foreman who mistakenly began using an iron tamping rod to tamp down an explosive charge before the protective layer of sand was in place. Instead of striking sand, he struck rock, causing a spark, which caused the charge of dynamite to explode, sending the "pointed, 3-cm thick, 109-cm long tamping iron . . . through his face, skull, brain, and then into the sky."[21] Gage survived, his wound healed, and he lived for over eleven more years before a series of severe seizures finally ended his life. Yet it was clear to his friends and his family that, at least in the immediate aftermath of the accident, "Gage was no longer Gage," and that he had become intolerable as a person: rude, inconsiderate, and really quite immoral.[22]

No autopsy on Gage was ever done, but his damaged skull was recovered after his death, and is the basis of all subsequent analyses. Based on modeling procedures that sought to fit Gage's skull into the anatomical space of a standardized human skull model, and Gage's brain into the anatomical space of a standardized human brain, Damasio et al. determined that Gage sustained brain damage that spared all of his dorsolateral areas, but that completely lesioned his ventromedial prefrontal cortices and the front of his anterior cingulate. Damasio and coworkers recognized the significance of these lesioned areas, and focused on the damage to the ventromedial prefrontal cortex, orbitofrontal cortex, and frontal pole. These areas are known to be associated with one's own perception of the emotional salience of an event or object, especially if it interacts directly with the body in any way, such as via touch, taste, etc.[23] Additionally, work by the Damasio group in the early 1990s had identified a group of twelve individuals with damage to these areas who were quite impaired both in their own emotional sense and in social judgments about the emotions, intentions, and preferences of others. Surprisingly, all of these individuals, while seemingly incapable of sensitive social interaction, were intact in "their ability to tackle the logic of an abstract problem, to perform calculations, and to call up appropriate knowledge and attend to it" in other contexts.[24] These converging lines of evidence led the Damasio group to infer that "emotion and its underlying neural machinery participate in decision making within the social domain."[25]

For the purposes of the current article, the paradigmatic example of Phineas Gage is critical not because of its supposed support of emotion as a critical player in decision making, but because it serves as an important lesson in the importance of caution when drawing larger implications from limited scientific data. The story told by Damasio and others has been overwhelmingly helpful in attracting attention to the importance of the ventromedial prefrontal cortex and orbitofrontal cortex as critical for effective social judgment and action, and thus for emotion's role in both. However, this effort has overlooked several aspects of Gage's story that undermine his status as a scientific paradigm in this regard.

First, even if one accepts Damasio and coworkers' model of the damage to Gage's brain, it would suggest that Gage also sustained damage to the dorsal anterior cingulate, which is an area not associated with emotional processing but strongly associated with processing cognitive conflict and the realization of one's errors in the efforts to achieve goals one has in mind. Thus, this area is directly in line with nonaffective accounts of reasoning, and the damage to it in the Damasio model is often overlooked in favor of the larger story about emotions. Second, no one really knows where Gage's brain was damaged, since no autopsy or complete examination of the extent of the damage was ever done. The Damasio model is one convincing model; but other models, using newer technologies and insights about the mechanics of the skull during the impact of the iron bar, suggest that Gage's ventromedial prefrontal cortex and frontal pole survived largely intact, and that the damage was confined largely to the left side of his brain.[26] To be sure, this new model includes damage to the left orbitofrontal cortex, but also to the left dorsolateral prefrontal cortex, which is strongly associated with working memory and reasoned judgment.[27] Thus, it is more helpful to focus on more recent work linking impaired social reasoning to focal damage in the ventromedial cortex, orbitofrontal cortex, and frontal pole, since such work clearly identifies both the damage and the decision making impairments in great detail.

The Affect of Reason Revisited: Damage to the Prefrontal Cortex in Adulthood and Early in Life

Several converging lines of evidence from research conducted by the Iowa group, of which the Damasio laboratory is a part, including work by Antoine Bechara, Daniel Tranel, and Steven Anderson, provide strong evidence for the "affect of reason" theory about how emotion relates to reasoning in the social domain. One set of findings involves common behavioral impairments in reasoning in a group of adults that overlap in lesions to the ventromedial prefrontal cortex (including ventral anterior cingulate), orbitofrontal cortex, and frontal pole.[28] This group shows an overall sparing of dorsal anterior cingulate and dorsolateral prefrontal cortex, areas associated with cognitive conflict processing, error detection, and working memory. Hence, these individuals share profound damage to neural areas strongly associated with emotional salience, while showing much less consistent or no damage to those areas more associated with nonaffective components of decision making. These patients exhibit clear deficits in social judgment, reasoning, and behavior in their personal lives, and are often characterized as socially insensitive and incapable of sustaining relationships that were strong prior to their lesions. Moreover, when this group of patients is rigorously compared to other lesion groups with damage to the prefrontal cortex outside of the three critical areas (prefrontal control group) or with damage to cortex outside of the prefrontal area (non-prefrontal control group), they show much more seriously impaired social relationships[29] and impaired behavior on tasks requiring strategic thinking in terms of evaluation and emotional salience.[30] Tranel and colleagues used the Multiple Errands Test, which is a neuropsychological assessment that tests real-world monetary evaluation by requiring patients to economize while running a number of errands at a shopping mall.[31] Patients in the affective processing lesion group, whose dorsolateral prefrontal cortex and dorsal anterior cingulate cortex was spared damage, had more errors and fewer task completions than patients with complete lesions to areas strongly associated with working memory and explicit reasoning, and compared to patients with lesions outside of the prefrontal cortex. It is important to keep in mind that these patients show average to above average IQ scores, and generally are not impaired on tests of logical reasoning in abstract contexts that do not involve decisions about their own valuations or those of the people around them. The evidence in this study is representative of a larger body of work with such patients, and underscores the potential importance of neural areas associated with emotional processing to real-world reasoning, especially in the evaluative and social domains.

Perhaps more convincing in this regard is a series of studies conducted by Steven Anderson and colleagues, investigating the long-term implications of damage early in development (within the first five years of life) to ventromedial prefrontal cortex, orbitofrontal cortex, and frontal pole. Early reports from this group showed that adults who had sustained such lesions when infants (less than twenty-four months of age) developed amoral behaviors that were accompanied by a complete lack of any evidence of guilt or remorse.[32] They also showed a failure to achieve moral reasoning beyond concern for egoistic consequences, as determined by the Kohlberg Moral Judgment Task. Anderson and colleagues recently expanded on this work by examining the consistency of social impairments in a larger group of these patients, again comparing them to patients with childhood onset damage outside of the prefrontal cortex.[33] The findings again support the critical role that ventromedial prefrontal cortex, orbitofrontal cortex, and frontal pole play in social judgment and decision making. Critically, and quite poignantly, the authors convincingly make the case that "emotional dysfunction (both diminished experience of emotion and emotional overreactivity) is a strong predictor of real-world social dysfunction in patients with [prefrontal cortex] damage," and then point out that "it remains the case that the impairments stemming from childhood [prefrontal cortex] damage often persist into adulthood despite well-intended intervention, at considerable personal and societal cost."[34] It is important to note that damage to emotionally relevant neural regions so early in development creates social judgment and reasoning dysfunctions that last a lifetime, especially since the brain is known to be quite plastic and flexible in response to damage to other areas, including areas for language, at this early stage.

The Emerging Consensus in Affective Neuroscience: Emotion as Cognition

By the late 1990s and into about 2003, a consensus about the importance of emotion for reasoning had emerged, in response to the body of research summarized above, and other similar lines of evidence coming from the work of neuroscientists like Ralph Adolphs, Richard Davidson, Jaak Panksepp, and others. Adolphs and coworkers had shown that focal damage to the amygdala in humans strongly impaired the ability to recognize fear in the faces of other people and the ability to show normal social judgment based on a person's appearance.[35] The amygdala is also strongly associated with personally relevant emotional salience, particularly in the area of fear.[36] Affective neuroscience, which had long battled to be taken seriously in the area of cognitive neuroscience, was emerging victorious at last. Cognitive neuroscience, a relatively new interdisciplinary field joining experimental cognitive psychology[37] and neuroscience, which began in the late 1970s and early 1980s, had maintained that cognition was to be defined as any kind of information processing or transformation that had relevance to measurable outcomes in the traditional loci of cognitive psychology: perception, attention, memory, imagery, language, problem solving, and decision making.[38] Emotion, according to early conceptions of cognitive neuroscience, did not really belong to the field, since it could not be reliably measured, nor was it clearly relevant to adaptive behavioral outcomes in the traditional areas of investigation.

These views began to change in the 1990s, and Richard Davidson, whose work contributed much to change them, published a paper in 2003 summarizing the outdated views on emotion. The paper, entitled "Seven Sins in the Study of Emotion: Correctives from Affective Neuroscience,"[39] addressed the first and major sin as maintaining that "affect and cognition are subserved by separate and independent neural circuits." Drawing on much of the research briefly summarized above, Davidson's corrective emphasized the "overlap between circuitry involved in cognitive and affective processing," and argued that emotion "is a set of differentiated subcomponents that are instantiated in a distributed network of cortical and subcortical circuits." On this view, emotion really amounted to cognition, in the definition of cognitive neuroscience, because emotion entailed information processing and transformation. The long-held divide between cognition and emotion had been breached by a failure to find such clear divisions in the circuitry of the human brain, and by the positive findings relating areas known for emotional salience processing to effective reasoning and decision making in the social domain. Davidson also criticized outdated views that confined emotion and affective processing to the subcortical limbic region, or the so-called reptilian brain. In fact, the old model of the "triune brain,"[40] which divides the brain into reptilian, paleomammalian, and neomammalian subcomponents is no longer viable in cognitive neuroscience. Finally, Davidson challenged the views that emotions are (or necessarily involve) conscious feeling states, and cognitive and affective neuroscience have followed him, Damasio, and others on this point. Current views of emotion in these sciences distinguish between emotions and feelings, where the former are cognitive information processes that activate dispositions for action, while the latter entail conscious awareness and reflection upon such processes.[41]

The emerging consensus that rejected a dichotomous view of emotion and cognition implied a rejection of another dichotomy built upon the emotion/

cognition divide. This second dichotomy is between explicit and implicit information processing, where explicit processing is that seen and guided by awareness (i.e., is deliberative) and implicit processing is that outside of awareness and often viewed as independent of it (i.e., is automatic). Once again, it was difficult to find clear breakpoints in the neural circuitry that supported such a clear conceptual break between one's conscious awareness and the numerous processes outside of awareness that nonetheless support that awareness and are likely guided in some way by it. One of the clearest examples of this relationship was a brief report in 1999 by a French team of neurologists and neuroscientists working at the Centre d'Investigation Clinique, Fédération de Neurologie and INSERM.[42] A patient who had been implanted with electrodes deep in her brain for the purposes of deep-brain stimulation for the treatment of Parkinson's had a highly unusual and terrifying experience once the electrodes were turned on. The patient was a sixty-five-year-old woman with no history of depression or mood disorders, or psychiatric disorders of any kind, even after a thirty-year struggle with Parkinson's. Yet she became depressed, despondent, and even suicidal, after approximately only five seconds of stimulation via an electrode implanted in her substantia nigra, a subcortical area. She was completely aware of herself and her surroundings, she spoke intelligibly to the physicians, and she experienced no hallucinations at all during the period of depression accompanying the implicit signal of electrical stimulation. She made statements to the doctors as follows: "I'm falling down in my head, I no longer wish to live, to see anything, hear anything, feel anything. . . . I'm fed up with life, I've had enough. . . . I don't want to live any more, I'm disgusted with life. . . . Everything is useless, always feeling worthless, I'm scared in this world. . . . I'm tired. . . . I want to hide in a corner. . . . I'm crying over myself, of course. . . . I'm hopeless, why am I bothering you? . . ."[43] This profound turn in her self-aware emotional state and subsequent expression of her self-valuation, brought on by an external stimulus applied directly to her brain (i.e., an implicit signal), was completely gone within ninety seconds after the stimulation was switched off. Then she returned to her normal self, "and she laughed and joked with the examiner, playfully pulling his tie." She was also able to recall the entirety of what she had experienced during the stimulation.

Surprisingly, and courageously, this patient endured the stimulation at least one more time, with a complete replication of her experience, only this time she underwent simultaneous neuroimaging via positron emission tomography (PET). The PET scan showed increased activity in the left orbitofrontal cortex and left amygdala, both known for associations with one's own emotional experiences and evaluations, and in the right superior parietal cortex. That the increased activation was confined to areas associated with emotional salience and did not involve increases in areas like the anterior cingulate or the dorsolateral prefrontal cortex (i.e., those areas typically associated with cognitive conflict, error monitoring, and online working memory), and that such activation was accompanied by explicit changes in self-awareness and decision making, shows that dichotomous views separating emotion and cognition, on the one hand, and implicit from explicit processing, on the other, are limited in explanatory power. The case articulated by Davidson and others, supported by an impressive stream of mounting evidence, seemed to promise the quick development of alternative models to human decision making and reasoning in the social domain that would integrate emotional processing into reason, rather than continue to keep the two apart. However, such a goal has so far proved elusive, and new developments within social and affective neuroscience have in contrast advanced by building instead on older dichotomous, dual process models of decision making.

Dual Process Theories in Social and Affective Neuroscience

A brief overview of the appeal and explanatory power of dual process models is necessary to capture something of the current state of the debate within the neuroscience of emotion, particularly in social judgment and decision making. However, it will not be possible within this chapter to do full justice to the history of dual process models in experimental cognitive psychology, social psychology, and the newer fields of social neuroscience, decision neuroscience, and neuroeconomics.[44] What should be clear in what follows is that almost every manifestation of dual process theory is actually *oppositional process theory*, in that the two proposed processes are not just theorized as separate, but as forever in opposition to one another, with no possibility of integration for unified, motivated action. It is this strong emphasis on oppositional processes that is the primary focus for the subsequent discussion.

Oppositional dual process models may have gained influence by the long-running division between reason and emotion, or reason and "the passions," within Western philosophy. In experimental psychology, dual process models were influential already in the 1960s and 1970s in discussions applying artificial intelligence to human thought and reason.[45] Schneider and Schiffrin, Simon, Broadbent, and others appealed to formal dual process models to make sense of data within information-processing frameworks based on computational architecture.[46] Dual process models hypothesize two distinct cognitive and/or neural systems mediating, on the one hand, the top-down or goal-directed or endogenous control of thought and activity (e.g., attention), and, on the other hand, mental processing that is not controlled, labeled bottom-up or automatic or exogenous. Controlled processing is often associated with processing that is consciously, even reflectively, directed; and a recent account has labeled such consciously aware processing "refleCtive" processing, in contradistinction to automatic, or "refleXive" processing, yielding a "C"- and "X"-system dichotomous model of decision making.[47]

As noted above, once neuroscientists interested in the study of emotion failed to find clear neural dichotomies that mapped onto the conceptual divisions of dual process models, they challenged the dualisms and sought integrative accounts. However, social and affective neuroscience began to see a growing influence of experimental social psychology soon after 2000, with the result that dual process models were once again introduced in force. Social neuroscience began as an attempt to apply cognitive neuroscience to social cognition and decision making, but has evolved to a more complete interdisciplinary engagement between cognitive neuroscience and experimental social psychology.[48] In the latter field, dual process models have always dominated, and they are a prevailing influence in social neuroscience as a result.[49] Yet, as pointed out by Feldman Barrett and co-workers,[50] controlled, or top-down, processing need not always be under conscious control. For example, someone with a conscious goal of desiring a good meal at a restaurant and who makes a conscious decision to look at the menu to accomplish this goal, most often will not be consciously controlling detailed visual scanning of the menu. Nonetheless, in this case the person's visual attention to the menu is under top-down control, since attention was the result of a goal-directed decision, and a conscious one at that. That is, instead of looking out the window or at the salt shaker on the table, the person decided to look at the menu.

While there is clear experimental evidence for some distinction between behaviors that are influenced by conscious control and those that are not, it is unclear that postulating separate, non-overlapping, and forever oppositional systems—one for controlled the other for automatic, processing—aids in understanding the mechanisms behind the data. Oppositional dual process models can cloud such understanding, since they deemphasize the fact that implicit processing is always involved in human activity, even during conscious control of decision making. For example, the controlled focus of attention in recalling a specific memory involves millions of changes in the brain that are not under the conscious control of the person doing the remembering. Further, dual process models tend to neglect the role of controlled processing in activating and modulating implicit processing, as would be the case when someone tries to remember a person she likes versus a song she cannot stand. Controlled processing can have clearly observable effects on the processing of stimuli—such as words or faces or memories which are processed—even though the control does not extend to the millions of brain events in such processing. For example, the outcome of a visual search for a lost item in a room cluttered with objects will be influenced strongly by the image of the item one consciously has in mind while searching for it. If one has a false image of the item in mind, finding it may take much longer, if it is found at all. So the conscious image exerts an effect on all of the processing in the millions of brain events going on during the search, even without conscious control of those implicit events.

Upon careful consideration of the ubiquitous presence of implicit process-ing with deliberative processing, and of the demonstrable effects of delibera-tive processing upon implicit brain processes, it is clear that postulating two distinct processing systems obscures more than it reveals. Recently, some authors have acknowledged the intricate interplay of controlled and automatic processing, and have called for "drastically revising the dual-process story as we now know it."[51] Others more sympathetic to dual process frameworks have even called for abandoning the dichotomous nature of dual process models in favor of a temporally recursive model, in which deliberative processes modu-late implicit processes which in turn give rise to changes in the deliberative processes.[52] However, these newer statements, such as the well-argued paper by Cunningham and Zelazo,[53] still attempt to create neural dichotomies by assigning more implicit, "relatively automatic," processing to "emotional" areas like the amygdala and orbitofrontal cortex, and more explicit, "relatively reflective," processing to cognitive areas like the dorsal anterior cingulate and the dorsolateral prefrontal cortex. The problem with such models is not that they are inconsistent with neuroimaging data; in fact, they are consistent with a significant body of neuroimaging experiments motivated by dual process accounts, though they are not the only models to show such consistency. The primary issue, as we have seen, is that they do not adequately take into account the large body of lesion-deficit data showing that so-called implicit areas like ventromedial prefrontal cortex, orbitofrontal cortex, and frontal pole figure more greatly for social judgment and reasoning than so-called deliberative areas like dorsolateral prefrontal cortex and dorsal anterior cingulate. So dual process models, derived in part from a pre-affective stage of cognitive psy-chology and imported from social psychology, fail to explain a set of critical findings in the neuroscience of emotion and reasoning, especially in the social domain. It is perhaps for this reason that a renewed interest in integrationist approaches, which seek a unified conceptual system where emotion is consti-tutive of reasoning, is now gaining momentum.

A Renewal of Interest in Integrationist Approaches

This renewal stems from two primary areas in the neuroscience of emotion and decision making, briefly described here. The first area supporting renewed interest in integrating emotion and models of reasoning in the social domain is the area of simulation theoretic approaches to the theory of mind.[54] Simula-tion theoretic approaches to the neuroscience of social understanding and decision making investigate neural networks for evidence of *simulation processes*. Simulation theories constructed from data demonstrating these pro-cesses have made it clear that emotionally relevant conceptual processing is essential for adaptive and efficient social engagement.[55] Such frameworks in affective and social neuroscience identify similar processing involved in both the *experience* of an intention or emotion in oneself and the *perception* of an intention or emotion in another. The networks carrying out this double duty of self- and other-representation are termed "shared circuits," or sometimes, "mirror neurons." These networks are then supportive of empathy, which is the ability spontaneously to reconstruct in oneself what another is feeling, thinking, and intending.[56] Importantly, it is known that these simulation processes increase with the conscious awareness of increased similarity between oneself and another person, in terms of age, gender, political attitude, and even sports allegiance. Simulation processes are also modulated by the consciously perceived morality of another person, specifically how fair they are perceived to be. What is not known as yet is whether the conscious awareness of similarity or morality gets the simulations started to begin with, whether it is the other way around, or how much these processes integrate in a recursive network.

The second source of increased interest in integrative approaches to the neuroscience of emotion and reasoning comes from new applications of social and affective neuroscience to moral action.[57] Early work in this area by Joshua Greene advanced the case for a dual process account of moral judgment, in which emotional biases hampered the cool, reasoned exercise of utilitarian criteria.[58] These arguments were driven largely by utilitarian commitments that shaped the interpretation of neuroimaging data. More recently, scholars advancing these arguments sought support from lesion-deficit studies showing that patients with lesions to ventromedial prefrontal cortex, orbito-frontal cortex, and frontal pole, engage in almost perfect utilitarian decision making when encountering hypothetical moral dilemmas.[59] Greene argued that this result is predicted exactly by dual process accounts of the kind he advocates, and took the evidence as strong support for a dual process in moral judgment and action, where emotion just gets in the way of reasoned moral judgment.[60] Recall, however, that these same patients (those with damage to ventromedial prefrontal cortex, orbitofrontal cortex, and frontal pole), show profound real-life social deficits and moral insensitivity in their everyday lives. In fact, Jorge Moll and Roberto de Oliveira-Souza made this point, and argued that what was in fact happening was that the lesion patients suffered from an inability adequately to perceive and reason about human situations, preferences, desires, etc., and so were left with only utilitarian criteria available to them.[61] Thus, the utilitarian judgment exhibited by the patients in the moral dilemma task gave evidence of a further deficit in their reasoning, rather than evidence of an improvement, as Greene would have it. Such a view is more consistent with what is known about these patients' reasoning in real life and on other socially and evaluatively relevant tasks, as summarized above.

Taking their lead from this interpretation and its potential importance for the understanding of moral action, Moll, Davidson, and others have renewed investigations and theoretical arguments which again attempt to see emotion as constitutive of human reasoning.[62] They are being joined by other social and affective neuroscientists who continue to find no clear evidence for dichotomous views of emotion and reasoning when investigating neural systems in detail.[63] Rather than dichotomous, opposing systems, what is emerging is a complex interconnection of circuits in which emotional signals cannot be separated from adaptive reasoning and decision making when such judgment and action are relevant for oneself and others. That this emerging account has implications for moral theology, especially any system that values human relationality, should be clear. We may soon have a descriptive account that motivates a more careful consideration of the claim, made by Bonhoeffer and others, that a morally virtuous person is one who is "not a double psyche, a person of two souls."[64]

NOTES

1   See Robert Merrihew Adams, *A Theory of Virtue: Excellence in Being for the Good* (Oxford: Oxford University Press, 2006); Romanus Cessario, O. P., *The Moral Virtues and Theological Ethics*, second edition (Notre Dame, IN: University of Notre Dame Press, 2009); Rosalind Hursthouse, *On Virtue Ethics* (New York: Oxford University Press, 1999); Alasdair MacIntyre, *After Virtue: A Study in Moral Theory* (Notre Dame, IN: University of Notre Dame, 1984); John McDowell, "Virtue and Reason," *The Monist*, Vol. 62 (1979); Kieran Setiya, *Reasons without Rationalism* (Princeton, NJ: Princeton University Press, 2007).

2   Linda T. Zagzebski, *Divine Motivation Theory* (Cambridge: Cambridge University Press, 2004).

3   Or so I argued in Michael L. Spezio, "The Feeling of the Other," at the Annual Meeting of the American Academy of Religion, 2000.

4   See especially Allan Gibbard, *Wise Choices, Apt Feelings: A Theory of Normative Judgment* (Cambridge, MA: Harvard University Press, 1990); Simon Blackburn, *Ruling Passions* (New York: Oxford University Press, 1998); Mark Schroeder, *Slaves of the Passions* (New York: Oxford University Press, 2007); Michael A. Smith, *The Moral Problem* (Cambridge: John Wiley, 1994).

5   Christine M. Korsgaard, "The Authority of Reflection," in *The Sources of Normativity*, ed. Onora O'Neill (New York: Cambridge University Press, 1996), pp. 98 and 100. Note that it is not claimed here that current neuroscientific investigations have shed any light on this as yet. In fact, as long as neuroscientists persist in studying how people make decisions about others' benefits and harms in the absence of any explicit Kantian instruction or mental set, it is unclear how any progress in these areas could be made.

6   J. Greene, "From Neural 'Is' to Moral 'Ought': What Are the Moral Implications of Neuroscientific Moral Psychology?," *Nature Reviews Neuroscience*, Vol. 4, no. 10 (2003), pp. 847–850; J. Greene and J. Cohen, "For the Law, Neuroscience Changes Nothing and Everything," *Philosophical Transactions of the Royal Society of London B: Biological Sciences*, Vol. 359, no. 1451 (2004); J. D. Greene et al., "The Neural Bases of Cognitive Conflict and Control in Moral Judgment," *Neuron*, Vol. 44, no. 2 (2004), pp. 389–400; J. D. Greene et al., "An Fmri Investigation of Emotional Engagement in Moral Judgment," *Science*, Vol. 293, no. 5537 (2001), pp. 2105–2108.

7   See Edmund Husserl, *Logical Investigations: Volume 1*, ed. Dermot Moran (London: Routledge, 2001), pp. 40–100.

8   An unconcern with psychologism, and sometimes an outright endorsement of its principles, is the case in the following essays (most of which are considered in this paper): J. Greene, "From Neural 'Is' to Moral 'Ought'"; J. Greene and J. Cohen, "For the Law"; J. Greene and J. Haidt, "How (and Where) Does Moral Judgment Work?," *Trends in Cognitive Sciences*, Vol. 6, no. 12 (2002), pp. 517–523; J. Haidt, "The Emotional Dog and Its Rational Tail: A Social Intuitionist Approach to Moral Judgment," *Psychological Review*, Vol. 108 (2001), pp. 814–834; J. Haidt, "The New Synthesis in Moral Psychology," *Science*, Vol. 316 (2007), pp. 998–1002; J. Moll and R. de Oliveira-Souza, "Moral Judgments, Emotions and the Utilitarian Brain," *Trends in Cognitive Sciences*, Vol. 11, no. 8 (2007), pp. 319–321; J. Moll et al., "Opinion: The

Neural Basis of Human Moral Cognition," *Nature Reviews Neuroscience,* Vol. 6, no. 10 (2005), pp. 799–809; F. Cushman, L. Young, and M. Hauser, "The Role of Conscious Reasoning and Intuition in Moral Judgment: Testing Three Principles of Harm," *Psychological Science,* Vol. 17, no. 12 (2006), pp. 1082–1089; M. Hauser, "What's Fair? The Unconscious Calculus of Our Moral Faculty," *Novartis Found Symp,* Vol. 278 (2007), pp. 41–50; discussion pp. 50–55, 89–96, 216–221; M. Koenigs et al., "Damage to the Prefrontal Cortex Increases Utilitarian Moral Judgements," *Nature,* Vol. 446, no. 7138 (2007), pp. 908–911; L. Young et al., "The Neural Basis of the Interaction between Theory of Mind and Moral Judgment," *Proceedings of the National Academy of Sciences U S A,* Vol. 104, no. 20 (2007), pp. 8235–8240; F. B. M. de Waal, "Morally Evolved: Primate Social Instincts, Human Morality, and the Rise and Fall of 'Veneer Theory'," in *Primates and Philosophers: How Morality Evolved,* eds. Stephen Macedo and Josiah Ober, (Princeton, NJ: Princeton University Press, 2006), pp. 1–80; F. B. M. de Waal, "The Tower of Morality," in *Primates and Philosophers: How Morality Evolved,* eds. Stephen Macedo and Josiah Ober (Princeton, NJ: Princeton University Press, 2006), pp. 161–181.

9   Moll et al., "Opinion: The Neural Basis of Human Moral Cognition."
10 See for example the recent interdisciplinary program on Law and Neuroscience, directed by the neuroscientist Michael Gazzaniga (University of California Santa Barbara) and the law professor Owen Jones (Vanderbilt University), (url: http://www. lawandneuroscienceproject.org/Default.aspx). Both scholars are committed to determinism with regard to human action and interpret neuroscientific evidence to support only this conclusion. This results in a commitment to substituting neuroscientific interpretations, about matters within the science that are far from settled, for interpretations of human action that rely on intentions, motives, and choice. Take, for example, this statement in a recent paper emerging from the project, which leaves no role at all for the mind in influencing behavior: "All behavior results from the interaction of genes, environments (including social contexts), developmental history, and the evolutionary processes that built the brain to function in the ways it does." (Owen D. Jones et al., "Brain Imaging for Legal Thinkers: A Guide for the Perplexed," *Stanford Technology Law Review,* Vol. 5 [2009], p. 7.) With regard to how neuroscience should influence the practice of law, the Program says in its Mission Statement: "More generally, neuroscience raises fundamental challenges for criminal law as a whole. According to some commentators (Greene and Cohen), our practice of punishment assumes a kind of free will that is refuted by psychological and brain sciences. Furthermore, most legal systems prescribe greater punishment when harms are intended (as in murder) than when they are not (as in involuntary manslaughter), and yet some experiments have been interpreted so as to suggest that conscious intentions do not affect actions at all or, at least, as much as we think, because our brains start to produce our actions before any intention becomes conscious (Libet, Wegner). The very notion of intention is also problematic insofar as it requires courts to decide whether a defendant did or did not intend a harm, whereas scientists have long recognized a wider variety of mental states that cause acts, or increase the probabilities of those acts, only as parts of larger sets of circumstances. (Sapolsky 2006) These apparent conflicts between science and law suggest that our criminal law might need to be radically reconceptualized. Defenders of traditional criminal law find this skepticism overblown, but radical proposals based on neuroscience are becoming so widespread, even in the popular imagination, that they cannot be ignored" (http://www.lawandneuroscienceproject.org/About-Us/ Mission.aspx). The proponents of determinism in the Law and Neuroscience project see only that determinism will result in more humane policies for criminals. However, it is not clear why determinism would not yield radical reconceptions of the law in directions that would entail greater erosions of human rights. One should also note that other writings from the project seem to resist a thoroughgoing psychologism: "Norms, though influenced by biology, can never be justified by biology alone." See Jones et al., "Brain Imaging for Legal Thinkers: A Guide for the Perplexed," p. 8.
11 Philip Clayton and Jeffrey Schloss, eds., *Evolution and Ethics: Human Morality in Biological and Religious Perspective* (Grand Rapids, MI: Eerdmans, 2004), p. 3.
12 Gottlob Frege, *Foundations of Arithmetic,* trans. Dale Jacquette (Upper Saddle River, NJ: Longman, 2007 [1884]); Husserl, *Logical Investigations: Volume 1.*
13 Such is the case in some of J. Greene's earlier writings. See especially Greene, "From Neural 'Is' to Moral 'Ought'"; Greene and Haidt, "How (and Where) Does Moral Judgment Work?"; Greene et al., "The Neural Bases" and Greene et al., "An Fmri Investigation." Importantly, the

238   *Michael L. Spezio*

statistical associations emerging from neuroimaging research that Greene and other neuro-scientists rely upon should be taken as hypothetical associations only. Recent work by Bruno Wicker and co-workers shows that when a neural region associated by Greene with rational, utilitarian judgment is temporarily inactivated, personal biases are actually *reduced*, and not enhanced, contrary to Greene's model. See B. Wicker et al., "Disrupting the prefrontal cortex diminishes emotional biases in moral judgment" (paper presented at the Annual Meeting of the Organization for Human Brain Mapping, Barcelona, Spain, June 6–10, 2010).

14   Schroeder, *Slaves of the Passions*, pp. 170–175.
15   In other words, influences that are not measured at all, and that may not be even taken account of in theory.
16   In Jones et al., "Brain Imaging for Legal Thinkers: A Guide for the Perplexed," p. 9.
17   Blackburn, *Ruling Passions*, pp. 125–134.
18   A. Damasio, *Descartes' Error: Emotion, Reason and the Human Brain* (New York: HarperCollins, 1994).
19   Hanna Damasio et al., "The Return of Phineas Gage: Clues About the Brain from the Skull of a Famous Patient," *Science*, Vol. 264, no. 5162 (1994), pp. 1102–1105.
20   Damasio, Macmillan, and others generally quote from the original studies by the physician who treated Gage, John M. Harlow. See John M. Harlow, "Passage of an Iron Rod through the Head," *Boston Medical Journal*, Vol. 39 (1848), pp. 389–393 and John M. Harlow, "Recovery from the Passage of an Iron Bar through the Head," *Publications of the Massachusetts Medical Society*, Vol. 2 (1868), pp. 327–347. Sometimes the secondary summary of Bigelow is also consulted: H. J. Bigelow, "Dr. Harlow's Case of Recovery from the Passage of an Iron Bar through the Head," *American Journal of Medical Sciences*, Vol. 20 (1850), pp. 13–22. See Malcolm Macmillan, "Restoring Phineas Gage: A 150th Retrospective," *Journal of the History of the Neurosciences*, Vol. 9, no. 1 (2000), pp. 46–66; Malcolm Macmillan, "Phineas Gage: Unravelling the Myth," *The Psychologist*, Vol. 21, no. 9 (2008), pp. 828–831 and Damasio et al., "The Return of Phineas Gage."
21   Damasio et al., "The Return of Phineas Gage," p. 1102.
22   Macmillan, "Restoring Phineas Gage: A 150th Retrospective."
23   E. T. Rolls and F. Grabenhorst, "The Orbitofrontal Cortex and Beyond: From Affect to Decision-Making," *Progress in Neurobiology*, Vol. 86 (2008), pp. 216–244; E. T. Rolls et al., "Representations of Pleasant and Painful Touch in the Human Orbitofrontal and Cingulate Cortices," *Cerebral Cortex*, Vol. 13 (2003), pp. 308–317.
24   Damasio et al., "The Return of Phineas Gage," p. 1104.
25   Ibid. See also Antoine Bechara, "The Role of Emotion in Decision-Making: Evidence from Neurological Patients with Orbitofrontal Damage," *Brain and Cognition*, Vol. 55 (2004), pp. 30–40.
26   Peter Ratiu and Ion-Florin Talos, "The Tale of Phineas Gage, Digitally Remastered," *New England Journal of Medicine*, Vol. 351, no. 23 (2004), p. e21. For a favorable account of the new model, see Macmillan, "Phineas Gage: Unravelling the Myth."
27   See Greene et al., "The Neural Bases"; O. Monchi et al., "Wisconsin Card Sorting Revisited: Distinct Neural Circuits Participating in Different Stages of the Task Identified by Event-Related Functional Magnetic Resonance Imaging," *Journal of Neuroscience*, Vol. 21, no. 19 (2001), pp. 7733–7741.
28   Joe Barrash, Daniel Tranel, and Steven W. Anderson, "Acquired Personality Disturbances Associated with Bilateral Damage to the Ventromedial Prefrontal Region," *Developmental Neuropsychology*, Vol. 18, no. 3 (2000), pp. 355–381; Daniel Tranel, Julie Hathaway-Nepple, and Steven W. Anderson, "Impaired Behavior on Real-World Tasks Following Damage to the Ventromedial Prefrontal Cortex," *Journal of Clinical and Experimental Neuropsychology*, Vol. 29, no. 3 (2007), pp. 319–332.
29   Barrash, Tranel, and Anderson, "Acquired Personality Disturbances."
30   Tranel, Hathaway-Nepple, and Anderson, "Impaired Behavior."
31   See Ibid. for more details.
32   Steven W. Anderson et al., "Impairment of Social and Moral Behavior Related to Early Damage in Human Prefrontal Cortex," *Nature Neuroscience*, Vol. 2, no. 11 (1999), pp. 1032–1037; Steven W. Anderson et al., "Long-Term Sequelae of Prefrontal Cortex Damage Acquired in Early Childhood," *Developmental Neuropsychology*, Vol. 18, no. 3 (2000), pp. 281–296; Barrash, Tranel, and Anderson, "Acquired Personality Disturbances."

33   Steven W. Anderson et al., "Consistency of Neuropsychological Outcome Following Damage to Prefrontal Cortex in the First Years of Life," *Journal of Clinical and Experimental Neuropsychology*, Vol. 31, no. 2 (2009), pp. 170–179.
34   Ibid., p. 178.
35   R. Adolphs, D. Tranel, and A. R. Damasio, "The Human Amygdala in Social Judgment," *Nature*, Vol. 393, no. 6684 (1998), pp. 470–474.
36   D. Pare, G. J. Quirk, and J. E. Ledoux, "New Vistas on Amygdala Networks in Conditioned Fear," *Journal of Neurophysiology*, Vol. 92, no. 1 (2004), pp. 1–9.
37   For a very helpful overview of experimental cognitive psychology and its relation to cognitive science, see G. A. Miller, "The Cognitive Revolution: A Historical Perspective," *Trends in Cognitive Sciences*, Vol. 7, no. 3 (2003), pp. 141–144.
38   See E. Bruce Goldstein, *Cognitive Psychology: Connecting Mind, Research, and Everyday Experience* (Belmont, CA: Thomson Wadsworth, 2008, 2005).
39   R. J. Davidson, "Seven Sins in the Study of Emotion: Correctives from Affective Neuroscience," *Brain and Cognition*, Vol. 52 (2003), pp. 129–132. With apologies to Evagrius.
40   For a more detailed description, see Constance Holden, "Paul Maclean and the Triune Brain," *Science*, Vol. 204, no. 4397 (1979), pp. 1066–1068.
41   See also R. Adolphs, "The Neurobiology of Social Cognition," *Current Opinion in Neurobiology*, Vol. 11, no. 2 (2001), pp. 231–239; R. Adolphs, "Neural Systems for Recognizing Emotion," *Curr Opin Neurobiol*, Vol. 12, no. 2 (2002), pp. 169–177; R. Adolphs, "Cognitive Neuroscience of Human Social Behaviour," *Nature Reviews Neuroscience*, Vol. 4, no. 3 (2003), pp. 165–178 and N. Tsuchiya and R. Adolphs, "Emotion and Consciousness," *Trends in Cognitive Sciences*, Vol. 11, no. 4 (2007), pp. 158–167.
42   Boulos-Paul Bejjani et al., "Transient Acute Depression Induced by High-Frequency Deep-Brain Stimulation," *New England Journal of Medicine*, Vol. 340, no. 19 (1999), pp. 1476–1480.
43   Ibid., p. 1476.
44   For a more complete consideration of dual process models, the reader is encouraged to consult the works cited here.
45   See J. Evans and K. Frankish, eds., *In Two Minds: Dual Processes and Beyond* (New York: Oxford University Press, 2009).
46   W. Schneider and R. M. Shiffrin, "Controlled and Automatic Human Information Processing: I. Detection, Search, and Attention," *Psychological Review*, Vol. 84 (1977), pp. 1–66; W. Schneider and R. M. Shiffrin, "Controlled and Automatic Human Information Processing: II. Perceptual Learning, Automatic Attending, and a General Theory," *Psychological Review*, Vol. 84 (1977), pp. 127–190; Donald E. Broadbent, *Decision and Stress* (London: Academic Press, 1971); and H. A. Simon, "Information Processing Models of Cognition," *Annual Review of Psychology*, Vol. 30 (1979), pp. 365–396.
47   Matthew D. Lieberman, Darren Schreiber, and Kevin N. Ochsner, "Is Political Cognition Like Riding a Bicycle? How Cognitive Neuroscience Can Inform Research on Political Thinking," *Political Psychology*, Vol. 24, no. 4 (2003), pp. 681–704.
48   Compare Adolphs, "The Neurobiology of Social Cognition" and Adolphs, "Cognitive Neuroscience of Human Social Behaviour" with K. N. Ochsner and M. D. Lieberman, "The Emergence of Social Cognitive Neuroscience," *American Psychologist*, Vol. 56, no. 9 (2001), pp. 717–734. The former two articles are written from the perspective of a cognitive neuroscientist addressing social cognition, while the last article is written by two experimental social psychologists who entered social neuroscience well after being established in social psychology.
49   K. N. Ochsner and J. J. Gross, "The Cognitive Control of Emotion," *Trends in Cognitive Sciences*, Vol. 9, no. 5 (2005), pp. 242–249.
50   L. Feldman Barrett, M. M. Tugage, and R. W. Engle, "Individual Differences in Working Memory Capacity and Dual-Process Theories of Mind," *Psychological Bulletin*, Vol. 130 (2004), pp. 553–573.
51   Ibid., p. 567.
52   William A. Cunningham and Phillip David Zelazo, "Attitudes and Evaluations: A Social Cognitive Neuroscience Perspective," *Trends in Cognitive Sciences*, Vol. 11, no. 3 (2007), pp. 97–104. See also R. Adolphs and M. Spezio, "Role of the Amygdala in Processing Visual Social Stimuli," *Progress in Brain Research*, Vol. 156 (2006), pp. 363–378.
53   Cunningham and Zelazo, "Attitudes and Evaluations."

54   R. Adolphs, "How Do We Know the Minds of Others? Domain-Specificity, Simulation, and Enactive Social Cognition," *Brain Research*, Vol. 1079, no. 1 (2006), pp. 25–35; L. W. Barsalou, "Simulation, Situated Conceptualization, and Prediction," *Philosophical Transactions of the Royal Society B: Biological Sciences*, Vol. 364, no. 1521 (2009), pp. 1281–1289; J. A. Etzel, V. Gazzola, and C. Keysers, "Testing Simulation Theory with Cross-Modal Multivariate Classification of Fmri Data," *PLoS ONE*, Vol. 3, no. 11 (2008), p. e3690; A. Goldman, "Simulation and Interpersonal Utility," *Ethics*, Vol. 105, no. 4 (1995), pp. 709–726; S. Hurley, "The Shared Circuits Model (Scm): How Control, Mirroring, and Simulation Can Enable Imitation, Deliberation, and Mindreading," *Behavioral and Brain Sciences*, Vol. 31, no. 10 (2008), pp. 1–58; P. M. Niedenthal et al., "Embodiment in Attitudes, Social Perception, and Emotion," *Personality and Social Psychology Review*, Vol. 9, no. 3 (2005), pp. 184–211.

55   Adolphs, "How Do We Know the Minds of Others?"; Michael L. Spezio, "Narrative in Holistic Healing: Empathy, Sympathy, & Simulation Theory," in *Spiritual Transformation and Healing*, eds. Joan D. Koss and Philip Hefner (Lanham, MD: Altamira, 2006), pp. 206–222; and Adolphs and Spezio, "Role of the Amygdala."

56   T. Singer and C. Lamm, "The Social Neuroscience of Empathy," *Annual of the New York Academy of Science*, Vol. 1156 (2009), pp. 81–96; T. Singer et al., "Empathy for Pain Involves the Affective but Not Sensory Components of Pain," *Science*, Vol. 303, no. 5661 (2004), pp. 1157–62; T. Singer et al.,"Empathic Neural Responses Are Modulated by the Perceived Fairness of Others," *Nature*, Vol. 439, no. 7075 (2006), pp. 466–469.

57   For a more complete discussion, see James A. Van Slyke et al., "The Rationality of Ultimate Concern: Moral Exemplars, Theological Ethics, and the Science of Moral Cognition," *Theology and the Science of Morality: Virtue Ethics, Exemplarity, and Cognitive Neuroscience* (London: Routledge, 2012).

58   Greene and Haidt, "How (and Where) Does Moral Judgment Work?" and Greene et al., "An Fmri Investigation."

59   Koenigs et al., "Damage to the Prefrontal Cortex."

60   J. D. Greene, "Why Are Vmpfc Patients More Utilitarian? A Dual-Process Theory of Moral Judgment Explains," *Trends in Cognitive Sciences*, Vol. 11 (2007), pp. 322–323.

61   Moll and de Oliveira-Souza, "Moral Judgments, Emotions and the Utilitarian Brain."

62   J. Moll et al., "Functional Networks in Emotional Moral and Nonmoral Social Judgments," *NeuroImage*, Vol. 16, no. 3. Pt 1 (2002), pp. 696–703 and J. Moll et al., "The Self as a Moral Agent: Linking the Neural Bases of Social Agency and Moral Sensitivity," *Social Neuroscience*, Vol. 2, nos. 3–4 (2007), pp. 336–352.

63   See especially Luiz Pessoa, "On the Relationship between Emotion and Cognition," *Nature Reviews Neuroscience*, Vol. 9, no. 2 (2008), pp. 148–158.

64   Dietrich Bonhoeffer, Clifford J. Green, eds., trans. Reinhard Krauss, Charles C. West, and Douglas W. Scott, "Ethics as Formation," in *Ethics* (Minneapolis, MN: Fortress Press, 2005), p. 81.

16

INTELLECTUAL EMOTIONS AND RELIGIOUS EMOTIONS

PETER GOLDIE

A Simple Model of Emotion

There is a model of emotion to be found in the current debate on the emotions, both in philosophy and in the interdisciplinary activity of cognitive science, in which philosophy plays its part. According to this model, the emotions are quite simple phenomena. In support of the model, we are often given an example—a paradigm. Here is one such. We see a bear approaching us in the woods, and we react with fear. This fearful reaction involves certain visceral changes and changes to the autonomic nervous system (in this case increased heart rate, increased adrenalin flow and so on), which changes are felt. This is just what emotional feelings are—*bodily* feelings. The fearful reaction also involves certain action tendencies (in this case the tendency to escape from the threat, by running or hiding perhaps).[1] Something like this model is often attributed to the work of William James, and there certainly is some truth in the idea. According to James, emotions—or to be precise what he called the "standard emotions"—are just the feeling of certain bodily changes which "follow directly the PERCEPTION of the exciting fact"; "our feelings of the changes as they occur *is* the emotion."[2] Anyway, perhaps we can safely call the model *Jamesian*, bearing in mind that it continues to be advocated today in one form or another by people who call their accounts Jamesian.[3]

On this simple—Jamesian—model, the emotions have certain important characteristics. First, they are short-term reactions to events in our immediate environment, or to what is sometimes called an "eliciting event"—the approaching bear in this case.[4] Secondly, these reactions are selectionally advantageous to us; they are adaptive.[5] On our example, the fearful responses to the approaching bear, including the bodily changes and action tendencies, increase our chances of survival and thus of being able to pass on our genes,

Faith, Rationality, and the Passions, First Edition. Edited by Sarah Coakley.
© 2012 Blackwell Publishing Ltd. Book compilation © 2012 Blackwell Publishing Ltd.

always on the assumption that the environment in which we now live shares relevant properties with the environment in which the emotions evolved—the so-called environment of evolutionary adaptedness. Thirdly, the emotions on this model are universal, or at least pan-cultural amongst humans, with pan-cultural facial expression, and are shared with, or homologous to, emotions in other animals.[6] Fourthly, the emotions do not need to involve reasoning through higher-level cognitive processes; indeed, the very immediacy of the response to the bear is evidence for this, and for the fact that the immediate non-cognitive response is more adaptive than slower cognitive processing; it is what is called fast and frugal or quick and dirty.[7] And fifthly, because the emotions on this model are quite simple phenomena, involving measurable bodily changes, they are operationalizable: one can conduct empirical studies in psychology, biology and neuroscience to throw light on what processes are involved.

I am sympathetic to much in this model of emotion. But my sympathy comes with two very substantial qualifications. The first qualification is that the model must not claim hegemony; it must not claim that emotions in general have all these features. For if it does, it skews the class of emotion towards this particular paradigm. Some emotional experiences, including fear of the approaching bear, no doubt do have these features. But to insist that all emotions have these features either denies the phenomena, or it redefines emotion in a way that eliminates the rest of our emotional life by what is more or less a definitional fiat, in effect insisting that what lacks the features outlined above isn't *really* an emotion.[8]

The second qualification is really more of a disagreement. I would contend, although I cannot argue for it here, that not all emotional feelings are bodily feelings. Feelings can also be directed towards things in the world beyond the bounds of the body—towards the bear for example; these feelings, bound up with thought, are what I have called *feelings towards*.[9]

What the Simple Model Neglects

There is much more to our emotional life than is captured by the simple Jamesian model, and there is today a considerable reaction against it.[10] Here I want briefly to discuss three aspects of emotion that the simple model neglects, focussing in particular on the second and third. With these three aspects in place we have, I suggest, a more complex model of emotion, one that is better placed to capture the role of emotion in religious life—better, that is, than the simple model that takes as its paradigm our reaction to the approaching bear in the woods.

The Life of the Mind

First, then, we humans are capable of having emotions that are directed in thought and feeling towards the past and future. We can, for example, feel shame at the silly and irresponsible thing we did at that party on the beach all those years ago. This shame that we now feel might not be what we felt at the time; perhaps then, being younger, we thought our behavior to be rather insouciant and stylish, and only now do we see it as it really was. And in respect of the future, emotions can be involved in our forming intentions and in making plans. We can, for example, consider doing something rather reprehensible and feel guilty at the very thought: we shrink from the action "as an impossibility," to use J. S. Mill's nice expression.[11] So in us humans our emotions are not just concerned with "eliciting events" in our immediate environment, but with what I like to call the life of the mind.[12] Moreover, we can be reflective about our emotions, assessing them as appropriate or inappropriate, and even having emotions about the emotions which we have or imagine having.

The Intellectual (and Aesthetic) Emotions

The second aspect of human emotion that the simple model neglects is that emotions can be directed in thought and feelings towards matters of intellectual or aesthetic import, where the characteristic features of the simple model are much less readily applicable. I will not be discussing the aesthetic emotions here,[13] but will focus on the intellectual emotions, although I might quickly note that in the neglect of both these kinds of emotion we might again see a trace of William James, who thought of intellectual, aesthetic and ethical emotions as other than what he called "standard."[14]

A number of philosophers have recently argued persuasively for the existence of intellectual emotions.[15] These include emotions such as delight, wonder, awe, fascination, courage, surprise, worry, doubt, curiosity, concern, tenacity, and hope, some of which are found elsewhere, other than when directed towards intellectual objects, and some of which are more exclusive to intellectual matters. As Michael Stocker in particular has argued, these emotions have an eminent history in philosophical writing, which makes it even more notable that they are neglected today, and even more notable that one needs to argue for their existence. Moreover, they have an eminent history in biographies and autobiographies of philosophical and scientific enquiry, where we often find accounts that refer specifically to the emotions experienced by the philosopher or the scientist. The psychologist Theodule Ribot, who was writing just after William James, remarked, "The biographies of learned men furnish us with innumerable examples: the perpetual physical sufferings of Pascal, Malebranche nearly suffocated by the palpitations of his heart when reading Descartes, Humphrey Davy dancing in his laboratory after having made the discovery of potassium," and so on.[16] Many such examples, including Davy's discovery of potassium, are discussed in Richard Holmes's very nice book *The Age of Wonder* (2009). Holmes mentions there that Coleridge said that science was "necessarily performed with *the passion of hope*"[17]—a thought with which his friend Davy was very much in agreement. A nice example is Isaac Newton, who, in his letter to the then Secretary of the Royal Society, reports his first response to seeing light shone through a prism: "It was at first a pleasing divertissement to view the vivid and intense colors produced thereby, but after a while applying myself to consider them more circumspectly, I became surprised to see them in an oblong form; which, according to the received laws of refraction, I expected should have been circular. . . . Comparing the length of this colored spectrum with its breadth, I found it about five times greater, a disproportion so extravagant that it excited me to a more than ordinary curiosity of examining from whence it might proceed."[18] In this short paragraph, we can count at least four intellectual emotions.

One thought about the intellectual emotions is that their value is merely as a non-necessary instrumental aid to intellectual enquiry which an enquirer could manage perfectly well without, although they might be epistemically helpful. Although I can't argue for it here, I prefer the idea that we should think of what it is to have the intellectual virtues (I intend no elitist connotations here in the term "intellectual") as being analogous to what it is, according to Aristotle, to be an ethically virtuous person.[19] According to this idea, the virtuous intellectual enquirer, like his ethical counterpart, will have, as Aristotle put it, the right emotions at the right time in the right place and towards the right kinds of object,[20] and being able to do this is part of what it is to be virtuous. In other words, doing the right things is not sufficient for intellectual virtue; without the appropriate intellectual emotions, we cannot be a fully virtuous enquirer, and emotion is a necessary component of intellectual activity. On this view, then, in scientific or philosophical enquiry—what one might think of as the paradigm of rational activity— emotion is not just an instrumental aid, but essential to the activity itself. And, I believe, just the same is true of the artistic virtues: having the right emotions is essential here too. Furthermore, given that ethical, intellectual and aesthetic emotions aren't just an added extra but essential to their related activities, and given that engaging in these virtuous activities is constitutive of well-being, it follows that one cannot live a good life, a life of virtue, without these emotions.[21]

Virtues are, of course, a kind of disposition, and therefore, I am suggesting, the ethical, intellectual and aesthetic virtues will include dispositions to have the right emotions. And this leads me neatly to the third aspect of human emotion that the simple model neglects: emotional dispositions.

Emotional Dispositions

In discussing this third neglected aspect of emotion, I want to begin by recalling an ambiguity in our way of talking of emotion. If I say that I am envious of Mary's successes, I might be referring to the occurrent emotion, to the feeling of envy that I am now experiencing. Or alternatively I might be referring to the emotion as a dispositional attitude, an attitude that I have towards

Mary's successes. On this latter alternative, then, it can truthfully be said of me that I am envious of Mary's successes without in any way implying that I am at this moment feeling envious; I might be asleep or thinking of something entirely different.[22]

We typically use the term "emotion" for both episode and disposition, but the simple view focuses only on the episode. And yet our emotional dispositions are an integral part of our psychic economy. They make us what we are: our love of our children and parents; your hatred of oppression; his fear of large dogs; her sympathy for the homeless.

It is an important feature of emotional dispositions that they are not simply dispositions to have a single kind of emotion. For example, your enduring love of your children or parents is not just a disposition to have loving feelings towards them when they are in the offing. It can be expressed in a complex structure of possible responses: delight if they succeed in their endeavors; anger if you hear them insulted behind their backs; fear and concern if you think they might be ill; hope if you think that their illness might have a cure; and so on.[23] Even my envy of Mary's successes isn't just a disposition to feel *envy*; it can be expressed in a feeling of delight when I hear that her latest success looks after all as if it's turning into something of a poisoned chalice; I wouldn't be feeling this delight if I weren't envious of her.

Another important feature of emotional dispositions is their changeability—their vicissitudes. Part of this is to be explained by the ways in which emotional dispositions interact with experience: an experience can change the disposition—by consolidating it, or by attenuating it, or in other ways.[24] For example, one's sympathy for the homeless might be permanently damaged or even disabled completely as a result of a single experience of being attacked by a homeless person. Emotional dispositions can also be changed as a result of changes in other dispositions elsewhere in one's psychic economy. For example, her disposition to delight in the natural beauties of open spaces might disappear altogether as a result of an agoraphobia that only arrived as she reached middle age.

There are other possibilities here, however, possibilities that give rise to significant epistemic questions in understanding the mind—both one's own mind and the mind of others. For it is possible that certain factors can have the effect of blocking off or preventing the response that one would otherwise expect from the disposition, whilst the disposition remains in place.[25] For example, if I am depressed, as a loving father I might not feel the delight that I otherwise would when I hear of the success of my son in his exams, although I really am still a loving father. If I am overwhelmed with troubles of my own, as a fervent campaigner for civil rights I might not feel the compassion that I normally would when I hear of the arrest of a prisoner of conscience somewhere in the world. In these cases I might *judge* that these events are a good or a bad thing, and much to be celebrated or bemoaned, but still, I don't *feel* as I should, or as I used to feel. The expression of the emotional dispositions is blocked, and the judgements are no longer emotionally laden as they were.

Earlier I said that, in emotional experience, thought and feeling are bound up together, directed together towards the object of the emotion. As a corollary to that, I would add that we should resist the idea that these judgements are just the same with or without the feeling, so that if the feeling later returns, it is simply to be added on to the content of the judgement. This is what I call the add-on view; against this, I prefer the view that, with feeling bound up into thought, both the content of the judgement and the attitude itself are different.[26]

But the epistemic questions should be clear. In each case we might not know whether the disposition has ceased to exist, or whether the disposition is temporarily blocked from its normal expression. Would she still delight in open spaces if her agoraphobia could be cured? Am I no longer a loving father, or am I a loving father who is depressed? Is it just temporary compassion fatigue or don't I really care about political freedom any more?

Intellectual Emotion, Virtue, and Varieties of Weakness

Now, let's connect this discussion of the vicissitudes of emotional dispositions to the earlier discussion of the intellectual emotions and the intellectual virtues. I hope it is immediately obvious that the emotions that are appropriate to intellectual activity can be effected just as can my feelings about my son's successes, or her feelings about political freedom. So, if being disposed to have the right intellectual emotions is part of what it is to be intellectually virtuous, then these vicissitudes can prevent one from virtuous intellectual activity.

I dare say that we have all, at one time or another, been susceptible to this loss of affect in our intellectual activities, and, if we have, we will surely appreciate just how debilitating it can be. We *know* that this new book or paper on just the topic that we are ourselves researching will be interesting and challenging, and we *know* that we ought to read it. But we have no curiosity, no wonder at what we read, no feeling of hope that we will find some answers, and no courage to keep on reading, to keep on asking questions. We no longer feel the keenness to write new material, merely going through the motions, driven by mere habit or by the requirements of one's job, churning out more and more variations on the same old stuff. Our intellectual life has gone cold on us.

We have names for the variety of causes of such loss of affect: depression, apathy, lack of resolution, demoralization, a feeling of hopelessness, sloth, lassitude, tiredness, and so on; terms which are often simply names of a problem, rather than explanations.[27] What can you do? In part, the answer will depend on prior answers to the epistemic questions I have just been posing. If it's a temporary blocking of the emotional disposition, then perhaps you should try to take exercise in the morning before starting work. But if it's permanent, then perhaps the best thing is not to keep on flogging the dead horse, but to give up altogether.

Religious Emotions

I would like to suggest that these ideas about intellectual emotions can be brought to bear on the religious emotions—that we have here a good model of how religious emotions are properly located in a good religious life. Let's see how things would look if I were right.

First, the right model for religious emotions wouldn't be the simple model, which skews the class of emotion towards what William James called the *standard* emotions. So religious emotions needn't involve just bodily feelings; they needn't be immediate reactions to eliciting events in the environment; they needn't be selectionally advantageous, pan-cultural, and shared with other animals; they needn't typically arise without cognitive processing; they needn't be operationalizable.

Secondly, the better model for religious emotion would be the intellectual (and aesthetic) emotions—emotions directed in thought and feeling towards the object of the intellectual (or aesthetic) activity. Many of these emotions—such as delight, wonder, awe, courage, doubt, tenacity, and hope—will be common between the intellectual and the religious sphere; others—reverence and contrition perhaps—will be particular to religious experience. With this in mind, we can see a striking parallel between Newton's thoughts and feelings, bound up together, directed towards the colored spectrum, and Descartes's thoughts and feelings directed towards God, as he expressed it in the final paragraph of his Third Meditation: "Here let me pause for a while and spend some time in the contemplation of God...and gaze at, wonder at, and adore the beauty of this immense light, so far as the eye of my darkened intellect can bear it."[28]

Thirdly, as with intellectual activity, we would find that having the appropriate religious virtues would involve having the appropriate emotional dispositions so that one would not be able to act or think virtuously without having the right feelings, towards the right objects, at the right time, and so on. And without the virtues one would not be able to lead a good life; so emotional engagement wouldn't merely be an optional extra but a necessary part of what it is to lead a good religious life.

And fourthly, religious virtues, including the relevant emotional dispositions, would be fragile. They would be susceptible to vicissitudes as they are elsewhere, or they would remain in place whilst their expression is blocked off by depression, apathy, weakness, accidie, sloth, tiredness, and so on, so that one's religious life goes cold on one—both judgement and action lack the emotionality that is a requirement of virtue. And then we would be faced with the same epistemic questions: what is the explanation of the failure of virtue—the failure to have the right feelings? And what would one be able to do about it in any particular case? Answers to these questions would not be easy to find. But that is surely to be expected once we have given up the simple model of emotion.

NOTES

1 For discussion of action tendencies, see Nico J. Fridja, *The Laws of Emotion* (Mahwah, NJ: Lawrence Erlbaum Ass., 2007).

2 William James, "What is an emotion?" *Mind*, Vol. 9 (1884), pp. 188–205, at pp. 189–190.

3 See, for example, Antonio Damasio, *Descartes' Error: Emotion, Reason, and the Human Brain* (New York: Grosset/Putnam, 1994); Jesse Prinz, *Gut Reactions: A Perceptual Theory of Emotion* (Oxford: Oxford University Press, 2004); and Jenefer Robinson, *Deeper Than Reason: Emotion and its Role in Literature, Music and Art* (Oxford: Oxford University Press, 2005).

4 For this kind of view, see Klaus Scherer, "Emotions in Everyday Life," *Social Science Information*, Vol. 43 (2004), pp. 499–570.

5 For this kind of view, see John Tooby and Leda Cosmides, "The Evolutionary Psychology of the Emotions and their Relationship to Internal Regulatory Variables," in *Handbook of Emotions*, eds. M. Lewis, J. Haviland-Jones, and L. Feldman Barrett (New York: Guildford Press, 2008), pp. 114–137.

6 For this kind of view, see Paul Ekman, "An Argument for Basic Emotions," *Cognition and Emotion*, Vol. 6 (1992), pp. 169–200; Paul Griffiths, *What Emotions Really Are: The Problem of Psychological Categories* (Chicago, IL: University of Chicago Press, 1997); and Charles Darwin et al., *The Expression of Emotion in Man and Animals*, with an introduction, afterword and commentary by P. Ekman (London: Harpercollins, 1998). Joseph LeDoux discusses how the amygdala is implicated in fear responses in rats and humans in *The Emotional Brain* (New York: Simon and Schuster, 1996).

7 Many scholars are particularly struck by the experiments of Robert Zajonc, which purport to show that affect can occur prior to, and without, cognition. See his "On the Primacy of Affect," *American Psychologist*, Vol. 39 (1984), pp. 117–123, and "Evidence for Non-Conscious Emotions," in *The Nature of Emotions*, eds. P. Ekman and R. Davidson (New York: Oxford University Press, 1994), pp. 293–297.

8 See Griffiths, *What Emotions Really Are*.

9 This is of course not to deny that bodily feelings are a significant aspect of emotional experience; what is being denied is that bodily feelings are the *only* feelings which are involved. For discussion, see my *The Emotions: A Philosophical Exploration* (Oxford: Clarendon Press, 2000), and "Getting Feelings into Emotional Experience in the Right Way," *Emotion Review*, Vol. 1 (2009), special edition on emotional experience, eds. S. Döring and R. Reisenzein, pp. 232–239.

10 See, for example, Ronald de Sousa, *The Rationality of Emotion* (Cambridge, MA: MIT Press, 1990); John Deigh, "Cognitivism in the Theory of Emotions," *Ethics*, Vol. 104 (1994), pp. 824–854; Martha Nussbaum, *Upheavals of Thought: The Intelligence of Emotions* (Cambridge: Cambridge University Press, 2001); Robert Roberts, *Emotions: An Aid in Moral Psychology* (Cambridge: Cambridge University Press, 2003); Robert Solomon, *The Passions* (New York: Doubleday, 1976); Aaron Ben-Ze'ev, *The Subtlety of Emotions* (Cambridge, MA: MIT Press, 2000); Bennett Helm, *Emotional Reason: Deliberation, Motivation, and the Nature of Value* (Cambridge: Cambridge University Press, 2001); and my *The Emotions*. There is insufficient space here to argue for the alternative model of emotion that I am putting forward in this chapter; the aim, rather, is to begin with the assumption that this model is more or less correct, and then to see how it might be applied to the religious emotions.

11 John Stuart Mill, *Utilitarianism*, ed. R. Crisp (Oxford: Oxford University Press, 1993), Chapter 3.

12 See my "The Life of the Mind: Commentary on 'Emotions in Everyday Life'," *Social Science Information*, Vol. 43 (2004), pp. 591–598.

13 For discussion, see my "Towards a Virtue Theory of Art," *British Journal of Aesthetics*, Vol. 47 (2007), pp. 372–387; and "Virtues of Art and Human Well-Being," *Proceedings of the Aristotelian Society Supp.*, Vol. 82 (2008), pp. 179–195.

14 For a very helpful discussion, see Michael Stocker, "Intellectual and Other Non-Standard Emotions," in *The Oxford Handbook of Philosophy of Emotion*, ed. P. Goldie (Oxford: Oxford University Press, 2010), pp. 401–423.
15 See in particular Stocker, "Intellectual and Other Non-Standard Emotions," and Adam Morton, "Epistemic Emotions," in *The Oxford Handbook of Philosophy of Emotion*, pp. 385–399.
16 For this citation from Theodore Ribot, see Michael Stocker, "Intellectual and Other Non-Standard Emotions," p. 411. See also Ribot's *Psychology of the Emotions* (New York: Scribner's, 1897).
17 Richard Holmes, *The Age of Wonder: How the Romantic Generation Discovered the Beauty and Terror of Science* (London: Pantheon Books, 2009), p. 268.
18 Cited in Lorraine Daston and Katharine Park, *Wonders and the Order of Nature, 1150–1750* (New York: Zone Books, 1998), p. 303.
19 For a recent survey in this area, see Guy Axtell, "Recent Work on Virtue Epistemology," *American Philosophical Quarterly*, Vol. 34 (1997), pp. 1–26.
20 Aristotle, *Nicomachean Ethics*, trans. T. Irwin (Indianapolis, IN: Hackett, 1985), 1099a16-20.
21 According to Aristotle, artistic activity (both in producing and in appreciating art) is not part of well-being or *eudaimonia*; intellectual activity, of course, is; see especially *Nicomachean Ethics*, Book X. For discussion, with reason for disagreeing with Aristotle about the place of artistic activity in well-being, see my "Towards a Virtue Theory of Art" and "Virtues of Art and Human Well-Being."
22 Emotions as dispositions are central to Richard Wollheim's account of emotion; see his *On the Emotions* (New Haven, CT: Yale University Press, 1999), and for discussion see my "Wollheim on Emotion and Imagination," *Philosophical Studies*, Vol. 127 (2006), pp. 1–17.
23 This kind of structure is at the heart of Bennett Helm's account in his *Emotional Reason*.
24 For detailed discussion, see Wollheim, *On the Emotions*.
25 These issues are discussed in Justin D'Arms and Daniel Jacobson, "Demystifying Sensibilities: Sentimental Values and the Instability of Affect," in *The Oxford Handbook of Philosophy of Emotion*, pp. 585–613.
26 For discussion, see my *The Emotions*, and my "Getting Feelings into Emotional Experience in the Right Way." See also Tim Bloser, "The Content of Emotional Thoughts," *Philosophical Papers*, Vol. 36 (2007), pp. 219–243; and Michelle Montague, "The Logic, Intentionality, and Phenomenology of Emotion," *Philosophical Studies*, Vol. 145 (2009), pp. 171–192.
27 Matthew Ratcliffe has a very helpful discussion of loss of hope, one kind of which is demoralization. He notes that the latter has even been identified as a medical condition which is distinct from depression. See his "What is it to Lose Hope?" (unpublished paper), and D. W. Kissane and D. M. Clarke, "Demoralization Syndrome: A Relevant Psychiatric Diagnosis for Palliative Care," *Journal of Palliative Care*, Vol. 17 (2001), pp. 12–21.
28 *The Philosophical Writings of René Descartes*, Vol. II, trans. J. Cottingham, R. Stoothof, and D. Murdoch (Cambridge: Cambridge University Press, 1985). Thanks to John Cottingham for this reference.

POSTSCRIPT: WHAT (IF ANYTHING) CAN THE SCIENCES TELL PHILOSOPHY AND THEOLOGY ABOUT FAITH, RATIONALITY, AND THE PASSIONS?

SARAH COAKLEY

The concluding chapters in this volume have begged some fundamental questions in the philosophy of mind about the relation of mind and brain. Even to discuss what such news from neuroscience or cognitive psychology might mean for philosophy of religion, and for its own historical and systematic reflections on the relation of "intellect" and "affect," is to presume that the empirical sciences can deliver information about the processes of the brain which involves either correlation or causal connection (in senses in need of clarification) with "mental events." Further, the very notion of a "mental event" may be opaque or ambiguous without closer analysis.[1] So here we enter several contentious areas of philosophy of mind in which it might be said that "loose talk costs (philosophical) lives."[2] In the circumstances it is as well for the philosophical theologian at least to be aware of the range of possible philosophical choices to be made in these contested areas, and especially of the current hegemony of physicalist and reductive accounts in secular philosophy of mind. This makes philosophy of mind unusually hostile territory for the Christian believer.[3]

In this brief final postscript I shall therefore attempt only three succinct, but I hope suggestive, comments for philosophy of religion and its potential response to new neuroscientific discoveries about rationality and "emotion." The first comment relates to a stringent recent critique, coming from a Wittgensteinian direction, of the significance of neuroscience for the philosophy

Faith, Rationality, and the Passions, First Edition. Edited by Sarah Coakley.
© 2012 Blackwell Publishing Ltd. Book compilation © 2012 Blackwell Publishing Ltd.

of the "emotions," *tout court*.[4] Such an approach certainly puts a firm wedge in the door against crass physicalist reduction; but it also seems to deny that advances in neuroscientific research on the neurophysiological substrata of "emotions" could have *any* obvious or straightforward implications for everyday human language about feelings and affective states more generally. This is a serious and sophisticated challenge which has to be faced squarely. The second comment outlines a possible range of alternative responses to this first critique. It adumbrates some non-reductive contemporary models for the mind/body relation which are capable of taking the deliverances from the neuroscience of emotion seriously, but which neither succumb to a reductive physicalism nor to crass confusions about the specifically *human* language of emotion. The third and last comment simply notes the particular difficulties for *theology* of joining these highly technical secular debates in philosophy of mind, and muses in closing on how contemporary philosophy of mind might potentially be enlivened by re-considering some models for the mind/body relation (including the significance of affect or will in that relation) that take the sustaining matrix of the divine for granted from the outset.

1. *Some Confusions in Neuroscientific Accounts of Emotion.* A stringent critique of Antonio Damasio and other recent celebrated neuroscientific researchers on emotion has been mounted from a Wittgensteinian perspective of late by M. R. Bennett and P. M. S. Hacker.[5] Their core arguments, which cannot be gainsaid, may be expressed succinctly thus. First, a particular functioning of the brain does seem to be *one* causal condition for the feeling of human emotion. But it is misguided, say Bennett and Hacker, to "assimilate" such causal conditions for the feeling of an emotion to the cause of a *specific* emotion on any given occasion. So, for instance (the pointed example given by Hacker here): it is right to say that the "cause" of one's fear is the sound of a shot coming from the street; but it is misleading to say (as if in competition with this supposition), that it is the condition of one's brain that is the cause of one's fear. Further, the "object" of an emotion may not always be coincident with the "source" of an emotion: what one is frightened *by* (in this case, the sound of a shot) may not be the same thing as what one is frightened *of* (in this case, dying). We need to take account of all the complexity of our language and thinking about emotion at these various levels. Secondly, it is surely the case that animals (even higher mammals) and humans experience emotion significantly differently as a result of humans having the capacity for *language*; what Bennett and Hacker call the "horizons" of emotion and feeling are vastly expanded by linguistic expression. Indeed, there are certain kinds of emotion that animals are for this reason not capable of (fear of bankruptcy, for instance, as compared to fear of physical attack). Thirdly, one cannot therefore say (without significant rejoinder) that emotions have simply evolved *as* "brain states and bodily

responses." To be sure, human emotions do involve these factors, but cannot be reduced to them, since these factors do not capture the distinctively human *intentionality* ("directedness towards an object") involved in human emotions. Finally, it follows, according to Bennett and Hacker, that "Emotion words do not apply to brain states *at all*, but to creatures, who feel emotions and exhibit them in their behaviour."[6]

2. *Alternative Non-Reductive Models for the Mind/Brain Problem and Its Relation to Emotions.* It might be wondered, however, whether Bennett's and Hacker's conclusion here has overstepped the implications of their own case. It certainly does follow from the arguments they mount that naïve or ideologically physicalist reductions of "emotions" to brain states or bodily perturbations are ruled out by attention to the richness and complexity of human language; but it does not follow thereby that talk about emotions does not relate to those other arenas "at all" (ask any doctor who listens to patients describing the physical features of their anxiety states). Were that to follow, it would lead to a kind of inverse reduction in which the appeal to human "language" about emotion seemingly erased all interest in the accompanying physiological responses and neurological circuitry of such states in giving an account of emotion.

What are the options that remain, then, for philosophers of mind who remain sensitive to the irreducible difference of human emotion from animal emotion (thereby resisting reductionist "identity" accounts of the mind/brain relation), who note the particular importance of human language in expressing emotion, and yet also take seriously the possibility that neuroscientific and psychological investigations may add dimensions of understanding to our linguistic analysis of such states?

Roughly speaking, there would seem to be three distinct possibilities (with obvious room for internal variation) for those resisting physicalism of a reductive sort in this area.[7] First, there are various possibilities for non-reductive physicalism, that is, accounts of the mind/brain relationship (including the emotion/brain relationship, as a subset) which staunchly resist reduction of mind states to body states, and are able to give some convincing account of how the "I" (first-person) perspective is an irreducible feature of the person as a whole. One such account is that of Lynn Rudder Baker, who likens the relation of person to body as akin to the relation between "marble sculptures and the pieces of marble that make them up."[8] The point of this analogy is that "A marble sculpture has a physical nature in virtue of being constituted by a piece of marble and an aesthetic nature of being (nonderivatively) a sculpture":[9] the "nonderivative" dimension is clearly crucial on this account, although it also constitutes the most difficult part of the picture to give a clear account of.

A second possible approach is some form of emergentism. On this view (which has the merit of taking evolutionary developments from animal to human particularly seriously), the specifically human capacities of the person "emerge" from the physical into that which transcends it (the mind: including mental, linguistic and emotional capacities). Emergence, in the words of Philip Clayton, takes the view that "new and unpredictable phenomena are naturally produced by interactions in nature"; and that these newly evolved realities are then capable of exercising "a causal influence on the parts out of which they arose."[10] However, this does not imply any "substance" dualism of a classic Cartesian sort, since there remains an organic relation to the physical and a constant integrative interrelation between emergent mind and that on which it is based. On this view, acts of intention can impinge on the physical without denying that the physical also has some sort of causal relation to the constitution of (say) emotions. The main problem with this general approach is in giving a coherent account of the very idea of emergence—when and why it occurs and what can explain it.

The third possibility is some sort of recuperation of substance dualism in a form attuned to modern evolutionary and neuroscientific discoveries. This is by far the most unfashionable of the options mentioned; but Richard Swinburne's *The Evolution of the Soul*[11] heroically undertakes such a project. On this view "pure mental events" are distinct from physical events, and the occurrence of one "does not entail the other or vice versa, although one may cause the other."[12] Swinburne makes great efforts to accommodate the backcloth of animal evolution into his picture of substance dualism, and to mitigate the well-known difficulties of Descartes's attempts to explain the relation of soul to body by coming up with a theory of the soul's "structuring" or shaping the brain.[13] The main problems on this Swinburnian model inhere in the wholly speculative nature of the theorizing of this relation of "structuring."

3. *Philosophy of Mind Without God?* It is clear from even the briefest survey of trends in current philosophy of mind that no consensus is in sight, and that the various attempts to avoid the currently regnant reductive physicalism all have significant difficulties. This is true whether or not feeling and emotion are to the forefront of discussion, and it might be said that it witnesses to a set of profound *aporiai* in the field at large. As Richard Swinburne wryly notes of the current resistance to any form of dualism, "These days one gets a far more sympathetic hearing for arguments for the existence of God than one does for arguments for the existence of the soul."[14] And this is an odd state of affairs, given the confident moves in post-foundationalist philosophy of religion favor of *presuming* God's existence as "properly basic." It might then in closing be worth commenting that the philosophy of mind (and, *a fortiori*, of the emotions) could well be regenerated if new thought experiments were conducted on the supposition of God's existence rather than on the dogmatic presumption of God's non-existence. One might even hope that this volume could spawn some new philosophical creativity along those lines amongst philosophers of religion.[15]

NOTES

1 One of the best recent introductions to these disputed areas in contemporary philosophy of mind is Tim Crane, *Elements of Mind: An Introduction to the Philosophy of Mind* (Oxford: Oxford University Press, 2001). Crane himself takes a non-reductive approach focusing especially on the importance of intentionality.
2 Peter Goldie's chapter has of course already alerted us to some of these potential philosophical pitfalls when discussing "emotion" and the mind/body relation.
3 This is particularly clear in an introductory collection of essays such as eds. Richard Warner and Tadeusz Szubka, *The Mind-Body Problem: A Guide to the Current Debate* (Oxford: Blackwell, 1994), although one or two contributors to this book do still maintain forms of dualism and/or defend the notion of the "soul."
4 At the "Faith, Rationality and Passions" conference this view was pointedly posed by Stephen Mulhall.
5 M. R. Bennett and P. M. S. Hacker, *Philosophical Foundations of Neuroscience* (Oxford: Blackwell, 2003). For the particular critique of Damasio, and of his reliance on William James's concept of emotion, see esp. ibid., pp. 203–216. The Wittgensteinian background to this analysis may be traced in G. P. Baker and P. M. S. Hacker, *An Analytical Commentary on Wittgenstein's Philosophical Investigations*, Vol. 1 (Oxford: Blackwell, 1983), esp. pp. 267–317.
6 Bennett and Hacker, *Philosophical Foundations*, p. 209, my emphasis.
7 I here present a variation on the analysis of Crane, *Elements of Mind*, Chapter 2.
8 Lynne Rudder Baker, *Persons and Bodies: A Constitution View* (Cambridge: Cambridge University Press, 2000), p. 228.
9 Ibid.
10 Philip Clayton, *Mind and Emergence: From Quantum to Consciousness* (Oxford: Oxford University Press, 2004), p. vi.
11 Richard Swinburne, *The Evolution of the Soul* (Oxford: Clarendon, second edition, 1997).
12 Ibid., p. ix.
13 See ibid., Chapter 14, esp. the diagram on p. 291. Oddly, Swinburne has very little to say in this book about emotions (though see ibid., pp. 140–141), given his interest in the evolutionary background to human bodies.
14 Ibid., p. ix.
15 One hopeful sign in this regard is the recent appearance of the excellent essays in eds. Mark C. Baker and Stewart Goetz, *The Soul Hypothesis: Investigations into the Existence of the Soul* (New York: Continuum, 2011), which present various forms of argument in favor of recovering a dualist concept of "soul," with or without any pre-existing presumptions about God's existence. (The issue of bodily "emotion," as such, is not however at the forefront of the discussion in this volume.)

INDEX

References to notes are entered as, for example, 11n.

Faith, Rationality, and the Passions, First Edition. Edited by Sarah Coakley.
© 2012 Blackwell Publishing Ltd. Book compilation © 2012 Blackwell Publishing Ltd.

Printed and bound by CPI Group (UK) Ltd, Croydon, CR0 4YY

09/06/2025

14686120-0004